Recently Published by Paraglyph Press:

Degunking Linux
By Roderick W. Smith

Game Design Complete
By Patrick O'Luanaigh

Game Coding Complete, Second Edition
By Mike McShaffry

A Theory of Fun for Game Design
By Raph Koster

Degunking eBay
By Greg Holden

Degunking Your Email, Spam, and Viruses
By Jeff Duntemann

Degunking Windows
By Joli Ballew
and Jeff Duntemann

Degunking Your Mac
By Joli Ballew

Acknowledgments

As usual, my family suffered for the time period when I was writing this book. My thanks go out to Max, Bailey, Adam, and Katrin, who helped me more than I can say.

Thanks also to Deifante Walters and Eric Yeung who did most of the work on the code for *Manic Mars Racer*, and to my Computer Science 585 class for helping in other ways.

The folks at Radical Entertainment deserve a mention, especially Neall Verheyde and Nigel Brooke.

Also, a final thanks to Ben Sawyer for thinking of me when the book idea was first bounced about.

About the Author

Dr. Jim Parker (Alberta, Canada), an expert on driving and racing games, has been a programmer and game designer for many years. In 2000, he pioneered Canada's first curriculum to train and educate aspiring game developers at the University of Calgary in conjunction with Radical Entertainment of Vancouver, B.C.

Jim is an academic and author. In 1998 he went to the Game Developers Conference to see what was up and he was captivated by the energy, skill, and enthusiasm of the group. He has been offering his course in Computer Game Programming at the University of Calgary since 2000, and is the capstone of the first program in computer games at a Canadian University. A driving game is always the project in this class.

Jim has worked in graphics, computer vision, artificial intelligence, and computer audio for numerous years. He has written two previous books (you can find them on the Internet). One of the books is a "bestseller" on computer vision.

A firm believer that almost anyone can create a game if they want to spend the time, he has been a champion for the democratization of game creation. This book is but one step in that process, of teaching others that they, too, can make a game that someone will want to play. Games can promote agendas, they can teach, they can be subversive, and they can tell a story as well as be entertaining.

Jim lives on a small farm near Cochrane, Alberta, Canada, in the foothills of the Rocky Mountains with his family.

Contents at a Glance

Contents

Part III
Advanced Techniques

Chapter 11
Cinematography for Driving and Racing Games 285

Chapter 12
Creating Terrains 303

Chapter 13
Designing the *Manic Mars Racer* Game 331

Chapter 14
Coding the *Manic Mars Racer* Game 351

Introduction

If you are interested in learning how to design and program driving or racing games, you've certainly come to the right place. I've written this book to be the first hands-on programming guide that shows you how to build and customize driving and racing games. It features the graphics, physics, AI, user interface, collision detection, audio, cinematography, and 3D techniques to create different types of driving and racing games.

In setting out to write this book, I was amazed to discover that no one had approached the subject of driving and racing games for a book up until now. Numerous books have been written on myriad game programming topics from graphics to interface design to AI programming, but the topic of driving and racing has been ignored. This is surprising considering that driving and racing games is one of the most popular genres of games.

Who this Book Is For

This book is for anyone who wants to learn how driving and racing games are put together. In automotive lingo, this book presents a "look under the hood." This genre represents about 12% of games on the market, and is therefore a substantial portion of the overall game market.

Why driving games? There are many reasons. I teach a university course on computer game development, and the project in the class has always been a driving game. I do this because driving games involve speed, motion, collisions, AI, and control of a moving object. Driving games at a basic level have a certain simplicity about them, yet to do them well and accurately requires a great deal of sophistication. Still, they illustrate the basic features that all computer games have in common. Taking a detailed look at a driving game really teaches you about *all* games.

Of course, there are important prerequisites to developing a computer game. You should be a programmer, and this book assumes that you are. You should have access to the Internet, and I assume that you do. I also assume that you are not afraid of math, and have creative leanings. These are all requirements for any game developer, even amateur ones. Most importantly, you must be willing to learn.

How this Book Is Organized

Take a moment to look over the table of contents for this book. You'll see that all of the chapters have been arranged into three parts. Part I covers the essentials of developing driving and racing games, Part II shows you how to build more realistic simulations, and Part III covers more advanced techniques of building driving and racing games. In Part III we'll apply much of what we learned so that we can create the *Manic Mars Racer* game. This game won't use every technique presented in the book, but it will incorporate many features including 3D graphics, AI, audio, physics, continuous time, cinematography, and terrain mapping.

Here's a little more detail on what you'll encounter in each part:

- **Part I**: We'll start learning about the features used in successful driving and racing games by looking at some of the best games of all time. We'll build a simple two-dimensional (2D) game called *Gopher-it* to see what the components of a game are and how they interconnect. All driving games—in fact, all video games of any kind—use computer graphics technology, and I'll show you how to use the OpenGL system to display graphics on the computer screen. Once we know how to create 2D graphics for our games, we'll learn how to use three-dimensional graphics (3D) by converting the simple 2D game we built in Chapter 2 into a 3D version, complete with sound. This new version of the game is called *Gopher-it 3D*. Once you complete Part I, you'll understand what a driving game should do and how the software accomplishes what we want. You'll also have two simple games to take apart, modify, and play with!

- **Part II**: In this part of the book we'll focus on techniques to develop the playability of driving and racing games. In particular, you'll learn how to build more realistic simulations. The playability of a game, the *fun* part, is provided by the artificial intelligence code. The AI not only enforces the rules of play, but connects the simulation parts of a game to the user, and provides extra entertainment by creating intelligent opponents to play against. I'll present most of the AI techniques we need in Chapters 5 through 10.

Sound is an essential part of a game and is responsible for much of the emotional impact and entertainment value. I will show you how to implement audio for a game using a platform-independent package called OpenAL. This will permit you to play sounds that have been stored as WAV files. I'll include special advanced material on how to create sounds in real-time and play them. This is unique to this book, so take advantage.

Many code demos will be provided in this part of the book, and I encourage you to compile and run them to get a good understanding of the concepts that are presented.

Although you'll encounter some mathematics in this part of the book, especially in Chapter 9, the math is essentially what you would encounter in high school courses. I'll also provide a short math tutorial at the end of the book if you missed math class on the wrong day.

- **Part III**: The goal is to build a real 3D racing game—*Manic Mars Racer*. This game will be much more than a demo game like the one we built in Part I of this book. The game will take place on Mars and it will allow you to you drive, collect objects, and race against a Martian on a model of the Martian surface.

In addition to building our final game, we'll discuss cinematography and terrain mapping. The cinematography in a driving game can be more advanced than what you'll find in other types of games, so we'll need to devote some time to this topic. We'll also cover how terrain is built and displayed in a game, since racing games tend to use outdoor scenes where terrain is an issue.

We'll then design and build the *Manic Mars Racer* game by creating some important design and implementation documents. They will help us focus on how the game will really work and what we'll need to do to implement the game. It is essential that a workable game design be created before you start to write code for any game. The complete source code for the game can be found on the website for this book. I encourage you to play the game, compile it, modify it, and ultimately improve it. Then tell me what you like and don't like about the game. The best mods will get posted to the site.

The game has flaws, but is certainly the coolest complete game provided in a book at this point in time. I designed it, but my thanks go to Deifante Walters and Eric Yeung who were students in my *Video Game Programming* class at the University of Calgary for their insights and assistance.

Using the Code and Examples with this Book

The computer programs provided with this book are all written in C. This is because C is more portable than most other languages, and will compile under a large collection of different tools. Similarly, I use the portable graphics system

OpenGL, which is available on Unix, Linux, Windows, and Mac systems. I use the portable audio system *OpenAL* for the same reason. The nature of your computer or operating system will not be a limitation in your use of this book to learn about computer games.

The code examples are provided to give you a means to experiment with actual working game code. Creating a large enough program to experiment with on your own may take too long, and you may become disheartened with the process before you can learn what was intended. On the website associated with this book, you will find graphics and audio demos, camera models, terrain rendering, and even entire games.

As always, please feel free to modify the programs.

How to Use the Website

All of the code and development files can be found at the website **http:// www.paraglyphpress.com/startyourengines/**. The major directories in the website are named as chapters: **Chapter 2** is a directory that contains the source and executable code for the first simple game *Gopher-it*. The **Chapter 3** directory contains some simple graphics demos, and so on for most of the chapters in the book. The code is written for Microsoft Visual Studio Version 6, except that the *Manic Mars Racer* gives ".net" build files. The code will compile under version 6 also; it's just that I gave the project files for the ".net" version in this case. All demos are called out in the text so you know what they're supposed to do.

I am also providing online figures from the book, because many of them were originally in color and were printed in gray level. You get to see them the way I originally created them—full color and full size.

Chapter	Directory	File	Explanation
2	Chapter2\GopherIt	Gopher-it.exe	The executable 2D *Gopher-it* game, with 1 second time steps.
3	Chapter3\myfirst	myfirst.exe	Opens a GLUT window.
3 a	Chapter3\teapot	teapot.exe	Draws a wireframe teapot into GLUT window.
4	Chapter 4\GopherIt3D	GopherIt3D.exe	Initial 3D version of *Gopher-it*.
4 of	Chapter 4\v2	main3d.exe	Final version of the 3D version *Gopher-it*, with sky box and texture maps.
7	Chapter 7\1myfirst	main.exe	Plays a specific WAV file.
7	Chapter 7\StopandPause	main.exe	Plays an engine sound: typing an odd number (followed by a return) pauses the sound, an even number resumes it.
7	Chapter 7\3moving	main.exe	Plays an engine sound. Typing in a floating point number between –12 and + 12 as aY position for the sound, left to right in the audio field. Try typing 1001!
7	Chapter 7\4frequencyChange	main.exe	Plays an engine sound. As you enter floating point numbers starting at 0, the pitch of the engine changes. Type –1 to exit.
7	Chapter 7\5audioFromMemory	main.exe	This program generates pure sine tones, ascending in frequency.
10	Chapter 10 Time\Demo 1	camera.exe	A 3D environment with a vehicle (a prism) that you can move using the numeric keypad. Some flicker.
10	Chapter 10 Time\Demo 2	demo2.exe	Basically the same as Demo1 above, but uses basic Windows WGL functions instead of GLUT. No movement, though.
10	Chapter 10 Time\Demo 3	demo3.exe	Same as Demo 2, but movement is allowed.
10	Chapter 10 Time\Demo 4	demo2.exe	Same as with Demo 1, but uses GLUT double buffering to eliminate flicker.

Chapter	Directory	File	Explanation
10	Chapter 10 Time\Demo 5	demo5.exe	Same as with Demo 3, but uses Windows double buffering to eliminate flicker.
11	Chaper 11 Camera\Demo 1	camera.exe	Simplest camera model, view from behind and up, no seperate camera motion.
11	Chapter 11 Camera\Demo 2	camera.exe	Camera view point is delayed slightly based on current velocity.
11	Chapter 11 Camera\Demo 3	camera.exe	Practical third-person camera: height and focus change as a function of velocity.
11	Chapter 11 Camera\Demo 4	camera.exe	Slight variation on parameters of demo 3. Type 'v' for bumber level camera.
11	Chapter 11 Camera\Demo 5	camera.exe	Introduction of time lag into camera pointing logic.
11	Chapter 11 Camera\Demo 6	camera.exe	Bumper cam, multiple auto-switching cameras, ceiling camera, all selected by typing 'V'.
12	Chapter 12 Terrain\Demo 1\gen	gen.exe	Creates a 128x128 synthetic terrain.
12	Chapter 12 Terrain\Demo 2	demo 2.exe	A drivable demo that has a terrain rendered; quad strips are used, but there are commented code blocks that do it other ways.
12	Chapter 12 Terrain\ textured terrain	textured terrain.exe	A drivable demo that has a terrain rendered and textured to look like Mars. Drops are changed to red also.
14	Chapter 14 Mars Racer		Contains all sources and binaries for the *Manic Mars Racer* game, this time as a .net project.
15	Chapter 15 Charged		All sources and binaries for the *Charged!* game. Warning: uses DirectX, not OpenGL. Windows only.

Chapter 1

Starting Your Engines—
Basic Design Elements

- Learn that racing and driving games are designed around six key properties.

- Explore the top ten racing/driving games that have been developed over the past 15 years.

- Learn how the popular driving and racing games use features such as venue, conflict, speed, physics, graphics and sound, props, and interface.

Most people below driving age hold a secret burning desire to jump into a car or truck and drive way too fast. Before the release of driving and racing games in the early 1990s, this desire would have led to juvenile court or would have gone unrequited. I know because my nine-year old son loves cars, loves the idea of driving and racing, and especially loves "monster trucks." Fortunately, he has a few years until his learner's permit is within reach.

Computer games are a way to live a fantasy. And a driving or racing game in particular is a way to cut people off without getting the "bird," a way to bounce off of dividers and other cars without getting a huge bill, and a way to bound down a freeway at 120 miles per hour without guilt of fines while the police are on your tail. Not only the young can appreciate these games, but those of us who regularly get bogged down in traffic can also appreciate them.

As fun as driving and racing games are to play, they are just as enjoyable to program. They offer a huge amount of entertaining play for a moderate degree of programming effort. I'm not saying that a driving game is easy to write, but I am saying that these genres of games are based on components and design features that are within the reach of programmers having relatively little game programming experience, as you'll learn in this book.

Many games require complex animation. Driving games require little or no real-time animation, and can be written to avoid character animation, which can be quite difficult and time consuming. The animation you do see displayed is pre-rendered and thus it can be quickly displayed. There are a wide range of graphics that would be considered acceptable in a driving game, so the highest quality photo-realistic graphical technology is not required. The physics needed to create a good driving simulation are complex, but simpler than the physics needed for most other sports games. Moreover, in the area of game design, the driving aspect can be connected with other game-play features to create a range of games including mission games, combat driving games, track, rally, and drag racing games, touring and exploration games, pursuits, motorcycle races, boat races, and even some space games.

In this chapter I'll introduce you to the basic features of driving and racing games. This will help set the stage so that you'll be able to explore the architecture of driving and racing games in Chapter 2. We'll start by looking at the top ten driving/racing games that have been developed and then we'll dicuss how these games share a set of common features.

The Key Properties of Driving Games

Let's first look at the six key properties that characterize a racing/driving game:

- *The primary interface feature involves guiding a vehicle.* That is, most of the characters typed or mouse movements used to communicate with the game are used to control the speed or direction of a vehicle. Of course, the vehicle could be a boat, aircraft, or spacecraft. (In this book, we'll focus on working with wheeled vehicles.)

- *Speed is a key element.* Usually, a part of the game involves getting to a destination faster than any other driver, or faster than you did before.

- *High-quality graphics are not essential.* When high-quality graphics are used, vehicles are usually very well rendered, then the scenery is rendered.

- *Character animation is not a key element.* Sometimes the driver can't even be seen, and frequently the characters in a game never leave their vehicles. In fact, animation in general is not essential to most driving games.

- *Audio can be limited in scope and quality.* Engine sounds and crashing noises don't have to be recorded in 5.1 channel Dolby at 44KHz. Background music is often used, and it competes with sound effects for the player's attention. When developing a driving game, you don't want to "cheese out" on the sound, but compared to a game like *Myst* or *Ghost Recon*, the audio you use can be relatively simple.

- *Little or no narrative is required.* Stories or a story can exist, usually as an excuse to go somewhere fast, or to explain why ominous black vans are chasing you.

These properties might make you think that some games that you used to consider driving or racing games actually belong in some other catgeory. For example, I wouldn't consider the *Grand Theft Auto* franchise games as driving games because driving is not a key element of the games. For this book, we'll be focusing on how to design and program games that incorporate these six important properties.

Let's next explore some good driving games to see what features make them interesting and fun, and we'll then return to a more practical discussion of function and design.

The Top Ten Driving Games

By taking a little time to look at what I think are the ten best drving games, you'll gain a better understanding of how basic design features are used to create different types of games. I have resisted the temptation to assign these games ranks, so you won't know which one I think is number one. You'll almost certainly disagree with me on some of them, and you might resent the fact that your favorite has been omitted. Sorry.

I'll also point out why I think each game is important, and I'll describe the basic game play features and the features that are especially significant.

Crazy Taxi

Let me state up front that I biased the top ten list with games that I like personally. Although, when it comes to *Crazy Taxi* (see Figure 1.1), I must confess that I don't like this game. The voice-over is irritating and repetitive. The green arrow that frequently points in a misleading direction makes me want to bend my controller. Having people leap from my cab when I'm ten feet from the destination makes me nuts. So, why is this game important to us?

The idea behind this game is to pick up passengers who have large dollar signs floating above them, and take them to their destination as quickly as possible. Your car is not damaged by smashing it into walls or other cars, you don't have to stay on the road, and your passenger alternates between whining about how much time it is taking and complaining that you are not driving carefully enough. You must make a certain amount of money in a specific time period or the game will end. Your passenger, as I mentioned before, will leap out of the car and not pay their fare after a specific time period has passed. Then there's the annoying arrow to deal with.

A large green arrow floats at the top of the screen and points in a destination. The arrow would be more useful if the car could fly, but of course it can't. Sometimes you can use the arrow to drive over lawns and such, but other times it seems to point straight into a building. Even more irritating, I have seen it spin 180 degrees in a few seconds for no visible reason.

So, why is this game in the top ten? The design is really quite excellent. If this was not the first crash-em up driving mission game, then it was an early entry, and a great many games have been designed by following its lead. The game makes it fun to ignore traffic laws, jump the curb, and bounce off of oncoming traffic, especially when there are no consequences. The floating arrow idea is also now ubiquitous in driving games. Fortunately, game designers have learned how to use it to actually help players find things.

I first played this game on a GameCube. The sound was not especially good, and the graphics was medium resolution, but the game is not a new one and should not be judged by modern standards. It was released in 1999 on the Deamcast console. I think that players still remember it fondly and play it from time to time because of its playability and fun factor. The number of games that use at least some of its features speak well of its basic design.

Colin McRae Rally

This game was one of the first two or three rally games to hit the market, originally back in 1997 (see Figure 1.2). It has been a very successful game, and I think it is hard to beat the combination of features that the designers and implementers have built in.

Figure 1.1
Crazy Taxi—an early and manic crash-and-dash game.

Figure 1.2
Colin McCrea Rally 2.0 in a familiar setting.

You can find more of this style of game available today, and perhaps the quality of this game helped grow the genre. The high point of CMR is the graphics; the scenery and vehicles are first-rate. The graphics aren't photorealistic, but they are very attractive and reminiscent of actual rally settings.

I played the PC version, which had primitive controls that made the game too "touchy." I have rallied some, summer and winter in Canada, but I'm certainly not a pro. Still, I have never been on soapier roads than the Finland track in CMR. Controlling the car using a PC is quite difficult, and I regularly damaged the car—again, something that I never did in real life. I found the night driving quite realistic, although I did not encounter any deer jumping into my windshield. As I played, I discovered that all of the roads were too soapy, and it seemed to be impossible to corner at a reasonable speed without sliding into the audience. By the way, I love the audience. They are surreal, ghostly figures that never come into focus. Cool.

The physics appear to be fairly good, in spite of what I said about slippery roads. The engine sound is somewhat irritating, but accurate for the kind of vehicle it propels.

The game uses the types of stages that you would find in a real rally. I find that my eyes get sore and sticky after a while, and I need to take a break periodically. The stages allow me to get a drink and splash water on my face without pausing at an arbitrary moment and losing focus.

Simpson's Hit and Run

I must say at the beginning, by way of being completely honest, that I know some of the people who worked on this game. Radical Entertainment, the developers of *Hit and Run* and its predecessor *Simpson's Road Rage*, work with me on a game programming class at the university where I work. Does this mean that I can't be fair and impartial about this game? I don't think so.

I love the Simpsons, too. The *Simpson's Hit and Run* game (see Figure 1.3) is a licensed issue that involved close collaboration with the creators and actors from the television program. The voices are those of the original actors. Some of the program's writers worked on the script for the game, and the producers of the show had some veto power and contributed ideas and art. The result is a fan's dream: you can drive around Springfield to your heart's content, seeing many familiar sights and meeting many familiar

Figure 1.3
Here's Lisa driving the "Malibu Stacey" car in *Simpson's Hit and Run*. She is about to run down a bystander.

characters. There is even a consistent story line about Mr. Burns and a conspiracy to spy on the... (Okay, I can't give away too much!) Let me just say that you should keep your eyes on the bees, and on the mysterious black vans.

This game is essentially a mission driving game—a relative of *Crazy Taxi* and many others, put in a familiar setting. Unlike other games in this genre, the damage you do is tracked, and when you exceed a pre-set limit, the police track you down and fine you. You can collect items and cash, and use these resources to buy new cars and clothing. Each level has many races that you can opt for, and many of the missions are timed, which makes this game a racing game. There are also actual races as missions in almost every game level.

The physics simulation is fairly good, and does not interfere with game play. Sound is excellent, and the voiceover is hardly irritating at all. The music is custom-made and quite interesting if you listen closely. Each character has their own theme, which varies according to whether they are walking, driving, or running; the segues are also really good. This kind of feature adds a lot to a game like this, both in quality and expense.

One good thing about the game is that you get to play a different character in each level. There are lots of things you can explore and do, including taking any car you see on the street (as a passenger, it seems, but it goes where you direct it) and jumping onto any car and having it drive you around town.

The basic game play is expertly done, and the game is fun even for people who are not Simpsons viewers. There are 56 missions and a great many other treats—enough to keep most players amused for weeks. You are even given a significant degree of control over the camera position.

What don't I like about the game? I think that the degree of difficulty of the races is not consistent with the level you are on. The way to accomplish the mission goal is not always clear. And if I had coded the audio engine, Bart would never say the same phrase three times in a row.

Mario Kart Double Dash

I was never a fan of the Mario Brothers franchise. I didn't like *Donkey Kong*, and I find the entire genre to be surreal and not interesting. This is just me, since Mario and Co. sold millions of dollars worth of games. But *Mario Kart Double Dash* (see Figure 1.4) is not about the Mario Bros. and the plot is non existent (fortunately, for me). This game is hugely entertaining as a driver, and I'm not sure I know why.

Figure 1.4
Mario Kart Double Dash provides split-screen action for two players.

The characters are the ones from the Mario universe. The first thing you do is select a pair of characters and a car—I should say cart, since these are go-cart looking vehicles and not really race cars at all. You can then select a track or a course of multiple tracks that you wish to race on. Note that the race concept is fundamental here. All of the action takes place on a track. Once the race starts, the opponents are very good at leaving you behind, meaning that the artificial intelligence used is good.

Not being a fan, it took me a few games to realize that picking up and using weapons was a critical part of the game. There are things to throw at opponents ahead of you that slows them down, and mine-like things to drop for the opponents behind you. I especially like a device that shrinks a car and the occupants to about 1/4 their usual size. Of course, they move relatively slower too. Naturally, the opposing vehicles pick up things to throw at you, making life interesting.

Actually, this game illustrates quite a few concepts that occur repeatedly in the driving genre. The physics seem quite good; there is a track that is all ice, and the traction is quite different from the desert track. The vehicles move much too fast, of course, but the skids are pretty realistic, especially for a cartoon-style game. There are objects that accelerate the car rapidly when you hit them, and objects that do the same when you pick them up and use them. There are interesting obstacles to avoid, like a tornado and giant worms, and various surfaces to get used to. The game grew on me very quickly.

I very much like the multi-player split screen views, and I'm a big fan of the "ghost" racer. Basically, the game remembers your previous race and you can race against a ghostly previous version of yourself. These are features I would steal (I mean borrow), if I were building a track racer game.

Road Rash

Most guys seem to love motorcycles for some reason. It may be that they like being close to the road, having the wind in their hair, or getting bugs in their teeth. When I first played *Road Rash* (see Figure 1.5), I got that feeling again. But this game actually made me feel a little disoriented at first because it was so fast. The graphics aren't stellar; after all, the game was released in 1991 on the Genesis and in 1996 on the PC. The game creates the sensation of speed by using a combination of techniques, including using a moving backdrop, rendering low resolution but fast graphics, and focusing the player's attention on a small part of the screen.

The game has little narrative. It is essentially a race, and everything else in the game is a set up for the race. You can collect winnings in cash and buy different bikes, you can select different characters to be, and you can select different tracks to race on. You race on streets with traffic, and there are other vehicles and obstacles on the track. Unlike some games where you can bounce off of almost anything, *Road Rash* will knock you of your bike and leave you in a ditch if you hit an oncoming car. You'll then have to walk

Figure 1.5
In this game of *Road Rash,* two racers are fighting it out to see who should be in 7th place.

back and get it going again, and you'll drop back 5 to 7 positions in the process. The game also has cops, although they don't chase you as they do in *Need for Speed*, but you can get busted.

The music is loud and fast, and contributes greatly to the feel of the game. I'm told that this game sold very well and was quite popular—I easily got addicted playing it.

Driver

The driving you do in this game has a practical application—it lets you successfully escape the law and be rewarded by the criminal overlords. Or you can play as an undercover policeman posing as a getaway driver.

The landscape is urban and fairly detailed and gritty (see Figure 1.6). The cities presented are real. Miami is good, but San Francisco is my favorite. *Driver* is an early mission-type game, but the missions in *Driver 1* do not allow you to leave the car. Later versions change this, making the game less of a driving game by my narrow definition. It is obvious to me that many later mission games owe a huge debt to the *Driver* series.

Figure 1.6
The car in *Driver* seems to float in mid-air.

The original game starts with some driving practice to let you get familiar with the controls. You can skip over the practice sessions, but doing so is not a good idea; the missions are more fun if you know how to control your car. The controls in the PC version are quite difficult to master, so the practice sessions are valuable. Once you complete the practice sessions, you'll start a mission that requires you to perform all of the practiced maneuvers to shake off pursuit. The game is also very rally-like, not only in the driving but in the scheduling as well. If you arrive too late or too early, you'll encounter a problem. And bringing ten police cars with you to a pick up is a *really* bad idea.

The graphics aren't sparkling, but they are interesting and convey speed. The narrative and missions are interesting, and the game has been rated highly by many sources.

Gran Turismo (1,2,3,4)

This game (see Figure 1.7) was advertised widely as being a *real driving simulator*, and this is no exaggeration. The simulation aspects of this game are exceptionally good and the physics are superb, especially considering that *GT1* likely pre-dates the availability of really good third-party physics engines. When researching this book, one of the things I did was go to game rental shops and ask questions like "What's the most popular driving rental over the past 4 to 5 years?" Whatever I may think of this game, I

Figure 1.7
This screen in *Gran Turismo 4* shows the proper view of the opposition.

must confess that all of the rental places ranked this game, or rather the franchise, in the top three. No other game featured in this chapter had that degree of popularity.

For simulator fans, this game offers a huge collection of cars to choose from. The cars can be customized to a great extent, not only with new parts but also by specifying the parameters of your car. The ability to build your own car and earn cash racing it so you can improve it is a clever one, and also simulates, in some sense, the real situation in racing circles.

The graphics are just acceptable. As we'll see later, one must sacrifice one thing for another, and the sacrifice here was likely graphics for physics. The details are remarkable, considering this, including stickers from well-known sponsors. (I wonder if they paid to be in the game?) Being able to watch the race from any of the other cars is also a clever idea.

The successors to the first version of this game are, in my opinion, not as good, in the sense that they don't improve much on the original game. Most of them just offer more of the same—more cars, more races, and much better graphics, especially *GT3*. The original was fairly good, and really set the stage for simulation racers that followed.

Need for Speed (All Versions)

Need for Speed (see Figure 1.8) is a beautiful game. One of the original 32-bit driving games, its high resolution graphics really set the standard for many later games, and the high level of physical accuracy was impressive for the time. Realism seems the operative word here. In one sense, the game sacrifices realism over features since there are not many options, in terms of "missions" and opponents.

The original version of this game is your basic highway race, not quite *Gumball Rally* style but close enough. The police catch wind of the race, which takes place in highway traffic at reckless speeds, and attempt to put an end to it. You can hear the police radios identifying your car, and others, setting up roadblocks, and losing track of your whereabouts.

The first version of this game was a big success, and quite a few versions of the game have been developed. I certainly have not played them all, and they are not all up to the same high quality standard when it comes to details and resolution. Still, the franchise is a sound one, founded on the basis of simulation quality.

I'm fairly sure that this game has significantly influenced games like *Grand Theft Auto* and other popular games of this era.

Figure 1.8
Need for Speed shows my favorite yellow Spyder as it is about to slip away from the authorities again.

Project Gotham Racing

Project Gotham Racing II (see Figure 1.9) is an Xbox game that was released in November 2003. Like many Xbox games, the graphics and sound are phenomenal. At first glance, this game looks like your fairly standard racing simulation, with the added feature that you race though real cities that are rendered quite realistically. The cars are very well rendered as well. The game provides you with a selection of cars to choose from and the selection grows as you earn points with which to purchase them.

The most interesting feature to me was the variety of race types that the game offers. Well, "offers" is not really the right word; the game actually forces you to play through a sequence of the races before opening up other tracks, venues, and cars for your selection. Naturally, the standard race types are provided: one-on-one, trials, and so on. Interesting variations are also provided. For example, one variation provides a situation where you must pass three cars to win and another offers a pylon course. You'll even encounter a situation where you must be traveling at a certain speed or faster at a particular place to win.

Driving at high speed through the streets of Barcelona, a city I know, is a hoot. Oddly, though, the city seemed very quiet. That's because this game seems to have no other traffic. Perhaps this is a realistic situation because if you are going to have a high-speed race through a busy town, you'd better clear the streets. This game is clearly in the category of racing simulator.

Figure 1.9
In *Project Gotham Racing* my convertible is trying to pass a Volkswagen.

On the down side, I found that the cars were sluggish at first. There is a real temptation to take corners too fast and then end up on the sidewalk. This may occur because
there are insufficient cues as to how fast you are really going, making it easy to underestimate your ability to control the vehicle. Some games, as irritating as it can be in
excess, make the car more difficult to steer as it goes faster. This warns the driver that
cornering would be a poor idea. *Project Gotham* cars seem to understeer and are quite
stable at high speeds in a straight line.

Burnout

This game is a very popular recent one (April 2003) developed for all of the major
platforms (see Figure 1.10). I didn't like it at first because it seemed like the game was
based on one or two gimmicks, and that it offered limited play value. However, the
more I played it, the more interesting it became. I think that the hidden interest factor
is its raw speed.

Burnout (I actually played *Burnout 2*) is not a track racing game. It takes place on city
streets with traffic, including your opponents, semi-trailer trucks, and buses. Given
this, a lot of collisions take place, which tie-in with the first gimmick: slow motion and
detailed collision views. When you hit another car, the collision is played using multiple distant cameras, slowly, and with added detail. For example, extra cars often pile

Figure 1.10
Burnout 2 really grows on you the more you play it.

into the stopped and damaged vehicles. This technique has limited appeal to me, but is interesting at first. I am now thinking about what would be needed to implement this feature because I have not seen it previously.

The other gimmick is the *boost-burnout* itself. This is an instant increase in acceleration, like an afterburner on a jet plane. You earn the ability to boost by spending time in the air over bumps and hills, and by engaging in close calls with other vehicles. Don't get *too* close, though, because accidents subtract from the points you need to get a boost. There is a bar-type indicator that tells you how many points you have collected and how close you are to being able to burn out. The boost allows you to achieve speeds well over 160 MPH, depending on your speed when you get boosted. The *burnout* occurs when the boost is exhausted, and is obviously an important enough event to be the actual name of the game. Usually, all that happens is that you slow down again.

The game provides a few interesting race variations. One is to see how much damage you can cause in accidents. A dollar value is accumulated each time you are involved, including incidental damage by third-parties piling on. Still, for me the best feature was the speed, and the simulated appearance of speed. This was enhanced by placing the camera lower than in many games, by placing a lot of objects near the road, and by having a lot of tunnels.

Burnout 3 is due for release shortly after the publication of this book.

Learning from the Best?

The top ten games we just explored are not just my personal favorites. Although I have evaluated all of these games and many others, the list was compiled from Internet rankings by game sites and magazines, and from historical sales numbers.

Now that you've been introduced to these games, let's look at them a little closer to find the common elements and the features that make these games as good as they are. If three or four of these games have a common design element, it's likely that this element is important enough to help create an engaging driving or racing game. While you may see different things in this collection (feel free to tell me so!), I see seven major features worth discussing.

Venue

Most of the top ten games take place in interesting locations, often real places that you may have visited—San Francisco, New York, or Paris. I have never driven in any of these cities, but I have visited them and can recognize some of the places in the games. Many people have seen these places in movies and on television, which gives the sites an extra degree of familiarity. This makes the venues important, and not just because they are often distant and exotic to many of us. If you could create a game that would let you drive through your own home town, for example, I'm sure that the game would interest you.

Of course, simply placing the action in an exciting place is not good enough—you must portray that place using 3D graphics and sound accurately enough so that the player can identify it. This is an implementation issue more than a design issue, but it is important, and I'll discuss it in more detail.

Placing a driving game on a racetrack is an obvious thing to do, but it can actually take away from the fun *unless* the track is familiar to the player. The track at Indianapolis is well known, for example, and a racing fan would quickly identify it. This is where racing games overlap with sports games. In a basketball or hockey game, the designers and implementers go to some significant efforts to try to make the players look and act like the real players. Fans know their sport, and can be very critical when the players are not behaving properly. Similarly, in racing games that are more realistic (*Colin McRae Rally*, for example) the players are more likely to be racing fans, and will expect the tracks and the cars, maybe even the drivers, to behave as they do when seen on TV and in person. This kind of accuracy is hard to achieve, and requires regular game updates to keep the game accurate from year-to-year.

It is a little unusual to permit a driver to get too far away from the path that the game designers have set out. In *Driver* and *Hit and Run*, you can go anywhere in the city, and the game play continues. However, the virtual cities are small subsets of the real cities and can be thought of as a track that is all bent and convoluted. On the other hand, *Crazy Taxi* actually allows you to drive just about anywhere, even underwater. This feature gives the player the experience that they have much more freedom than they really do; they appear to have many choices but the choices all seem to lead to the same few consequences. This illusion of complete freedom is very important to computer games in general, not just racing games. It is necessary because as game designers we just can't simulate the entire universe.

Not *yet*, anyway.

Conflict

A race is a game that has winners and losers. Clearly the goal is to win, and any game that does not allow the player to win will not be popular. This is the minimum conflict requirement of a racing game. Observe that many of the games we explored earlier are more than just simple races, although they may include them. There are a variety of other conflict sources in the games, and they are essential to game play. Indeed, any narrative depends on a degree of conflict to be interesting. While narrative in driving games usually just provides background information (an excuse for the action), the conflict provides interest and engagement.

So, what kind of conflict am I talking about? In *Crazy Taxi* we have customers refusing to pay if a taxi gets there late, and they berate drivers for going too fast or slow. *Hit and Run* has a collection of conflict-creating scenarios, since the TV show the game is based on has a degree of conflict in every episode. Homer dislikes Smithers, Bart and Skinner get on each other's nerves, there is a distinct criminal element in town, and so on. These elements are carried into the game. *Double Dash* has weapons that can slow your opponents.

Road Rash allows you to kick your opponents off of their bikes. Finally, the police in *Driver* and *Need for Speed* are always trying to impede the player's progress.

In my top ten list, only *Colin McRae Rally* lacks a source of conflict other than the competition of the race itself. This leads me to believe that there are two main classes of racer/driver: the simulation and sport racer (SSR), and the theme driver (TD).

The simulation/sport racer is about sports, cars, drivers, and racing. The accuracy of the physics and graphics are an important fun-imparting aspect of the game for the intended audience, usually race fans. These are, in my opinion, hard to construct because the audience is relatively narrow and critical of flaws. The fun lies in competing with the pros, with devising accurate strategies, and with implementing them successfully.

The theme driver uses driving and racing as a key theme, and adds other aspects. These other aspects might include hiding, searching, fighting, performing missions, and so on. Unlike the simulation/sport racer, the fun here lies in doing things that are *not* realistic—shooting a missile at a road hog or taking a short cut across your neighbor's lawn. Driving is still a key element, and the main user interface remains the vehicle controls. The addition of the extra themes, however, provides a wider canvas for having fun, and this gives a broader scope to the designer. It's also true that there is a greater opportunity for narrative in this genre. The narrative appeals to both players and designers.

Speed

The driving games that are the most fun to play typically allow you to go *fast*. Not CPU-fast, although that's good too, but MPH-fast. The good racing games provide a good illusion of speed. This can be achieved using many tricks, and I'm certain that I don't know all of them.

One simple trick is to have objects near the road move past a driver at a high speed. This is often done using buildings because they have a lot of detail that flashes past a driver in a similar way to what would be seen in movies or real life. In fact, a range of objects in a range of distances is effective in conveying the illusion. Buildings, being closer to the car, move past quickly, while the distant forest moves by a little slower, and the mountains move by even more slowly. The illusion of reality is made more complete by having objects move past at appropriate speeds.

Sound is crucial as well. All you need to do is play *Need for Speed* or *Road Rash* without sound to see the difference. A fast moving music track helps a lot, as does a good set of speed-implying sound effects: engine sounds, 3D audio, doppler, and so on.

One nice idea that is simple to implement and is now a standard feature in games is a backdrop with scenery painted on it. This effect is also used in movies; the Borg ship internal shots on *Star Trek* are actors in front of paintings. Many science fiction productions depend on paintings to convey distance and strange environments. The use of drops in a game can add a depth that is noticed if absent, but usually draws no comment otherwise.

The 3D scene of a race consists of a terrain model on top of which we have a road, vehicles, and stationary objects. As shown in Figure 1.11, these objects are placed in the near and medium distance. There is usually a distance beyond which objects will

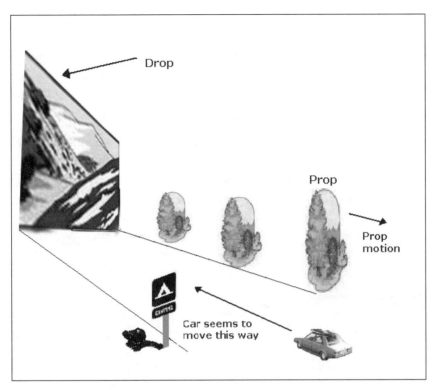

Figure 1.11
Creating the illusion of speed by using a backdrop and props of various sizes.

not be rendered (far clipping plane). As objects get closer, they seem to "pop" into existence when they pass that distance. In the far distance, we have an image painted on a surface that passes for the horizon. In *Road Rash*, this image often has hills and a sky painted on it, while in *Driver* the image is sometimes an ocean, sky, or an urban backdrop. In any case, the drop has no depth. A well-produced game will have the drop rotate as the player turns the vehicle, which gives the illusion that the car changes direction. This is essential in maintaining the impression that the player is actually moving.

Physics

Creating a game involves creating an entire universe. You get to decide where things are, how big they are, what they eat, and so on. In particular, the rules of physics as we understand them in the *real* universe are flexible, and you get to decide how they work in *your* universe. If you are building a game of the SSR variety, the physics must be an accurate rendition of actual car and driver physics. The gear ratios must transform the engine torque appropriately because your players will know if you are wrong.

In many other instances of games, the accuracy of the physics takes a back seat to playability and entertainment value. In a game like *Doom,* a player can run quickly through a level. If you actually measured the speed of how fast the player moves, you might be surprised to learn that a top speed of 60 MPH can be obtained! This does not detract from the fun; on the contrary, restricting game objects to real-world speeds would slow a game down a lot.

Physics includes a variety of topics including how collisions are handled, how fuel is consumed, how fast the vehicles can accelerate and what the top speeds are, how fast cars can enter a turn before they skid, and how a vehicle can become airborne if it reaches the peak of a hill. The games in my top ten list do take liberties with physics to enhance game play, especially *Hit and Run* and *Double Dash.* We will discuss this further after we get a chance to look at how physics are implemented in a game in Chapter 9. Just remember that any rule can be violated if it makes the game more fun.

Graphics and Sound

All of the games in the top ten list excel in some aspects of graphics or sound or both. *Colin Mcrae Rally* has exceptional scenery and cars, *Need for Speed* focuses on the cars, and *Driver* has excellent urban backdrops. *Hit and Run* offers its players the ability to explore a town that they are familiar with—Springfield, home of the Simpsons. Do not underestimate the value of *sandbox mode.* This is essentially a mode in which you can explore the game world without having to be timed or perform a mission. If the world is interesting, just looking around can be entertaining.

Sound may be more important than graphics, especially for imparting a mood, such as excitement. A fast moving rock and roll audio background adds energy to a game in the same way the ethereal themes from *Half Life* make this game's world seem dangerous and spooky. Having great sound doesn't need to be a tradeoff; you can have good graphics and audio if you just have the wherewithal to create both.

Of course, the SSR-type games tend to use better graphics because they need to provide a more faithful simulation. The TD games, such as *Double Dash,* can be very "cartoony" and still offer a huge degree of entertainment value.

So what do the top ten games have in common when it comes to graphics and sound? They offer an appropriate level of detail in graphics, with good audio and appropriate and entertaining objects and backdrops rendered predictably.

Props

Props are items that can be manipulated in a game. Sports games in general have fewer props than most games, but racing games may be an exception. Mission-based TDs in particular will have the player pick up passengers, money, fuel, and objects. They may knock down trees, smash lampposts and mailboxes, and run over small critters. Some games even have weapons; a missile can be a prop—and a very sophisticated one at that, because it can move on its own.

Props have an immense potential for making a game more interesting. Without the possibility of picking up weapons and speedups, *Double Dash* is just a cartoon race game. Being able to slow down your opponent from a distance, and having him be a threat from behind, adds an element of excitement to a game. Combat-style driving games are really two games, or two styles, in one package.

Props also allow a more interesting narrative, since entire missions and levels can depend on moving props from one place to another. Props can be protected, and your opponent's props can be destroyed. They can impart important properties that remain from level-to-level, like magic icons, fuel, and skill points. This leads to the conclusion that complexity makes a game more interesting. There is some truth to this, as long as a game remains playable. Although I do think it is more likely that *a degree of unpredictability makes a game more interesting*. A driving game must be consistent, but it is best if it does not repeat itself exactly each time it is played. Props can be used both to make a game more complex and to make it less predictable. The location of the props can change, which in turn can help prevent a repeatable character from becoming too dull. A pattern of play can be useful sometimes, but it's rarely entertaining.

Interface

There has been a significant effort to standardize some game interfaces. For example, console games have tried to standardize on how controls are used to perform similar tasks. Driving games tend to use consistent control sequences, like arrow keys. Still, the games presented in this chapter vary some on how they use the keyboard and controls. In the games we explored, I've found the controls for *Driver* hardest to remember and master.

There are other variations on how simple keys, such as arrow keys, are used. Some drag racing games use the mouse to control speed and direction, which I feel is an error. The mouse has more degrees of freedom in directional control, and the faster a car goes, the harder it is to control with a mouse. One tends to oversteer, and mouse position is relative, not absolute.

So the lesson of the top ten games is to standardize the interface as much as possible, making it simple and effective. You don't want to force the player to remember awkward key sequences in the heat of play.

Fortunately, when it comes to interface devices, things have changed in the past few years. Special game interface devices are now available at low cost. Most of these devices use the USB interface, which is much better than the old parallel port or the even older "game port" that was available on PCs. These were almost always used to plug in a joystick—a curious term for a game control.

I have two interfaces that I really like, other than the usual. One is the steering wheel and pedal set that converts wheel and pedal motions into character sequences. There are a few brands available, most of which now use the ubiquitous USB interface. The fact that they can be configured to send any sequence you like means that game interfaces don't have to be standard anymore, at least in the long run. More and more people will acquire the special interfaces until the keyboard becomes old fashioned. Figure 1.12 shows one particular brand, the Logitech.

Figure 1.12
A USB steering device and pedal set.

Another USB interface device is the game controller; the idea is to make the computer look more like a game console by giving it a similar control device. Unfortunately, these devices seem to be just a little different. At least, I can't find one that mimics my Gamecube controller very well. In any case, the idea is a good one, and it should be possible to create a controller that can be assigned key values and behaves very much like the real thing, again limiting the requirement of the games themselves to provide a sensible key assignment.

There are many other possibilities, including a nifty plastic control unit that straps over a keyboard. The controls are levers and buttons that are used to manipulate simulated heavy construction devices like cranes. Pulling a lever results in a key being pressed. I tried one that came with a child's game, which allowed an inexpensive "feel" of driving and I enjoyed it myself.

I could easily get carried away discussing possible interfaces for games. My own university research includes some work on hand gesture recognition, and we have applied this research to controlling games on the PC—hand motions are interpreted as requests to move, pick an object up, and so on. We were able to combine this with a gaze recognition system, so that the position control was based on where the player was looking! We are also going to use gaze to control the path of a missile fired by a player. Ultimately, games will become an invisible technology, like telephones and TV. They will be anywhere we like, and will require no special knowledge or hardware to play.

Summary

We have looked at a collection of very good draiving games. In some cases these games are seminal, in that they have provided the basic idea or theme for an entire generation of similar games, on many platforms. While looking at these games, I have tried to point out the features that made them great. A list of these features, in no particular order, is: venue, conflict, speed, physics, graphics, sound, props, and interface.

We'll spend the remaining fourteen chapters discussing how to actually implement most of these features, in at least a basic and functional way.

Chapter 2

Game Architecture for Driving and Racing Games

- Learn that driving and racing games are developed using a standard architecture.

- Design a simple game called *Gopher-it* that shows how basic game components are constructed.

- Learn how you actually go about making a driving game function on a computer.

architecture *n.* **3. Construction or structure generally; any ordered arrangement of the parts of a system: the *architecture* of the universe.**[1]

According to this definition, the architecture for a driving or racing game should be about the structure of a game—the way that the parts are arranged to create a working system. And to truly understand the structure of a driving or racing game, you need to know something about programming, although it is possible to have a general appreciation without being a programmer. You need to know what the parts are, not just the visible parts such as cars and roads, but also the structural and functional parts, such as the audio system and the graphics rendering code. You need to understand how the parts communicate with each other, and what each part needs to know to accomplish its important work.

A game player cannot be required to know this. The player needs only to know about the things needed to *play the game*—the game's rules, tasks, and interface. In fact, my students have told me that after studying games and actually writing one, they never look at a game in the same way again. They still play games but find themselves asking, "Why did the game's developer put that building there?" and "How did the designers create the torches?" Knowing how a game functions under the hood can sometimes interfere with the experience of playing the game.

In this chapter we'll look at the architectural components of driving and racing games—the graphics system that presents the virtual universe, the audio system, the user interface, the scheduler, and the artificial intelligence system. As you'll learn, all of these components are needed to create a realistic simulation-style game. You'll also learn how these components interact with each other. Rather than just present the theory of driving and racing game architecture, I'll take you through the process of designing a simple game called *Gopher-it*. Although this game is just a sample 2D maze/chase game, it will show you how the key game components, such as the AI system, need to be designed and incorporated into your games.

The Components of a Driving/Racing Game

In a technical sense, any video game, including any driving and racing game, is an interactive real-time simulation with a graphical display and an audio system. Such a simulation requires a number of components including a graphics system, audio system, user interface (which I define to include the *front end*), scheduler (main loop), and an artificial intelligence (AI) system.

Figure 2.1 shows a diagram of the basic components and how they are connected. Notice that the AI system is assigned the important job of keeping track of the simulated objects in a game. Of course, this organization is not the only one that is used to build driving and racing games, and it certainly doesn't show all of the details involved, but it should be good enough to help you get started. I'll be using it throughout this chapter as I peel away the layers to show you how racing and driving games operate.

I'll introduce each of the components presented in Figure 2.1 and you'll learn how they communicate with each other and what information is shared between the components. This will give you a much clearer idea of how a basic driving or racing game functions as a software system. In later chapters, we'll work with each component in much more detail.

Presenting the Virtual Universe

All computer games offer their players worlds that don't really exist. Without getting too philosophical, what is displayed on the computer screen is a rendition of data that represent a simulated situation. The player sees a real screen with real images, but the environment that is being drawn doesn't quite exist in the real world—it is a virtual environment in which a computer program controls the laws that dictate how objects interact. A significant part of the code used in a game is dedicated to displaying the images and playing the sounds that form the imaginary world for the player to interact with.

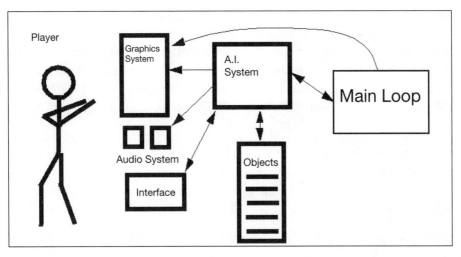

Figure 2.1
Architecture of a computer game.

Before proceeding, keep in mind that there are many types of games, and that each type has its own design requirements. I'll be focusing on racing and driving games in this book, and thus I won't be presenting a general discussion that includes other game genres, as you'll find in other game programming books. When I discuss how we should go about displaying a game world, I'll concentrate on the view from behind the wheel.

We perceive the universe from our particular point in space. What is going on a mile away is unknown to us, and doesn't affect us. The road ahead for the next few hundred yards is crucial, and how we respond to it will influence the hundred yards following that. The important thing you need to consider as a programmer of driving and racing games is how to display the things that the player needs to experience so that the player can make game-play decisions and feel that the simulated world is realistic. Processing key data involves two main aspects: the visual data, which require a computer graphics system, and the sound data, which require an audio system. Let's look at both of these components in a little more detail next.

Inside the Graphics System

The graphics needed to render a driving game can consume numerous CPU resources. And because a driving game requires much more than just graphics, you'll need to have an efficient graphics system so that you'll have enough CPU resources to devote to other aspects of your game system. A good driving game uses an appropriate level of detail for the application, and that's important too. The basic problem addressed by graphics systems involves placing enough frames (images) on the screen every second to give the illusion of motion and realism. Movies use 24 frames per second to achieve their degree of realism, while television uses almost 30 frames per second. However, a television displays an image that is about 525¥525 pixels, while a motion picture has a much higher resolution.

Another aspect of picture display that must be considered is the number of distinct colors that can be shown. This is sometimes called *quantization*, and television, for example, can display far fewer colors than a motion picture can. A computer screen falls somewhere in between.

To understand the basics of how you'll need to render frames in a driving game so that you can create realistic simulations, there is some basic math you'll need to know. If you render images at 24 frames per second on a computer screen that has a resolution of 1024×768 with 24-bit colors, you would need to calculate and write out 56 Megabyes per second. This is quite a lot of data, even on a modern PC, so we must use a few little tricks. First, and most importantly, the video card needs to take a greater role in calculating screen updates. Fortunately, newer video cards can draw millions of polygons per second, perform texture mapping, support stencil buffers and mip-mapping, and perform many other essential operations. This means that your CPU does not have to do these things. It can focus more on organizing critical data for the video card.

Another essential trick is to group the objects to be drawn according to their position and visibility. If you are driving a car and looking through the front windshield, your field of view will be restricted to the region in front of you, say 60 degrees each side of dead ahead. Objects that are not in that region can be ignored, and should not require any significant amount of computation. Also, objects that are too far away should be ignored, as they will be too small to see. The same applies to objects hidden behind buildings and hills. Of course, determining what can and can't be seen requires effort, but not as much as drawing these objects.

Some of this must be done by your game, but your graphics card can handle much of it. A number of these cards are available, and each has its own capabilities and interfaces. If you want your game to run on more than one computer, you cannot code your graphics system for a specific device. Fortunately, software packages are available that form a layer between your game code and the graphics card, hiding the differences between the cards while presenting a consistent interface. This is really essential for a commercial game, and is also important for us.

The two major competitors in this field are DirectX and OpenGL. Both are freely available, and both probably exist on your computer right now. We'll discuss these interfaces later but for now you just need to know that they exist. I'll be using OpenGL in this book for the driving and racing games that are presented. (Chapter 3 will be dedicated to graphics generally and OpenGL specifically.) The thing to remember about most game graphics systems is that they are based on polygons, because polygons can be drawn quickly using a graphics card. We can represent any object as a collection of polygons, and we can quickly shade them, place textures on them, rotate and scale them, and perform other operations using very fast algorithms.

If you read a number of game programming books, you will frequently encounter the phrase *graphics pipeline*. The idea is that if you can keep a number of software modules busy at the same time, you can increase the number of polygons that can be processed per second. There are a few ways that the pipeline can be organized, but I take the view that there are three basic parts: the object level, the geometric level, and the rasterization level. Let's take a closer look at each of these parts.

The Object Level

At a conceptual level, objects are conceived and manipulated as units. Of course, they are really displayed as polygons and lines, but when designing a game it is preferable to think of a rock as having the properties of a real object. A rock can be seen, but offers resistance when it is moved, and can be collided with. Operations such as animation, morphing, and collision detection are performed at this level. Basically, we can perform any operation that needs to know about the objects themselves. At the end of this phase, a set of polygons or lines is sent to the geometric level.

This part of the pipeline is the most sensitive to the game itself. The game designers and creators implement the object level in software because they understand the game objects the best.

The Geometric Level

The geometry part of the pipeline has a variety of functions that can be arranged into distinct modules, as shown in Figure 2.2.

The first step converts model-based coordinates, which are often based on an object-centred coordinate system. These coordinates are converted into a more global system of coordinates so that objects can interact with each other.

Next, based on the position of the viewer (camera), a coordinate transformation is computed to align the polygons of the objects to a common system based on the viewer. One result of this is that some polygons become impossible to see; they may be behind us, or too far away.

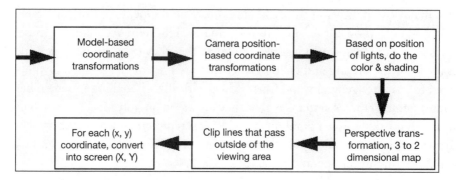

Figure 2.2
Functions performed in the geometric part of the graphics pipeline.

Let's consider the position and color of the lights and create an appropriate shading and color transformation of the object's polygons. The sun, for example, is positioned a great distance away and is colored yellow-white, while a nearby headlight might be a brighter blue. The color of a pixel is a function of its own intrinsic color and of the brightness, color, and position of the illumination sources.

Now we compute the viewing transformation, most often a perspective transformation. This gives us the view we would expect of a three-dimensional object, including the fact that distant objects look smaller than ones that are nearer. The view of the scene will be realistic if it represents what we expect, and we expect a perspective view. The objects that were 3D polygons are now two-dimensional ones.

The polygons that fall outside of the computer screen area, or viewing area, must be eliminated, or *clipped*. This is the next stage. Polygons that are too close or too far away would have been clipped in the previous stage. Clipping is a non-trivial operation. For example, a triangle that is partly outside of the screen area is cut by a vertical or horizontal line, and this often means that it will not be a triangle anymore.

Finally, all coordinates of all lines and polygons are converted in screen (or window) to X, Y coordinates so they can be drawn quickly.

The Rasterization Level
In this stage we convert lines and polygons into pixels. Pixels are the only thing that can be displayed on a screen, so it is essential that this step be performed accurately as well as quickly. After this is done, we can do any other operations that need to be done on a per-pixel basis: the Z-buffer visibility algorithm is an example of one such operation.

Comments on Optimization

It should be obvious that code must be written efficiently because the graphics system must render a sufficient number of frames per second so that a game will look smooth. The algorithms we choose must be able to deal with the number of polygons likely to appear in the objects, in both space and time considerations.

The game we are going to create will, first and foremost, have to display scenes on the screen with the correct positions and colors, follow the game rules as designed, and play sounds at correct moments. Although we won't be intentionally wasteful, efficiency will not be the most important thing. Why? It is because code optimization can become boring very quickly, and is not our main interest. There are many reference works on the subject for those interested, including *Game Coding Complete, Second Edition*[2] and *Core Techniques and Algorithms in Game Programming*[3].

Inside the Audio System

In general, the purpose of the game's audio system is to play music and sound effects. This is supposed to be a simplistic view, and yet even after decades of technological changes in game technology and design, the game audio system still does pretty much what it always did, and still works in a similar way. Much progress has been made in the area of graphics, but, as an acquaintance of mine likes to say, "Game audio is a train wreck."

Most sounds that we'll need, such as engine sounds, sounds of doors opening and closing, noises of crashes and scrapes, and even background music, will be read in from files, usually one file per sound. A very common format for sound files is the WAV file, which is basically a Microsoft standard that is supported on most platforms. These can contain compressed or uncompressed audio, can have mono or stereo, and can store audio at a variety of sample rates, including the CD standards. The WAV file format is simple and it is very convenient for our purposes.

However, you may need an audio system that has more sophistication so that you can perform tasks such as playing positional audio, in which each sound appears to originate from a particular point in space. This can be done with stereo, but is much better suited to modern 5.1 channel audio systems, and can be truly impressive. Sound cards have recently been designed with some capacity for sound synthesis, and some degree of synthetic sound and music, especially using MIDI. However, the basic structure of the audio system is simple, and its job is obvious.

Playing the Game by the Rules

The game architecture that I've presented earlier in this chapter is what I would call the *game board*—the part that the user sees and manipulates. There are many programs that have very sophisticated graphical and audio interfaces that are not games. What's the difference? A driving game works in real time, processing user choices and updating the display accordingly. A driving game is a simulation and, most importantly, is one that has a goal. To be a game, there must be a way to at least keep score and usually there is a way to win. The part of the game program that does this is called the *game logic* section, the *artificial intelligence*, and some other things too.

The graphics and audio parts of a game can largely be shared by games that are quite different from each other. The game logic is what makes each game what it is. It is the code that reflects the game designer's intent. Even here, the structure of this program has a certain consistency from game-to-game; it is in the details that the code differs.

Most of a Computer Game Is Hidden

The player actually sees a world drawn by the graphics system, but this world is particular to the game at hand and changes according to rules that are largely invisible to the player, at least at first. Part of the game play is figuring out what the rules are. For example, you might not know how fast you can drive into a corner before skidding. That is actually a kind of rule. You also might not know the ratio of brake to gas pedal for a proper 180 degree turn. Again, this is a rule that the player discovers while playing the game. The number of damage points you can take before your car blows up, on the other hand, is an *explicit* rule that is stated up front. Personally, I don't read a lot of rules before starting to play. I discover a lot of the explicit rules as I go along.

When I say that a lot of a game is hidden, I mean that the rules, interrelationships between game objects, goals, and even a player's particular progress through the game are saved in code and internal data structures, and are not necessarily displayed. Indeed, their internal representation does not lend itself to be displayed.

The Artificial Intelligence

The artificial intelligence (AI) subsystem of a game is responsible for many things that the game does that are not seen directly, but are reflected in the game play and how the game simulates the real world. The AI system controls object management, including the physics and the direction of the independently simulated objects such as opponents. In our case, these opponents would be opposing drivers. Specifically, the AI keeps track of the current position and velocity of all of the objects. It is the logical system to use to perform collision detection. It keeps track of attributes of objects, including earned attributes such as hit points, damage, and found objects (ammunition, money, and so on).

Artificial intelligence has a connotation amongst the general population, supported by movies and TV, of computers that can think. In the movies, these computers are also frequently evil, but we'll leave that for later. Computer scientists and programmers know more about the details, and they realize that AI is about making a computer *appear* to be intelligent. The techniques that computer professionals use are many and varied, but the truth is that game AI is very simplistic compared with the techniques found in research labs, and the goals are also quite different.

The basic problem is that game AI has to function in real time, and must steal CPU cycles from what is perceived to be really important work—the processing performed by the graphics system. Thus, the really complex and sexy functions of an advanced AI system are simply too time-consuming for a game. For example, a voice recognition system would be cool for some games, but really isn't needed. Games are rarely required to prove theorems, recognize faces, or invent novel answers to complex questions. They *are* required to decide what to do next or plan a route through a building or a forest to reach a goal. In a racing game, the AI might need to perform a function such as determining how a machine-generated opponent will pass you on a hairpin curve. Although it is sometimes useful to use an advanced AI technique like a neural network to accomplish a game goal, it is unusual.

One thing that all AI systems must do is keep track of everything that is and isn't displayed on the screen. Not only must a game determine when you hit a wall, but it must also keep track of all of the other cars, even the ones you cannot see, and slow them down when they hit an obstacle. Most of the AI system focuses on supporting simple rules implying simple choices. The most common implementation of such a rule is:

```
if (condition is true) then { do this thing }
```

This is not especially sophisticated, but it does the job quickly. The same thing can be implemented as a table or a tree, as you'll learn in Chapter 6.

An Example AI System—A *Simple 2D Maze/Chase* Game

Let's look at an example of how a simple AI system can be set up for a game. For our example, we'll use a two-dimensional game that I will refer to as *Gopher-it*. This is the first game that we'll build in this book. It is a simple game that is played on a board like the one shown in Figure 2.3. The black lines represent the walls of a maze. The grey ellipses are gas stations, and the small squares are progress markers that show how far the player has progressed through this level of the game. These will, in fact, represent gophers, which the player runs over to generate points. The player will drive a car starting at the point marked with "X" and attempt to collect all of the squares (gophers). Two police vehicles, marked "P," will attempt to stop the player. As the player moves one unit per turn, their vehicle will move in the last direction indicated. The police cars generally move a little faster than the player's vehicle—the cops always get the faster cars for some reason! If a police car collides with the player's, the player's car vanishes and the player loses. When the player's car touches a gopher, the gopher vanishes, and the player collects one point.

Finally, the game uses a special feature in the form of a gas station. When the player touches one, the player's car is refueled and the station disappears. The player's car becomes invincible, and if it touches one of the police cars *it* vanishes. Police cars will attempt to get away from an invincible car, and move a little slower than usual to give the player a chance. The game ends when the player captures all of the counter squares, or when an enemy car touches the player's car.

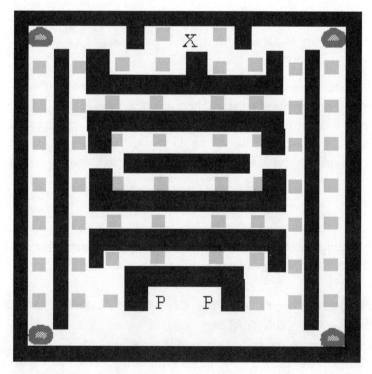

Figure 2.3
The playing surface for *Gopher-it.*

The AI for this game is simple but educational. Here is one implementation:

```
AI-step:play_audio (step_tone)
Move_user: s = compute_next_user_square;
   piece = contents_of (s);
   if (invincible_counter > 0) invincible_counter -= 1;
   if (piece != WALL)
   {
      if (piece == POLICE)
      {
         if (INVINCINBLE) contents_of (s) = EMPTY;
         else game_over();
      if (piece == COUNTER)
      {
         score++;
         contents_of (s) = EMPTY;
      }
      if (piece == GAS_STATION)
      {
         contents_of (s) = EMPTY;
         INVINCIBLE = TRUE;
         invincible_counter = 15;
      }
      contents_of (s) = USER_CAR;
   }
```

The point I was trying to make earlier should now be clear. The use of if-then-else statements to make decisions is ubiquitous, and no fancy decision making algorithms have been used. Instead, a lot of small decisions are made quickly. The control of the enemy cars is missing at this point, but we will return to this game later on.

Creating Design Documents

The design and implementation of even a simple game is a complex process, and there are some ways to make the process more transparent and less error prone. One way is to have a very clear idea at the outset of what the game will do in all circumstances, and know how each task will be performed. In other words, you'll want to create a set of design documents that specify how your game will work. These are not just for software engineering projects or projects that require big teams. In a game, they help nail down the concise explanation of the operation and structure of the game—a blueprint, if you like. No sensible builder would start construction on anything, not even a small shed, without doing some drawing, and no technician would think about building a new electronic circuit without making a diagram. The description above is not sufficient for implementation, but it is the basic idea.

What documents should we have? Well, game developers all have their own detailed sequence of documents that they use, and their publishers sometimes specify these documents. We want the minimum needed for our task, which is to build a small game in our basement using only a few people—perhaps only one person. My opinion is that we need, as a minimum, the following two documents:

- **High Concept Design**: A professional HCD can be 25 to 30 pages, and is used to sell a game to a publisher, among other things. Ours will be 1 to 2 pages, and will be used mainly to crystallize our thoughts on how the game will be played and why you believe the game will be fun.

- **Technical Design**: This document starts with the basic game objects and goals, and explains how each of the game's components is implemented, from architectures down to data structures. This will be the major document that we'll use to build the game. Its existence prior to writing code is essential for success, since it provides the blueprint for the actual code. A professional tech design could be hundreds of pages, but for our purposes we can stick with one that is between 10 and 25 pages.

A complete, if simple, high concept design for *Gopher-it* appears in Appendix A of this book. The table of contents for a technical design appears also, with sample technical design documents provided on the website for this book.

Defining the Game State

The state of a game is collection of information that represents the game at any given time. Given a particular state, a game can be started from that point. The information needed for the game state includes:

- Position, orientation, and velocity of all dynamic entities
- Behavior and intentions of AI-controlled characters
- Dynamic and static attributes of all gameplay entities
- Scores, health, powerups, damage levels, and so on

All subsystems in a game are interested in some aspect of the game state because the state variables are exactly those things that are essential to the look of the game and the play options possible from any point in the game. For instance, the graphics renderer needs to know the positions of objects so that they can be drawn, their damage levels, and so on.

How is the game state made available to subsystems? As always, there are many options, each with their own advantages and disadvantages, but for a straightforward driving game, there are only a few that make sense. Let's look at the different techniques that we could use to code our simple *Gopher-it* game, and then we'll select the one that best fits our sample game.

Global State Variables

This approach is just what it sounds like. State variables are global, shared by all of the modules. A lot of programming language design and sotware engineering practice has tried to show why using global state variables is a poor idea. After all, imagine every module having access—complete access mind you—to every other module's variables. This could create real chaos!

There is a certain convenience, however, to this scheme. If the graphics system wants to know where a tree is, it simply gets this information from where the tree is stored. The problem is that the graphics system can change the data, and before you know it, the tree might turn into something else. If you are writing a quite small system with very tight modules, and you are disciplined, using state variables could work. The more complex your game is, however, the more likely this scheme will create a lot of problems.

Push/Pull (Client-Server)

This approach is one of my favorites. In this scheme, subsystems have incomplete knowledge of one another, and can request information from each other in a structured fashion (a *pull*) or send a new value to a module (a *push*). This is what we will use in our sample *Gopher-it* game, and what you often see in Java and C++ as accessors and modifiers. For example, if we want to find the location of a police car, we could ask for it using a function such as:

```
getPosition (POLICE_CAR, &x, &y);
```

This is a pull. If we wish to notify the AI system that an object has been destroyed, we could perform a push:

```
setExist (object[i], FALSE);
```

This function call would set the *exist* attribute of the object to false.

This scheme is elegant. It also has another big advantage—it can be used across great distances with equal simplicity. For online multi-player games, the push-pull scheme operates on a server at a remote site, and one of various remote invocation schemes can be used transparently.

Managers

In some sense, using a manager is like the push-pull model with an intermediate system for handling the requests. The AI system does not own position and orientation attributes in this scheme, for example. They are owned by a management subsystem that has the simple task of hiding the variables and structures and permitting access to them using standard accessor and modifier functions.

Using this scheme, the AI system would have to ask for the position of an object just like the graphics system, and would also have to request a modification to position from the manager:

```
manager.getPos (OBJECT1, &x, &y);
manager.setPos (OBJECT1, &x+1, &y+1);
```

This is not much more complex than the client-server approach, and has a similar feel. Because there are few tools that support this model, discipline is needed to maintain it. I have seldom seen a situation where this scheme has an advantage over the client-server approach, and so I don't actively promote it.

Broadcast-Listener

For a certain amount of overhead, we can change the client-server model into one in which modifications to state attributes can be sent to other subsystems by issuing an event. When the position of an opponent changes, for example, an "opponent-change" event could be sent to the graphics system so that the opponent could be correctly drawn. Given a system similar to the Java **interface** scheme that uses *listeners*, all subsystems interested in this change can be alerted at the same time! Objects or subsystems interested in a particular event, like a position change of a police car for instance, would register with the listener so that they would receive the events.

Using a Java-like syntax, we could have:

```
public class Z extends q implements PoliceListener
{
...
t1.addPoliceListener(this);
...
public void policeMotion (GameEvent e)
{
    if (e.getSource() == t1) ...
}
```

This shows the three essential parts of the setup: declaring the use of the **PoliceListener** interface in the class header, adding this class instance to the list of those interested in receiving police motion events, and writing a handler (a callback, really) named **policeMotion()** that will be called when a police motion event takes place. No direct communication between subsystems is used in this scheme. Information is only sent to those interested, and is queued in the case where there are multiple events occurring simultaneously.

If you can make this technique work properly in a language that doesn't specifically support it, you'll certainly get a programmer rush. However, after studying software systems for many years, I came to realize that on almost all PC systems *there is only one CPU.* We can pretend that processes are independent if we like, but switching between software processes takes time on our single CPU, and treating software events like variable modifications as if they were asynchronous processes is a little wasteful and obscures the flow of the code. This is my opinion, of course. Still, some systems profit from using threads and such, and this is the way to deal with state on such systems.

Database Management System

Most games can't afford the overhead of a real database management system, and their developers can't afford the cost of developing and maintaining one if speed was not an issue. However, for massively multi-player online games (MMORGs), this may be the only option. Since I can't think of any MMORGs that are driving games, we shall ignore this scheme.

Shared and Global Entities

This technique uses the inheritance characteristic of an object-oriented programming language. Think of it as global state, but with references to classes and inheritance. With this approach, both the AI and the graphics system would have a reference (pointer) to a police car object, and could, by manipulating the accessor and modifier methods, get and change the object's position, orientation, and other attributes. This is the classic object-oriented way of doing things. It's cleaner than using globals.

Within this scheme, many options are available: a single rooted hierarchy, ownership, multiple inheritance, and so on. This approach has, in fact, become the standard practice in many colleges and universities that teach programming (mine too!), and as a result, this method, or family of methods, has become the most common scheme for manipulating game objects and system state.

My main complaint with this set of schemes is that they tend to become dependent on a particular language, usually C++, and the decision to use them becomes a "religious" one. I say this because I have had many an argument with software engineers over the proper use of multiple inheritance, for example. Since C++ is one of the few languages that permits multiple inheritance, a scheme that depends upon it has limited options for implementation. The problem is that a single class hierarchy does not scale well, and the inheritance structure starts looking like nonsense after a while. The most complex subsystem of a game (graphics, in general) tends to be able to specify the structure of the rest, simply by virtue of its complexity. Multiple inheritance scales better, but is hard to change later, and becomes difficult to manage when a system gets too complex. These schemes can also slow down performance. Many games need all of the help they can get, especially when they try to simulate the real world.

My personal favorite technique for defining game state is one based on the client-server scheme in which a standard procedural language (such as C) is used to create a class-like structure of functions. Each module contains a set of variables and data structures that cannot be accessed from the other modules except through the accessor functions provided by the module. However, when needed for testing or while merging modules, global variables and shared entities can be used such as a log file for dumping test information while performing a task like debugging. There is nothing to prevent the user of this scheme in using Java or a scripting language like Lua, or even C++, as a language for creating small specific-purpose sub-modules, as the controller for an opponent, for instance.

However you do it, the management and control of the system state in a complex system like a computer game must be done carefully and with discipline. While the best way has yet to be determined with certainty, it is absolutely clear that you should use modularity, planning, and discipline to achieve success. Sitting down in front of your computer and typing in code without having a good design is sure to fail, later if not sooner.

Making a Game Function on a Computer

We now know enough about the inner workings of a game to sketch the basic code. At the center, a game is a loop that checks for user input, moves each object that can be moved, schedules needed sounds, and draws the next frame. This sounds simple, but the phrase "moves each object" could require thousands of lines of code. The following loop, called the game main loop, shows the pseudo-code for performing the needed steps:

```
do
{
    ai.check_input();
    ai.move_objects();
```

```
    graphics.draw_frame();
    audio.play_sounds();
} while (game_continues);
```

There are many things wrong with this simple loop, but it does describe the operation of a game at a high level of abstraction. In fact, this is pretty much what *any* game does, at its heart.

The above organization of the *game loop* is of the type referred to as *monolithic*, and this is appropriate only for a variety of games provided the control of time is appropriate, as we shall see. The game loop usually handles most of the different game states, such as playing, paused, terminated, and so on. It must organize the correct order for the essential modules, such as movement and collision tests. The monolithic scheme is a clear way to organize, but discipline must be maintained during its design or it ends up having to know too much about lower software levels and variables.

Of course, no one scheme works for everything. The audio subsystem, for example, is often a distinct thread. Once a sound starts playing, the game should not wait for the sound to finish! It is also common for file operations to be sent to a parallel thread, since input and output do not require the attention of the CPU. Waiting for data from a file would be a waste, while waiting in a thread is not.

A game frequently requires a number of setup tasks before it can be played. It also requires a degree of take-down afterwards so that the computer can be used for something else. In addition to the game loop, we may have:

```
        Display startup screen
        Read initial audio files
        WHEN user types ENTER or startup screen is complete
        Display initialization screen
        Read initial graphics and other data files.
resume: loop
        Allow user to set parameters
        until user selects START_GAME
        execute main-loop
        confirm user exit, else goto resume
        save game state is needed
free game resources: sound and graphics
        exit.
```

The code before the **resume** label is sometimes called the *front end*, and serves the dual purpose of getting initial information from the player and loading the essential data from the files used. The program can read quite a lot of data from a file while the user finds a box on the screen with the mouse and clicks the button. We want the user to appear to be doing something rather than just waiting for the game to start.

After the game ends, it is normal practice to free up memory that the game allocated, close any open files, and so on. Some games allow you to save the state and resume from that point next time, and others keep a file of players and their high scores. All of this is done in the *back end*, after the main loop is complete. The main loop is never complete until the user says so, or unless an error occurs. And of course, an error will never occur. Right!

Controlling Time

All simulations must be able to control time. Time in a game or simulation does not move at the same rate as time in the real world. Therefore, we must have a way to keep track of the simulated time and the corresponding real time. Activities must appear to happen at a reasonable rate—a rate that does not depend on how fast your computer runs!

Non-game simulations normally do not execute in real time, and thus don't care about time. Simulated events must synchronize in simulated time. A common simulation scheme is to claim that the current time is the time of the current event, and the next time is the time of the next event. This is clearly not suitable for a game because, for one thing, the display should not appear to freeze when not much is going on. We could create *next frame* events that occur every 1/24 of a second, but then there will be other such things that occur. Here is the *next event* method in simulation jargon, and the *variable time step* method used in games:

```
do
{
    currentTime = time of next event that occurs;

    deltaTime = currentTime - time;
    time = currentTime;
    evaluate (time);
} while (GAME_NOT_OVER);
```

However, some types of dynamic simulations break time into fixed duration increments, and examine the world every t seconds to see what things need to be updated. The code to perform this might look like the following:

```
do
{
```

```
   time = time + deltaTime;
   evaluate (time);
} while (GAME_NOT_OVER);
```

This code has the huge advantage of simplicity, and if the time step is a nice multiple of a good frame rate, the graphics will also look good. This technique also permits the programmer to debug the code because the program should behave in a repeatable fashion. Debugging a simulation is a huge problem because there are necessarily random behaviors taking place, and random times occurring between events. The technique above, the *fixed time step*, allows the simulation to be repeatable, provided we use a standard set of random number seeds.

A problem surfaces if the **evaluate()** function, whose job it is to see what's going on now and implement it, takes longer than **deltaTime** to execute. The longer the game runs, and the more objects there are, the more likely this will occur. There is also a trade-off between accuracy, which is assisted by many small-time steps, and efficiency, which would dictate a few large ones.

The two methods we just looked at can be combined into one very useful scheme sometimes called *multiple fixed steps*. If the time **current_time** is the time of the next significant event (perhaps a collision), the time between now and then can be broken into fixed time intervals as shown here:

```
do
{
    current_time = time of next event;

    while (time < current_time)

    {
       time = time + deltaTime;
       evaluate (time);
    }
} while (GAME_NOT_OVER);
```

This is still fairly simple, but there is one obvious problem: If many events occur in succession, the code must process a lot of events all at once. This can happen in any of the schemes we looked at, and it means that we have to choose which ones to deal with and which ones to ignore. We could change the scheme so that each time interval (between events) has at least one or two subintervals, or we could place a minimum value on the **deltaTime** value. In general, this seems to be a good compromise between complexity and efficiency, and appears to permit good graphics display rates.

Controlling Objects

Any modern game contains a vast number of objects or entities (or whatever you want to call them). *Gopher-it*, our toy game shown in Figure 2.3, contains five basic types of objects, but its implementation requires 56 gophers, 2 police vehicles, the player's vehicle, 4 gas stations, and walls consisting of 131 wall cells or pixels—a grand total of 194 objects! Three of these can move, and therefore can collide with other objects. Sixty of them can either be visible or not at any given time, depending on whether or not they have been touched. For being a very simple game, numerous objects are required and a huge number of possibilities are available. Imagine the number of objects in a game like *The Simpson's Hit and Run*! We definitely need a way to keep track of all of our objects.

It certainly makes sense to have one place for storing moving objects and another for storing still ones (obstacles). Still objects cannot interact with each other, only with the moving ones. We could keep a table of objects, indexed by an integer code that is unique for each object. The table would store properties of each object: position, velocity, and orientation (if needed). Graphical rendition information could also be stored. If the object is one that can move, we might need to store information about its current goals and behaviors.

Finally, there are objects that contribute to the score or the actual plot and play of the game. A fuel-up, for example, can increase the speed or range of the player's car, and some games have collectable items that are worth points towards winning the game. The *object management system* or *OMS* (object is used in the generic sense) we are building here may contain a lot of information, but the organization is nothing that a programmer who has a few years of experience has not seen before

We also need to be able to retrieve and store attributes for our objects. There must be an interface to the table that permits us to make efficient inquiries as to the position of the enemy vehicle. We will be implementing their motion, so we also need to be able to update positions. In an object-oriented language like Java, the object's attributes would be an integral part of the implementation for the object itself, and the table would simply contain references to objects organized in a convenient way. In a language like C or Pascal, the table would be spread out over multiple arrays, each containing a structure holding relevant data.

Nothing could be more relevant at this point than to give another real code example that shows one way to handle entity management.

Objects in Gopher-it

The first thing to do is classify the objects into moving ones and stationary ones. The player's car is special; there is only one, and the computer does not control it. Objects are coded as integers, and the player's car will be object zero. The two police cars will be objects 1 and 2. The gas stations will be objects 3 through 6, and the gophers will be objects 7 through 62. The walls will not be stored in the table, but will instead be saved in a 2D board array where a wall is **true**, and anything else is **false**.

A first draft of the structure is shown here:

```
struct objectStruct
{
    int posx, posy;      /* Position on the board */
    int direction;       /* Where are we headed */
    unsigned char exists; /* Still there? */
};
typedef struct objectStruct OBJ;
#define MAXOBJECTS 61
OBJ all_objects[61];

#define USER_CAR    0
#define POLICE1     1
#define POLICE      2
```

We also need accessor and modifier functions as shown:

```
void setObjectPos (int object, int x, int y)
{
    if ( object>=0 && object < MAXOBJECTS )
    {
        all_objects[object].posx = x;
        all_objects[object].posy = y;
    } else error....
}

void getObjectPos (int object, int *x, int *y)
{
    if ( object>=0 && object < MAXOBJECTS )
    {
        *x = all_objects[object].posx;
        *y = all_objects[object].posy;
    } else error....
}
```

We need such a pair of functions for all object attributes. A complete list of these is:

```
void setObjectPos (int object, int x, int y)
void getObjectPos (int object, int *x, int *y)
```

Object direction of motion; must be either left, right, up, or down:

```
void setDirection (int object, int dir)
int getDirection (int object)
```

Most objects can be destroyed. We need to know whether an object still exists or not:

```
int objectExists (int object )
void exist (int object)
```

Objects also have graphical icons by which they are known, and that are displayed on the screen in the relative position of the object:

```
void setIcon (int which, unsigned char *icon)
void setPlayerIcon (unsigned char *icon)
void setPoliceIcon (unsigned char *icon)
void setFuelupIcon (unsigned char *icon)
void setGopherIcon (unsigned char *icon)
```

We also want a couple of classifiers—predicates that tell us what group a particular object is a member of:

```
int isPolice (int k)
int isGopher (int piece)
```

This is essentially our object management system as viewed from the outside. Since we are looking at the AI subsystem right now, we may as well finish it. The initialization steps are carried out by three simple functions:

```
void game_over ()
void initializeAI( void )
void terminateAI ( void )
```

Mostly, these functions just free up space that was allocated by the AI system. The **game_over()** function can be called from anywhere, and it calls all subsystem terminate functions and ends the program.

My implementation of *Gopher-it* uses a two-stage scheme for keeping track of objects. All objects except WALL objects have an entry as an **object_struct** structure in the

all_objects array, indexed by the integer code for the object. This means that we can look up the position, existence, and so on of any such object. In addition to this, the program keeps a map as a 2D array in which all stationary objects can be represented as their code stored at their 2D coordinates in the map.

Figure 2.4 shows the map that was used for the game. This is a character array in which 0 represents an empty space and 1 represents a wall. Storing walls in this way makes it easier to perform collision tests. Using the object table, we need to look at 131 table entries to determine whether a moving police car has struck a wall. Using the map, we need to only look at four array entries, those that surround the police car being tested. Of course, having two representations means keeping them both current at all times—a more complex (error prone) situation.

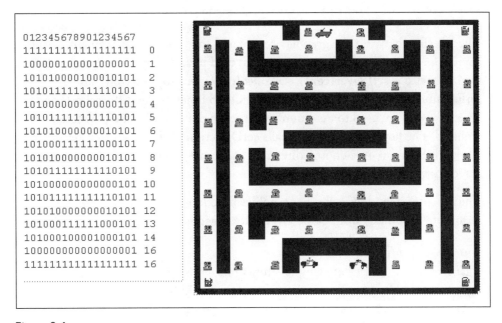

```
012345678901234567
111111111111111111  0
100000100001000001  1
101010000100010101  2
101011111111110101  3
101000000000000101  4
101011111111110101  5
101010000000010101  6
101000111111000101  7
101010000000010101  8
101011111111110101  9
101000000000000101  10
101011111111110101  11
101010000000010101  12
101000111111000101  13
101000100001000101  14
100000000000000001  16
111111111111111111  16
```

Figure 2.4
The file representation for the *Gopher-it* maze is shown on the left and the actual maze displayed on the screen is shown on the right.

Graphics in Gopher-it

The graphics module is quite simple, and since we have not yet discussed graphics in any detail, I will not analyze the actual code. However, the graphics subsystem contains functions that perform quite recognizable tasks, even though we may not know how they perform them just yet. The graphics module consists of the following two initialization functions:

```
void initializeGraphics( void )
void terminateGraphics ( void )
```

To display the screen and handle the mouse and keyboard, the following functions are used:

```
void display(void)
void mouseClick (int butt, int updown, int x, int y)
void keyPress (unsigned char key, int x, int y)
```

Finally, here are the functions needed to read icons from files and display them:

```
void readIcon (unsigned char **icon, char *filename)
void drawIcon (unsigned char *icon, int x, int y)
void getPPM (char *infname, unsigned char **buf)
```

The interface between the graphics system and the Object Management System is straightforward. The graphics system must read in and assign icons to objects, and the OMS functions **setPlayerIcon()**, **setPoliceIcon()**, **setGopherIcon()**, and **setFuelupIcon()** do the assignments. The OMS functions **getObjectPos()** and **objectExists()** are used to determine whether to draw an object and where to draw it, if required. The **keyPress()** function calls **setDirection()** when an arrow key is pressed to let the player move in a chosen direction, and **game_over()** is called if a mouse click is detected within the game window.

The AI subsystem does call other graphics functions, but OMS calls only **terminateGraphics()** from **game_over()**, for obvious reasons.

Sound in Gopher-it

Again, the audio subsystem contains functions whose internal workings will be a mystery (until Chapter 7) but whose function should be clear. Specific sounds must be played to correspond to specific actions in the game, and the AI will call sound system functions to do this. In particular, these two functions are used for initialization:

```
void initializeSound ( int argc, char **argv )
void terminateSound ( void )
```

There are six sounds that are needed by the game: the sound played every step, the one played when you run over a gopher, the one played when you capture a police car, the one played when you win the game, and the one played when you lose. The sixth, the "ambient" sound, is played when you hit a gas station (fuel_up); at this point, you become invincible and can capture police cars. A special piece of music plays for the entire time you are invincible. This is the ambient sound. Note that it is the one sound that has a function to stop it:

```
void audioPlayAmbientTone ( void )
void audioStopAmbient (void)
void audioPlayStepTone (void)
void audioPlayGopherTone ( void )
void audioPlayLoseTone ( void )
void audioPlayPoliceTone ( void )
void audioPlayWinTone ( void )
```

Object AI Subsystem

The Object AI (OAI) is the part of this game that is responsible for controlling the actual game play. The AI subsystem consists of the OAI and the object management system. Essentially, the OAI is in charge of moving objects and evaluating the consequences of the move. Based on the design document, we see that there are three objects that can move: the player's car and the two police cars. The player controls the player's vehicle, and so all we have to do is implement the move as indicated by the user's input and evaluate its consequences. The player is handled by this function:

```
POSITION compute_next_user_square ( void )
```

It determines the position on the board where the user's car will be if we move it one space in the current direction. It returns a **POSITION**, a simple vector with X and Y coordinates in it.

The following function is called when the game determines that the player's car has occupied the same square as a police car:

```
void collide (int piece)
```

The appropriate sequence of steps for either the police car capturing the player, or vice versa, is coded in this function.

Every second, a timer causes the following function to be invoked. It handles the activities associated with the player's move, as described in the code a few pages back, starting at the label **AIstep:**

```
void timedAILoop (int a)
```

The two police cars are the only independent moving objects in the game, and must be controlled in a somewhat clever way by the game program. If the police (opponents) are too stupid, the game won't be fun. Also, if they are too good, the game cannot be won, and it likewise won't be fun.

Each police car has a timer associated with it that causes it to move periodically. The appropriate functions are:

```
void moveCop1 (int a)
void moveCop2 (int a)
```

These move the associated police car. Two functions are needed so that the two cars can exhibit different behaviors, although in this first simple game they both do the same thing. When the timer for each police car expires, one of these functions is called:

```
void movePolice (int a)
```

This actually moves the police car. I use a simple method to do this: I assume that the player's car is the beginning point of a maze, and the police car is the exit. I then use a simple region fill algorithm to find the shortest path from the player to the police car, and move the police car to a square that would permit it to follow this path. For example, consider the situation shown next. Let P be the player and X be the police car:

```
################# 0          #################
#0P000#0000#00000# 1         #1P123#6000#00000#
#0#0#0000#000#0#0# 2         #2#2#3456#000#0#0#
#0#0#########0#0# 3          #3#3#########0#0#
#0#00X000000000#0# 4         #4#45X000000000#0#
#0#0#########0#0# 5          #5#5#########0#0#
#0#0#00000000#0#0# 6         #6#6#00000000#0#0#
```

The first (left) picture is of the upper portion of the board, where 0 designates an empty cell. On the right is the same position after the fill algorithm has marked empty cells with the distance to the player's car. A quick scan of the neighbors of the police car shows that the smallest non-zero value is 5, and so the police car will take a step onto that cell. The police cars have been set up to move a little faster than the player's car, so they will catch up with the player sooner or later.

If the player captures a gas station, their car becomes invulnerable, and can capture and destroy a police car. In this situation, a counter is set to the number of turns that the player will remain invulnerable, and for those turns it would be suicidal for the police to chase the player. Instead, they try to move in the opposite direction. This method makes good use of existing code: the same fill algorithm is used to compute the distance to the player as before. We simply move away from the player's car instead of towards it.

The only code remaining in the AI system of any consequence is **KillObject()** and **getBoard()**. The first function

```
void KillObject (int object)
```

performs the bookkeeping associated with deleting an object. This includes processing used gas stations, gophers, and destroyed police cars. The second function

```
int getBoard(int i, int j)
```

reads the ASCII description of the game board into the in-memory array.

Front-End/Back-End

We expect there to be a front-end and back-end to a game, but little thought is put into these components—or too much, actually. A common beginner's error is to spend a lot of time on a really classy front-end animation that does not add anything to the fun parts of playing the game. As a hobby, this is not a problem. In the industry, the time may be better spent on coding a better collision system.

As we'll see later, the tricky bit is to switch the graphics system between the rendering needs of the three subsystems. However, the basic function of the front-end needs to simply introduce the game, and sometimes to stall while files are being loaded.

The back-end, at least in our case, is used to display the player's score and time. The hard part here is getting the characters to be displayed. Graphics systems usually don't deal with characters very well. Anyway, the front-end functions include:

```
void frontEnd( int a )                               Initialize: read image, etc.
void feDisplay (void)                                Display the screen
void femouseClick (int butt,int updown,int x,int y) Handle the mouse

void beLoadFont ( void )                             Read the digit images
void backEnd ( void )                                Initialize back end
void beDisplay (void)                                Display back end, score, etc.
void BEmouseClick (int butt, int updown, int x, int y)
```

We will discuss some of the details of front images and display control in the next two chapters. For now, take some time and play with the game, look over the code, and see how it all fits together. Think of this as your first big assignment.

Summary

In this chapter, I've tried to show you what the basic parts of a game are, from the perspective of a game designer and programmer. I used a simple game (*Gopher-it*) to show you what the various functions of the AI system are, and I provided a quick summary of the types of design documents that are useful for creating a game. A lot of what I discussed actually applies to other sorts of games.

We'll finish implementing the *Gopher-it* game in Chapter 4, after we explore computer graphics in Chapter 3.

Chapter 3

Basic Graphics for Driving and Racing Games

- Learn the basic concepts required to program the types of graphics that you'll need to create driving and racing games.

- Brush up on the math that is needed to program game graphics.

- Learn how to use the basic features of OpenGL to program real-time graphics.

As we discussed in Chapter 2, many people think that computer games are all about graphics. I guess that some games might require an extensive amount of graphics, but graphics are not what make a game play well. Naturally, driving and racing games need some graphics. After all, you can't drive if you can't see the road, and you certainly can't race if you can't see other cars. The degree to which a game depends on its graphics is one way to classify the game, but even in the racing/driving genre you'll find a wide variety of graphics.

Our goal now is to focus on the basic graphics techniques you'll need to master so that you can create driving and racing games. This requires that we do two things. First, we'll need to discuss all of the important graphics concepts such as working with polygons, translation, rotation, scaling, shading, texture mapping, and so on. As we discuss these techniques, we'll need to work through the basic math that is required. I'll also provide some references at the end of this book so that you can study more on your own if you need to brush up on some of the concepts presented. The second thing we need to do is discuss the basic techniques of using OpenGL—the graphics library that we'll be using in this book to create the games.

A modern PC has a wide variety of multimedia devices attached to it that a game needs to use. The graphics and audio cards are the key ones. Each specific brand of device works a little differently than the others. There are basically two systems that game developers use to isolate themselves from these hardware dependencies: DirectX and OpenGL. DirectX was developed by Microsoft, and works mainly on PCs running Windows. I find that DirectX has a fairly complex interface, and is not intuitive. It does, however, handle just about any kind of device you'd like to use, and most professional games use it.

Silicon Graphics created OpenGL. It first ran on just their computers but now it is a part of most PCs and Macs, and runs on Linux and Unix systems that run the X-windows graphics system. OpenGL has its difficult parts, but it has a simpler interface than DirectX and is clearly more portable. For these reasons, we'll code our example driving games in this book using OpenGL.

Essential Review of Computer Graphics

A typical computer screen consists of hundreds of thousands of dots in a rectangular array. Each dot can be made to light up in a variety of colors, like the old toy "Lite-Bright," and is used as a component to create a bigger picture. The dots are called picture elements, or *pixels* for short. Computer graphics are really all about connecting pixels into geometric shapes that look like what we are trying to draw.

A goal of most graphics systems is to distance the artist or programmer from having to work at the pixel level. After all, we don't really think of pictures as being a collection of pixels and we wouldn't likely draw them pixel-by-pixel with a pencil or a brush. The OpenGL system has very few operations for drawing pixels specifically. Instead, we draw basic geometric shapes using polygons. When we wish to draw a polygon, we specify the coordinates of the vertices, a color, and perhaps a texture to be mapped onto the polygon, and OpenGL converts this information into a set of low-level pixel operations. We don't manipulate pixels directly. OpenGL converts our wishes, via a set of function calls, into a raster image. The mechanism is hidden from us, for the most part, as it should be.

We want to think of a scene as consisting of high level objects that we move around, and not as consisting of pixels that we need to draw. So, how do we draw objects? What are the basic components of a race car that we wish to draw? Polygons!

Objects Are Polygons

Any object we wish to draw can be created from simple polygons, usually triangles. For example, Figure 3.1 shows a sphere constructed out of triangles. From left to right, each sphere is drawn with more triangles. Notice that the representation looks more and more like a sphere as more triangles are used. Of course, there is a limit to the number of polygons that can be used, but generally the more polygons used to represent an object, the better it looks. The act of building an object from triangles is called *tessellation*, or sometimes *polygonization*. The polygonalized object is sometimes referred to as a *mesh*.

Why do most games use polygons to represent objects? Mainly because using polygons is easy and fast. Algorithms for determining whether an object can be seen are easy when polygons are used. Polygon intersections can be calculated simply and quickly. It's

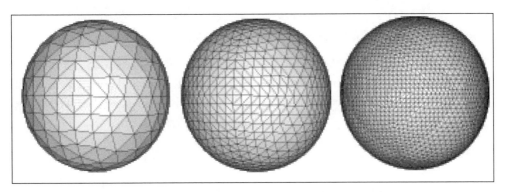

Figure 3.1
A sphere as it is being built from triangles only.

also easy to determine if a point is inside or outside of a polygon. Polygons can have shading applied so that a collection of them will look like a smooth surface, and they can also have textures applied very easily. Using this approach can improve the simplicity and speed of a computer game.

Meshes can be created in a few distinct ways. The easiest way involves using a drawing tool to create an object and simply saving it as a mesh. Most tools used for building graphical models, such as Maya and 3D Studio Max, save objects as a polygonal mesh. The other main way to create a mesh is to define a surface somehow, perhaps by defining it mathematically or digitizing a real object, and then running the data through a special polygonalization algorithm. Both methods are complex in their own way, and so we will simply assume from now on that any objects to be drawn into our game exist as a polygon mesh, however it was created. I get most of the objects I use from websites that offer free 3D models. A list of these sites is presented in the references section at the end of this book.

Storing and Drawing Polygons

It's time to learn how we can store and draw triangles as a special case. This is what we'll probably be doing in practice. A triangle has three sides, or *edges,* and three points where their edges meet, also called *vertices*. In three dimensions, each vertex has three coordinates: X, Y, and Z. These coordinates would usually be stored as a three dimensional vector:

```
float vec3d[3];
```

A triangle will need three of these, so you could save a triangle using a data structure such as:

```
float triangle[3][3];
```

Here, **triangle[1][2]** represents the second vertex (the first has index 0) and the Z coordinate of that vertex. (The X coordinate would be 0 and the Y coordinate would be 1.)

Of course, any object we'll want to draw will consist of a collection of triangles. We won't always know how many triangles are used in advance, and not all objects will have the same number. To handle this flexibility, we'll need a special data structure as shown here:

```
struct object3dstruct
{
    int Ntriangles;
    float *vertices[3][3];
};
```

In an object-oriented language, we'd encapsulate these variables within a class. In C, we need a function to allocate an object, determine the object's size in polygons, and free an object. Here's an example:

```
typedef struct object3dstruct * OBJECT;
OBJECT newobject (int N)
{
    OBJECT returnValue = 0;

    if (N <= 0) return returnValue;
    returnValue = (struct object3dstruct *)
    malloc(sizeof(struct object3dstruct));
    if (returnValue)
    {
       returnValue->Ntriangles = N;
       returnValue->vertices =
           malloc(sizeof(float)*9);
    }
    return returnValue;
}
```

Each object needs to have its own structure, which is just big enough to hold the object's polygons. There can be as many objects as needed, and these can also be stored in an array.

Drawing the objects is easy, especially because we won't need to write the whole program. If we have a procedure that draws lines, we draw a triangle **T** by simply doing the following:

```
drawLine   (T[0][0],T[0][1],T[0][2],
            T[1][0],T[1][1],T[1][2]);
```

```
drawLine    (T[1][0],T[1][1],T[1][2],
            T[2][0],T[2][1],T[2][2]);
drawline    (T[2][0],T[2][1],T[2][2],
            T[0][0],T[0][1],T[0][2]);
```

The graphics package that we'll use will have a **drawLine ()** function, and will also have a draw polygon function. All we need to understand is how to represent our universe (that which we wish to plot) as polygons, and everything else will fall into place.

We need to have an appreciation of other aspects of the scene, though. Lighting, point of view, scale, and perspective all affect the way things will look. Fortunately, it is not necessary to do all of these things ourselves. They have been implemented by the graphics system and thus, all we need is a knowledge that these aspects exist, an appreciation of how these things affect the graphical version of the scene, and knowledge of how the graphics system implements them.

Working with Geometry

You've now seen how basic polygons are stored and drawn. But how can we move polygons around to create animated scenes? To do that, we'll need to use a little geometry. This geometry consists of all of the manipulations of an object that affect its position and orientation in space. Unfortunately, we'll need to use a little bit of math here. As we go along, I'll be referencing some of the sections from the math tutorial presented in Chapter 15. Mostly these operations will be performed by the graphics system (OpenGL, remember?), but we will need to know about them so that we can see how to use them and when they are needed.

All geometric operators work by systematically changing the coordinates of the vertices of the polygons that comprise an object. These coordinates can be defined by their use. They can be absolute coordinates, which is to say they are based on some arbitrary point (0,0,0) in space, or they can be relative, which means they are based on a system of coordinates relative to the object itself—a system in which the origin is a point in the object. In any 3D graphics system, multiple coordinate systems are used, which become the source of much confusion. I'll try to keep this discussion as simple as possible.

Translation

Translating an object involves changing its position in three-dimensional space. To see how this works, let's align the X-axis to what we think of as the horizontal and the Y-axis to the vertical. Now, imagine a triangle with vertices (0,0,0), (0,1,0), (1, 1, 0) as shown in Figure 3.2. A translation in the X direction by 1 unit corresponds to simply adding a value of 1 to each of the X coordinates in the triangle. We can translate an object by different amounts in all three coordinate directions at the same time by simply adding a different amount to each coordinate. The new (X,Y,Z) coordinates

could be written out (in terms of the old ones and the three translations) using the
following notation:

Equation 3.1 $X_{new} = X_{old} + T_x$

$Y_{new} = Y_{old} + T_y$

$Z_{new} = Z_{old} + T_z$

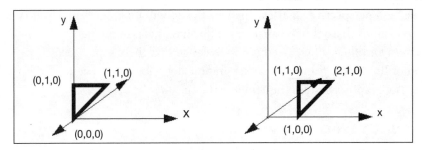

Figure 3.2
Translation of a triangle by 1 unit.

If you have some familiarity with linear algebra, you will understand that the new
(X,Y,Z) and old (X,Y,Z) are vectors. The actual vectors are notated as:

Equation 3.2 $new = (X_{new}, Y_{new}, Z_{new})$

$old = (X_{old}, Y_{old}, Z_{old})$

Note that the translation is specified relative to a set of coordinates for which (0,0,0) is
a special place (the *origin*). Note also that we can create a matrix that represents the
translation, and a matrix equation that represents the transformation of coordinates.

Before we show the final form of the translation, you might be wondering why a matrix
is being used. After all, why make the math more complicated? Because using a matrix
results in a more general formulation in which we can implement a matrix multiplication and then use it to perform the translation. In addition, it will turn out that we can
do many geometric operations and store them in a single matrix. Efficiency and
modularity in a game are very important to us. Also, OpenGL uses matrices to do
translations, rotations, and scaling, so we need to stick with a consistent notation.

In summary, a matrix can be used to implement a translation. There are two ways to do
this. One way simply adds a translation vector (which is technically a matrix) to the old
vector to get the new vector:

Equation 3.3   new = old + T

Here the line over the symbol means the symbol is a vector. However, as you will see later, this leads to inconsistencies—the matrix form of other geometric operations involves multiplication, not addition.

The other way involves what are called *homogeneous* coordinates. Perhaps the best way to explain these is to work backwards from the answer. Take every 3D vector and add an extra fourth element, always a 1:

Equation 3.4 $new = (X_{new}, Y_{new}, Z_{new}, 1)$

$old = (X_{old}, Y_{old}, Zold, 1)$

We want a multiplicative equation; that looks something like this:

Equation 3.5   new = T * old

In this case, **T** is a matrix. The rules for matrix multiplication tell us that if **new** and **old** are 4 dimensional, **T** must be 4x4. If **T** looks like the following

Equation 3.6

$$T = \begin{matrix} 1 & 0 & 0 & T_x \\ 0 & 1 & 0 & T_y \\ 0 & 0 & 1 & T_z \\ 0 & 0 & 0 & 1 \end{matrix}$$

it is called the *translation matrix*. Multiplying out the matrix equation (Equation3.5) gives us

Equation 3.7 $X_{new} = X_{old} + T_x$

$Y_{new} = Y_{old} + T_y$

$Z_{new} = Z_{old} + T_z$

$1 = 1$

which is what we wanted!

In summary, we can translate a set of 3D coordinates by multiplying the translation matrix by the coordinate vector. This has the effect of moving the object within the specified system of coordinates.

Rotation

Rotation is a circular motion about a specified axis by a specified angle. It is easier to explain rotation in two dimensions first. Look at Figure 3.3 and you'll see the X,Y coordinate axis on the left side with a pixel drawn at the point (2, 0). On the right we see the same axis, but now the pixel has been rotated about the origin point (0,0) by 45 degrees. What are the coordinates of the rotated point? To answer this, we'll need to use some high school trigonometry.

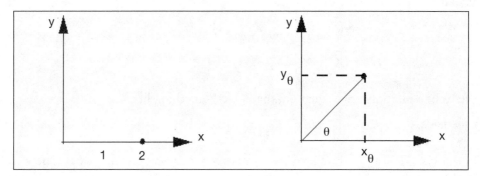

Figure 3.3
Rotation of a triangle by q degrees about the origin.

In this case, the angle θ is 45 degrees, and the length of the line joining the origin to the point (the hypotenuse) is still 2 units. So the following trigonometric equations hold:

Equation 3.8 $\sin \theta = x_\theta / 2$

$\cos \theta = y_\theta / 2$

We can now rearrange these to find the point (x_θ, y_θ) as $(2\sin \theta, 2\cos \theta) = (1.41, 1.41)$. However, this only works if the point was on the X-axis in the first place. If not, we can rotate the point around so that it *is* on the X-axis. Then we rotate it to the correct position. To eliminate a lot of boring math, the equation needs to rotate any point (X,Y) about the origin by q degrees:

Equation 3.9 $x' = x \cos \theta - y \sin \theta$

$y' = x \sin \theta + y \cos \theta$

If the rotation is not supposed to be about the origin, but instead is to be about some point P, then the process is as follows:

- Translate the object so that P becomes the origin (that is, translate all points in the object by -P)

- Perform the rotation

- Translate back (by +P)

In three dimensions, a number of things change. First, we don't rotate about a point. Instead, we rotate about a line, usually one of the three coordinate axes. Second, there are three coordinates, not two, and so there are three equations. Finally, a rotation about an arbitrary line can be implemented as a translation and a number of rotations about the coordinate axes, up to three of them. The basic rotation equation about the Z axis is

Equation 3.10 $x' = x \cos \theta + y \sin \theta$

$y' = -x \sin \theta + y \cos \theta$

$z' = z$

which is the matrix equation **x' = R$_z$*x where the matrix R is:**

Equation 3.11

$$\begin{matrix} \cos \theta & -\sin \theta & 0 & 0 \\ \sin \theta & \cos \theta & 0 & 0 \\ 0 & 0 & 1 & 0 \\ 0 & 0 & 0 & 1 \end{matrix}$$

Similarly, the rotation matrices for the other two axes are:

Equation 3.12

$$R_x = \begin{matrix} 1 & 0 & 0 & 0 \\ 0 & \cos \theta & -\sin \theta & 0 \\ 0 & \sin \theta & \cos \theta & 0 \\ 0 & 0 & 0 & 1 \end{matrix} \qquad R_y = \begin{matrix} \cos \theta & 0 & \sin \theta & 0 \\ 0 & 1 & 0 & 0 \\ -\sin \theta & 0 & \cos \theta & 0 \\ 0 & 0 & 0 & 1 \end{matrix}$$

We could use these matrices to perform the rotation for an object in a game we were creating, but we don't need to. OpenGL will build these matrices for us and apply them to any object we choose.

Scaling

A scaling transformation reduces or increases the size of an object as it appears on the screen. It seems obvious that if we want an object to get bigger, say twice as large, we would multiply each coordinate in each vertex by two (see Figure 3.4). We can, of course, scale each dimension by a different amount by multiplying each dimension by a different value. If the object is not centered at the origin, scaling it also appears to translate it; the multiplication by a scale factor makes the coordinates larger or smaller, and this changes their distance from the origin by the same factor.

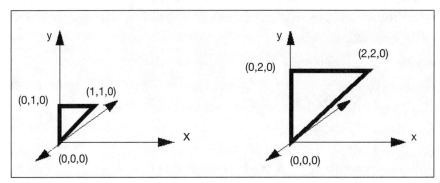

Figure 3.4
Scaling a triangle to twice its size by multiplying all coordinates by 2.

The new coordinates can be expressed in terms of the old ones as shown here:

Equation 3.13
$$X_{new} = S_x * X_{old}$$
$$Y_{new} = S_y * Y_{old}$$
$$Z_{new} = S_z * Z_{old}$$

As a homogeneous matrix equation this is **new = S * old**, where:

Equation 3.14

$$new = \begin{matrix} X_{new} \\ Y_{new} \\ Z_{new} \\ 1 \end{matrix} \quad S = \begin{matrix} S_x & 0 & 0 & 0 \\ 0 & S_y & 0 & 0 \\ 0 & 0 & S_z & 0 \\ 0 & 0 & 0 & 1 \end{matrix} \quad old = \begin{matrix} X_{old} \\ Y_{old} \\ Z_{old} \\ 1 \end{matrix}$$

At this point, we can calculate all of the important geometric transformations using simple matrix operations. Assume that we have a function called

```
VECTOR4 matTransform4 (MATIX4 mat, VECTOR4 vec);
```

which multiplies the matrix **mat** by the vector **vec** and returns the resulting vector as the function result. This single function can perform any of the geometric operations we have examined, depending on the matrix that is passed to it. Also, assume that we have a function that multiplies two 4-dimensional matrices together:

```
MATRIX4 matMultiply4 (MATRIX4 m1, MATRIX4 m2);
```

It turns out that matrix operations can be accumulated into a single transformation matrix simply by multiplying the respective matrices together. Given a rotation matrix **R**, a translation matrix **T**, and a scale matrix **S**, let's first scale, then translate and rotate the vector **V**. Scaling **V** involves multiplying **V** by the matrix **S**, giving us **SV**. Performing the translation involves multiplying this result by the matrix **T**, giving us **TSV**. Finally, a rotation of this result vector involves multiplying it by **R** giving us **RTSV**. If the same set of transformations is to be applied to multiple vectors, it can be done by multiplying the matrices together and saving them: **A = RTS**. The matrix **A** represents all of the transformations **R**, **T**, and **S**, in the order they were applied, and any vector **V** can be transformed as **AV**. The **matMultiply4()** function would be used to create the matrix **A** from the individual transformation matrices.

Any number of transformations can be saved in a single matrix, but care must be taken to multiply them together in the correct order. The first transformation to be applied is the matrix on the right of the chain of multiplications, and the last one is the one on the left. The basic code for matrix and vector multiplication can be found on the website for this book.

Shading

You've already seen how a sphere can be built out of polygons. I've also indicated that any object can be reduced to a set of polygons that can then be manipulated by simple matrix operations. Figure 3.1 showed what an object built from polygons looks like—a wire frame mesh of lines. But in our games we want a polygonal surface to present the effect of a solid object. This can be accomplished by shading the polygons so that they appear to be a smooth surface. We can do this using a technique called *interpolation*, assuming that we know what the brightness and color of the polygons are at a very few special places.

Let's explore two methods for doing this. The first assumes that we know the *normal* at each vertex of each polygon on the surface. A *normal* is a line perpendicular to the surface, and it can be defined in many ways. We need to know the angle that this line makes with, for example, the coordinate axes, or some other standard of comparison.

Then, the normal is used to calculate what the brightness of the pixel will be at the vertex; this is called the *vertex intensity*. Finally, we interpolate (estimate) intensities of points along the edges between vertices, and use these in turn to estimate (interpolate) the intensities of th2e interior pixels. Whew! In case you want to look this up on the Internet, it is called *Gouraud shading*. Figure 3.5 shows the steps, without getting into too much detail yet. The image on the left shows normal vectors to the surface at each vertex. The image in the center uses the normals to compute the intensity of the vertex pixels. The image on the right interpolates other pixels along the edges, then inside the polygons.

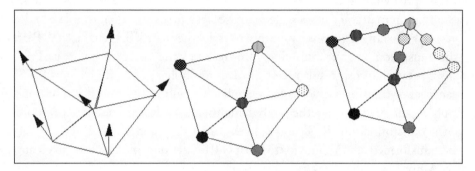

Figure 3.5
Using the Gouraud shading technique.

The algorithm used to perform the shading actually involves four steps:

1. *Calculate the normal at each vertex.*

    This step can be performed in one of two ways. First, if the polygons represent a surface whose equation is known, it would be possible to use that equation to calculate the normal of the surface at each point that corresponds to a vertex. Unfortunately, this is not true in most cases, but it is possible to estimate the normal at a vertex from the normals at all adjacent triangles.

    Finding the normal to a triangle is actually pretty easy. Since a triangle is a planar surface, all points on and in a triangle have the same normal—a line that is perpendicular to the plane of the triangle. If the vertices of the triangle are named V_1, V_2, and V_3, the normal will be $(V_1-V_2) \times (V_2-V_3)$ where "x" is the vector cross product. The normal at a vertex can be estimated to be the average of the normals of all touching faces.

2. *Calculate the brightness at each vertex.*

   Obviously, we calculated the normal **N** at the vertex for a reason—so we can calculate the brightness or intensity at that point. There are a few possible illumination models we could use to compute brightness given the normal. Most require that we know where the light source is and that we have a vector **L** that points in that direction.

   If at some point labeled X, the vector **N** points in the same direction as **L**, the illumination at X will be as bright as it can be; if **N** points in the opposite direction to **L**, then the point X will be facing away from the light and will be dark. At positions in between, the intensity will vary from light to dark in proportion to the angle between **N** and **L**. The relationship can be written as

Equation 3.15 $\quad I = I_p k_d \cos \theta$

   where θ is the angle between the light source and the surface. Using the vectors **N** and **L,** this relationship can be re-written as:

Equation 3.16 $\quad I = I_p k_d (\mathbf{N \cdot L})$

   The variable $\mathbf{k_d}$ represents the material of the surface. Some surfaces, such as metal, reflect light better than, say, wood or chalk. The variable $\mathbf{I_p}$ represents the brightness of the light itself. The dot product **N·L** clearly represents the angle made by the light "beams" with the surface. Figure 3.6 attempts to illustrate the geometry of this situation, and shows why the intensity dims as the angle between the light and the surface approaches 90 degrees. The strongest reflection is seen at an angle equal and opposite to the angle between the normal and the light.

3. *Interpolate the brightness between vertices along the edges.*

   We now know the intensity or brightness of two points, and we know these points are vertices of a triangle. It is easy to estimate the intensity of any point between these two points along the line formed by the edge. For example, the point exactly in the middle of V_1 and V_2 will have intensity exactly in between the intensities at those two points. We could repeat this process recursively, or simply use the *interpolation* formula. Let's say that V_1 and V_2 are positioned as shown in Figure 3.7.

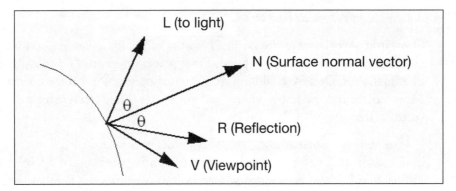

Figure 3.6
How the brightness at a point depends on the normal and direction to the light.

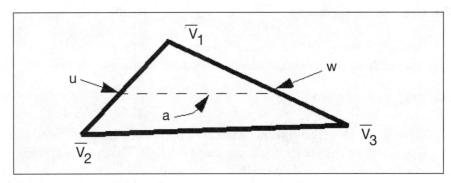

Figure 3.7
Using the interpolation formula to determine brightness between vertices.

The intensity at V_1 is I_1, and at V_2 is I_2. What is the intensity at the point **u**? It is

Equation 3.17 $I_u = I_1 - (I_1 - I_2) * (V_{1y} - u_y)/(V_{1y} - V_{2y})$

where V_{1y} is the Y coordinate of V_1, u_y is the Y coordinate of **u**, and so on.

You should be able to see that any point on any edge of the triangle can be given a reasonable estimate for the intensity at that point. The point **w**, for example, is directly to the right of **u** (X coordinate changes only) and is between V_1 and V_3. Its intensity is:

Equation 3.18 $\quad I_w = I_1 - (I_1 - I_3) * (V_{1y} - w_y)/(V_{1y} - V_{3y})$

4. *Interpolate the brightness of the interior pixels.*

Using Figure 3.7, note that we now know the brightness (intensity) of the points **u** and **w**, and that these are on a line that divides the triangle horizontally. By an identical interpolation process, we can determine the intensity at any point between **u** and **w**, which is to say at any point inside the triangle; for example, the point labeled **a**. We could interpolate the intensity I_a at point **a** as:

Equation 3.19 $\quad I_a = I_w - (I_w - I_u) * (w_x - a_x)/(w_x - u_x)$

Now all points inside the triangle have an interpolated estimate of intensity/brightness.

Why do all of this work? Because now an object rendered as a set of polygons can be shaded so that it looks like a smooth surface. The location where two polygons meet is shaded smoothly on both sides, and the join is now invisible!

Having done all of this, you should know that OpenGL would simply do it for you if you give it the right instructions. You should also know about Gouraud shading for many reasons, though, not the least of which is that other game programmers know about it, and you need to talk to them.

There is another popular shading scheme called *Phong* shading that performs shading in a different way. Instead of finding the brightness at the vertices and then interpolating from there, Phong shading involves interpolating the normal vectors at all points in the polygon (starting from the vertices), and then computing the brightness at these points using Equation 3.13

Viewing

The viewing transformation takes the objects and the lights that have been defined by the programmer and creates a two-dimensional projection as seen from a particular point in space. This projection can then be displayed on the computer screen as pixels—obviously the goal of any graphics program. The viewing transformation needs to know where all of the polygons are, where the viewer is (in three-dimensional space), and what the parameters of the viewer are—perspective or orthographic. It also needs to know what direction the viewer/camera is looking, the focal length, and so on.

The most common projection is the perspective projection because it is the one nearest to what we would expect in real life. For example, objects that are farther away appear smaller than ones that are nearer. The position of the view can change, even while the game is being played. It is common in a driving game to allow the player to apparently look through the windshield, and just as common to adopt a position behind and above the car (see Chapter 12 for more details about this). All we know right now is that we have to be flexible and allow for multiple-viewing positions. However, any projection that did not show farther away objects as seeming smaller than ones that are nearer would be rejected by our common sense, and would be difficult to incorporate into a 3D game.

I have been tossing about terms like projection, viewing position, and perspective as if they are already understood. In fact, the whole concept of taking three-dimensional objects in a virtual space and creating a planar representation (as would be seen from a virtual position) is conceptually very difficult. My experience from teaching these concepts have taught me that people have trouble with them. There are two common ways to cover the needed material: the entire thing could be abstracted and described as geometry and algebra, or it could be described as images where the intention is to create 3D mental models.

Why do this at all? Since OpenGL will do the work for us, why not just explain how it does it rather than show all of the details? Because experience again shows that the result of getting the OpenGL calls wrong is often a view of nothing at all. This won't tell you what you did wrong, and trying to get it right by trial and error is a bad idea. Although you may get lucky, there are just too many ways to get nothing drawn on the screen. So, I will give you the basics in a few pages, and you can follow up in the references if you wish to know more.

Projecting the Image of a Scene onto a Plane

Imagine that a scene consists of a simple prism and that the center of the front face of the prism is distance **d** from your eye. This situation is diagrammed in Figure 3.8.

Simply put, the projection of the scene, or the prism here, is a two dimensional view obtained by placing a plane in between the viewer and the scene (see Figure 3.9). Rays drawn from all points on the prism to the eye will intersect the plane, and those places are indicated by a change of color on the plane. This will create an image of the scene.

From the game writer's point of view, all we really want is the projection. The screen is two dimensional, and *is* the plane above where the scene is projected. We wish the projection to have the basic properties of the real situation. If we move the plane closer to the prism, the projection of the prism gets larger until it becomes the same size as the prism itself. Moving the plane away from the object reduces the size of the image projected.

The plane being discussed is referred to as the *viewing plane* or *projection plane (PP)*, and the location of the eye above is often called the *center of projection (COP)*. We need to have a simple numerical description of what's happening so we can calculate the

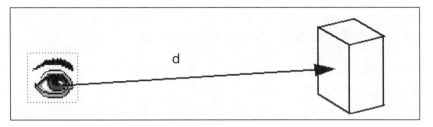

Figure 3.8
A prism that is placed distance d from your eye.

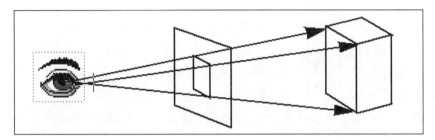

Figure 3.9
Placing a plane between the viewer and the scene.

view at any time in our game. Remember, we will want to determine what the driver sees at each time, and display that for the player in close to real time. In particular, we need to know how big things should appear on the PP when objects are a specific distance from it. If we look at the geometry of the situation, it is surprisingly simple. In Figure 3.10, we wish to be able to compute the height of the prism in the projection, **h**. Its actual height is **x**, and its distance from the viewpoint is **z**.

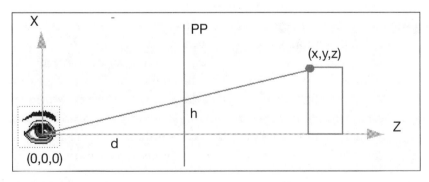

Figure 3.10
Computing the height of the prism.

This is what in high school we called a *similar triangle*—the triangle defined by the viewpoint, and the projected top and bottom of the prism have the same angles as the one defined by the viewpoint and the actual top and bottom of the prism. This means that the ratios of the height to distance (from 0,0,0) are constant; or in other words:

Equation 3.20 $\dfrac{h}{d} = \dfrac{x}{z}$

It is possible to calculate apparent sizes quite simply. In fact, we can create a matrix to do this, as we did for rotations and translations. I will spare you the details—the matrix is shown here:

Equation 3.21
$$\begin{bmatrix} 1 & 0 & 0 & 0 \\ 0 & 1 & 0 & 0 \\ 0 & 0 & 1 & 0 \\ 0 & 0 & 1/d & 0 \end{bmatrix}$$

This agrees with the notion that the apparent size of an object is inversely related to the distance it is positioned from us.

The discussion so far has concerned itself with the perspective transformation, which is commonly used in games and animations. If the viewpoint (COP) is moved away so that **d** is infinite, the lines from COP to the object become parallel and we get an *orthographic* or an *oblique* projection, depending on other details. There is no decrease of size with distance in this case (**d** is so large you could not see anything at all!), and these are of limited use in games. We did use it in *Gopher-it*, since we were looking down on an essentially 2D object anyway. More on parallel projections can be found in the references, especially *Foley and van Dam*[3].

Eliminating Things You Can't See Anyhow

There are always things that you cannot see in the real world from a particular location. They might be hidden behind something else, or they may simply not be in your field of view. If you hold your arms out from your sides, you will be aware that your hands are to your left and right, but you likely won't be able to see them. If you wiggle your fingers you can detect the motion, but not count the fingers themselves. Moving your hands towards each other in front of you will allow you to see them clearly at some point. There is an area in front of your eyes, for a certain angle on each side, which can be clearly seen. Simulating this involves *clipping* the objects outside of this area.

In fact, it's not an area; it's a volume, because there are things that are too far away to be clearly seen, and there is a region very close to you where you can't see very well either. We thus have a volume that contains things you can see, and all objects outside of that volume should be ignored. In truth, this volume is cone shaped, but in computer graphics, we usually create a polygonal viewing volume of the sort illustrated in Figure 3.11.

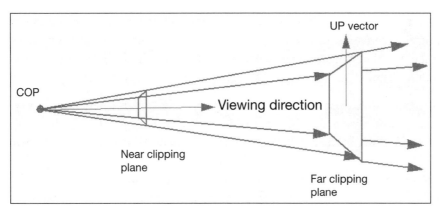

Figure 3.11
Defining a perspective viewing volume.

Every polygon, vector, and point that lies outside of the truncated prism that is the viewing volume doesn't have to be drawn. However, some objects will reside partly inside the volume and partly outside. Any method that rejects vectors that can't be seen must also cut (clip) them so that the visible part is present and the part outside of the view volume is not drawn. This is involved, but fortunately we don't have to get into the details, provided that the problem is clear. OpenGL will perform the clipping for us once we define the viewing volume.

Hidden Object/Surface Removal

I already mentioned that there are two ways in which an object won't be visible; one is when it lies outside of the viewing volume. The other is when it is hidden by another object. The subject of hidden surface removal used to be discussed by academics and practitioners until the development of the very popular *Z-buffer* algorithm. This algorithm is only practical when a relatively large amount of memory is available, but fortunately, memory has become cheap and most graphics cards now come with at least 64 megabytes.

So, let's take a quick look at the Z-buffer algorithm. Not only is it used for hidden surface removal, but similar methods are used by OpenGL for performing other tasks such as transparency, shadows, and blurs.

Simply put, a Z-buffer or depth buffer is a two-dimensional array the same size as the viewing area. Each pixel displayed on the screen has an entry in the Z buffer. When a pixel is drawn on the display, it is associated with a distance from the viewer (COP). Objects are drawn one at a time, and if the Z-buffer has no entry in it for a pixel to be drawn, we save the distance from the viewpoint to the object at that point in the Z-buffer. If the Z-buffer has a distance in it already, we compare that distance against the distance of the pixel we are drawing; if it is greater than the current one, we draw the current pixel and save its distance. We never draw a pixel that is farther away than the value in the Z-buffer. Thus, any object that is behind another will not appear on the screen.

One thing that can happen in practice is *Z fighting* or *Z flicker*, where polygons seem to flick in and out of existence rapidly as the point of view changes. This is the result of approximation errors in the pixel-depth values. Frequently (and this can occur with OpenGL), depths are stored as floating point numbers in a narrow range, and these are sometimes converted from integer user coordinates. Increasing the accuracy of the values of the buffer usually solves the problem. For example, if a 16-bit Z buffer is being used, changing it to a 24-bit or 32-bit buffer will solve the problem.

Texture Mapping

Textures are present in just about everything that we see around us. Wood, stone and tile all have texture, as well as brick, concrete, skin, fur, and scales. If we had to draw the textures in the same way that we draw people and cars, we would need a huge number of polygons. Shading and rendering would be hugely time-consuming, even if it were possible to do it at all. Fortunately, there is another option we can use—map a small texture image, pixel-by-pixel, onto an arbitrary surface. This involves a lot of work and a certain amount of math. Fortunately, computers are good at math and do not get bored.

This kind of thing is useful in more cases than simply creating basic textures. Drawing a building, for example, can be as simple as drawing a cube and then mapping the face of the building onto that. The texture in this case can be a high resolution image of a real building, a cartoon drawing of an imaginary building, or anything in between. The trick is to calculate where each pixel in the 2D texture image ends up on the 3D surface of the object. This is especially important as the object changes position with respect to the viewer. For example, as you drive past a building, the mapped face of the building must change perspective according to rules that you can't state out loud, but know intuitively, especially when they look wrong.

Mapping onto Simple Surfaces

Because images are usually rectangular arrays of pixels, mapping them onto rectangles is especially easy. If the texture image T has N rows and M columns and the rectangle R being mapped onto T has NxM pixels, the map will essentially be a scaling operation, and it can be implemented as an interpolation. For example, a pixel in row i of the texture is i/N of the vertical distance from the top of the image. The corresponding position in rectangle R is $(i/N)*N$ from row 0.

This mapping is actually backwards, because by going from texture to object we may have object pixels that are never set (see Figure 3.12). Going from object pixels to texture pixels will ensure that every pixel visible to a viewer will have a reasonable value.

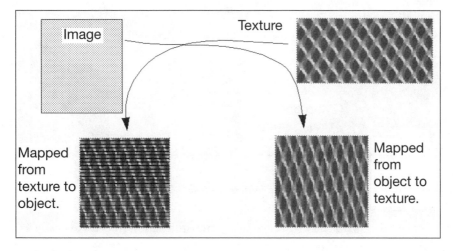

Figure 3.12
Using simple texture mapping.

The essential code for mapping a texture onto a rectangle is:

```
for (i=0; i<NÆ; i++)
{
    y = (float)i/(float)N;
    I = y*N;
    for (j=0; j<=M; j++)
    {
        x = (float)j/(float)M;
        J = x*M;
        mapped[i][j] = texture[I][J];
    }
}
```

If the rectangle being mapped is in 3D space, it may be viewed from an oblique angle. If this happens, the rectangle will look like a parallelogram or a rhombus, and the mapping from the texture image (a rectangle) seems harder than before (see Figure 3.13). This isn't the case; the object coordinates can map pixels from the texture before the perspective transformation is done. Without actually showing you the mathematics,

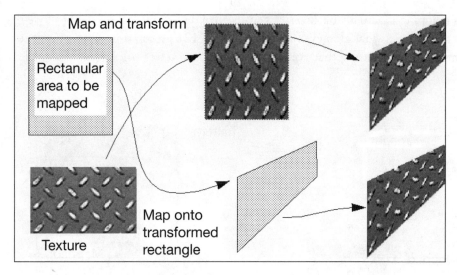

Figure 3.13
Mapping a texture onto a perspective-transformed rectangle.

the texture pixel is transformed by the viewing transformation in the same way as any other pixels, and we don't have to do anything special.

On the other hand, mapping a texture onto a sheared rectangle is not difficult. The following code will do it, assuming that the function **I(j)** returns the minimum index in column **j** and that **II(j)** returns the maximum index in column **j**:

```
for (j=j0; j<jn; j++)
{
    i0 = I(j);
    i1 = II(j);
    x  = j/M;
    jj = x*M
    for (i=i0; j<=i1; i++)
    {
        y = (i-i0)/(float)(i1-i0);
        ii = y * N;
        mapped[i][j] = texture[ii][jj];
    }
}
```

The code that will actually execute is a bit more complex, and can be found on the website for this book in the Chapter 3 directory.

Texture Mapping onto a Triangle

The polygons most likely to be used to represent objects in a driving game are rectangles and triangles. We have discussed how to map a texture onto a rectangle and a rhombus, but we still need to map a texture onto a triangle—although I'm sure you could figure it out for yourself by now. As before, the idea is to do an interpolation, but the sides of a triangle are not parallel to each other, so there is a slight variation.

As shown in Figure 3.14, a first step is to determine the texture pixel values at two points along two of the triangle's sides. This is done by interpolating the values between the common point **A** and the two other vertices. Then, we look in the BC direction and interpolate between the two points we just computed on the sides.

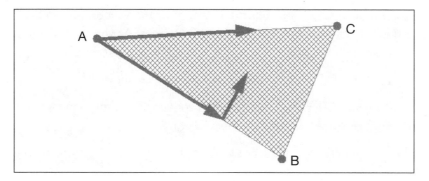

Figure 3.14
Texture mapping onto a triangle.

It is sufficient to see how this can be done. OpenGL performs the details of the mapping, and does it by asking the graphics card to do it if that facility is available.

Introducing OpenGL

The OpenGL system consists of many parts, but from the perspective of a game programmer, the key components are the *window system*, *graphics system*, and the *performance utilities*. The window system consists of procedures for creating, manipulating, and removing windows, either on PCs, Macs, or Unix systems. This is provided by OpenGL so that the programs don't call the system functions for window operations, and the program can run on different operating systems. The graphics system is obviously used for drawing objects onto the computer screen, and has facilities for color manipulation, texture mapping, geometry (rotation and translation), and rendering polygons—the basic operations needed to draw cars and buildings. Finally, the performance utilities are provided so that scenes can be rendered quickly. For a realistic impression of motion, the screen must be redrawn at least 24 times each second. If a scene is complex; some accommodation must be made for drawing it quickly.

While OpenGL is a fairly complete basic graphics system, it does not draw complex objects; you must build them out of simpler ones, like polygons, and draw them using the basic operators it does provide. OpenGL does not support event handling either, nor is it a window system. It does provide an auxiliary library called *GLUT* (Graphics Language Utility Toolkit) that performs window management functions. GLUT is especially useful because it draws graphics into a window and not directly to the screen. It also gives you the functions you need to create and destroy windows and to move them around.

By the way, because OpenGL is a worldwide standard there are a lot of web pages with code, examples, and documentation about it. I have provided a set of links in the references for this chapter to help you get more information. As you start to work more with OpenGL, here are some abbreviations you should be familiar with:

- GLUT is the OpenGL Utility Toolkit, as I mentioned above.

- GLU is the OpenGL Utility Library, which contains coordinate-mapping functions, surfaces, and texturing options.

- GLX is an X-windows specific set of tools for hardware acceleration, off-screen rendering, video input and more when using Unix or Linux.

- GLC is the OpenGL character renderer, used for drawing text in scenes.

Manipulating Windows in OpenGL

Because OpenGL draws into a window on the screen, we need to first learn how to create and manipulate a window. This is really quite simple but, like all window system programming that I know of, it requires that we know something about *event driven* software.

An event is simply some relevant thing that occurs. To a window, what is relevant is to be covered by another window, to be uncovered, to be resized, to be moved, or to be made the active window. Any mouse or keyboard activity performed on the active window is also a relevant activity. There are others but these will certainly do for now. The thing about events is that they can happen anytime. When a normal program is awaiting input from the keyboard, it knows that it is to expect a real number, string, or whatever. An event-driven program must be able to deal with any of the possible events that occur, and at any time. As mentioned before, the library that deals with window manipulations is called GLUT. GLUT also allows us to handle events.

GLUT

GLUT is essentially a system-independent interface to the native window system that can be used on any of the major operating systems. We'll deal only with the details of using GLUT with Windows, and for consistency, we'll use the Visual Studio or Visual C++ compiler from Microsoft. The location of the GLUT libraries and the OpenGL libraries on the disk must be given to Visual C++. My version of the compiler seems to know about them already, but in case your version is different, the details are shown here:

3

GLUT requires three files:

1. The include file **glut.h** should be in the include directory of your compiler, in a subdirectory called **gl**. On my system, this directory is *C:\Program Files\Microsoft Visual Studio\VC98\Include.* You could add an additional directory by clicking on the project->settings->C/C++ item in the Visual Studio window, and placing path names into the *Additional Include directories* text field.

2. The file **glut32.lib** must be linked into the runtime version of your program. In Visual Studio, choose the select the *project->settings->link* window, and add glut32.lib to the *Project Options* text box. The lib file itself must be in the compiler's lib folder, which on my system is located at *C:\Program Files\Microsoft Visual Studio\VC98\Lib.*

3. The **glut32.dll** file must also be made available at runtime; it must reside in the directory *C:\WINDOWS\system32.*

   NOTE: Keep in mind that these compiler settings are required to be able to compile programs that use GLUT.

I mention this stuff first so that you can set up a VC++ project that will allow you to compile sample GLUT code. I like to play around with a new system as I learn it.

By the way, when you create a new project in VC++, if you wish to avoid the Windows-dependent code that is normally needed for XP, Win98, and so on, the common thing is to create a new *Console Application.* Unfortunately, when you run such a program, an extra window opens (the *console,* apparently) and remains even after your program has terminated. You need to type a character in the console window after program termination for the window to go away. This is irritating.

I have learned a recipe to fix this:

- First, while running Visual Studio with your program active in the workspace, select the *project->settings->link* window. There is a combination box named *Category* that has choices like *General, Customize, Debug, Input* and *Output*. Select *Output*. Now in the box named *Entry- point symbol*, you should type *mainCRTStartup*.

- In the same window, you should now look in the box named *Project Options*. Look for the string *subsystem:console* and replace that with *subsystem:windows*.

- Build the application and execute it. The console application will now execute as a windows application, although GLUT is going to do the windows stuff instead of Visual Studio code. The console window will not be gone!

It's now time to write our first program.

Creating Our First Windows/GLUT Program

The first program we write won't actually appear to do very much, but it will have the skeleton of the windowing features needed to write our example game. It will create a window and close it on command from the user; to do that, it must handle at least one simple event. We will actually use two events; the program will handle input from the keyboard and it will deal with mouse button clicks. Any character typed or any mouse button press will cause the window to close.

The first thing that is always done in a GLUT program is to initialize the system, allocate storage, and so on. This is done by the following function:

```
void glutInit (int *argc, char **argv);
```

This is always the first OpenGL function called. The **argc** and **argv** parameters are the same as the ones passed to the main program, and **glutInit()** needs to look and see if any of the strings passed to main are intended for OpenGL. If so, it extracts them and does whatever it needs to with them.

The next thing we need to do is tell the window system what color model to use: RGBA full color, or color-index (also called color map). To do this, we call the following function:

```
void glutInitDisplayMode (unsigned int mode);
```

This function also performs a few other initializations that I'll explain later on. The integer value we pass it (**mode**) is usually a symbolic constant found in the glut.h include file. For example, to specify the RGB color model, we would pass the constant **GLUT_RGB**.

Next, we tell the system where to put the window on the screen, and how big the window should be. We need two functions for this:

```
void glutInitWindowPosition (int x, int y);
void glutInitWindowSize (int width, int size);
```

The x and y position arguments specify the location of the upper-left corner of the window on the screen, which has (0,0) as its upper-left coordinate. The width and height arguments are represented in pixels as their units.

Finally, we can create the window. This complex operation is performed by the following simple-looking function:

```
int glutCreateWindow(char *string);
```

The string passed to this function is the title of the window, and normally appears in the solid band at the top of the window. This function returns a unique integer identifier for this window; we can create many windows, and it pays to know which one you are referring to when communicating with OpenGL.

This new window now exists, technically, but is not yet visible. Because the GLUT system handles events, it contains the main loop that simply repeats forever waiting for an event to occur. Here is the function that will make the window visible:

```
glutMainLoop();
```

We can call this function without having set up any code to deal with events, but the result will not be very useful. The program that we've been constructing so far is shown next. This program should compile correctly under Visual Studio 6 with no errors or warnings. When you run it, a window will appear briefly on the screen and then vanish. This is possibly the simplest OpenGL program that does anything at all. Before we can make the window visible, we need to learn a bit about events and how to handle them.

```
#include <gl\glut.h>

int main(int argc, char **argv)
{
/* First, we must initialize and set the display mode */
   glutInitDisplayMode(GLUT_RGB);

/* Create window, size it at 512x512 pixels, and position it */
/* so the upper-left corner is at screen coordinates 200,200 */
```

```
    glutInitWindowSize (512, 512);
    glutInitWindowPosition (200, 200);
    glutCreateWindow("My First OpenGL Window");

/* The GLUT Main loop simply executes a test of all possible events */
/* When one occurs, the relevant callback function is executed.*/
    glutMainLoop();
    return 0;


}
```

Events and Callbacks

Since the occurrence of an event cannot be predicted, or even detected by us directly, we must tell the system what to do when an event occurs. We do this by writing a function. The function that deals with an event is called an *event handler*, and in OpenGL, it is a class of functions known as *callbacks*. We call OpenGL to tell it what our function is, and OpenGL "calls it back" whenever the event occurs. This is really a very simple way to deal with a complex operation. Let's look at an example in detail.

Consider the event that occurs when a character is typed. The GLUT system defines a key press as a keyboard event, and the handler for such an event must have three arguments, as shown here:

```
void keyPress (unsigned char key, int x, int y);
```

The first parameter, **key**, is the character connected to the key that was pressed. Thus, pressing the 'a' key results in the ASCII character 'a' being returned in this variable; pressing the shift and the 'a' keys would result in a 'A' being returned. The **x** and **y** parameters represent the coordinates of the screen cursor when the key was pressed; these coordinate are window relative, with the upper-left of the window being (0,0) as usual.

Of course, every time a key is pressed while the window is active, this same function is called. It must therefore handle all possible key presses. When the function returns, it returns to the main GLUT loop, in the function **glutMainLoop()**. For our simple program, any key press is supposed to result in closing the window and terminating the program. Thus, I propose the following actual code:

```
void keyPress (unsigned char key, int x, int y)
{
    exit (0);
}
```

We don't care what key was pressed or when the key was pressed. If we did, there would be a **switch** statement that assigned actions to each relevant key, such as:

```
void keyPress (unsigned char key, int x, int y)
{
   switch (key)
   {
     case 'q':   exit (0);
     case 'r':   rotate(theta);
                 break;
     case 'z':   increase_contrast ();
                 break;
   }
}
```

Here each key has a different action attached to it by virtue of the activity of the **switch** statement.

In order to tell the system that the function **keyPress()** is to be called whenever a key is pressed, we pass a pointer to the function using a *callback registration* function, in this case, specifically:

```
glutKeyboardFunc(keyPress);
```

The fact that the function was named **key Press()** has no significance to the system. We could call it **functionA** because it would not matter. Until we make the association between a key press event and the function **keyPress()** by calling **glutKeyboardFunc()**, no such association exists.

Before adding this code to our example and testing it, let's look at mouse events because they are a little bit different. First, the function that handles mouse events has a different set of arguments. For example:

```
void mouseClick (int butt, int updown, int x, int y);
```

When this function (or any mouse event handler) is called, the parameter **button** will tell us what button was pressed; its value will be one of **GLUT _LEFT _BUTTON** or **GLUT _RIGHT _BUTTON** (sometimes there could be a **GLU T_MIDDLE _BUTTON**). The **updown** parameter tells us whether the mouse button was pressed (**GLUT_UP**) or released (**GLUT_DOWN**). Each time a "click" occurs, one event of each of these two types will be generated. Again, the **x** and **y** parameters tell us the window coordinates of the cursor when the event occurred.

To establish **mouseClick()** as the mouse callback function, we must call this function as shown here:

```
glutMouseFunc (mouseClick);
```

You can call **glutMouseFunc()** with **NULL** as a parameter to disable mouse events. The program we are writing simply closes the window when the mouse is clicked inside of it. The mouse event handler **mouseClick()** looks very much like the key press handler we just finished writing:

```
void mouseClick (int butt, int updown, int x, int y)
{
    if (updown == GLUT_UP)
        exit (0);
}
```

This function exits when the mouse button is released—the last part of a "click."

GLUT provides us with 19 callback registration functions, so we have clearly just scratched the surface. Further documentation can be found on the Internet at various places, of course, so I'll only describe one more callback, but it is a crucial one.

The display callback is called by OpenGL whenever the screen may need to be redrawn; that is, if something changes, the window is exposed or resized, or if a request to redraw the screen comes from the user (that's us). The registration function for this is:

```
void glutDisplayFunc (void (*func) (void) );
```

The function parameter, according to the definition above, has no parameters, but it does have a crucial job: it draws all of the graphical elements that are to appear in the window. Yes, all of the graphics operations are called from the display handler. For users of X-windows, or even Java, this should not be a foreign idea. That's the way they do things, too. X-windows even uses explicit callback functions (although Java accomplishes the same thing using *Interfaces*).

Our first OpenGL program does not really involve any graphics. However, without a display callback, the window will not exist for more than a second or so. The simplest display callback I can think of is:

```
void display(void)
{
    glFlush();
}
```

This simply causes any OpenGL graphics commands that are pending to be executed now. It has a side-effect of keeping the window open until you can type or click in it to close it.

The complete program exists in pieces above. Here it is a finished program so that you can see how it all comes together:

```
#include <gl\glut.h>

void keyPress (unsigned char, int, int);
void mouseClick (int, int, int, int);
void display (void);

int main(int argc, char **argv)
{
    glutInitDisplayMode( GLUT_SINGLE |
                    GLUT_RGB);
    glutInitWindowSize (512, 512);
    glutInitWindowPosition (200, 200);
    glutCreateWindow("My First OpenGL Window");
    glutMouseFunc (mouseClick);
    glutDisplayFunc(display);
    glutKeyboardFunc(keyPress);
    glutMainLoop();
    return 0;
}

void display(void)
{
/* Graphics operations will go HERE */
    glFlush();
}

void mouseClick (int butt, int updown, int x, int y)
{
        if (updown == GLUT_UP)
            exit (0);
}

void keyPress (unsigned char key, int x, int y)
{
    exit (0);
}
```

When the program executes, the window will be drawn over the top of whatever stuff happens to be on the screen at the time. Since we never clear the window, the stuff will remain there, and will move with the window.

There is one final important item in GLUT that we need to discuss right now. If your program modifies the graphics in the window, the window will have to be redrawn. The right way to do that is to call the following function:

```
glutPostRedisplay(void);
```

It sets a flag someplace that **glutMainLoop()** detects. It also calls the display callback, which then redraws the screen. We will need to do this very soon.

A small change to the program will actually draw something into the window. GLUT has a dozen or so built-in drawing functions for spheres, cubes, and even a teapot. So, replace the **display()** function above with the following one:

```
void display(void)
{
    glClear (GL_COLOR_BUFFER_BIT);
    glutWireTeapot(0.5);
    glFlush();
}
```

When this program is compiled and executed, the resulting window shown in Figure 3.15 is displayed.

Basic Graphics Operations

It's unlikely that the objects you wish to draw will have pre-defined OpenGL functions that will render them (unless you write a racing teapots game, of course). OpenGL will render objects that are defined as polygons, and will do so quite rapidly. This is the desired operation of the graphics system of our game, in almost all cases. Graphics cards these days describe performance on the basis of the number of polygons they can

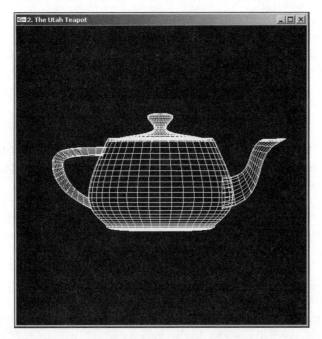

Figure 3.15
A rendition of the famous Utah teapot created by a call to the glutWireTeapot() function.

process per second. Thus, we should describe the graphical components of our game as polygons, and we need to understand how to use OpenGL to draw these.

Drawing Polygons

There are multiple ways to draw polygons in OpenGL, and multiple ways to specify objects that consist of polygons. The basic scheme encloses a set of polygon descriptions, coded as procedure calls, between a *begin* and an *end* procedure call. Specifically, we could draw a triangle in the following manner:

```
glBegin (GL_TRIANGLES);
glVertex3f (x0, y0, z0);
glVertex3f (x1, y1, z1);
glVertex3f (x2, y2, z2);
glEnd();
```

The triangle drawn by this code is shown in Figure 3.16.

The constant **GL_TRIANGLES** indicates that an independent set of triangles will be specified as vertices, between the **glBegin()** and **glEnd()** calls. There will, in this case, be three vertices specified per triangle. Their coordinates are (x_i, y_i, z_i) as indicated

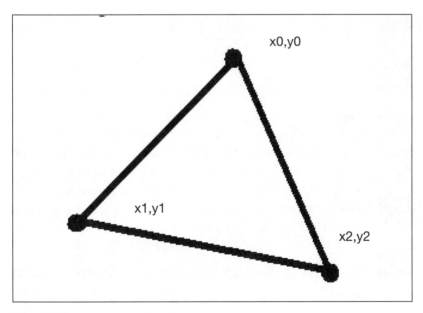

Figure 3.16
Drawing a polygon (triangle) using a set of glVertex3f() calls.

above. You can specify as many triangles as you like between the **glBegin()** and **glEnd()** calls. In fact, the more you use, the better—initializations are inexpensive.

The calls to **glVertex3f()** specify the coordinates of the vertices as three floating point Cartesian coordinates: x, y, and z. Each three consecutive calls defines one triangle here, because that is what **GL_TRIANGLES** means. By default, the coordinate values range between 0.0 and 1.0, but previous initializations can alter this, as we shall see.

> **WARNING!** A common error is to specify a set of triangles or other polygons using glVertex3f() but forgetting to enclose these triangles between glBegin() and glEnd(). This is legal syntax, but will not result in any polygons being drawn.

The specifier **GL_TRIANGLES** implies that distinct triangles are to be drawn. It is more efficient to draw a connected grouping of triangles, and have them share vertices. For example, you could use a set of triangles that share edges in a strip-wise fashion: OpenGL calls this a **GL_TIANGLE_STRIP**, and the code looks like this:

```
glBegin (GL_TRIANGLE_STRIP);
glVertex3f (x0, y0, z0);
glVertex3f (x1, y1, z1);
glVertex3f (x2, y2, z2);

glVertex3f (x3, y3, z3);

glVertex3f (x4, y4, z4);
glEnd();
```

The image drawn is shown in Figure 3.17. The first three coordinates specify the first triangle, as before. Then, each new coordinate defines a new triangle, using the previous two vertices plus the new one. This is a more efficient way to draw polygons because it is only necessary to specify N+2 vertices to draw N triangles instead of N*3 vertices as before. Another way to do this kind of thing is by using a fan of triangles, or **GL_TRIANGLE_FAN**, where the first vertex defines the center of a fan of triangles, and successive pairs of vertices define consecutive triangles.

I should point out that the triangles do not have to be in the same plane. It would defeat the purpose, in fact, since we wish to use triangles/polygons to represent an arbitrary surface in three dimensions, like a car or a boat. Thus, a 3D surface like the one shown in Figure 3.18 would be possible to easily define using the triangle drawing facility of OpenGL.

3

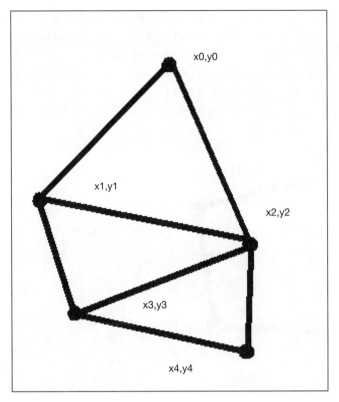

Figure 3.17
Drawing a set of triangles that share edges.

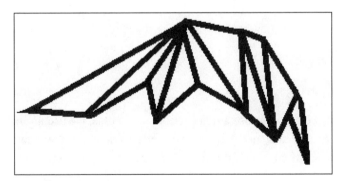

Figure 3.18
Drawing a 3D surface using triangles.

Triangles are not the only kind of polygon that we can draw. My favorite polygon is a quadrilateral or a *quad* in OpenGL terms. This group of polygons includes squares, rectangles, parallelograms, and rhombuses. Drawing an independent quadrilateral (see Figure 3.19) is accomplished by starting the vertex block with a call to **glOpen ()** specifying **GL_QUAD**, and then specifying each quad as four vertices:

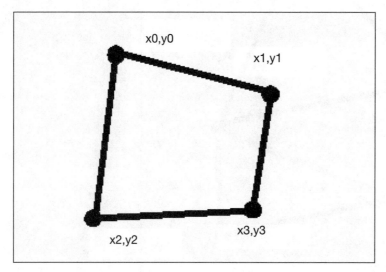

Figure 3.19
Drawing an independent quadrilateral.

```
glBegin (GL_QUADS);
glVertex3f (x0, y0, z0);
glVertex3f (x1, y1, z1);
glVertex3f (x2, y2, z2);
glVertex3f (x3, y3, z3);
glEnd();
```

As we found with triangles, we can also use a quad strip. In this case, we use an initial quad that requires four vertices. Each successive pair or vertices define a new quad as shown in Figure 3.20. Here are the calls required:

```
glBegin (GL_QUAD_STRIP);
glVertex3f (x0, y0, z0);
glVertex3f (x1, y1, z1);
glVertex3f (x2, y2, z2);
glVertex3f (x3, y3, z3);
```

```
glVertex3f (x4, y4, z4);
glVertex3f (x5, y5, z5);
glEnd();
```

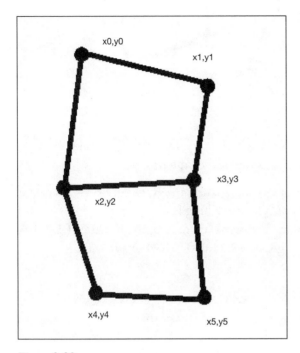

Figure 3.20
Using a quad strip.

Again, as with triangles, you can use rectangles to define a 3D surface (see Figure 3.21). However, it is also normal to think of each quad as being in a plane, even though it is obviously possible to have a quad that is not.

Between the **glBegin()** and **glEnd()** calls we can have a limited variety of OpenGL calls. These are defined in the reference manual. However, the calls to define the vertices can be contained within user-defined procedures, so we can write procedures that draw cubes, trees, and cars and have one **glOpen() – glClose()** pair bracket all of the polygons that are drawn. For example, we can draw a cube using the following calls:

```
glBegin (GL_QUADS);
draw_cube();
glEnd();
```

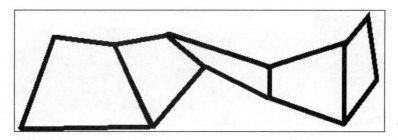

Figure 3.21
Using rectangles to define a 3D surface.

Here, the **draw_cube()** function draws each of the eight faces of the cube as six distinct quads. (I'll leave this as an exercise until the next chapter.)

Color is specified by calling **glColor3f()** and passing the R, G, and B values desired. This effectively sets the *current* color, and everything is drawn in that color until the color is changed. The color values are between 0.0 and 1.0, so **glColor3f (1.0, 1.0, 1.0)** sets the current color to white, and **glColor3f** (1.0, 0.0, 0.0) sets it to red.

Viewing Transformations

OpenGL maintains a stack of transformation matrices, and is always currently using the one on top. Specifying modifications to the current transformation matrix is easy, and is always the default. Creating and pushing a new one has to be requested. Also, there are multiple stacks, one for each type of matrix: viewing, model transformations, and projection transformations. When manipulating the matrices, you enter the correct mode using the **glMatrixMode()** function: either **glMatrixMode(GL_MODELVIEW)** or **glMatrixMode(GL_PROJECTION)**. In modelview mode, you can rotate, scale, or translate polygonal models before plotting them. In projection mode, you can change the way the world looks.

The viewing operations involve a few processes: defining the transformation, specifying the viewpoint, and specifying the clipping volume. The viewing transformation used in the *Gopher-it* game I introduced in Chapter 2 was orthographic—the simplest to specify. In the game I use

```
gluOrtho2D (0.0, 19.0*CELLSIZE, 19.0*CELLSIZE, 0.0);
```

which sets up a two-dimensional viewing transformation having the min (left) and max (right) X coordinates as the first two parameters (0.0 and 19.0***CELLSIZE**) and the bottom and top coordinates being the final two. In this case, the bottom is greater than the top. Y runs in ascending values from the top of the image to the bottom. Because **CELLSIZE** is 32, the entire region is 19*32, or 608 pixels square.

Establishing a perspective viewing transformation is a matter of creating and pushing a perspective transformation on to the projection stack. The whole process is coded as follows:

```
glMatrixMode (GL_PROJECTION);
glLoadIdentity ();
gluPerspective (90.0, 1.0, 1.0, 350.0)
```

The call to **glLoadIdentity()** pushes an identity matrix on the current stack (projection stack, in this case). This new matrix is modified according to the parameters given to the **gluPerspective()** call. Specifically, the first parameter is the field of view in the vertical direction specified in degrees; the second is the *aspect ratio*—the ratio of x to y for the field of view. The final two parameters are the near and far clipping planes specified as Z coordinates, where 0 is the nearest possible coordinate. Positive values represent an increase in distance.

This sets up the basic viewing transformation, but that's not usually enough. Where is the center of projection, or where is the location from which we are looking? What direction are we looking? These aspects can be specified by using the call

```
gluLookAt (MyX, MyY, MyZ, dirx, diry, 0.0,
           0.0, 0.0, 1.0);
```

where **(MyX, MyY, MyZ)** are the current 3D coordinates of the place from where we are looking. The parameters **(dirx, diry, 0.0)** represent the direction we are looking, or the *viewing direction* as defined back in Figure 3.7, and the last three parameters represent the vector that identifies the vertical, in this case **(0,0,1)** or the Z axis. This call will create a matrix that will be multiplied by the current one (i.e., top of stack) to give a resultant viewing matrix.

We should now define the clipping volume. First, we need to make sure that hidden surface removal is turned on by calling this function:
```
glEnable (GL_DEPTH_TEST)
```
This call basically enables the Z-buffer. It can be done anytime before drawing. Clipping can next be turned on using the following function:

```
glViewport (0.0, 0.0, 700.0, 700.0)
```

This function specifies the 2D coordinates of the part of the projected scene that can be seen. If you want to actually clip in 3D, then you call the following function:

```
glFrustrum (left, right, bottom, top, near, far)
```

Here, all of the parameters are **double**. This function calls specifies the six clipping planes as the relevant coordinate only; if Z is distance, for example, we need only specify Z for the *near* and *far* clipping planes. I'll provide detailed examples of how to use this function in subsequent chapters.

Practical Texture Mapping

Getting OpenGL to perform texture mapping onto polygons requires three basic steps.

1. You must read the texture into memory. Textures are images, and are stored in an image file format such as GIF, JPEG, or PPM. OpenGL does not read images, so we'll use images in PPM format because this format is simple and we already wrote a function to read them.

2. You must map the vertices of the polygon onto texture coordinates "by hand." That is, every polygon vertex plotted must be associated with row and column coordinates in the texture image. Remember, the polygons are in 3D space and the texture is in 2D space.

3. The polygons must be drawn, covering them in the process with portions of the texture. Once you have defined the mapping, as in step two above, this part is almost automatic, taking place when you draw the polygons because OpenGL keeps track of the polygons that have textures.

As you can see, texture mapping is all about setting things up so it can be done automatically.

OpenGL thinks of textures as objects, and the image used to map onto a polygon is merely one property or parameter of the texture. Textures are referred to by names, which are in fact unique integers. OpenGL assigns a texture a name using this function:

```
glGenTextures (N , &textureObject)
```

It returns the name of a texture. If **N** is set to 1 it returns the next integer we can use to define a new texture. In general, this function returns **N** such names. The name(s) get returned as the second parameter **textureObject**. This merely gives you a unique name. A new texture object is given properties using two functions, and this means that the name is associated with a texture image, pixel color scheme and implementation, size, and so on.

Once we have a name, we must *bind* it to a *target*. The official documentation on this subject seems to me to be a bit fuzzy, especially for beginners. Please bear with me or skip ahead if you are an advanced user, but I think the following is essential:

- *There is only one target that is important.* That target is called **GL_TEXTURE_2D**. It represents the two dimensional texture that is being used at the present time. There are one- and three-dimensional targets that we will never use.

- *Only one texture can be active at a time.* Only one texture can be bound to the target **GL_TEXTURE_2D** at a time. If you map a texture, it will be the one bound to **GL_TEXTURE_2D**. If you modify a texture parameter, it will be to the texture bound to **GL_TEXTURE_2D**.

- *An OpenGL function call binds a texture to a target*—glBindTexture (GL_TEXTURE_2D, textureObject). Binding means to connect or to link. From now on, the name in **textureObject**, which is an integer, will be associated with a particular set of parameters referring to a texture. The name operates more like a *handle* than a name. (If you have experience programming with DirectX, you should be familiar with how handles work.)

- *The binding can be redone.* Each time glBindTexture() is called, another texture object, specified by name, becomes the one currently active; it becomes bound to the target **GL_TEXTURE_2D**. If you want to use multiple textures—a very common thing to do—you must bind the texture you wish to use before you plot the polygons to be texture mapped.

- *You can't change the binding while drawing.* Inside of a **glBegin()- glEnd block()**, a call to **glBindTexture()** will cause an error. The error will not cause the program to halt, but the desired texture mapping will not occur.

Once you have a name bound to a texture object, you can assign that object properties. Specifying the actual texture image is a simple matter (with complicated parameters):

```
glTexImage2D (GL_TEXTURE_2D, 0, 3,
    width, height, borderWidth,
    pixelFormat, pixelType, image)
```

The first parameter specifies the kind of texture, always **GL_TEXTURE_2D**. The second is called the *level of detail*, and will be discussed more in a future chapter. Suffice to say that the usual level is zero, and higher levels refer to images that give differing images that represent what the texture looks like at different sizes. The third parameter specifies the number of color components in a texture pixel. This can be 1, 2, 3, or 4; the 3 specifier above actually indicates 3 components are used: r, g, and b.

The width and height parameters refer to the size of the image itself, and there are size limitations. Both must be a power or 2 plus the total size of a specified border. The size of this border is the sixth parameter, **borderWidth**. It can be 0 or 1. The **pixelFormat** can be one of a few values, specified as constants, and is specified the way pixels are represented. I typically use **GL_RGB** or **GL_RGBA**. The **pixelType** specifies how the pixel values are stored: reals, ints, chars, and so on. **GL_UNSIGNED_BYTE** is typical. Finally, we have a pointer to the pixels themselves, stored in the form described by the parameters.

This assumes that the properties of the texture image are known (i.e., it has been read into memory). This call does not really do anything except note what the values of certain image parameters are and where the image can be found. The image is actually at least four parameters (image location, sizes, format), and this one call sets them all. Setting other parameters is done more simply by calling the following function:

```
glTexParameter (GL_TEXTURE_2D, pname, pvalue);
```

There are 16 texture parameters that I know of, but not all of them are equally important and the default values work just fine. These will be explored later also.

Now we're ready for the final step—drawing a texture-mapped polygon. This involves specifying the texture coordinates of each vertex as it is drawn. Believe it or not, that's all that is required! In practice, here's how you can draw a quad that is mapped to a texture:

```
glTexCoord2f (1.0, 0.0); glVertex3f (x0, y0, z0);
glTexCoord2f (1.0, 1.0); glVertex3f (x1, y1, z1);
glTexCoord2f (0.0, 1.0); glVertex3f (x2, y2, z2);
glTexCoord2f (0.0, 0.0); glVertex3f (x3, y3, z3);
```

Each texture coordinate, specified as an (x,y) index into the texture image, is associated with the vertex coordinate in 3D that follows.

The complete (more or less) code needed to map a foliage texture onto parts of a cube is shown here:

```
/* Read the texture image */
    readIcon (&hedgeIcon, "hedge1.ppm");
/* Assign a name */
    glGenTextures (1, &hedgeTex);
/* Make it the current texture */
    glBindTexture   (GL_TEXTURE_2D, hedgeTex);
/* Assign an image to the current texture */
    glTexImage2D    (GL_TEXTURE_2D, 0, 3, 128, 128, 0, GL_RGB,
        GL_UNSIGNED_BYTE, &hedgeIcon[2]);
/* Filter for varying viewing distance */
    glTexParameterf (GL_TEXTURE_2D, GL_TEXTURE_MIN_FILTER,
        GL_NEAREST);
```

```
/* The environment setting - MODULATE */
   glTexEnvf       (GL_TEXTURE_ENV, GL_TEXTURE_ENV_MODE,
                    GL_MODULATE);
/* Switch on texture mapping */
   glEnable        (GL_TEXTURE_2D);
   glBegin         (GL_QUADS);
     /* START DRAWING */
/* East face of the cube */
   glTexCoord2f (1.0, 0.0); glVertex3f ((x0, y0,z0);
   glTexCoord2f (1.0, 1.0); glVertex3f (x1, y1, z1;
   glTexCoord2f (0.0, 1.0); glVertex3f (x2, y2, z2);
   glTexCoord2f (0.0, 0.0); glVertex3f (x3, y3, z3);
/* West face */
   glTexCoord2f (1.0, 0.0); glVertex3f (x0+WEST, y0, z0);
   glTexCoord2f (1.0, 1.0); glVertex3f (x1+WEST, y1, z1);
   glTexCoord2f (0.0, 1.0); glVertex3f (x2+WEST, y2, z2);
   glTexCoord2f (0.0, 0.0); glVertex3f (x3+WEST, y3, z3);
   glEnd();
```

This code appears to be the minimum needed to perform texture mapping in
OpenGL. There are three things that have not been mentioned yet:

1.   We need to switch on texture mapping in a way similar to the way we switched
     on hidden surface removal. This is done by using
     glEnable(GL_TEXTURE_2D).

2.   There is an environment in which textures take place, and there are global
     parameters that specify how it is done. The essential ones specify how the
     texture is placed on the surface: **GL_DECAL** pastes a texture over whatever is
     there; **GL_MODULATE** multiplies the background with the texture so that
     they both appear to some extent. The function **glTexEnvf()** allows you to alter
     environment parameters.

3.   There are parameters that operate as filters, specifying how the texture changes
     scale as you get nearer or farther from it. The parameter named
     GL_TEXTURE_MIN_FILTER specifies how a pixel being textured is mapped
     onto an area bigger than one texture element. In the code above, the call
     **glTexParameterf (GL_TEXTURE_2D, GL_TEXTURE_MIN_FILTER,
     GL_NEAREST)** specifies that we use the value of the texture element that is
     nearest (physically) to the center of the pixel being mapped onto. I discovered that
     this had to be specified or the mapping would not take place. I think it is because
     the default is not appropriate, although there may be another reason. I am looking
     into it.

Summary

I've covered quite a lot of territory in this chapter. It might seem to you that the basic graphics techniques we discussed are not just used to develop driving and racing games. All games have a foundation in graphics, audio, AI, and programming that is extensive, and as a teacher, I know that my job is to make sure that you have a solid background. I haven't yet covered everything you need to know about graphics so that you can program driving and racing games, but we have covered many of the fundamentals. In future chapters, I'll have much more to say about more advanced graphics topics such as performance issues, mipmapping, bump maps, and so on.

At this point, if you understand what has been explained, you'll be able to start designing and writing a 3D game. In the next chapter, we'll explore how we can turn the *Gopher-it* game into a 3D game, including using textures.

Chapter 4

Building a Basic 3D Driving Game

- Learn how the basic 2D *Gopher-it* game can be developed into a 3D driving game.

- Learn how to apply texture mapping and backdrops to create more realistic 3D effects.

- Use special techniques to eliminate texture seams in your game backgrounds.

In Chapter 2, I introduced the very simple 2D driving game called *Gopher-it*. Then, in the previous chapter you learned how to work with 3D graphics and OpenGL. In this chapter, we'll apply everything we've discussed so far and develop a 3D version of *Gopher-it*. Hopefully, you'll now feel up to the task. After all, you now know the basics of driving and racing games architecture, and you know how to piece a basic game together from components.

But we do have our work cut out for us. Knowing about 3D graphics and building a complex real-time display are very different. Still, it is our goal to delve into the depths of game coding and design, and to push the limits of our new-found knowledge.

Of course, there will still be some parts that we can't complete, so these parts will be built in successive chapters after we learn more about the relevant material. Audio, for example, was simply thrown into *Gopher-it* without explanation, and we won't cover audio until Chapter 7. Other things can be done, but they will require some redesign of the original *Gopher-it* engine. For example, the walls that define the maze will need to be given height. Perhaps we should texture map them as well so that they look like buildings or hedges. The gas stations should look more like what they are, and the police cars should be 3D cars that chase you.

The big thing that we cannot do yet is incorporate physics to give the game proper car control. The cars won't drive properly just yet, which means that you might feel you are pushing them around with sticks. This will be a good thing actually, since it will help you gain an appreciation of how important the physics simulation is.

How *Gopher-it* Actually Works

The 2D game presented Chapter 2 used a lot of code that might not have been completely understandable to you until we discussed 3D graphics and OpenGL in Chapter 3. Now that you have a good background, you might want to go back over some of the important details and see how we did them. This will give you a little more perspective before we jump into the 3D version.

Gopher-it 2D was written to explain how the components of a game might be combined. It's important to remember this because (as always) there are better ways to do many of the things we did.

2D Graphics and the Display

The board for *Gopher-it* is stored in a text file and is read in and displayed by the graphics sub-system. The board file contains only information about where the maze walls are and nothing else. The initial positions of all the other objects are hard-coded in the program. Because of a disagreement in coordinate systems (i.e., between OpenGL and me), the Y coordinates are reversed in the display system, as indicated by this call in the display routine:

The coordinates used by the objects are gross ones; they are specified at a higher scale than the screen coordinates. They are processed as array indices into the board matrix as the board data is read in. Each matrix element is **CELLSIZE** x **CELLSIZE** pixels, where our choice of **CELLSIZE** is 32. Thus, the entire board display is calculated as follows:

18 cells × 32 pixels/cell = 576 pixels wide, by 17 cells × 32 = 544 pixels high

The actual display matrix as defined in the call to **gluOrtho2D()** is 19×19 cells, which equals 608×608 pixels.

The components of the game, including the police cars, gas stations, gophers, and the player, are raster images of size 32×32 (one cell) that are displayed at the proper place on the board. The place is determined in advance by initializations in the AI system that set up the database of objects. The object images are displayed by calling the OpenGL function **glDrawPixels()**, passing it the address of a "bitmap" containing the image to be displayed. The **glDrawPixels()** function simply copies a set of pixels (a 2D set, usually) into a place on the display.

We still need to get our images from someplace, and games need a lot of them. They are stored as images in some standard image format, often GIF or JPEG. Some games even use a special internal representation. For the sake of simplicity, I suggest that we use a format called PPM, which is a standard file format available on the Internet and known to those who work with images. Utilities are available for converting from GIF and JPEG to PPM, and they can be downloaded from the Internet. Moreover, it is easy to write a program to read PPM images, and that's one big reason why I want to use this format here.

Reading PPM Images

A major advantage of the PPM format is that it has both an ASCII (text) and binary version. It is intended to store color images in 24-bit RGB format. A PPM file contains a text header that stores only the basic info:

ASCII file version	Binary file version
P3	P6
256 128 256	256 128 256
	... pixels ...

In all cases the header is text, so we are always guaranteed to be able to read an important part of the file. The "P3" indicates color and ASCII (text) format. The label "P6" indicates color and binary format. The next three numbers specify the number of columns, the number of rows, and the number or distinct values in each color (NL), respectively.

The data is stored as RGB values—red, green, and blue intensity codes. In the text version, three integers are stored in the file for each pixel—a red, green, and blue value. Each of these numbers is between 0 and NL (the number of levels). This file can be printed, although I'd recommend against it due to the typical large size of an image. In the binary version, the RGB values are written to the file as three bytes, in the usual order—red, green, then blue. It is customary to read these as unsigned characters.

The images used for icons in the *Gopher-it* game are all saved as binary PPM files, "P6" type. In fact, we will use this format for texture map images and all image types that we will need to read, since it makes sense to be consistent about these things. This approach takes less code, and therefore, less time.

It would be nice if OpenGL read in a few standard image formats, but it doesn't. Since OpenGL can't read images, we must write the code ourselves, knowing that we will use it not only for icons but also for texture maps.

The PPM header is read as text by using **scanf()** calls. Each pixel requires three read operations: one each for red, green, and blue. You can find code on the Web for manipulating PPM files (and its companion formats PGM and PBM) free for the asking. You can also find utilities for displaying them on the screen. Here is the basic code for reading the binary (P6) form of the PPM image file format:

```
void getPPM (char *infname, unsigned char **buf, int *NC, int *NR)
{
    FILE *inf;
    int i,j,k, N, m;
    unsigned char pixel;
    unsigned char *buffer;
    int nc, nr, ngl, XC, XR;
    char c1, c2;

    inf = fopen (infname, "r");
    if (inf == NULL) return;
    /* Read header - P6 */
    fscanf (inf, "%c", &c1);
    fscanf (inf, "%c", &c2);
    fscanf (inf, "%d", &nc);
    fscanf (inf, "%d", &nr);
    fscanf (inf, "%d", &ngl);

    *NR = nr; *NC = nc;
    m = 256/ngl;
    do {
        fscanf (inf, "%c", &c1);
    } while (c1 != '\n');

    XC = nc + (4 - nc%4);
    XR = nr + (4 - nr%4);

    if (XR*XC < 36*36) N = 36 * 36;
    else N = XR*XC;

    buffer = (unsigned char *)malloc (N*3+2);
    for (i=0; i<N*3+2; i++) buffer[i] = (unsigned char)255;
    *buf = buffer;
    buffer[0] = (unsigned char)nc;
    buffer[1] = (unsigned char)nr;
    k = 2;

    for (i=0; i<nr; i++)
    {
```

```
    for (j=0; j<nc; j++)
    {
        fscanf (inf, "%c", &pixel);
        buffer[k++] = pixel*m;
        fscanf (inf, "%c", &pixel);
        buffer[k++] = pixel*m;
        fscanf (inf, "%c", &pixel);
        buffer[k++] = pixel*m;
    }
}
    fclose (inf);
}
```

4

Drawing the Icons

The icons for the objects are 2D images that are the size of a cell on the board. All we need to do is draw them where they belong. Of course, the only ones that move are the cars, so keeping track of them is not difficult. OpenGL allows us to draw pixels at any point on the output window. We simply need to tell it where and how many we want to display.

The **getPPM()** function reads in the images. Note the way it stores them: as a one dimensional array of bytes. This happens to be the way OpenGL wants them. Each color is one byte, and the bytes are stored in the red, green, and blue order, one row after another. A quick call to our **getObjectPos()** function returns the position of the object to be drawn, as X and Y coordinates on the board. There are **CELLSIZE** pixels across the top and side of each object cell, so we must multiply by **CELLSIZE** to get absolute X, Y positions **XX** and **YY**.

The steps in OpenGL we need to follow to draw the icon are:

1. Set the OpenGL cursor to the correct position (**XX, YY**) in the following way:

    ```
    glRasterPos2i (xx, yy);
    ```

2. Copy the pixels that define the icon to the output buffer

    ```
    glDrawPixels (nc, nr, GL_RGB, GL_UNSIGNED_BYTE,
                  &(icon[2]));
    ```

    where **nc** and **nr** specify the size (in rows and columns) of the icon image, **GL_RGB** specifies the way the image is structured, **GL_UNSIGNED_BYTE** tells the system to assume bytes instead of floats, and **icon[2]** specifies the location of the first pixel in the icon, since the first two elements hold the size.

Timing

Gopher-it is not a game that allows continuous motion. Each second the player's car can move in a specified direction, and the police cars move slightly more or less often. So how do we make something happen every second?

The GLUT subsystem has a function called:

```
void glutTimerFunc
    ( unsigned int interval,
      void (*func)(int val),
      value);
```

When called, this function sets up a timer callback. The function to be called is specified as the second parameter, and please understand that it is not called immediately; it will be called in **interval** milliseconds. Also, understand that this timer only runs once. You must call **glutTimerFunc()** each time you want to execute the callback. The callback function will be written by you, and it takes one integer parameter. This is specified as the third parameter to **glutTimerFunc()**. For example, if the player gets to move every second, you would specify a parameter of 1000 milliseconds. This should be a named constant so let's call it **PLAYER_INTERVAL**, and the function to be called, the one that moves the player's car, is named **timedAILoop()**. The setup is:

```
glutTimerFunc (PLAYER_INTERVAL, timedAILoop, 0);
```

In this case, the **timedAILoop()** function will be passed 0 as its parameter. We don't care because it is not used. Inside of the **timedAILoop()** function, a call identical to the one above to reset the timer is made, so that the timer goes off *every* second.

Two police cars are used, and they can move in quite different ways if we like. Each police car has its own timer, and each timer can be adjusted to go off at different times. In fact, the interval must be variable because in normal mode the police cars are faster than the player, whereas when the player is indestructible, the police cars move slower. A possible way to do this is to use the following function call:

```
glutTimerFunc (COP2_INTERVAL+cop_slow,
               moveCop2, POLICE2);
```

The value of **cop_slow** is 0 in normal mode and is positive in invulnerable mode, so that the time between moves is longer (i.e., the car will move more slowly). The function **moveCop2()** must reset the timer each move, and moves only the one police car. If that car is destroyed, it is very important to stop setting its timer!

Gopher-it 3D Graphics I

Extending *Gopher-it* into the third dimension is not really the hard part of what we are going to do here. The really hard thing is the change in perspective—we can't look at the board from above anymore. We have to take a position as a driver, or at least from the perspective of the player's car. It is common to have a viewpoint that follows behind the car being driven, looking ahead and down a bit, as shown in Figure 4.1.

Figure 4.1
Example of the viewpoint taken in most driving games.

This means that all scenes must now be rendered because the car will be moving and the view will be different each time.

Another difference is that time can't really jump forward in one second increments anymore. We need, for a reasonable driving game, to provide a smooth advance of time, and thus we must allow the car to move at various speeds, and to turn in more than two ways. Turning a corner at a higher speed may take 4 to 6 time steps. This also has more consequences than initially anticipated. Let's examine each important change one at a time.

Adding the Third Dimension

Drawing a scene must be done from the OpenGL *display* callback function, so this is the place to begin with the creation of the third dimension. We must potentially draw any wall that is in front of the player's car, along with any gophers, gas stations, and police cars in that same region. By *in front*, we mean in a direction indicated by the player while the player is steering. Of course, we could draw all of the walls and cars and components and leave the task of sorting out visibility to the renderer, but that may take too much time.

The first step is to extend the walls upwards and give them thickness. Since a wall object occupies an entire square in the original game map, it makes sense to turn the walls into cubes. In the 2D version of *Gopher-it*, OpenGL was used in a somewhat unnatural way. I didn't tell you that at the time, but now that you know some graphics, using the orthographic projection to look down on a 2D board from a height is probably overkill, and not what was intended. You now know about projections, hidden surface removal, and polygons, and so it is a simple matter to create a cube for each original wall square and to draw them in perspective projection from the viewpoint of the player.

First, we turn on the Z-buffer hidden surface removal. Next, we define the viewport and set up the perspective projection. This is done once in the display function, at initialization time. The code for this is found in the same place where we used to set up the orthographic projection:

```
if (!InitFlag)
{
    glEnable (GL_DEPTH_TEST);
    glViewport (0.0, 0.0, 700.0, 700.0);
    glMatrixMode (GL_PROJECTION);
    glLoadIdentity ();
    gluPerspective (90.0, 1.0, 1.0, 350.0);
    glMatrixMode (GL_MODELVIEW);
    InitFlag = 1;
}
```

Next, we need to set up the "camera" position to be the player's position. This position is retrieved from the AI system as before. The **gluLookAt()** function is used for now to set the camera parameters. Oh, and don't forget that the board consists of 19×19 cells, each of which is 32 (**CELLSIZE**) pixels square. This is crucial to correct graphical positioning. Here's the code for this:

```
glLoadIdentity ();
getObjectPos (PLAYER, &x, &y);
dir = getDirection (PLAYER);
gluLookAt ((x+0.5)*CELLSIZE, (y+0.5)*CELLSIZE,
    1.5*CELLSIZE, dirx, diry, 0.0, 0.0, 0.0, 1.0);
glClear (GL_COLOR_BUFFER_BIT|GL_DEPTH_BUFFER_BIT);
```

Setting the Z coordinate to be **1.5*CELLSIZE** places the camera slightly above the height of the walls, so that we can see over them for some distance. During later versions of the game, this will be reduced to **0.5*CELLSIZE** so that the viewpoint is slightly above the car, and so that the walls obscure the player's view.

Finally, the walls are drawn almost as before. The **draw_cube (i, j)** function is used to draw each cube at its position. For now, we'll simply draw each face of the cube as a distinct color so that we can see where we are. This is useful for debugging the program. I have some trouble with coordinate systems, like many others, and I used the colors to help me figure out why I was not turning left when I typed the '4' key. Little tricks like this while coding a game are very useful, and can be turned on and off using flags. While debugging, I also had a flag that turned off police pursuit. This allowed me to run the program for a longer time than usual, so that I could test the motion commands and viewpoint considerations.

Figure 4.2 shows two views of the maze with these few modifications made. A significant change in the look of the game has been affected by a simple change in the display. The code for part of **draw_cube()**, which draws the wall squares as cubes, is shown next. Only half the function is shown. The rest is symmetrical and can be found in the source files on the website for this book.

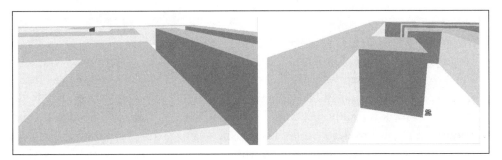

Figure 4.2
Views of the new 3D maze from a height of 1.5 CELLSIZE.

```
void draw_cube (int i, int j)
{
    /* Bottom */
    glColor3f (1.0, 0.0, 0.0);
    glVertex3f ((float)i*CELLSIZE, (float)j*CELLSIZE, 0.0);
    glVertex3f ((float)(i+1)*CELLSIZE,(float)j*CELLSIZE, 0.0);
    glVertex3f ((float)(i+1)*CELLSIZE,(float)(j+1)*CELLSIZE, 0.0);
    glVertex3f ((float)i*CELLSIZE, (float)(j+1)*CELLSIZE, 0.0);
```

```
/* Top ... omitted */
/* East face */
glColor3f (0.0, 0.0, 1.0);
glVertex3f ((float)i*CELLSIZE, (float)j*CELLSIZE, 0.0);
glVertex3f ((float)i*CELLSIZE, (float)j*CELLSIZE,
    (float)CELLSIZE);
glVertex3f ((float)i*CELLSIZE, (float)(j+1)*CELLSIZE,
    (float)CELLSIZE);
glVertex3f ((float)i*CELLSIZE, (float)(j+1)*CELLSIZE, 0.0);

/* West face ... omitted */
/* North Face */
glColor3f (1.0, 1.0, 0.0);
glVertex3f ((float)i*CELLSIZE, (float)(j+1)*CELLSIZE, 0.0);
glVertex3f ((float)i*CELLSIZE, (float)(j+1)*CELLSIZE,
    (float)CELLSIZE);
glVertex3f ((float)(i+1)*CELLSIZE, (float)(j+1)*CELLSIZE,
    (float)CELLSIZE);
glVertex3f ((float)(i+1)*CELLSIZE, (float)(j+1)*CELLSIZE,
    0.0);

/* South Face ... omitted */

}
```

Other 3D Objects

To keep things simple, I propose to draw the gophers and gas stations as simple prisms that have a texture-mapped image on their visible surfaces. This will reduce the amount of modeling we must do and it will reduce the number of polygons required. Reducing the polygons will certainly speed up the display. The fact that we'll need to do texture mapping is not a consideration because the plan is to texture map onto the wall faces as well; buildings, trees, and other scenes will make the maze look more like a scene.

I wrote a function named **prism()** that looked a good deal like **draw_cube()** except that the size of the faces are parametric. This same function is used to draw the gophers, the gas stations, and the cars in the second demo version of our game gopher-it2, found on the website.

Player Control

A viewing perspective from wall height or less makes it quite confusing to specify absolute directions for motion. It is better is to steer left or right relative to the current direction, just like steering a car. It is a little more difficult to implement, though, because any direction specified from the keyboard is added to the current direction. A simple way to do this is to use an array that holds the four directions as encountered by a consecutive series of right turns. We then increment or decrement the index to this array modulo the number of directions, in this case, four.

The code that must be changed lives in the keyboard callback function **keyPress()**. For a right turn we have:

```
if (key == '6')
{
    dirIndex = (dirIndex - 1);
    if (dirIndex < 0) dirIndex = 3;
    setDirection (PLAYER, directions[dirIndex]);
    dirx = directionsX[dirIndex];
    diry = directionsY[dirIndex];
}
```

The **directionsX** and **directionsY** arrays contain the X and Y direction values used in the **glutLookAt()** function for camera direction. They contain values of 0.0, -1000, or +1000 depending on the direction we are moving. The large value provides an offset from the player's position that will be a large distance outside of the playing area, and effectively parallel to the sides of the playing square.

All of these changes have been incorporated into the version of the *Gopher-it* 3D game found in the Chapter4/gopher-it1 directory. This is the first complete 3D version of the game.

Icons

In the original *Gopher-it* game, the gophers and fuel tanks were small images drawn on a flat surface. This is still the case so far in the new game, as you can see in Figure 4.2. There is a tiny gopher drawn near the lower-right portion of the screen. In a 3D game, we want 3D objects, and the gophers should not be flat. The easiest thing to do, not necessarily the best, is to draw the objects as cubes or prisms.

We can use a variation of the code shown in the previous section to draw a prism, simply by extending the cube in the vertical direction. We'll draw a prism at the point where each gopher, fuelup, or police car is to be drawn and draw an image of the object onto the prism. This works fairly well, and results in creating a playable game—my nine year-old played it for about half an hour. Still, it lacks a few things, especially in the graphics area.

Texture Mapping

I put a bit of effort describing the principles and practice of mapping textures onto 3D polygons in Chapter 3, and now we're going to actually put into practice what we learned. The prisms representing gophers and fuelups can be mapped with the same images we used in the original game. The gophers will not be convincing—they will actually look like drawings of gophers drawn on a box, but they will be three dimensional and will fit better into the game than flat images.

Let's look at a gopher. The image is read in and stored in the form of an icon as we did before. The image is rgb format with each component represented as an unsigned byte. To draw one, we'll use a function called **drawGopher()**:

```
void drawGopher (int x, int y)
{
    glBindTexture (GL_TEXTURE_2D, gopherTex);
    glBegin (GL_QUADS);
    texturedPrism ((float)(CELLSIZE/5),
        (float)(CELLSIZE/5), (float)(CELLSIZE/3),
        (float)(x+0.5)*CELLSIZE,
        (float)(y+0.5)*CELLSIZE, .6, .6, .2);
    glEnd();
}
```

The variable **gopherTex** is the gopher image as a 1D array of pixels. We make this the current texture using **glBindTexture()**. Next, we draw a prism that maps the texture on all faces. Chapter 3 shows how most of this is done. A draw prism function with texture mapping is a slight variation on the cube function, starting as:

```
void texturedPrism (float xwidth, float ywidth,
float zwidth, float x, float y,
float r, float g, float b)
{
/* East face */
    glTexCoord2f (1.0, 0.0);
    glVertex3f (x, y, 0.0);
    glTexCoord2f (1.0, 1.0);
    glVertex3f (x, y, zwidth);
    glTexCoord2f (0.0, 1.0);
    glVertex3f (x, y+ywidth, zwidth);
    glTexCoord2f (0.0, 0.0);
    glVertex3f (x, y+ywidth, 0.0);
/* ... other prism faces */
}
```

The fuelup is done the same way.

Finally, the walls of the maze themselves are texture mapped with a new texture—a hedge image was captured, edited, and saved in PPM format, then read in as an image and mapped onto all the faces of the cubes that represent the walls of the maze. It's possible to create distinct textures for each cube or face, and I could have used a higher resolution image. These are all details that you can change if you like. I did arrange it so that different cube faces are displayed in different colors. Since the texture mapping environment mode is **GL_MODULATE**, the color used to paint the face is visible in the texture. Thus, what I call the "East" face of each cube is tinted blue and each "North" face is white. The pixelized nature of the image is visible, and no effort was made to blend the textures into each other. We are game architects and builders, and we must be exposed to the seams, undersides, and basements of our constructions.

Figure 4.3 shows the way the game looks at this point. The point of view has been lowered to approximate the position of a driver. The rectangle in front of the viewing position represents the player's car. It is a cube, but we see it only from above.

Figure 4.3
Gopher-it 3D with lower point of view and texture-mapped objects and walls.

Backdrops

In Chapter 1 I discussed how backdrops are used in driving and racing games as a way to make the virtual world look realistic (see Figure 1.11). A backdrop is actually just a plane, or a set of planes, placed vertically in the far distance and mapped with a texture. For urban games, the texture could be a cityscape or a housing development. For other games it could be the sky, mountains, buildings, or seats in a grandstand around a track.

In *GopherIt-3D,* the backdrop is used for a sky image. I fetched an image from a database and resized it to be 1024 × 1024. (Recall that OpenGL specifies that images used for texture mapping be a power of two in size, plus the boundary that I set to zero.) I could have simply taken a photograph of the sky with a digital camera, though, or scanned an existing photograph. This image was mapped onto four rectangles placed just outside of the playing surface. This is really too close, but now you can see why. As you drive along one of the outer paths, the sky appears to move past, and the perspective transformation of the sky image gives it an unusual appearance, with clouds seeming to be foreshortened in a way that never really happens. In short, we are too close to the sky.

This problem can be repaired by moving the drop planes further away. At the same time, we need to make sure that our playing area is more or less in the middle of the planes, and that the far clipping plane, as specified by the function **gluPerspective()**, is past the drop so that we can see it. Finally, we should draw a rectangle right above us as a roof, and color it blue or map it (see Figure 4.4).

In the program that accompanies this chapter on the website for this book (Chapter4/ gopherit3d), I've placed a flag in the include file for moving the drops far away. If **NEAR_BACKDROPS** is 0, the drops will be positioned at a distance; otherwise, they will be drawn up against the playing surface. I set up a variable **dropdistance** that is initialized to a distance of 4000 pixels, but you can change this value. To center the surface in this area more or less, a variable **dropoffset** was defined to be 2000 if we are drawing distant drops. The drawing of a distance drop is now done in the following way:

```
glBindTexture (GL_TEXTURE_2D, drop1Tex);
glBegin (GL_QUADS);
glColor3f (1.0, 1.0, 1.0);
glTexCoord2f (1.0, 0.0);
glVertex3f (dropdistance-dropoffset, 0.0-dropoffset, 0.0);
glTexCoord2f (1.0, 1.0);
glVertex3f (dropdistance-dropoffset, 0.0-dropoffset, 1024.0);
```

```
glTexCoord2f (0.0, 1.0);
glVertex3f (0.0-dropoffset, 0.0-dropoffset, 1024.0);
glTexCoord2f (0.0, 0.0);
glVertex3f (0.0-dropoffset, 0.0-dropoffset, 0.0);
glEnd();
```

Figure 4.4
Gopher-it 3D with simple backdrops.

The image used for the sky textures is 1024×1024, which explains the Z coordinate values.

The top of our "sky box" is colored blue. To find the value to use, I displayed the sky texture image using the Windows Paint program and sampled a sky pixel. It turned out to be (58, 149, 246) in RGB coordinates. The maximum value is 255, and dividing these integer RGB values by 255 gives us (0.2274, 0.5843, 0.9647) as the OpenGL color value.

When the game is played you'll see a sky and a horizon. Because the joins between the texture images are still visible, you'll get the impression that the game is being played inside of a box, which is true. Figure 4.5 shows the "skybox" with its joins.

Figure 4.5
The "skybox" created by using the unedited texture images as sky textures.

Fixing Texture Seams

Making textures look realistic is not a programming issue, but it is most certainly an important issue that makes a game more enjoyable to play. We need to create an illusion here, and anything that detracts from that illusion is a *bad* thing. There are a few ways to fix these textures, and I will show you an easy way.

First, take the texture image you wish to use and import it into your favorite image manipulation tool. Anyone who wants to make games should have a collection of such tools including *Paint*, *PhotoShop*, *Gimp*, or others. Using your tool of choice, you cut the image down the middle vertically and discard half of it or so. Then save the half you have left, and flip it left to right. Read the half you saved a moment ago, and line up the two halves so that you cannot see the join. This is now possible, of course, because you flipped it, and one half is a mirror image of the other. When you use this texture the seams will line up, and will be invisible. Of course, you can now see that the images are tiled. Figure 4.6 shows this process being performed on a sky texture.

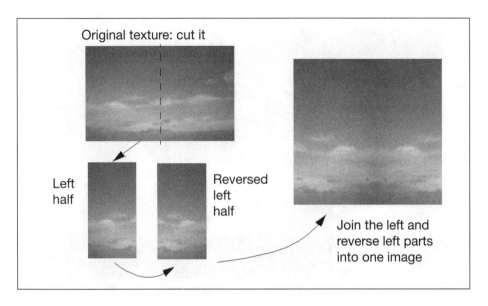

Figure 4.6
The process of making a seamless texture.

I created a sky texture and a new foliage texture in this way and made these the textures of the game. As shown in Figure 4.7, the seams that we were concerned with are indeed gone, but the join between the top and sides of the sky box are still easily visible.

Creating Custom Textures

There is no fast and easy way to fix the sky texture seam, and I think the best way is to create an image that can be used to specifically fit along the top edge of the sky texture images, and that will match them perfectly. My idea is to create an image S that is the color of the sky. This color is generated using the setting (58, 149, 246) as we determined previously. Next, we copy the upper row of pixels from the sky texture image into the top row of S. Then we copy the same pixel values along the outside columns of S to the bottom row. This creates a frame of pixels that matches the sky textures exactly.

The pixels neighboring the boundary are then modified. This is accomplished by taking all of the pixels in the row next to the boundary pixels in the image and storing them in the next row of S, and so on. Each row is only copied between the diagonals, and is then copied to the outside columns and the next unfilled row at the bottom. The effect is to build a triangle from the base upwards, copying lower, left and right symmetrical pixels as you go. Sounds simple, right? Unfortunately it isn't. Once again let's appeal to a visual display (see Figure 4.8). The triangular section is extracted using this simple bit of code:

Figure 4.7
Skybox and seamless, yet tiled, textures—a triumph of image editing.

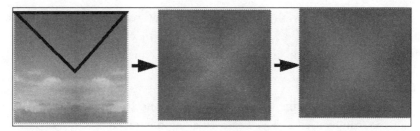

Figure 4.8
Creating a top for the sky using image manipulation.

```
for (I=half+1; I<nr; I++)
{
    colStart = half - (I-half);
    colEnd   = half + (I-half);
    for (J=colStart; J<=colEnd; J++)
    {
/* Now for each pixel in this quarter of the image, find the place
   where it belongs, by symmetry, in the other 3 quadrants and copy.    */
        copyPixel (I, J,   J, I);
        copyPixel (I, J,   half-(I-half), J);
        copyPixel (I, J,   J, half-(I-half));
    }
}
```

where half is 1/2 the width of the square image being altered. This code copies one section of sky into an entire image. There is sometimes an artifact along the diagonals, and I personally used *Photoshop's* Gaussian filter to minimize it, although there are other options.

The Pipeline

You may have noticed that the past few pages have not been about programming, but about creating and manipulating the art assets of a game, in this case, the images. A lot of time and energy is spent in creating and manipulating art and music in commercial games. When I started working on games, a typical team consisted of 6 to 7 programmers and 3 to 4 artists and designers. This has changed to about a 50/50 ratio, and I expect that the role of the programmer in game creation will continue to decline. Why? Because the third-party tools like game engines, physics, and audio modules are getting better. They allow games to be created by non-programmers in some situations.

One meaning of the phrase *graphics pipeline* is the chain of activities that is needed to incorporate graphics into a game. This includes some code that manipulates the pictures, scaling and matching them to the game environment. In the final touches to the images *for Gopher-it3D* described above, I have described a part of what might be a pipeline for the artistic assets of the game. It means that we need programs that can manipulate images; I use *PhotoShop*, *Paint*, *LView pro*, and on Unix/Linux I use programs called *XV* and *Gimp*. For audio manipulation I use *Sound Forge* and *GoldWave*. Common utilities for manipulating video are *Bink and Smacker* and *Adobe Premiere*.

It is beyond the scope of this book to cover all of the operations on audio, video, and images that can be used to create a game. I have written some books on image manipulation, and I know how complex it can be to devise just the right scheme to create the picture that you need. Still, I must point out how important it is to have the right artistic tools at your disposal, and to know how to use them.

Summary

We've now completed our development work for *Gopher-it 3D*. This game isn't the flashiest one, but it has served its purpose well. It has provided us with a model of the basic techniques used to build commercial games. We still have a lot to learn, especially driving-specific stuff, and there will be a new game to design and build called *Manic Mars Rally*. It's an off-road race that takes place on the planet Mars. We will use real Mars topographical data and images, and we'll try to model physics as well as possible.

The next steps are to discuss the AI, audio, and physics parts of a game, and then we'll design the *Manic Mars Rally* as a software project.

Chapter 5

Game AI and Collision Detection

- Learn that basic AI techniques are used in racing and driving games to help perform collision detection.
- Learn how to use techniques such as broad phase collision detection to make your games more realistic.
- Use narrow phase collision detection to determine if collisions actually occur.

The phrase "artificial intelligence" conjures up a host of advanced technology. Our first exposure to *AI*, as it has come to be known, is often through science fiction; the computers on *Star Trek* speak fluent English, and the robots serve drinks and pilot spacecrafts. In truth, AI has not advanced nearly this far. Although computers can now defeat humans at chess and checkers, this is a far cry from the scenes we see on television and in the movies.

So what is AI, really? Historically, this subject has been called *cognitive simulation*, which is probably a more descriptive phrase for what is happening. The mission of AI is to simulate the actions and responses of an intelligent creature. Why would a driving game need to have simulated intelligent creatures? There are hundreds of reasons. Most importantly, a driving game needs intelligent creatures so that it can simulate other drivers. At a high level, AI is used in games to implement other people performing intelligent tasks. These simulated characters, sometimes called *bots* or simply *opponents*, are expected to behave in a manner that would be consistent with how a real person would behave. They don't actually have to be intelligent, and a discussion of the differences would be interesting but would really sidetrack us now.

At a lower level, the AI in a game keeps track of things: cars, people, trees, roads, and all of the other objects that are used. One of the most important tasks the AI system performs is to determine when two objects collide. This is because collisions are often key points in a game. A missile collides with its target, and the target is destroyed. A hockey player collides with another player and loses the puck. A car collides with a concrete bridge support and gets damaged and changes direction. Each of these activities requires that a collision is detected, and that the location of the impact and its exact time is known.

It's also true that a good portion of a game's AI system spends most of its time performing physics calculations. After a collision occurs, something breaks, changes direction, or falls down. A good approximation of real-world physics is essential for a game to be able to simulate the real world, especially for a sports or driving game. And, as we'll learn in this chapter, accurately determining the properties of collisions is a crucial first step in correctly simulating physics.

Professional programmers and computer science students have some knowledge of "academic" AI, which is an exciting subject. It is, in fact, what *I* do at my university most days. Unfortunately, not many of the AI methods developed in the university labs find their way into computer games. Occasionally, a device such as a neural network that has been trained in advance to accomplish a particular task might get used by a game developer. However, there just wouldn't be the time to train such a network to handle changing situations or incorporate other types of complex AI in a real-time driving game scenario. As game programmers, we must have a practical view of AI, and in a game, this means we need to focus on speed and simplicity. Most decisions in a game are made using simple look-up tables or decision trees.

In this book, I will be presenting all of the parts of an AI system that can add much more realism to our driving and racing games. I'll be addressing opponents, automatic driving, and physics simulation. In this chapter, I'll start with collision detection because of its importance. After all, if collision detection doesn't work properly in a driving game—if it isn't fast or accurate—the game won't be very playable. It can't be added on at the last minute; it must be an integral part of the game from the start.

I must say up front that you might find collision detection to be dull. I won't try to convince you otherwise, but doing it correctly is essential, and thus we need to look at this subject carefully. You can use off-the-shelf packages for performing some of the work, but I think it is dangerous to have code in your program that you don't have at least some understanding of; so please review this chapter closely before downloading someone else's code! Having said this, there are entire books written on the subject, and this chapter is simply designed to provide you with the basics. You should use an existing collision detection system until you feel you are ready to code your own.

Basic Collision Detection

When two objects collide in the real world, the result is a physical response: sound, heat, energy transfer, and so on. In a game, the objects are not real; they are numbers representing how the objects look and where they are positioned in a virtual space. When they collide, the collision is a virtual one with no effect unless the collision is detected and visually simulated.

There are two major problems with collision detection in computer games. The first is complexity. A small game may have 100 or so objects active simultaneously. If they are all moving, a game must look at each pair to see if they will hit each other, which means approximately 10,000 tests (100 x 100) must be performed. A game must do this at each time interval, which is usually the time between two frames, say 24 times per second. This implies a quarter of a million tests must be performed each second for a collision in a small game, and over a million tests must be completed in a fair-sized game. Any solution we implement must be fast.

The second problem is that time in a game is quantized. Let's say we have 24 images per second displayed on the screen, which is the speed of a motion picture. It's possible, even likely, that two objects approaching each other fast enough will pass each other in the time between two frames—1/24 of a second. They should collide, but at time T they will be some distance apart, and at time T+1, they will have changed places. We can do two things in such a case: predict the time at which they will collide, or calculate the time in the past when they did collide. Even a game can't easily roll time backwards, so the former solution is best. We must determine when they will collide, determine the results of the collision, and draw only the result at time T+1.

There are other issues that can occur, some dependent on the algorithm we choose, but we just discussed the big ones. It's time to stop worrying about the problems and solve some of them. Let's pick an easy problem first.

Collisions in One Dimension

One-dimensional collision detection will never likely be interesting (or used in a game), but it will help us gain some insight into more complex collision detection in multiple dimensions. In one dimension, we only need to consider the motion of particles along a line. To make our discussion even easier, let's just use two particles. Only a few possible situations can occur as listed in Table 5.1.

Table 5.1   Possible collisions with two objects in a single dimension.

	Particle 1		Particle 2		
Case	Position	Speed	Position	Speed	Name
1	0	+2	4	-2	Approach
2	0	+2	4	+1	Overtake
3	0	+2	4	+3	Escape
4	0	-2	4	+2	Diverge

Position is a distance along a line that we'll assume is oriented along the X-axis. Time is represented in integral units—frames perhaps. In case 1, the two particles head towards each other until they collide. Here, the speed of the particles dictates that the collision will take place in exactly 1 step; both particle 1 and particle 2 will be at position 2. This is unusual because the time of the collision will fall between two time units if the particles are moving at different speeds (which is usually the case).

Case 2 also produces a collision, since at some point in time the faster particle (1) will overtake the slower one, colliding from behind. In the other two cases, no collisions will occur because the particles are moving in opposite directions (4) or because one is receding from the other (3).

The collision algorithm, as would be found in an imaginary one-dimensional game, would be:

1. Determine whether a collision will occur between any two particles between times T and $T+1$.

2. Compute the precise time of the collision.

I have always found that a precise statement of the problem and algorithm is essential for finding the best solution. A brute force solution would be a good first approach:

1. For each particle i at time T having position P_i, calculate the value of $D_{ij} = P_i - P_j$ for all other particles j. Think of this as the distance to all other particles.

2. Compute the position of the particles at time $T+1$, and call these positions P'.

3. Calculate $D_{ij}' = P_i' - P_j'$ for all i and j.

If the sign of D_{ij} is not the same as that of D_{ij}', particles i and j will collide between time T and $T+1$. In fact, this means that if at one time particle i is to the left of particle j, and then later on j is to the left of i, the particles must have passed each other. This would produce a collision in one dimension.

If $D_{ij} = 0$, the two particles will be in contact at time T, and if $D_{ij}'=0$ they will be in contact at precisely time $T+1$. Otherwise, if a collision occurs we still must determine the time of the collision. (Of course, if no collision occurs, this second step is not needed.)

Imagine the following situation:

- We have two particles A and B, and particle A is at position $P_{Ainitial}=0$ with velocity $V_A=2$.

- Particle B is at position $P_{Binitial}=4$ with velocity $V_B=-3$.

- At time T, $P_A-P_B = 0-4 = -4$. At the next time, $T+1$, $P_A=2$ and $P_B=1$. Thus, $P_A-P_B = 1$, and the sign changes implying that a collision occurs.

When does the collision occur? Well, simple high school physics tells us that the position of particle A is given by $P_A = P_{Ainitial} + V_At$, for any time t; similarly, $P_B = P_{Binitial} + V_Bt$. When the particles collide, $P_A = P_B$, so simple algebra tells us:

$$P_{Ainitial} + V_At = P_{Binitial} + V_Bt$$

-> $\quad P_{Ainitial}-P_{Binitial} = (V_B-V_A)t$

-> $\quad t = (P_{Ainitial}-P_{Binitial})/(V_B-V_A)$

This is the time at which the collision takes place. The value of t is between 0 and 1, and is relative to the initial time T. If the collision is perfectly elastic, meaning that no energy is lost, the final step is to determine where the particles will be at time $T+1$.

At time t, both particles will be at position $X = P_{Binitial} + V_Bt$. An elastic collision will then occur and the particles will reverse direction, with the same speed (we'll assume). Time $T+1$ is 1 time unit from time T, and is $1-t$ units from the collision time t. In that time, both particles will move: particle A moves with velocity -2 from position X for time $1-t$ units, and particle B moves with velocity +3 from position X for $1-t$ time units.

Plugging in the numbers, we get the following:

$t = 4/5 = 0.8$

$X = 1.6$

$1-t = 0.2$

The final position of A will be

$X-V_A(1-t) = 1.2$

and the final position of **B** will be:

$X-V_B(1-t) = 2.2.$

Newton never lies (he just approximates!).

In summary, a computer program that displays the positions of moving points in one dimension would have, in two consecutive frames:

Time T: point A at $P_A=0 V_A = 2$ point B at $P_B=4 V_B = -3$

Time T+1:   point A at $P_A=1.2$ $V_A = -2$ point B at $P_B=2.2 V_B = +3$

Figure 5.1 shows this situation. The points will never be seen to touch, since a collision will occur between two frames, and so won't be rendered.

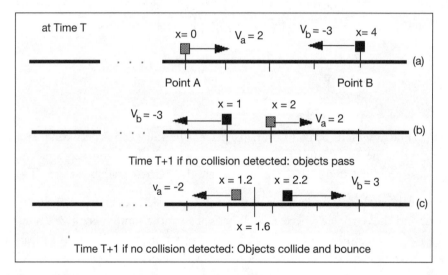

Figure 5.1
Examining the situation where two objects do not collide.

This simple collision in one dimension is not going to help us in a game, but it does give us an idea of how to solve the same problem in more than one dimension.

Collisions in Two Dimensions

The method for determining collision detection in two dimensions is similar to the method we just explored for collision detection in one dimension. There are, however, complications due to the extra dimension. In particular, just because two particles have changed places does not mean that they will collide. Each particle now occupies an area, and they will collide only if their areas also overlap. We must, therefore, perform a two-step test: we first determine if a collision could occur and then we determine if it actually happened. In a real game, most objects will not be involved in collisions during any particular time period, thus we can use a fast test to eliminate as many objects as we can.

In one dimension we were concerned with points. Unfortunately, mathematical points cannot collide in 2D because they have no area. We now need to focus on moving polygons in a plane, and detecting collisions between them. Again, let's name our two polygons **A** and **B**, and give them positions and velocities at time **T**. This time, a position will be specified by a 2D vector. The velocity will also be specified by a vector, and each component of a velocity vector will be the speed in that direction, X or Y.

Instead of computing a simple distance to determine if a collision is possible, we must do something more complicated. Since a polygon contains N vertices and all of them are moving at the same speed and direction, we can easily define a straight line that corresponds to the path taken by each vertex in the time between **T** and **T+1**. We can also easily compute the position of all of these vertices at both times. A simple rule that excludes a collision between A and B is:

If we compute a line L that represents the path of a vertex of A, then a collision cannot have taken place between that vertex of A and polygon B if B is on the same side of that line at both time T and T+1.

That doesn't sound very simple, does it? For a visual aide, take a look at Figure 5.2. Here we have a few polygons at two points in time, and with any luck at all my explanation will make sense in the context of the figure.

Basically, if any of the vertices of polygon **A** crosses any of the lines L_1 to L_3, a collision may have taken place. This is the same basic method we used for the one-dimensional situation, and has a similar solution.

The line labeled L_1 in Figure 5.1 is crossed by the triangle A if any vertex is on one side of the line at time **T** and on the other side at **T+1**. Every line has an equation that defines it, and this can take one of many mathematical forms. Let's use the standard normal form as shown here:

Equation 5.1 $ax + by + c = 0$

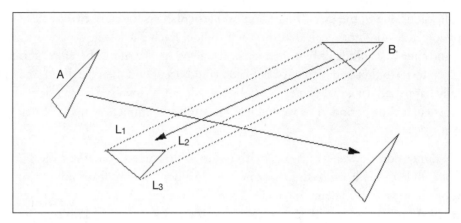

Figure 5.2
Determining if a collision occurs between two polygons.

A point (x,y) that satisfies this equation is *on* the line, and there are two other possibilities:

- **ax+by+c** is greater than zero, in which case the point (x,y) is *above* the line
- **ax+by+c** is less than zero, meaning that the point is *below* the line

Thus, if any vertex is above L_1 at time **T** and below it at **T+1**, we could have a collision; otherwise, no collision will occur.

This is an example of *broad phase* collision detection—the elimination of objects that can't possibly collide. The idea is to do this quickly, without using a lot of CPU time. The next step, or the *narrow phase*, involves accurately detecting collision events and determining the time and position of the collision. Breaking the problem into these two parts is about performance. The idea is to do the detailed and time-consuming narrow phase detection only if there is a chance the objects could collide in the first place. This has the effect of also making the whole process more flexible. There are many ways to solve each problem, and the solutions that are decided upon can be combined almost arbitrarily.

Let's look at each phase independently, making sure that there are ways to combine them. After that, we'll look at a few cases of single phase collision detection. Because collision detection is so fundamental, detailed execution time measurements will be made and the algorithms will be compared for efficiency. We'll also need to jump back into 3D, since most games take place almost exclusively in three dimensions these days.

3D Broad Phase Collision Detection

Determining if a collision could take place in 3D can be done in a number of different ways. The broad phase approach gives us the greatest savings of time if we carefully select an algorithm and implement it efficiently. This phase is about rejecting objects that cannot collide and eliminating collision tests that cost time but cannot yield fruit.

Operational Methods

In a game, there are many objects that could collide with each other. The general collision problem is $O(n^2)$; the time it takes to perform all of the calculations is in proportion to the square of the number of objects. However, consider that many of the objects don't move, as I have pointed out before. A game having four cars, a hundred trees, and twenty buildings would have 124 objects and would require up to 15,376 collision tests.

Oh, wait a second. Let's eliminate some of the tests. Testing an object A for collision with object B is the same as testing B for collision with A. We certainly don't need to test to see if object A collides with itself. This reduces the tests needed to a total of N^2-$N)/2$, which is a lot fewer than N^2. We've just reduced our problem down to 7,626 tests! Let's simplify the problem even more.

Now consider that some of the objects, such as the trees, do not move and thus they can't collide with one another. This same situation is found with the buildings—they are static and can't collide with trees or other buildings. We're now left with the following: the cars need to be tested against all other objects, but that is all we need to do! This represents 4*3/2=6 tests between cars and 4*120 = 480 tests with static objects, for a grand total of 486 tests. Any further efforts at broad phase detection won't likely yield any more significant savings.

Most games have many classes of objects, and computation time can be reduced significantly this way. Alien missiles, for example, need not be checked against alien spacecraft, and sometimes asteroids or meteors need not be checked against each other. This isn't as sexy as advanced code optimization, but a little common sense will give us a much greater benefit than almost anything else we can do.

You should always look very carefully to make certain that you are not making any tests that aren't needed. You can then focus on the more difficult things, and combine the two methods to achieve a combined time savings.

5

Using Geometric Tests

When we checked to see which side of the line the start and end point of a polygon vertex was on at times **T** and **T+1**, we were using geometry to eliminate possible collisions. This is a fairly efficient process, and we can also use it in three dimensions. In 3D, a line becomes a plane, and the test involves checking a polygon or node to see if it is on one side of a plane at time **T** and on the other at time **T+1**. If so, a collision is possible. If not, one has been eliminated.

Let's look at this a little closer. Imagine that two cars in our game are to be tested to see if they could collide with each other. We know that we're going to draw our cars as collections of polygons, as we have discussed earlier. So the question is: *will any of the polygons in the set A* (i.e., car **A**) *collide with any of those in set B* (car **B**). Each polygon is, in fact, a part of a plane. A mathematical plane is infinite in extent and a polygon is not, but in the broad phase approach we extend a polygon in one object (car **A**) to become the plane in which it is embedded and ask whether any of the vertices or polygons in another object (car **B**) are on opposite sides at times **T** and **T+1**. If so, a collision is possible; otherwise, a collision has been eliminated.

This can be done quickly using a technique like the one we discussed earlier when we explored 2D collisions. Let's look at an example. Two triangles **A** and **B** have vertices A0, A1, A2 and B0, B1, and B2. Both triangles belong to different moving objects, and we want to know if they can collide. Instead of simply plugging coordinates into the equation of a plane, I'll use vector math to do the equivalent thing, but in a manner that I think is faster.

First, close your eyes and picture a plane—or a triangle or rectangle—floating about in 3D space. Three points are needed to determine this plane; that is, any three points must belong to the plane in the same way that any two points are on a line and can be used to define the plane. However, consider any point on that plane and a line not passing through that point; this also defines a plane (most importantly, so does a point and the *normal* to the plane.) Normal means perpendicular, or 90 degrees to the surface of the plane. If we can quickly find a vector that is normal to a polygon, and if we have a point on that polygon, we can determine the equation of the plane.

Chapter 15 contains a summary of the math we need and a primer on key subjects. It also provides basic implementations of the important operations. It turns out that a simple operation known as the *cross product* takes any two vectors and creates a vector that is perpendicular, or normal, to the plane on which the two input vectors lie. For two vectors **h** and **j**, the cross product **h x j** is a vector:

Equation 5.2

$$h \times j = \begin{bmatrix} h_y j_z - h_z j_y \\ -(h_x j_z - h_z j_x) \\ h_x j_y - h_y j_x \end{bmatrix}$$

If we have a triangle (or a quad), we'll have two such vectors—any edges will do.

The *dot product*, another simple operation on vectors, computes the length of the projection of one vector onto another; for vector **a**, **a·a** is equal to the length of **a**, and if **a** and **b** are perpendicular, then **a·b** will equal zero. The dot product is defined as

Equation 5.3

$$a \cdot b = \sum_{i=1}^{n} a_i b_i$$

in **n** dimensions. (This might look like a simple distance calculation.) The usual form of the equation of a plane is shown here:

Equation 5.4 $$C_0 x + C_1 y + C_2 z = d$$

Returning to the triangles **A** and **B**, note that each vertex of **A** (i.e., A_i) has 3 coordinates, and is therefore a 3D vector. Thus, $A_0 \times A_1 = N$ is a vector cross product that is a normal to the triangle (plane) **A**. The dot product between **N** and any point in the plane of **A**, say any vertex, is the equation of the plane. So, $A_2 \cdot N$ is as follows:

Equation 5.5 $$d = N_x A_{2x} + N_y A_{2y} + N_z A_{2z}$$

This equation has the same form as the equation of a plane. It is also the equation of the plane that the triangle **A** lies in. This is what we want. We can store the plane as **N** and **d**, which are really just the constants for the equation of the plane, and we do this for every polygon we may want to test for collision. Testing is a matter of plugging in the (x,y,z) values of the target (i.e., what we are testing for collision, like another polygon vertex) before and after motion, and seeing if the target is on opposite sides of the plane. If so, we need to look further, and if not, we can ignore this target.

Using Enclosing Spheres

Two cars may consist of thousands of polygons each. If one of them is *my* car, and I am clever enough to pass your car in a race, it is possible that many of the polygons in my car will be candidates for collision with the polygons in your car. This could cost a lot of time in detailed collision tests that aren't needed. One way to avoid this is to process collisions at a higher level at first, looking at all of the polygons in my car as belonging to a single object that has a virtual shape, such as a sphere. If the sphere that encloses my car never intersects with the sphere that encloses your car, the cars couldn't have collided. We could save thousands of polygon collision tests!

Better yet, the enclosing sphere can be defined along with the car, or whatever object we're looking at, once, when a game is started. All we need to do is find the center of the sphere, which would be the *centroid* of the object, the radius, and the distance to the most distant vertex. The centroid of the car will be what we actually move; the car is drawn on the screen relative to that point, and the collision tests are initially performed on the sphere centered on that point too.

The centroid, or center of mass, can be approximated by finding the mean coordinate of all polygons in each dimension in 3D. The X coordinate of the center of mass is the sum of all polygon X coordinates for the object divided by the number of polygons. (The Y and Z coordinate are computed in the same way.) The distance to the most distant vertex can be calculated at the same time we calculate the centroid, which is to say at some time after an object is created but before the game is distributed.

Each object now has a center of mass and a radius associated with it, in addition to a big set of polygons. The question that faces us now is: for each pair of objects that could possibly collide, is it possible for the enclosing spheres to collide? If not, we can ignore all of the polygons that are part of those objects, and that will save us a large amount of time. Of course, if a collision *is* possible, we need to do more checking. Sometimes it is more useful to keep the object as polygons, as in the case of walls and buildings. Covering them with a sphere would be a waste of time because it's easier to keep their relatively few planar faces as planes.

Sphere vs. Plane Collision

The first step is to see if the sphere changes sides of the plane during the time interval. The situation is diagrammed in Figure 5.3.

The sphere at time T is labeled S_T, and its center $S = (Sx, Sy)$ is a distance D_T from the plane and the positive side as computed by Equations 5.4 and 5.5. At time $T+1$, the center of the sphere is at D_{T+1}, and is shown on the opposite (negative) side of the plane (see Figure 5.2). We must make sure that $D_T > r$, or the sphere will be intersecting the plane at the beginning.

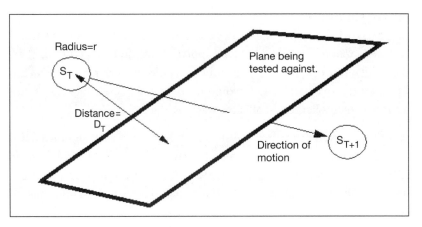

Figure 5.3
Determining if sphere passes through a given plane.

A sphere is not a point—it has volume. For this reason, the test concerning whether a sphere may have collided with a polygon is a little different than the one we performed earlier: if $\mathbf{D_T} > \mathbf{r}$, where $\mathbf{r}$ is the sphere's radius, and $\mathbf{D_{T+1}} < \mathbf{r}$, a collision is possible. A simple way of computing this is to use the calculation $\mathbf{d_T} = (\mathbf{S_T} - \mathbf{Z}) \cdot \mathbf{N}$ for some point on the plane $\mathbf{Z}$ and plane normal $\mathbf{N}$.

When a collision with a plane occurs, we know the collision took place some time between $\mathbf{T}$ and $\mathbf{T+1}$. But we need to check a little closer to see when the collision actually took place. We can parameterize time between $\mathbf{T}$ and $\mathbf{T+1}$ to be one unit using a new variable $\mathbf{t}$

Equation 5.6

$$t = \frac{d_T - r}{d_T - d_{T+1}}$$

where $\mathbf{t}$ is between 0 and 1. This ratio is the fraction of the difference in distance between $\mathbf{T}$ and $\mathbf{T+1}$ that is represented by the sphere's radius; it is the fraction the distance traveled in that time by the sphere. Thus, the location of the center of the sphere at the time of the collision is

Equation 5.7

$$x = S_{xT} + t\,(S_{xT+1} - S_{xT})$$

$$y = S_{yT} + t\,(S_{yT+1} - S_{yT})$$

$$z = S_{zT} + t\,(S_{zT+1} - S_{zT})$$

where, S_{xT} is the X coordinate of the center of the sphere at time $\mathbf{T}$.

Sphere to Sphere Collisions—Part 1

When checking two cars for collision, one car could be enclosed by a sphere and the other could be considered to be polygons. Each polygon would be a plane for the purposes of the collision test. On the other hand, it would be better to construct a single plane between the two cars, which would both be considered spheres. A single test could then determine whether a collision was possible.

The definition of a plane requires three points, or a point and a surface normal. One point would logically be the midpoint between the two spheres, P_m, found by taking the average of the coordinates of the sphere centers. A better point would be the midpoint P_0 between the two sphere *surfaces*, but that is harder to find and may not be much better.

Still, consider that the distance between the surfaces of the spheres is $P_m - R_0 - R_1$, with R_0 being the radius of S_0, and so on. The length of P_m is $||S_0 - S_1||$, and so the fraction of this length represented by the radius of S_0 is $R_0 / ||S_0 - S_1||$, and similarly for S_1. We can use this method to find the points of the sphere's surfaces along the line that joins the centers. The midpoint between those two points is what we want.

The total distance between the centers in the X coordinate is $S_{0x} - S_{1x}$, thus the distance along X to the surface of the sphere is $(R_0 / ||S_0 - S_1||) * (S_{0x} - S_{1x})$. Calculating the distance between the Y and Z coordinates is similar, and so we now can determine the 3D coordinates of the points on the spheres nearest to each other by simply taking an average. The code shown next calculates the midpoint fairly efficiently:

```
struct v3
{
    float x, y, z;
};
typedef struct v3 VECTOR3;
struct sph3
{
    float R; /* radius */
    VECTOR3 center;
};
typedef struct sph3 SPHERE;

/* Compute the length of vector 'a' */
float normV (VECTOR3 a)
{
    double t;
    t = a.x*a.x + a.y*a.y + a.z*a.z;
    return (float)sqrt(t);
```

```
}

/* Determine the difference between two vectors */
void diff3 (VECTOR3 a, VECTOR3 b, VECTOR3 *c)
{
   c->x = a.x-b.x;
   c->y = a.y-b.y;
   c->z = a.z-b.z;
}

void SurfaceMidpoint (SPHERE S0, SPHERE S1, VECTOR3 *mid)
{
   VECTOR3 a, b, c;
   float d, d1;
   float dx, dy, dz;

   /* Computer center between surfaces */
   diff3 (S1.center, S0.center, &a);
   d = normV (a);
   d1 = (S0.R/d);
   dx= d1*a.x; dy = d1*a.y; dz = d1*a.z;
   b.x = S0.center.x + dx;
   b.y = S0.center.y + dy;
   b.z = S0.center.z + dz;
   d2 = (float)(sqrt((double)(dx*dx +
   dy*dy+dz*dz)));

   /* Now do the same for S1 */
   diff3 (S0.center, S1.center, &a);
   d1 = (S1.R/d);
   dx= d1*a.x; dy = d1*a.y; dz = d1*a.z;
   c.x = S1.center.x + dx;
   c.y = S1.center.y + dy;
   c.z = S1.center.z + dz;
   mid->x = (b.x+c.x)/2.0;
   mid->y = (b.y+c.y)/2.0;
   mid->z = (b.z+c.z)/2.0;
}
```

Now we need two more points or the normal to the plane. Determining the normal is quite easy because it is the vector between P_0 in the S_1 direction, or from P_0 to S_0. Let's use $N=S_1-P_0$ as the normal. The equation of the plane is then

Equation 5.8 $\quad N_x(x-P_{0x}) + N_y(y-P_{0y}) + N_z(z-P_{0z}) = 0$

or, substituting for the normal vector coordinates we get:

Equation 5.9 $\quad (S_{1x}-P_{0x})(x-P_{0x}) + (S_{1y}-P_{0y})(y-P_{0y}) + (S_{1z}-P_{0z})(z-P_{0z}) = 0$

Any points on this plane will be equidistant from S_0 and S_1. The points P_1 and P_2 are two such random points on the plane (see Figure 5.4). These are points that are equidistant from the sphere centers at disparate angles. If *Equation 5.9* is truly the correct equation of the plane that bisects the two spheres, we can check this by computing the distance between P_1-S_0 and P_1-S_1; the two distances must be equal.

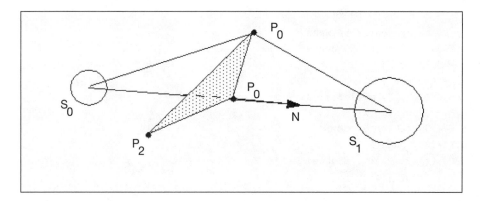

Figure 5.4
The geometry of two spheres separated by a plane.

Summary of Using Geometric Tests

This discussion has been a trifle complex. Sometimes it can be hard to focus on the big problem when there are lots of details to take care of. Here's a quick summary of what we've done so far:

1. Calculate the center of mass **C** for each moving object (i.e., average coordinate in each dimension) and store it with the object. Also calculate the maximum distance from the center of mass and every polygon vertex.V_n. The distance between **C** and V_n is the radius of the enclosing sphere, and won't need to be computed again.

2. When a collision occurs, detection needs to be done. We look at each pair of spheres and compute the equation of the plane that lies in-between the spheres (see Equation 5.9).

3. Compute the distance between the sphere and the plane for both spheres. This needs to be done before and after the current move. If either sphere crosses the plane (i.e., the sign on the distance changes), a collision is possible.

This technique allows us to enclose a complex object with a simple sphere. It reduces the number of tests required by thousands to one, in most cases. Also, the calculation to determine if the collision is possible is now reduced to a few addition and multiplication operations for each object.

Naturally, if a collision *is* possible, a more time-consuming test must be performed to determine if a collision actually occurs.

Sphere vs. Sphere Collisions—Part 2

In the previous section, we developed a method for testing spheres against planes, which was related to a two-dimensional comparison of points and lines. This is normally a solid test, but there are special cases.

If the spheres are moving in the same direction, and one is moving faster than the other, one sphere could pass through the plane without actually being able to catch up with the other sphere and collide with it. The technique we used works fine if one sphere is not moving, such as a sphere that surrounds a tree or a building, or other stationary object. The technique is quick, however.

One thing that could help would be to examine if the spheres are far enough apart so that they won't get close enough to collide during a specified time interval. In other words, the *net* movement vector between the two spheres must be greater than the distance between them, minus the radii, of course. A movement vector is the vector between the position of a sphere's center before and after the movement. It can be easily computed using the velocity vector, current position, and time duration. If both spheres are moving, we need to compute the *relative* movement, or the movement that would be seen from one of the spheres. This amounts to subtracting one movement vector from the other. If this relative movement vector is less than (shorter than) the distance between the centers of the spheres minus the sum of the radii, the spheres could collide. This is a very simple test to perform.

There are other collision rejection tests we could perform on spheres. For example, if two spheres are moving away from each other, they can't collide. How can we tell if this condition exists? We first create a vector that points from the center of sphere S_0 to the centre of sphere S_1. We can call this vector N_0 because it points in the same direction as the vector N (see Figure 5.4). Quite specifically, the calculation we perform is:

Equation 5.10 $N_0 = S_1 - S_0$

The next step is to project this vector onto the movement vector for S_0. This is done using the vector dot product that we've used before. If the movement vector is M, then $q = M.N_0$ will be the dot product of M and N_0. If $q <= 0$, the sphere S_0 will not be moving towards S_1, and there can be no collision. As before, if both spheres are moving, we use the relative movement vector.

At this point, we know that the sphere S_0 is moving far enough to collide with S_1, and that it is moving in the direction so that it could do so. For simplicity, assume that S_1 is stationary, realizing that we can make it so by transforming coordinates. The final question is, does S_0 get closer to S_1 than the distance R_0+R_1?

If not, the spheres cannot collide. Computing this last value is a little tricky, unfortunately. Figure 5.5 represents my effort to describe this situation better.[12] In this figure, M is the movement vector and N_0 is the vector joining S_0 and S_1, both as defined previously. We need to determine the point on the vector M. If we treat the point as a line, it will be near the center of S_1. When I did a *Google* search for "distance from line to point" I found a useful formula on the MathWorld pages[14]:

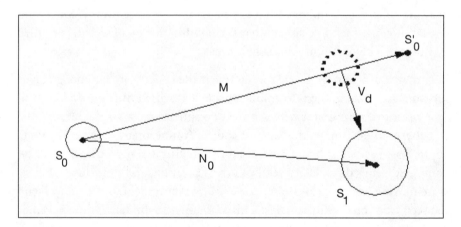

Figure 5.5
Determining that two spheres will not collide.

Equation 5.11

$$d^2 = \frac{((S'_0 - S_0) \times (S_0 - S_1))^2}{|S'_0 - S_0|^2}$$

I have substituted our variables for theirs in this equation. The d^2 value is the smallest distance (squared) between the line from S_0 to S'_0 and the point S_1, the center of the sphere S_1. If this value is greater than $R_0 + R_1$, the spheres cannot collide. Note that the 'x' in the formula indicates a vector cross product, not a multiplication. All of the variables except **d** are vectors. If none of the tests above fail, a collision between the two spheres could occur.

Using Bounding Boxes

A bounding box is a rectangle or prism that completely encloses all of an object's polygons. Its sides are planes, and its volume is relatively close to that of the object. This bounding box turns out to be a better approximation than using a sphere. An *Axis Aligned Bounding Box (AABB)* is a specific type that has faces that are parallel to the three coordinate axes. It has the advantage of being very simple to calculate; we simply run a plane through the most distant point in each coordinate axis direction. That is, to find the minimum and maximum X coordinate in the object, we construct a plane through these points that is parallel to the YZ plane. This is done for the Y coordinate (XZ plane) and the Z coordinate (XY plane). Figure 5.6 shows an example of how this works.

No complex calculations are needed to find the AABB. We simply scan through all of the polygons for the object and note the minimum and maximum value found in each dimension—six values in all. Of course, this must be done using the polygon coordinates in the *world domain;* that is, we use the coordinates as drawn in place in the scene. Once we have the minimum and maximum values, it's a simple task to use them to detect whether a given point is inside or outside of the box, and whether two boxes are overlapping. A point is inside the AABB *if its coordinates are greater than the minimum and less than the maximum in each dimension.* Two AABBs will overlap *if any of the vertices of either one lies inside of the other.* Another similar test we can use to see if two AABBs overlap involves checking to see *if their extents overlap in each of the axes.* This is quite fast and simple to compute.

This is, of course, not good enough. The two boxes may pass completely though each other and not touch either at the beginning or the end.

How do we, as before, determine if a collision has occurred between the start and end of the time interval? First, consider a one-dimensional problem. A moving one dimensional box can be represented as two real numbers: **s** (start) and **e** (end) that describe the position of the box at two times. The set of all intervals can be represented as a list L of (s_i, e_i) values. It would be best to keep this list sorted in ascending order. What we need to do is find all values of (s_i, e_i) and (s_j, e_j) that overlap.

We create a fresh list, initially empty, that will contain entries for all objects currently "active." We call this the *active* list. As we scan the sorted list of intervals L, a new s_i that is encountered results in the active list being output as a potential collision in interval **i**, and the interval **i** is added to the active list. When a new e_i is seen while scanning L, interval **i** is removed from the active list.

The great thing about using AABBs is that they can be expanded to work in 3D. We do this simply using a list for each dimension. If all three dimensions report an intersection between $AABB_i$ and $AABB_j$, they intersect, and a collision may have occurred.

A new AABB must be determined each time an object changes direction. This is an expense not incurred by using spheres, but we shall see if there is a compensating trade-off. Another, more minor, problem is that the AABB can sometimes be a poor fit for an object. Consider a triangle, circle, and rectangle shown in Figure 5.6. As the objects rotate, the AABBs fit more or less well in the box. The closer the fit, the more accurately the collision between boxes will predict an actual collision.

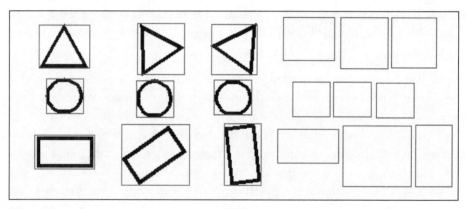

Figure 5.6
Using an axis aligned bounding book (AABB)to process three simple shapes in three orientations.

Object-Oriented Bounding Boxes

An object-oriented bounding box (OOBB) is always aligned along the primary axes of the object. This box is defined when the object is first created, and is read in along with the polygon coordinates or computed as it is read in. The box is translated and rotated along with the object, and so it should be clear that the edges of the OOBB will not necessarily align with any axis.

Why use these? In general, they hug an object better than an AABB or a sphere as shown in Figure 5.7.

This means that a collision can be more accurately determined. On the other hand, it takes a lot more code and time to determine whether two OOBBs collide or not.

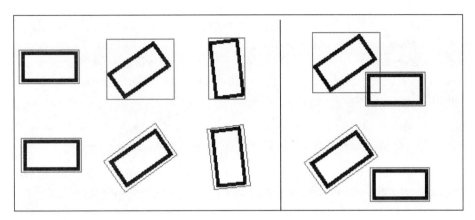

Figure 5.7
Using an object-oriented bounding box.

I won't cover the details on OOBB collision detection (See references 4 and 5), but there is an interesting issue here worth discussing. It is true that a new AABB must be computed each time the object changes direction, and this can be time consuming. However, a nifty idea is to construct the OOBB at the outset and build AABBs that surround this. There is a small problem with extra space, but this is a small price to pay for the extra efficiency. The OOBB, you see, has eight points around which you construct the AABB, instead of possibly thousands of polygon vertices if you use the raw data.

Space Subdivision

In the game *Manic Mars Racer* that we'll be developing later in this book, relatively few objects are used, and the game has a lot of empty space. The process of looking at every pair of objects to see if a collision has occurred is slow. If the objects are spread out over a large area, we can break up the entire playing volume into small pieces. Each piece will be large enough so that moving objects won't pass completely through one, but small enough to contain only a few objects that might collide. The basic idea is to check for collisions only among objects that are within the same piece of space.

To implement this approach, we only need a simple data structure. Space is divided into equal sized blocks, and an array can be used to represent each block. A block contains a list of objects that reside in it; these are all cleared out at the beginning of each frame. The list of objects is processed and each object is placed into the appropriate list. The blocks that contain objects also have a count of the number of objects that are in that block. Finally, we can look though the list of all blocks for those with more than one object.

If a game has a lot of 3D interactions, this method could require a lot of storage. A driving game mostly takes place on the ground—a "flat-ish" surface. A driving game is at best 2 1/2 dimensional. What? By this I mean that we will consider squares on the terrain surface and a small volume above, and ignore the rest of the playing volume, which can't be driven on.

There are a variety of uses and implementations of the *block map* method, but in the context of a driving game, I think we can restrict it in the following ways:

- A vehicle will be in one block, as a general rule. This will be the block in which resides the center of mass, or the center of the enclosing sphere.

- The size of the block will be such that the object/vehicle, and any other object with which it can collide, cannot pass through a whole block in one interframe time interval. This means we only have to check the starting block and the ending block in the worst case, and in most cases the object will stay in one block.

- We want a reasonable number of blocks, so they must be big enough so we have fewer blocks than objects.

- We can't have more than a few (4 to 5 max) objects in any block.

So, consider the *Manic Mars Racer* game. Let's say that the playing area is 22 kilometers. Let the maximum speed of the vehicle be a highly unreasonable 100 Km./hr. At 24 frames per second, a frame takes 1/24 second, or about 42 milliseconds (100 Km./hr. is 28 meters/second, or 0.28 meters per millisecond, or 1.176 meters/ frame). The rules we just discussed give us the following limits:

- The block should be at least the size of the vehicle. A car is rarely less than 3 meters long, so let's say the block must be at least 6M.

- In one frame the car will pass through 1.176 M, so 6 M is large enough so that the car cannot pass through a block in one frame at 24 FPS. If we get to 60 FPS, we'll have to make it 2.94 M. 3M is still big enough.

- We'll have about 250 objects in the game at most. 6M is too small; at this size, we'll need more than 100,000 blocks. At 250 objects, the block size will be about 125 Meters.

- At a block size of 125 meters, we'll still want to have fewer than 4 to 5 objects per block that can be interacted with. In the race portion of the game, the opponent will sometimes be very close. If we are careful about how we place objects, a block size of 100 meters should be fine. This size gives us a little less room but lets us put objects closer together.

At a block size of 100×100 meters, a vehicle can pass though in about 4 seconds, but objects can be placed far enough apart so that it takes a while to get to one. How many blocks are there then? Ten blocks per KM is 20×20 blocks, or 400 blocks all together. This is a bit large, but small enough to be reasonable to search. Most of the blocks will be empty after all.

Another advantage of using a block map is that only the moving objects will need to be updated each frame. Everything else is placed in its block at the beginning of the game and will remain there. A moving object can be quickly placed in a block by mapping the coordinates of the object center onto block map grid coordinates. For the 2×2 Km. map above, we first map the object's (x, y, z) coordinates onto block indices. We can do this using the following formula:

X coordinate in Kilometers/100 = column index = J

This same formula is also used for the Y coordinate, which we will call I.

Each block is represented by a structure stored in a 2D array, indexed by (I, J). Each structure contains the number of objects in that block and indicators that allow access to each object. These could be pointers or indices to an array of objects. If a complex structure is used to store them, it would be no worse than a simple linear list. I suggest that we use a maximum of six (6) objects per block, and use a fixed-size array of indices of objects within each block structure. Here's an example:

```
struct blockStruct
{
    short Nobjects;
    short objIndices[6];
};
```

To speed things up even more, we'll create a global list of all blocks containing more than one object. This could also be a fixed-size array. Whenever an object moves, we can check to see if it stays in the same block. If not, we decrease the object count for the old block and increase the count for the new one. The old block from the global list is removed if it has less than two objects, and we add in the new one if it has more than one.

Before starting collision detection, we add the blocks where objects will end up after moving to the global list. Next, looking only at the global list, we check for collisions between objects within every block in that list. Finally, we update the global list to remove the blocks no longer having more than one object.

Narrow Phase Collision Detection

Once we determine that a collision is possible, the next step is to determine if the collision actually occurs. If we get a collision, we then need to determine at what point on the surface the impact occurs. Because our surfaces are drawn as polygons, we're really trying to determine which polygon on the model suffers the impact. Determining this can rarely be done as fast as we'd like. And, as always, the more accuracy we need, the more expensive it will be. The hope is that this detailed and expensive calculation will not have to be performed very often.

A wide variety of narrow phase algorithms are available, and an entire book could be written on this topic. However, we only need to consider the most obvious methods. A narrow phase algorithm is invoked when a collision occurs between two objects consisting of polygons. These objects were enclosed by spheres or boxes, but now we must look at the details. Let's assume that the polygons are triangles—each has three vertices. If an object consists of 1,000 triangles, we'll need 3,000 vertices, right?

No, because most of the vertices in an object are shared. We could estimate that we would have 1,000 *distinct* vertices in this object (2,000 would be shared). Each vertex will move in a known direction by a known amount, the so-called movement vector. This means that there are 1,000 *rays*, or directed-line segments, that we would need to examine. We can assume that the second object is stationary because if it were moving, we'd subtract its movement vector from both objects to determine a net movement vector on the object being tested, as just described when we checked for collisions using spheres.

We have 1,000 rays and a similar number of polygons in the other object we need to test against. This would require a million tests, each ray against each polygon. It's possible to eliminate some rays and some polygons, though. Only polygons that are on the side of the object facing the other object need to be tested, so we'll be left with 500 × 500 tests. This is still a significant number, but it's now only 1/4 of the previous value.

Ignoring the back-facing polygons can be done using something called *back-face culling*[16]. Each polygon (triangle) has a normal associated with it. (We could compute one every time we need it.) Back-face culling is really a visibility algorithm. The question is: *Can we see the polygon from where we are now?* We use the dot product between the normal to the triangle and a vector from the viewer's position to determine the angle between these vectors. If it is between 90 and 270 degrees, we'll know that the polygon is facing the viewer; otherwise, it is not and can be ignored. In this case, we replace the viewer with the centroid of the object being tested against, and the method is the same. Of course, this must be done from both objects involved in the collision, each taking turns being the viewpoint. There are also tricky ways to speed this method up[15].

Ray/Triangle Intersection

The core of the collision test is determining which polygons intersect, where, and when. From the previous discussion, we have selected some polygons (perhaps all of them) to test them against each other, we have determined what the movement vector is, and we know that an object **A** is moving while **B** remains stationary (or at least has been made stationary by computing a relative movement vector). Now we'll select vertices in **A** and determine their positions before and after movement. Next we'll see if that line segment or *ray* intersects a polygon in **B**. If so, it is easy to determine when and where this happens. Here is what we must do, step-by-step:

1. The movement vector expresses relative movement, so by adding it to a point, we find where the point moves. Vertices in **A** will be named V_A. They are numbered from 0 to n, so they are V_{A0} to V_{An}; finally they have x, y, and z coordinates named V_{A0x}, V_{A0y}, V_{A0z}, and so on. The point V' is the same point as V, but is a position after the motion is complete.

    The ray associated with a vertex **VA**, given the movement vector **M**, is a vector **R** from **VAi** to V_{Ai}**+M**. Here's the math:

    Equation 5.12
    $$R_x = V_{Aix} + M_x$$
    $$R_y = V_{Aiy} + M_y$$
    $$R_z = V_{Aiz} + M_z$$

    The line that needs to be tested runs from V_{Ai} to **R**. We call this line **L**, and it is

    Equation 5.13
    $$L_x = V_{Aix} + (tR_x)$$
    $$L_y = V_{Aiy} + (tR_y)$$
    $$L_z = V_{Aiz} + (tR_z)$$

    where **t** runs from 0 to 1 to give any point on the line segment.

2. We now compute the equation of the plane in which the selected triangle in object **B** resides. This equation is was shown in 5.8. —you will recall that we need the normal **N** and a point in the plane **P** to get the plane:

    Equation 5.14 $\quad N_x(x-P_{0x}) + N_y(y-P_{0y}) + N_z(z-P_{0z}) = 0$

3.   Substitute the line **L** into the plane equation to solve for **t**—the time at which the collision will occur.

4.   Use the value of **t** found in step 3 to plug into Equation 5.13 to find the point **(x,y,z)** at which the collision will occur.

5.   Finally, determine whether the point found in step 4 resides inside the triangle. This can be done in a few simple ways:

■ **The interior angle test**: Compute the angle between the point and all three triangle vertices in order. The sum of the angles should be 360 degrees, within rounding error, if the point is inside the triangle.

■ **The odd intersections test**: Draw a line from the point being tested to a far away point. If this line intersects exactly one edge exactly once, it is inside the triangle. If the intersection is a vertex, through some bad luck, select a new direction and draw another line. (A vertex is part of two edges, and can't be used in this test.)

■ **Area test**: Make all triangles between the point being tested and consecutive points on the triangle—there are three. If the sum of the areas of these triangles equals the area of the big triangle, the point is inside. This test is approximate, partly again due to vagaries of floating point arithmetic.

These three tests are illustrated in Figure 5.8.

All five steps we just discussed can be accomplished in a remarkably small time period, and actually are performed in many games. You can implement any or all of the collision detection schemes I have described using the techniques introduced in this chapter, combined with a few details found on the Web. Or you could use someone else's code, as we'll discuss next.

Collision Detection Packages

Given the complexity of collision detection, the variety of methods possible, the relationships between the broad and narrow phases, and the difficulty of implementing some of the methods, I recommend using a package that is known to work correctly. There are quite a few packages that can be downloaded from the Internet in a few minutes. Almost any of them will save you a huge amount of time.

You should understand that, while it is possible to use my basic description of collision detection to implement your own system, you may be better off using someone else's. Personally, I prefer to spend my time on audio because I enjoy that aspect more than writing code for collision detection. Your passion might be graphics. Let's take a quick

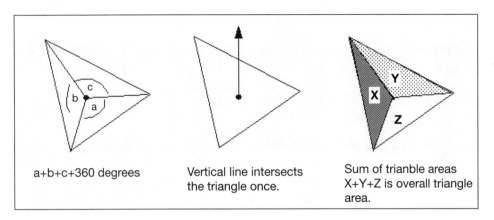

Figure 5.8
Using three tests to see if a point is in a polygon.

look at some of the collision detection packages that have been developed by others who have made their passion collision detection.

QuickCD

This package is implemented in C and has been tested over a period of years. It is based on a hierarchy of bounding volumes (called BV trees). It also has been used by many people and the worst of its problems have been fixed. It can be found at **www.ams.sunysb.edu/~jklosow/quickcd/QuickCD.html**. The basic implementation is for Unix/Linux, but it could very easily be converted for a PC or Mac. It seems to have been developed in about 1995.

Vclip

This system works for convex polyhedra, and is coded in C++ and Java, originally in 1997 by Brian Mirtich. It can be downloaded from **www.cs.ubc.ca/spider/lloyd/java/vclip.html**. The problem with this package is that cars and trees and such are not convex. Good thing that the system includes a program for computing 3D convex hulls. However, as a result, the collision detection is approximate for non-convex objects.

ColDet

This is a cool system that seems to work with what is called a *polygon soup*—a random appearing set of polygons, not convex, not necessarily even connected. Another good thing about this package is that it compiles on the GNU C++ compiler or Visual C++, and others. It uses a hierarchy of bounding boxes, and can achieve a very high degree of accuracy. It can be found and downloaded from **http://photoneffect.com/coldet/**.

I-Collide

This package claims to give *exact* collision results for complex polyhedra. It was first released in 1996, but the most recent version I have was released in 2004. You can find it at **www.cs.unc.edu/~geom/I_COLLIDE/index.html.**

Swift

This library is a C++ system that works on convex polyhedra or objects that are expressed as a hierarchy of convex polyhedra. It is faster than V-Clip or I-Collide, but it is also (in my opinion) more difficult to use. It can be downloaded from **www.cs.unc.edu/~geom/SWIFT/.**

RAPID

Like ColDet, this system works on polygon soups—the most general class of collision detection problems. It has a relatively simple interface and is coded in C++. This may be the easiest system to use with OpenGL, although this is clearly a matter of opinion. It uses a structure called an OBB tree (hierarchy of object-oriented bounding boxes) to achieve high speed yet general collision detection. It can be downloaded from **www.cs.unc.edu/~geom/OBB/OBBT.html.**

Summary

The collision detection scheme I suggest you use is to enclose the moving objects in spheres or bounding boxes and check to see if the enclosing objects could collide. If this is possible, you then check to see if any of their actual polygons might collide. This two level approach can save a lot of work and processing time. It is also possible to use region subdivision to avoid checking for collisions against objects that are too far apart for a collision to occur. This is a technique that we'll be using later in this book when we develop the *Manic Mars Racer* game. I have provided you with the basic methods for doing all of this.

I have also given you links to existing code that you may use to avoid writing your own collision system. Using an off-the-shelf package can possibly saving you a lot of time but the tradeoff is that using other people's code will require you to structure your program around somebody else's style. I guess all programmers have to do that someday.

Chapter 6

Incorporating Intelligent Opponents

■ Learn the basics of how to control an intelligent opponent vehicle.

■ Use waypoints and finite state machines to implement opponents.

■ Learn techniques for getting opponent vehicles back on track when they crash.

In Chapter 5, we learned how basic AI techniques are used to help us determine when objects collide. I hope your head is not still spinning from all of the math that we discussed. I promise that I'll give you a "math break" in this chapter.

We'll now turn the corner and look at how AI techniques can be used to create intelligent drivers (or intelligent opponents, as we like to call them). You'll actually learn how to write some of the code that expertly controls the vehicles you race against in your games. These are the vehicles that are not actually controlled by people. As you'll learn, there are many differences between driving a vehicle in the real world and driving a simulated one in a virtual world. You'll also learn that the basic strategy of AI game programming is to cheat! Keep in mind that it is only important that the simulated vehicles (I'll call them *opponents*) appear to behave as if a person is driving. The game that controls the opponents doesn't have to guide the vehicle using vision, and has advance knowledge of everything that is in the game. In addition, markers are placed all through the terrain that the AI uses to guide the vehicles. These markers are not visible to a human player because they are not rendered as objects; they are merely points in 3D space that are used to create a path.

The opponents will, in fact, either take the same path at the same speed each time through a course, or will at most have a finite number of variations, each one taken with a particular probability when encountered. We can even change those probabilities each time a choice is made, but that too is programmed and well-defined. Most opponents do not act in an intelligent way, but are guided by quite simple and quick algorithms.

We'll look at some of those algorithms in this chapter, but there are many that are not public knowledge. Game developers guard some of their secrets quite jealously, and although I have managed to pry open the vault a little, I am under no illusions. I can't tell you all of the secrets because I don't know all of them!

The Basics of Autonomous Control

The word *autonomous* implies that an object has independence or operates on its own. Autonomous control of opponent vehicles in a game is essential for making the game fun and exciting. The opponent vehicles provide a sense of competition and they serve as obstacles to have to be avoided, thus creating a more complex problem to solve. Opponents that are autonomous are controlled by software, and so we treat the problem as one of software design. The first question is: *What is the problem?*

Another way of asking this is to flip the question around: *What is the goal?* This is a question we can answer in general, at least partly. The goal of a player in a racing game is to have fun, and this means winning, right? Oddly, the answer is no. Winning a game regularly amounts to beating it, which frequently means that it is time to purchase another game! The entertainment value is in the game play, the puzzle, and the contest; beating a game too easily is the kiss of death, for a commercial game at least. Word will get out, and the game will not sell.

On the other hand, if a game is impossible to beat, then it is just as bad. Players simply give up, and again word gets out that the game is impossible to beat. We start to find them in garage sales.

A carefully worded high-level goal for the opponent cars in a racing game needs to be:

> **Goal 1**: The opponents should provide a challenge to the player without being impossible to defeat.

This goal is too vague to implement as it is. However, I think it leads to a logical set of sub-goals that *can* be implemented:

> **Goal 1.1**: If at all possible, the human player should beat some opponents if there are many. The player should not be humiliated by a computer if they are still actually playing.

> **Goal 1.2**: Some opponents should decrease their skill level as they get a distance ahead of the player, allowing a chance to catch up.

Goal 1.3: The goal of an opponent is not to win, but to provide entertaining competition. If the game involves objects such as weapons, the opponent must be able to use them. The opponent should play the game much as a human would play the game.

Goal 1.4: When there are many opponents, they should not all act the same. They should have variable skill levels, and should in some sense respond to the displayed skill of the player.

Goal 1.5: The player should be offered a choice of difficulty when starting the game so that easy opponents are available as well as difficult ones. Players can find their skill level and strive to improve it.

Most of these rules or goals are probably not a big surprise. You may not know that the AI system actually "dumbs itself down" to let you catch up, but you probably suspected as much. We will add to this set of goals, but for now, we have enough to get started. Since the precise nature of the game we are discussing is unknown, we'll keep things at a high level for the moment.

How to Control a Car

Users control their car using the keyboard, mouse, or game pad. A game receives character input that can be interpreted as a command. For example, left arrow might be used to turn a vehicle left; forward arrow makes the vehicle move forwards faster, and so on. We could control an opponent in the same basic way, except that we don't need input. So, we could have a function

```
void turnLeft (CAR x);
```

that would turn the opponent represented by x left by the standard turn angle. This would be done in the same way that the player's car would turn by angular increments. Or, we could enhance the opponents by allowing arbitrary relative angles:

```
void turnRelative (CAR x, float delta);
```

We could even use absolute angles:

```
void turnAbsolute (CAR x, float angle);
```

The idea is that a car is controlled using a set of very obvious primitive operations that can be combined into higher-level operations. We also need accessor functions that return key values to the AI system, such as a car's current speed, position, and direction. This would allow us to specify a high-level goal in terms of low-level operations and current parameters.

The high-level goals could be expressed in terms of minor goals, which may in turn be expressed in terms of local goals, and so on until at some level the goal is "go left," which can be done with a basic function call. The design would be from the high-level downwards, keeping in mind that the lowest level is pretty much defined at the outset. Let's take a detailed look at one of the possible intermediate goals: something called *cruising behavior.*

Cruising Behavior

The goal of this behavior is to maintain a set speed, more or less, while following a set track towards a geometric goal. It may also be important to avoid collisions. The "set track" I mentioned is a piecewise linear path drawn along the game's terrain, perhaps along the middle of the road or race track. Figure 6.1 shows a sample of the track and it labels a few interesting objects and locations.

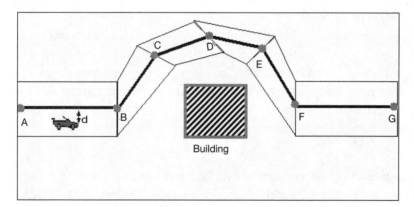

Figure 6.1
A simple set track and a set of line segments that allow driving behaviors to be defined.

The track can be identified as a connected sequence of straight line segments: AB, BC, CD ... FG. Points A and B are points in 3D space (A_x, A_y, A_z) and (B_x, B_y, B_z) that define the ends of a line segment. The car being controlled is at a known position $P=(x,y,z)$. Figure 6.1 shows the car moving towards point B; it is at a distance **d** from the track, and has a known speed **S** and desired speed S_{AB}. How do we keep the car on track?

Everything will be relatively simple as long as the car is moving in a straight line. The code must try to keep the car as near to the line as possible, and will attempt to keep the speed as near to S_{AB} as possible:

```
s = getSpeed (THISCAR);
if (s < Sab)
    /* Car going too slow */
    a = fmin(amax, k*(Sab-S));
else if (s > Sab)
    /* Car going too fast */
    a = fmax (amin, k*(Sab-S));

else a = 0.0F;
s = a*dt + s;

d = linePointDist (A, B, P);
if (d < RIGHTTHESHOLD) turnLeft (THISCAR);
else if (d > LEFTTHRESHOLD) turnRight(THISCAR);
```

This code does as follows:

- Uses a maximum and minimum acceleration

- If the car is going too slow, it increases the acceleration a little, up to the max.

- If the car is going too fast, it decreases the acceleration (increase the deceleration) with the limit being the minimum.

It then computes a new velocity based on the calculated acceleration and the time since the code last did this. The constant **k** is used to apportion acceleration between time frames, and should be determined by experiment.

We also need to pay attention to the steering. If the car moves right of the center line by a large enough distance, the car is turned to the left by one unit. If the car moves left of the center line by a large enough distance, the car is turned to the right by a unit. The system will straighten the steering angle automatically over the next few frames, but there is a risk of oversteer. We could fix that by only adjusting the steering angle every few frames.

Avoidance Behavior

While cruising, it is possible to encounter an obstacle. This would not usually be a wall or tree or the like, because the set track would not be placed where there were natural hazards like this. (I'm using golf terminology here, but it works). An obstacle on the track will usually be another vehicle on the track ahead, presumably one that is not moving as quickly. *Avoidance behavior* is what the opponent vehicle does when it comes upon this situation.

The first thing to note is that other opponent vehicles will be following the track, more or less. That's a reason the opponent vehicle is in your way. The first solution involves creating another set track to be followed in order to pass a car on the existing track. We can call the original set track, the *A-track*, and the new one, the *B-track*. Some (okay, most) game guys would call the A-track the *driving line* and the B-track the *overtaking line*. This arrangement is shown in Figure 6.2.

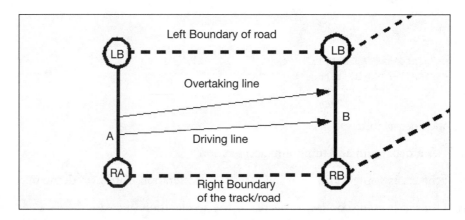

Figure 6.2
This AB sections of the road shows the driving line and the overtaking line.

As a vehicle V1 approaches another vehicle V0 from behind, it detects the potential collision, not by traditional collision detection, but by noting another vehicle ahead on the driving line. V1 then switches to the overtaking line and steers towards that line, thus avoiding the vehicle V0. If another opponent vehicle is already on the B- track, we simply slow down until it is gone. In a game like *Mario Kart*, we could also simply speed up and hit the other car, letting the collision sort things out—unless V0 is the player's car, of course.

If V_0 is the player's car, its behavior won't be predictable. If V_1 changes to the overtaking line, the player may just move over to block, but it could speed up, slow down, or hit something. Rather than having a fixed overtaking line in this case, we could create a new line by placing a target point in the middle of the largest gap, either left or right, between the player's car and the boundaries of the road. This point will move from frame-to-frame, but it does present a target to steer at until V_1 gets very close.

The speed of V1 also needs to be controlled. In principle, V1 must slow down a bit until a gap opens up that is big enough to take advantage of. The AI code could compute the trajectory of the player based on the current parameters and determine where the player will be in 3 to 5 frames. If the gap will be big enough at that time, V1 could speed up to fill that gap and force the player to decide whether to collide with it or to avoid it. This is how I would drive, and how I would code the game if I had the time.

Figure 6.3 shows how an opponent could react when coming up to a player's car from behind. Here, the new overtaking line uses the largest gap between the player and the side of the road. If the player moves over to block, it merely changes where the overtaking line resides.

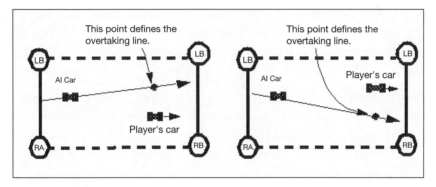

Figure 6.3
How to react if you come up to the player's car from behind.

Using nodes or points that connect to create a path is generally referred to as *waypoint pathfinding*. The waypoints can be saved as coordinates in a special structure in which there is a next and a previous waypoint. Every vehicle saves the current waypoint that it is using (the one immediately ahead) in its own structure so that we don't have to search for the point closest to the vehicle. When the vehicle passes that waypoint, the next one becomes current. The use of waypoints eliminates the need for path finding algorithms in general, and simplifies the task of keeping the opponent cars on the road and moving in the right direction.

In fact, there are a few ways to determine the path that an autonomous vehicle will use to traverse the race course. One is to create both a driving line and an overtaking line as we have described. The other is to create a different line for each opponent car that can be on the track at the same time. Each car then has a relatively simple task—it needs to keep as near to its driving line as possible. If another car is in its way, the cars simply collide, and the collision resolves the problem. Creating a number of driving lines requires some up-front effort, but it simplifies the game. The cars just don't have to be as smart because the designers have done the work. Most game players don't recognize that there is only one line per car, especially if the lines are assigned at random at the beginning of a race.

The driving lines can be associated with other information, like speed at each point. As a result, the line that is assigned to a car determines how well the car will do in the race. This practically eliminates the need for advanced computations while the game is being played.

Waypoint Representation and Implementation

The first thing to remember about waypoints is that they are basically points in 3D space. Thus, the first thing we need to keep track of is their X, Y, and Z coordinates. We also need a previous and next point, which can be stored as pointers. We may also have multiple previous and next points. Let's assume that we will have at most two of each. I will explain later.

I've already pointed out that we may want to specify a speed. This will be the desired speed at a specific waypoint. If the point is approaching a turn, it will be in a decreasing sequence, and will increase on straight sections. I should mention that the actual opponent vehicle may not travel at that exact speed when passing though the waypoint. The specified speed is a goal.

A C structure that could hold this information is:

```
struct waypoint_struct
{
    float x, y, z;
    float speed;
    struct waypoint_struct *next[2];
    struct waypoint_struct *prev[2];
    float Dnext[2];
};
typedef struct waypoint_struct * WAYPOINT;
```

The simplest way to use waypoints is to direct the vehicles toward straight lines that run through them. If we do, the cars will always pass through the waypoints, and will turn sharply whenever each one is encountered.

A different way to manage waypoint traffic is to approximate a path between them, and to look ahead more than one point.

Spline Paths between Waypoints

Originally, the term *spline* referred to a rubber tube with a wire running through the long axis. When you bent it, it would keep the shape you gave it. Engineers and draftsmen use them to draw smooth curves between non-colinear points on a piece of paper. These days the term "spline" usually refers to a mathematical construct that defines a continuous, smooth curve between any set of data points.

Think about a vehicle using waypoints to navigate across a surface. If we use more than one waypoint, we need a way to connect them so that the path driven is continuous, without angular turns or breaks. This means that the path will be smooth, and will permit simple accelerations. The more waypoints that are used to create the splines, the smoother the curve will be.

Catmull-Rom Splines

Although there are many kinds of splines, we'll focus on using one kind: Catmull-Rom splines. We'll use them to define driving paths in a racing game. In general, a spline provides a mechanism for representing a curved path using a sequence of points called *control points*. The position of a point on the curve between two control points is calculated using a special function that is different for each different kind of spline. It calculates the actual coordinates of a vehicle, given your relative position between the two enclosing control points.

One of the useful characteristics of the Catmull-Rom spline is that the spline curve actually passes through all of the control points. This is not true of all splines, and is a property that is important for navigation. Being a significant distance from the waypoints can be a problem when there is also other traffic trying to follow their waypoints.

To use a spline as a guide, we need to compute the position of a vehicle in 3D space given its relative position between the control points on each side of it. A parametric representation will be used, as we have done previously. We'll define a variable t that can take on values between 0 and 1, and let $t=0$ at waypoint P_1 and let $t=1$ at waypoint P_2, as shown in Figure 6.4. While we are between P_1 and P_2, the value of t specifies the fraction of the P_1-P_2 distance that the car is from P_1.

We also need the position of some control points to calculate the car's position. The path defined by a spline is smooth, and so we need to know the position of more than the two points P_1 and P_2 in order to create a smooth path; two points define only a straight line. Splines commonly use four control points at all times. In this case, two of them (P_0, P_1) are behind the car being driven and the other two (P_2, P_3) are ahead of the car. The spline itself is a combination of the four control points expressed as a cubic polynomial. A standard way to specify a spline mathematically is shown here:

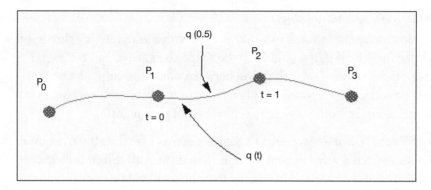

Figure 6.4
Using waypoints named P0 through P1 with a Catmull-Rom spline passing through them.

Equation 6.1

$$q(t) = 0.5 \begin{bmatrix} 1 & t & t^2 & t^3 \end{bmatrix} \begin{bmatrix} 0 & 2 & 0 & 0 \\ -1 & 0 & 1 & 0 \\ 2 & -5 & 4 & -1 \\ -1 & 3 & -3 & 1 \end{bmatrix} \begin{bmatrix} P_0 \\ P_1 \\ P_2 \\ P_3 \end{bmatrix}$$

Or, as a vector/matrix equation we can use:

Equation 6.2 $q(t) = 1/2\ T*M*P$

Changing the values in the matrix **M** yields different kinds of spline. When this is multiplied out, the polynomial for the Catmull-Rom spline is:

Equation 6.3 $q(t) = 0.5 * ((2 * P_1) + (-P_0 + P_2) * t + (2*P_0 - 5*P_1 + 4*P_2 - P_3) * t^2 +$

$(-P_0 + 3*P_1 - 3*P_2 + P_2) * t^3)$

Now that we have the equations, what do we do with them? First, the opponent vehicle will start at some point on the spline that we will call P_0. It will move towards the next waypoint P_1, and steer left or right so that it can remain as close to the spline as possible. Each part of the curve depends on four nearby points. When it passes a waypoint, the specific points used will change. We'll start out using P_N, P_0, P_1, and P_2. When the car passes P_1, the active control points become P_0, P_1, P_2, and P_3. This continues along the path until the path ends, or we return to the beginning.

Motion is about distance traveled per time unit, and we need to know where we are (i.e., we need to know the value of **t**) between each two control points on the spline at every moment. Unfortunately, the distance between two points is not a simple thing to calculate because we want the distance along the curve, not the straight line distance.

Fortunately, we only need to compute the distance between waypoints once, when the track is designed. We can save these distances in a data structure; the waypoint structure defined above has a field D_{next} that is used to store the distance to each of two possible next waypoints.

We could use calculus to determine the distance between waypoints, but using a computer makes it easy to determine the position of 100 or 1,000 points equally spaced between the waypoints. We'll also assume that the path between each pair of these waypoints is a line. The more points we use, the closer we'll get to the actual distance along the spline. This computation is made for each pair of waypoints.

The last thing to mention is that Catmull-Rom splines can be built in three dimensions, but it may be better to use 2D splines and simply add the height of the surface at that point as the third dimension. This is because we need to determine what side of the spline curve the car is on for steering purposes. It would not be wise to complicate this activity with a third dimension.

Spline Waypoint Implementation

Let's look at how we use splines and waypoint navigation to control an AI vehicle at the detailed level. The code is related to the code we saw earlier in this chapter. We must be given our previous position, **P**, our current position, **Q**, the current speed, the waypoint structures for all waypoints, **W**, and the index for the current waypoint (the one behind us), **W**$_i$.

The first thing to do is to determine where we are on the spline. This is done by taking the current position and plugging the coordinates into the spline equation:

```
t = estimateT(W, Wi, P, Q);
```

Next, we interpolate the desired speed from the two waypoints:

```
Sab = interpolate (W[Wi].speed, W[Wi+1].speed, t);
```

Then we adjust the current speed:

```
s = getSpeed (THISCAR);
if (s < Sab)                    /* Car going too slow */
   a = fmin(amax, k*(Sab-s));
else if (s > Sab)               /* Car going too fast */
   a = fmax (amin, k*(Sab-s));
else a = 0.0F;
   s = a*dt + s;
```

We can now determine where the spline curve is with respect to the car and steer towards it. My method takes two points on each side of the current point on the spline, say t- 0.001 and t+0.001, and draws a line through them. Then, we ask the question, "What side of the line are we on?" Here's the code that performs this task:

```
A = splinePoint (W, Wi, t-0.001);
B = splinePoint (W, Wi, t+0.001);
d = linePointDist (A, B, Q);
if (d < RIGHTTHESHOLD) turnLeft (THISCAR);
else if (d > LEFTTHRESHOLD) turnRight(THISCAR);
```

In very rare circumstances this method could turn the vehicle in the wrong direction. I like to think this gives it a human quality. The matrix **M** in equation 3.2 determines the kind of spline that is used to connect the waypoints; it is possible to use other cubic spline forms.

Splitting and Joining Distinct Paths

Using waypoints gives us a way to relieve the AI system of making complex decisions in real time, and allows game designers to make a system that has easy and hard paths, multiple paths for each vehicle, and strategies for managing otherwise complex situations. If a game involves driving off the road, you'll need to consider the idea of splitting paths. It could become obvious that a car is following a set track very quickly if the car always passes a certain object such as a cactus on the left, then turns right through a creek and around the south side of a little hill.

There is a way we can keep this from happening. When designing a game, we design the paths that the opponent cars can take, and we can have the track split into two parts anywhere we choose. This will occur at a waypoint, and when the car reaches that waypoint, it can follow one of two paths to the next waypoint, of which there would be also two possible paths. The choice would be made at random, possibly with a bias to the side of the spline the car is on just now or the direction it is traveling.

Assuming that we have a function named **random()** that returns a value between 0 and 1 uniformly distributed, the following code could be used to choose between two directions at random:

```
if (random() < 0.5) followLeftPath();
  else followRightPath();
```

The 0.5 value in this code can be any value at all between 0 and 1. To give the left path a preference, we set **W.leftProb** to 0.75 and then execute this code:

```
if (random() < W.leftProb) followLeftPath();
  else followRightPath();
```

If we want to give preference to the path that is nearest to the current direction the vehicle is traveling, we can do this using angular differences. We determine an absolute angle (i.e., compass heading) for each of the two paths and one for the vehicle. You may wish to presume that there is a maximum reasonable angular difference between the vehicle's path and the new track. Then, we perform the following:

```
leftAngle = angle2pointW (W, Wi, 0);
rightAngle = angle2pointW (W, Wi, 1);
vangle = angle2point (P, Q);
l = vangle - leftAngle;
r = rightangle-vangle;
if (random() < l/(l+r)) followLeftPath();
else followRightPath ();
```

You could allow a path to split into more than two parts, but why bother? Just create waypoints a little distance past the first split, and split again. Joining is easier because no decision is needed. Two paths that merge into one is not really a special case. The waypoint where the paths join is simply a control point in two different splines, which does not require any special treatment.

Using Finite State Machines

The idea that a vehicle can be cruising, chasing, or avoiding other vehicles is not especially profound. Clearly, different behavior can be assigned to each mode or *state*. It is also convenient from the perspective of design to be able to break up the different behaviors into distinct parts, which can then be implemented independently. The use of the traditional computer science tool, the finite state machine, is a pretty natural way to deal with this kind of situation. Finite state machines, also called FSAs, are used in programming languages, control systems, and artificial intelligence systems. Their properties are well known because they have been widely used, and efficient implementations abound.

A basic FSA is a collection of states and transitions between the states. An event, such as an input, allows us to move from one state to another. States are assigned numbers so that a state machine can be designed and implemented. So how can a FSA be used in a driving or racing game? Let's take a closer look.

An opponent vehicle can start out in the *cruising* state. If it encounters another opponent car on the road ahead, it enters the *overtake_AI* state. If it encounters the player's car, it enters the *overtake_player* state. The behavior of the AI is quite different in each

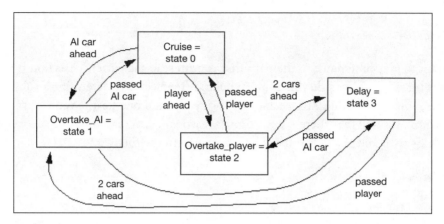

Figure 6.5
A finite state machine used to support opponent vehicles.

state; the goals and methods of achieving them are distinct. Figure 6.5 shows a diagrammatic representation of an FSA, specifically one for the three states we just looked at. It is essential to have a clear mechanism for moving between states, and a clear plan for what to do while in each state.

Mathematically, an FSA is a simulated machine or mathematical construction consisting of a set of states, which are usually integers. An FSA also has a special state called the *start* state, a collection of input symbols or events, and a transition function that takes an input symbol and the current state and decides what the *next* state will be. The FSA begins a computation in the *start* state, and enters other states based on input symbols/events and the transition function. A special state can be used called the *accept* state that can decide when a calculation is complete.

If we are in the *cruising* state (state 0) and an opponent vehicle appears in front of us, we enter the *overtake_AI* state (1); if we are in the *cruising* state and the player's car appears in front of us, we enter the *overtake_player* state (2). These are the only state transitions we can take from state 0 as shown in Figure 6.5.

While in the *overtake_AI* state, there are a couple of events that can occur. We can pass the opponent car or we can be blocked further. If we pass the car, we go back to the *cruising* state again. If we are blocked, we might need another state called *delay* in which we slow down and look for a change in the situation. The *delay* state could be state 3.

The *delay* state can mean different things to different vehicles, if we choose. Some cars will in fact slow down and look for a gap through which they can sneak. Other cars might aggressively try to push their way through, colliding with their opponents if the opponents refuse to move. Still others might leave the road, if they are allowed, to try to find a way around. Any of these options could be associated with the same state, depending on the actual vehicle.

FSA in Practice

Implementing an FSA is a simple matter. In this section I'll give you some good design and coding ideas to help you with style and convention. I'll use the FSA shown in Figure 6.5 as an example.

First, notice that states are represented as integers, from zero to some maximum value. They also have meanings, and so can be given names. Thus, I generally define states as constants as shown here:

```
#define STATE_CRUISE              0
#define STATE_OVERTAKE_AI         1
#define STATE_OVERTAKE_PLAYER     2
#define STATE_DELAY               3
```

We'll also need to define a state transition function. This function takes two parameters: the current state and a state transition event. The function will change the current state as defined by our particular FSA. This normally means that state transition events, however complex detecting one might be, need to be assigned integer labels and names, just like states:

```
#define   TE_AI_CAR_AHEAD         0
#define   TE_PASSED_AI_CAR        1
#define   TE_2_CARS_AHEAD         2
#define   TE_PASSED_PLAYER        3
#define   TE_PLAYER_AHEAD         4
#define TE_ERROR_XXX              9
```

The error state, **TE_ERROR_XXX**, is representative of many possible error states. For example, **TE_ERROR_103** could indicate that some transitions are actually illegal and result in some remedial action on the part of the program. Also, notice that the transitions are context sensitive; the event **TE_PASSED_AI_CAR** does different things depending on what state you are in.

The actual machine can be implemented in a number of ways. A particularly good way, from the point of view of efficiency, modularity, and portability, is to use a table. Transitions are integers, and these can be used to index into an array. States are also integers, and they can also be used as indices. Thus, a state transition table for the FSA shown in Figure 6.5 would look like:

		State			
		0	1	2	3
	0	1			
	1		0		2
Transition	2		3	3	
Event	3			0	1
	4	2			

This transition table contains state numbers, and is indexed by both current state and a transition event. If we are in state 1 (*Overtake_AI*), for example, and we pass the AI car (event 1=PASS_AI_CAR), we enter state 0 (*Cruise*). We do this using an assignment of the form:

```
new_state = transition_ table[TE_PASSED_AI_CAR][STATE_OVERTAKE_AI];
```

The missing entries in the table would be filled in with either error states or a null transition to indicate that a state can't be changed.

This is an effective implementation of an FSA, although it relies on a correct initialization of the table. If the table is read in from a file, it consists of integers that have no symbolic form, and this is somewhat error prone. If the table is initialized from a declaration, it is less simple to modify, but we can now use the declared state names. However we do it, the code is less clear than some options and needs good documentation.

Another way to implement an FSA is to use discrete code. The usual situation is to just use **if** and **switch** statements. The first two columns of the transition table above could be implemented using the following code:

```
switch (state)
{
   case STATE_CRUISE:
   if (transition_event == TE_AI_CAR_AHEAD)
       new_state = TE_PASSED_AI_CAR;
   else if (transition_event == TE_PLAYER_AHEAD)
       new_state = STATE_OVERTAKE_PLAYER;
   case STATE_OVERTAKE_AI:
   if (transition_event == TE_PASSED_AI_CAR)
       new_state = STATE_CRUISE;
   else if (transition_event == TE_2_CARS_AHEAD)
       new_state = STATE_DELAY;
```

```
     case STATE_OVERTAKE_PLAYER:
     if (transition_event == TE_2_CARS_AHEAD)
          new_state = STATE_DELAY;
     else if (transition_event == TE_PASSED_PLAYER)
          new_state = STATE_CRUISE;
     case STATE_DELAY:
     if (transition_event == TE_PASSED_AI_CAR)
          new_state = STATE_OVERTAKE_PLAYER;
     else if (transition_event == TE_PASSED_PLAYER)
          new_state = TE_PASSED_AI_CAR;
        default:
        /*          Error code          */
}
```

In this case, no anonymous integers are used. All names are symbolic, making it easy to read through the code to see what the transitions are. This makes the code much easier to maintain, and allows it to be more easily checked for correctness on a casual basis.

Both of the implementations above could be encapsulated within a simple function such as:

```
int transition (int state, int event);
```

This would return the next (new) state given the current state and the nature of the last event that occurred. The implicit assumption is, by the way, that two events cannot occur within the relatively small time interval between two consecutive frames. This is pretty standard, and what happens in practice is that we sometimes get two state transitions in quick succession if two events occur more or less at the same time.

Handling the "What Do We Do Now" Problem

We now know how to move from one state to another, how to implement transitions, and what the states mean. We haven't yet discussed what we should be doing once we are in a particular state. This is not actually a matter for the FSA to deal with. We need to determine what kinds of activities are associated with each state, and then to execute code that performs those activities when in the correct state. We also need to execute code that determines whether any of the transition events have occurred.

Here is a general sketch of how the FSA-based AI code would function:

```
switch (state)
{
case STATE_CRUISE:
        cruise (); break;
```

```
case STATE_OVERTAKE_AI:
        overtake_AI (); break;
case STATE_OVERTAKE_PLAYER:
        overtake_player (); break;
case STATE_DELAY:
        delay (); break;
}
event = test_all_transition_events(state);
state = transition (state, event);
```

This code causes the game to change between the feasible states as controlled by the events that have been defined by the designers and tested for in the function **test_all_transition_events()**. By the way, this function can be quite complex, and it would probably be a good idea to test only for those events that are significant from the current state. This is why the state is a parameter.

Other Useful States

It is impossible to describe the states that a driving game can be in without knowing the detailed context of the game being discussed. However, there are certain specific states that we can implement to better support the requirements of driving and racing games. I've tried to include some of the more obvious states here but you'll likely have some of your own, depending on the type of game that you'll want to create.

- **Start:** In racing games, it is common to start a race with all of the cars having predetermined start positions. The cars are stationary, and in fact they may not move until the starter fires a gun or waves a flag. The cars then accelerate to the desired speed and start racing on a selected driving track. This describes a state we could call the **Start** state.

In some games, an actual countdown to the start is used. If the player starts within a specified time of the actual start time, he gets a speed boost for a few moments. This can be done for opponent cars as well, but because the AI system knows exactly when the start will take place, an opponent car could easily cheat. Actually, it's hard not to cheat. The solution is to generate a random time at the start, and any opponent vehicle with a start time below the threshold would be given a boost.

Normally, the **Start** state would change to **Cruise** when a certain speed is achieved or a specific time interval has expired, and the car has been assigned a track.

- **Air:** A car that hits a big bump or crests a hill at a high speed may actually leave the ground for a few seconds. This has a few consequences: the engine usually revs up to a high value, causing the engine sound to change. The accelerator pedal has no practical effect because the car cannot accelerate forwards. The car also can't brake. The car cannot change direction, as the wheels won't be in contact with the ground and the vehicle cannot be steered. This could be described as the **Air** state.

A specific sound should be played when leaving the **Air** state to give the player the sensation that the wheels hit the pavement while spinning—a combination bump and screech. Then, we enter the state we were in before entering the **Air** state.

- **Damaged:** Vehicles can become damaged in many ways. The simplest way involves colliding with another car or with a stationary object, but some games involve weapons that can inflict damage, or processes that can cause a vehicle to deteriorate. Damage can result in an inability to perform normal tasks, such as steering or braking. It can reduce the top speed or the ability to switch tracks. Many damaged states could be used; in fact, a game could have one damaged state for every other "undamaged" state. For example, a game could have a **cruise** state and a **cruise_damaged** state, an **Air** state and an **Air_damaged** state, and so on. In the **cruise_damaged** state, a vehicle may not be able to reach the prescribed speed but should still behave in the same basic manner as in the **cruise** state.

Being damaged may also restrict the states that the vehicle can change into. For example, once in the **cruise_damaged** state, it may not be possible to move into the **overtake_ai** or **overtake_player** states, or their damaged equivalents. Perhaps a damaged vehicle should not try to pass another vehicle in the race, or at least one that is not also damaged.

From a **damaged** state, a vehicle should change into the equivalent non-damaged state when it is repaired; this would allow us to transition from **cruise_damaged** to **cruise**, for example.

- **Attacking:** In combat driving games, an attack can take a number of forms. A vehicle can simply fire missiles, intentionally collide with another vehicle, or attempt to push another vehicle off of the road. The **attacking** state corresponds to the AI system's effort to damage another vehicle, perhaps another opponent vehicle or the player's vehicle. The difference in behavior between **attacking** and **cruise** can be profound, since the attacking vehicle has a specific goal—destroy an opponent.

The **attacking** state may require that a vehicle actually *chase* another vehicle, be it the player or another opponent vehicle. This is quite a distinct change from the usual **cruise** or **Overtake_AI** state in which the goals are simply to make progress towards the finish line.

Defending: A set of circumstances that determine when an opponent realizes that it is being chased should be carefully defined. This would allow an opponent to adopt a strategy of avoidance, hiding, and perhaps high speed escape. These actions characterize a **defending** state that can be used in games where such conflicts are possible. The goal is obviously to hide from or destroy the attacker, and the previous goal indicated by the previous state is temporarily forgotten.

When the conflict is resolved, the vehicle should return to its previous state. Unfortunately, the chase could result in the vehicle being quite a large distance from where the chase began, moving in the wrong direction from the original goal. It may be best to move from the **defending** state to the **cruise state** and then have the system move between states based on the new local conditions.

Searching: Some games have objects that must be retrieved during the course of the game. In other cases, opponents move about and you must find them. To support these features, we'll need a **searching** state. In some ways, the **searching** state is similar to the **cruise** state, but the goals are a little different. No geographic goal is typically used in the **searching** state, only an objective one—locate something. Thus, the driving behavior results in large areas being covered and a minimum of backtracking or revisiting is required.

It would be reasonable to define searching tracks as a design feature of a game. Like a driving track, these would be defined using waypoints and could incorporate the goals of the search built into the layout of those waypoints. The AI would then have less "thinking" to do. It would only need to follow the waypoints blindly.

Patroling: Patroling behavior is very much like searching; you can think of it as searching for trouble. Consider a police car on watch, driving the city at night. This represents a **patroling** state, where an organized but random route is taken through an area. Of course, it should be random in practice so that bad guys cannot predict where the searching vehicle will be. Whether it is truly random in the game is up to you, the game creator.

The nature of what is being sought is also a bit different from what takes place in the **searching** state. A patrol might seek out a particular person, in which case it may be the same as searching. It may also be that the patrol looks for a complex set of behaviors to indicate that a crime is in progress or some form of enemy activity is taking place. This is harder to identify, and requires some careful definition of the goals in advance. For example, speeding is simple to spot because the AI code always knows how fast all objects are moving. An illegal lane change by the player may be more difficult to spot.

Skidding: When a car tries to turn a corner too quickly, its wheels could slide on the road. The wheels will try to keep moving in their original direction as indicated by Newton's law. We call this a skid, and it may be useful to have a **skidding** state to support this condition. This state is characterized by a lack of control, so steering will work differently than in other states. Turning into the skid may tend to align the axis of the car with the direction of motion, but the car continues in much the same direction as it was going before the skid. Turning away from the direction of the skid will tend to give the car a rotational velocity about its center, again without changing the direction of motion of the car very much. Braking may make the skid worse, but slowing down would permit the wheels to grab the pavement and give control back. It is a complex situation, but anyone who has been in a skid knows one thing—the original driving plan, be it going to the store or getting to work, goes out the window as the priority becomes one of just staying out of the ditch and getting control back.

Stopping: The AI might need to stop a vehicle from time to time. A vehicle might need to pick up passengers or to collect an object. A vehicle shouldn't just stop instantly, and it may be necessary to pull over to the side of the road to avoid being smashed into. This stopping behavior is certainly needed in some games, including the one we are going to discuss and build later.

It is necessary to enter the **stopping** state well ahead of the point where the vehicle wishes to stop. The goal is to stop at a particular place to conduct an activity, and so that place must be identified in advance and the vehicle needs time and space in which to slow down. Again, we'll need rules to dictate how far away to change states given the current velocity and direction.

Recovery—Getting Back on Track

When a vehicle controlled by the AI is knocked off of the driving line it has been assigned to, a game needs to have an intelligent way to recover. A collision could push the vehicle off of the track and into a building or a ditch. How does the AI get the vehicle back on the track? In some sense, the actions performed depend on whether or not someone is watching. If a player can see the vehicle, the vehicle must behave properly. Otherwise, who cares? Just dump the vehicle back on the track with a velocity of zero and let it catch up!

I suggest using this technique in cases where the player can't see an opponent vehicle. We can simply place the vehicle back on the track, plus or minus any damage points or similar penalties, at the point where it went off the track. Better yet, don't allow the vehicle to leave the track at all; simply assess the collision damage and set its velocity to zero. It will remain in the same state, or perhaps the equivalent **damaged** state. Some games have a high-level display, rather like radar, that shows where all of the cars are. On this radar the player will see the opponent vehicle stop, or merge with another and stop, and then proceed again. The next time the vehicle is seen it will show damage. This is sufficient for any driving game I can think of, and takes very little time.

If the player can watch the correction, then the AI system must drive the vehicle so that it looks like a person is doing it. What the AI does depends on the precise situation. Let's enumerate them and show how each situation can be resolved. We'll first look at how we can handle issues that relate to unobstructed paths and then we'll discuss obstructed path issues.

Handling Unobstructed Paths

Figure 6.6 shows the three types of conditions that can occur when a vehicle goes off the track of an unobstructed path. By "unobstructed path," I mean that no other vehicles or buildings will obstruct the path, making the situation more visible to the player. This occurs quite a lot, especially in off-road driving. Let's next look at each of the three conditions in the order of the simplest conditions first:

- Vehicle is facing in the correct direction, near the path

- Vehicle is facing in the wrong direction, near the path

- Vehicle is far from the path

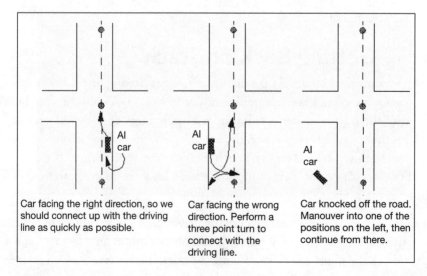

Figure 6.6
Three conditions that can occur when a vehicle goes off the track in an area having an unobstructed path.

Car Facing the Correct Direction

This is the simplest situation to resolve. The only difference between this situation and normal cruising is that the car is not moving. If there is enough room, all we need to do is to simply enter the **cruise** state and let nature take its course. The vehicle should automatically steer towards the driving line and accelerate to the correct speed. If there is not enough space (hard to tell sometimes, but let's say three car lengths), the vehicle can be backed up and then enter the cruise state. The automatic logic will take over and do the right thing.

Car Facing the Wrong Direction

If the vehicle is facing the wrong direction, it must turn completely about in a sensible way. One way to do this is to use a three-point turn. If performed on a road, this maneuver requires the following three steps:

1. Turn sharply left and drive until the vehicle is facing the curb, at an angle perpendicular to the sidewalk.

2. Crank the steering wheel around as far right as possible and back up, stopping when parallel to the street.

3. Move forward, straightening out the wheels until the vehicle is moving along the desired path.

There are a few ways you could program this. First, you could have two new states and associated behaviors: *three_point_1* and *three_point_2*. The *three_point_1* state corresponds with step one above, and results in the initial left turn. The state has a simple behavior: turn left slowly until you hit the curb, at the minimum turning radius. The *three_point_2* state also has a simple behavior; while in this state, the vehicle is moving backwards slowly with the steering wheel right as far as possible until the vehicle is nearly parallel to the street. At this point, we can enter the *start* or *cruise* state and resume the previous activity.

Another way to do this would be to take advantage of how the AI system uses waypoints. It is possible to place waypoints at locations that are relative to the vehicle. The first would be against the far curb so the vehicle would have to turn sharply left. This would be associated with a low velocity. When it was reached, the waypoint would reverse the vehicle's direction so that it would back up to the second temporary waypoint, placed at a location where the vehicle would reach at the end of step 2 above. When the temporary waypoints were reached, they would vanish.

When the second waypoint was encountered, the next one could be the next one on the original path that was being followed before the collision, or we could place a third temporary waypoint between the vehicle and the next permanent one.

The first approach that uses the two new states is easier to implement, I think, but the simple behaviors may have to be modified to suit specific circumstances, such as avoiding traffic or streets that are too narrow or too wide. Still, a good, simple solution is generally better than a complex, mediocre one.

Car Far from the Path

A severe impact can result in a vehicle being knocked quite a distance from its original path, perhaps off the road completely and even over a cliff! In real life, of course, such a collision would probably kill the occupants, rendering the vehicle immobile. In a game, these sorts of collisions occur all the time. You could even have a bad crash and the vehicle could catch on fire or explode. The player would then be under no illusions concerning its status. Having vehicles explode is not an option in many games, such as my favorite game, *Mario Kart*.

Since we are now dealing with the situation where the path is not obstructed, let's assume that no cliffs are involved. One way to get a vehicle back on path would be to place a temporary waypoint at the location where the vehicle was when it collided with an object. AI techniques can then be used to drive it back to where it needs to be. Another possibility, perhaps a more realistic one, would be to find the point on the original travel path closest to the current location of the vehicle, and place a waypoint there. The AI would drive the vehicle there, and then place the vehicle back on the course it was following.

A full AI solution would be to discover a path to the next waypoint on the vehicle's route. There are many such path-finding algorithms, including the famous A* algorithm that can be found in most game texts. A* attempts to find the "best" route according to some heuristic, usually based on the shortest distance. As a result, A* can be more time consuming than we might like, given that a game executes in real time and has a lot to do. What would be acceptable is a less than optimal but still feasible route that takes less time.

If the vehicle is off the road or path but still relatively near it, it might be possible to simply drive to a nearby location on the road. This would place it in one of the previous two situations: either it is facing the correct direction (situation 1 in Figure 6.6) or in the wrong direction (situation 2 in Figure 6.6). In either case, we now have a solution we can use to get back on the path.

One practical idea is to use a predefined grid of directions, indexed by using the vehicle's current position. This grid could be relatively coarse, containing perhaps a few thousand entries, and it should map onto the terrain of the game. Entries in this grid, easily implemented as a two-dimensional array, would be directions, either vectors or simply compass angles. The game designer would have to fill in the values at each location in the grid with the direction to steer to get back to the road or path. This is the usual trade off: to make the machine seem clever, a person has to do a lot of work in advance. (Recall that we had to do this with waypoints.) The other traditional trade-off in computer work is that of space vs. time, which you can see at play here. To speed up the path finding in this situation, a bunch of extra storage space is used (the grid).

If this method is used, the sequence of steps is as follows:

1. Find the grid element that corresponds to the current location of the vehicle. If the playing area is 1000×1000 yards, for example, we could break up this area into 25×25 grid elements, each being 40 yards square. Locating the grid is a matter of dividing the (x,z) coordinates by 40 and truncating.

2. Steer in the direction saved in the grid entry. This could be a byte value to save space, and could be in fairly crude terms, since we simply have to get back to the path, not find the best route.

3. Use a low speed because we're out of the race for the moment anyhow. The only obstacles that are a problem are moving ones, since the grid will be designed to avoid stationary objects. We could store a suggested speed along with the direction, again crudely quantized.

4. Grid elements that are near a path could contain a special value to indicate to the AI that the car should now be allowed to continue in its usual mode.

Figure 6.7 shows such a grid in a simple example. This example actually has obstacles so that it is easy to see how the grid is built. The directions are chosen to steer the car towards the path, not always directly at it, but sometimes around static objects. As the vehicle moves from one grid to another, it adjusts its steering direction to the new grid direction.

Anywhere that the vehicle ends up after a collision will have a grid entry that directs the AI how to control the car.

Obstructed Paths

Obstructions are always a pain. It takes a certain degree of intelligence to escape from some complex obstructed situations. In real life, people often have trouble doing this so getting a computer to simulate this is not easy. However, there must always be some way to escape from a situation that was gotten into, and a game must always have some way out for a vehicle trapped between buildings or trees. Figure 6.8 shows single examples of the three basic obstructed situations that we will discuss.

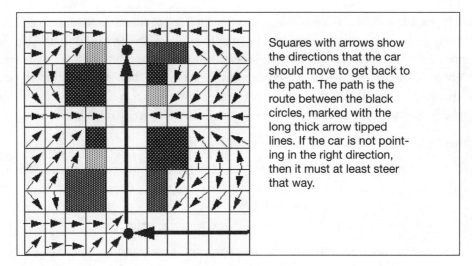

Squares with arrows show the directions that the car should move to get back to the path. The path is the route between the black circles, marked with the long thick arrow tipped lines. If the car is not pointing in the right direction, then it must at least steer that way.

Figure 6.7
Using a directional grid to find a route back to the road.

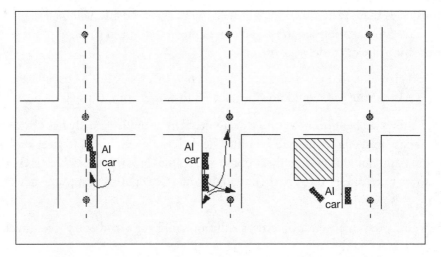

Figure 6.8
Obstructed paths for an AI vehicle after a collision.

Car Facing in the Correct Direction, Near the Path

In this situation, at least one obstacle will be found in front of a vehicle. One obvious solution is to back up until there is room to execute the solution for the unobstructed situation. We can then use the solution we discussed in the previous section. This will actually work in most instances, and can be implemented by associating this situation with a state and corresponding behavior, as can many of these situations.

If the vehicle is blocked in front and behind, the problem becomes more difficult. It is unlikely that both of the obstacles are static, so one possibility is to wait for one of them to move away. This is what I'd do unless poked very hard by the designers.

If poked, we could turn the wheel left hard and move forward as far as possible. Then we would turn the wheel right and back up as far as we can. We would repeat these two maneuvers until the vehicle is free of at least one obstacle. This takes a three-state FSA, and perhaps a certain amount of time. When free, we can use the unobstructed solution from that point on.

Car Facing in the Wrong Direction, Near the Path

Here we could try the same solutions as before: back up until free, wait for an obstacle to move away, or try to wiggle out. When free, we use the three-point turn that we used with the unobstructed solution.

Car Far from the Path

This is the most general case. There is no way to know in advance how far away from the path the vehicle is, nor what might be in between the vehicle and the correct place for it. It would still be possible to use the direction grid to guide the vehicle back to someplace reasonable. Even in off-road situations, this solution can be fast and quite reasonable in appearance. On the other hand, maybe this is the time and place to describe the A* algorithm for path finding. As I mentioned previously, most books covering game programming and AI search algorithms explain A*. I don't want you to feel cheated because I've ignored this topic.

A* Search

The A* algorithm is a method for searching though a set of states for a good path—one that should lead to the solution of a problem. This is a pretty vague statement, but A* can be used to solve a few distinct kinds of AI problems, and so it makes sense to be vague, I guess. In terms of finding a path, a *state* is a situation that has a position identified that is unique and is associated with a positional goal—a target position we are trying to get to. We also need a way to determine a *cost* associated with positions; in terms of paths, a cost may be how long it will take to get to the goal, or how much fuel it will take. The cost of moving from one position to another may well be connected to the terrain. Mud will cost more, and so will steep inclines, whereas paved roads will probably cost the least. The idea behind A* is to create a method for determining which route costs least without exploring all of the possibilities, which could be quite expensive.

It is important to realize that in order to use the A* algorithm, the playing area must be divided up into a grid, like we did when using the directional grid. Each grid element corresponds to a discrete state, and has a value that is related to the start and goal states. Each of these grid elements is called a *node* in A* terminology. Each node has a *cost* associated with it, which is related to how far it is from the goal or how expensive the route is from that point.

There are a couple of obvious things to be aware of before we get too far into the description of the A* method. The first thing is that it is logical to reduce the amount of computation that is done by remembering the cost associated with each node, and not recomputing it. Next we wish to keep a collection of nodes that are candidates for the next one in a path. A good way to do this is to have a set of nodes that are possible next ones. We call this the *open list* or *open set*. We will also have a list of nodes that do not need to be considered, possibly because they have already been examined. This is the *closed set*.

The A* algorithm is important enough in games and AI to spend a few pages on it, and I find that a picture can be very valuable in explaining how things work. Let's walk through an example that illustrates the method. Figure 6.9 shows the grid that gives the situation.

We first need to add the node **S** to the open list because we need to consider it as the 0th step in the path to the goal. The open list should be sorted so that the node with the smallest value of the total cost function (which we will call **F**) is first. The function **F** is a score traditionally composed of the sum of the function **G**, which is how much it costs to get to this node, and **H**, the estimated cost for the remaining nodes between this point and the goal. So **F** = **G**+**H**, but it seems as if **H** is impossible to calculate.

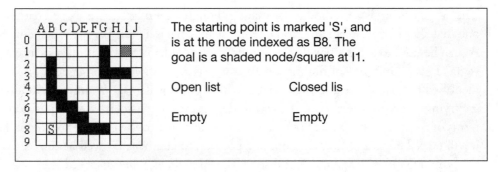

Figure 6.9
Initial situation in our A* example: find a path from B8 to I 11.

G is easy to calculate; each time we move horizontally or vertically to get to a node, we add 1 to the value of **H** for that route. We also add the square root of 2 for diagonal steps if they are allowed. To make the calculations a bit faster, we multiply by 10 and convert to integers, since integer math is much faster than floating point math. Horizontal or vertical steps cost 10 and diagonal steps cost 14.

How do we determine **H**? A common way is to use the *4-distance* or *Manhattan* distance between a particular node and the goal. This is simply the number of rows between the nodes, added to the number of columns between them. After **S** has been added to the open list and **F** is computed, Figure 6.10 shows the result.

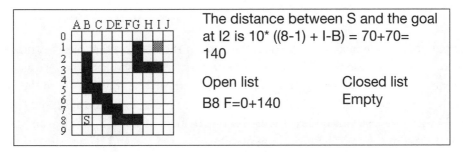

The distance between S and the goal at I2 is 10* ((8-1) + I-B) = 70+70= 140

Open list
B8 F=0+140

Closed list
Empty

Figure 6.10
Initialization for the A* first step. Add the first item to the *open* list.

Next, we take one of the nodes from the *open* list—the one with the smallest **F** value. Right now there's only one node in the *open* list, **S**. Then we add all of the nodes that neighbor **S** to the *open* list and move **S** to the *closed* list. We compute **F** for all of the new *open* list entries.

Remember, left-right and up-down neighbors are a distance of 10 from **S**, and diagonal neighbors are a distance of 14. A sample calculation of **F** for the node at B7 is:

H = distance to goal = 10*(6 + 7) = 130

G = accumulated distance from S = 10

F = **G**+**H** = 130+10 = 140

We do this for all eight neighbors in the *open* list to arrive at the result shown in Figure 6.11.

There's one more thing I need to mention at this stage. Whenever a node is added to the open list, we make a note of how we got there—we used the neighbor of a node that was on the path, and that node is the parent. We always remember the parent of a node because that's how we trace the route back to the start when the method is done.

Open list	Parent	Closed list
B7 F=140	B8	B8=140
B9 F=160	B8	
A8 F=160	B8	
C8 F=140	B8	
C7 F=134	B8	
C9 F=154	B8	
A7 F=154	B8	
A9 F=174	B8	

Figure 6.11
A* after examining all eight neighbors in the *open* list.

All right, let's do the next step. We pick the node in the *open* list that has the smallest value of F—in this case the C7 node—and put it into the closed list. Then we start examining its neighbors. We must ignore squares that can't be traveled on, so the black ones that represent an obstacle are ignored. Also, we ignore nodes in the closed list. Clearly, there are just four nodes that are legal neighbors of C7: C8, B7, B6, and D8. We add these to the *open* list if they are not already there. C8 and B7 are already there, so we don't add them, but we do check to see if the value of F for these nodes is smaller than it was before; that is, is the path that goes through the node C7 better than the one that has been computed already? If so, we change their parent to C7 and their F value to the new one; otherwise, we do nothing. For the new nodes B6 and D8, we add them to the open list and compute F values as shown in Figure 6.12.

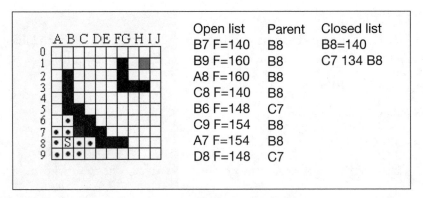

Open list	Parent	Closed list
B7 F=140	B8	B8=140
B9 F=160	B8	C7 134 B8
A8 F=160	B8	
C8 F=140	B8	
B6 F=148	C7	
C9 F=154	B8	
A7 F=154	B8	
D8 F=148	C7	

Figure 6.12
Next step of A*. Expand open and closed lists based on neighbors of current open.

Now we do it again. The node in the *open* list with the smallest **F** is B7. We move it to the *closed* list and place its eligible neighbors into the *open* list. There are only two nodes of interest here: node A6 and B6. Node A6 is new, and is added to the *open* list. Node at B6 is already in the *open* list, but the exciting thing about it is that the value of **F** computed through the new parent is smaller than the old one. Therefore, we change parents to B7 and adjust its **F** value to the new one, which is 140. The new situation is shown in Figure 6.13.

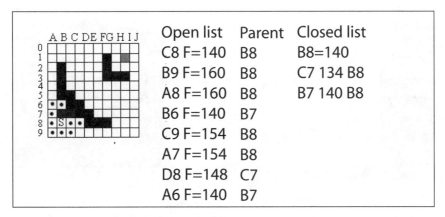

Open list	Parent	Closed list
C8 F=140	B8	B8=140
B9 F=160	B8	C7 134 B8
A8 F=160	B8	B7 140 B8
B6 F=140	B7	
C9 F=154	B8	
A7 F=154	B8	
D8 F=148	C7	
A6 F=140	B7	

Figure 6.13
And again: recomputed open and closed lists, repeat until I1 is in the open list.

And so we continue, pulling out the *open* node with the smallest **F**, putting into the *closed* list, and putting its neighbors into the *open* list.

We stop when the *open* list is empty. This means that the goal cannot be reached. The other termination condition occurs when we add the goal node to the *open* list. We trace the path of parents back from the goal node to read off the sequence of nodes in the "optimal" route.

The algorithm, in summary, is:

1. Create **start** and **goal** nodes.

2. Place the **start** node into the *open* list.

3. Repeat while there are nodes in the *open* list.

4. Select the node **P** from the *open* list with smallest **F** value.

5. If **P=goal** then we quit with the solution.

6. For each neighbor N_i of **P**

7. If N_i is unusable or in the closed list then continue from step 6.

8. Let the cost of N_i = $H(N_i)$+ distance to **P**.

9. If N_i is not in the open list then add it

10. else if N_i is on the open list and the path has a lower **F**

11. then change **F** to the new value, change the parent of N_i to **P**.

12. end of FOR loop

13. end of repeat

14. If the open list is empty, there is no path to the goal.

Did you forget what we were doing? Now we have a path from the AI vehicle that was knocked far off of its path by a collision to a waypoint that is on the original path the vehicle was following. In other words, we have a way to get back to the "normal" situation after being knocked off the path.

The Robot Auto Racing Simulator (RARS)

Before finishing this chapter, you should be aware that there is a way to use the Internet to test strategies for driving and racing. The Robot Auto Racing Simulator site found at **http://rars.sourceforge.net/** is an environment in which you write a program that controls a race car. There is a graphic display of the track and your AI program will compete with other programs submitted by other programmers, some of which are very interested in automated driving of actual vehicles.

The website contains a complete listing of race results since 1995, descriptions of control algorithms, a downloadable environment for developing code, and a host of other interesting items. I'm not certain how many game developers use this as a testbed, but I surely would. Even though the code does not port to a game platform, the algorithms certainly will, and competing against the best is always a good way to refine the methods. It's fun, too.

Summary

We have examined the basic technique for implementing artificial intelligence in a driving game: the finite state machine. In that context, we also discussed the use of waypoints as basic navigation tools. We have specifically described quite a variety of states, meaning situations that a vehicle might find itself in, and also how to detect them. We have also looked at a simple path-finding method called the A* algorithm. All of these techniques are used to implement intelligent opponents, which are an essential part of any driving game.

Chapter 7

Audio for Driving and Racing Games

- Learn how sounds are stored as digital files.

- Learn the basics of using OpenAL for loading and playing sound files.

- Use OpenAL to write programs that can stop, pause, and play sounds continuously.

When I first prepared for and taught a course on game programming, I had a huge amount of help from a professional game developer, Radical Entertainment. I had a lot of programming experience, and I had taught computer graphics and vision, data structures, algorithms, and operating systems. My experience with playing and developing video games was limited, however. One of the eye-opening (or ear-opening, I suppose) demonstrations that Radical performed for my class was to play a popular first-person shooter with the sound on. They then played the game with the sound off. We were all amazed by how much energy and emotional content was contained in the audio portion of the game. Before you read any more of this chapter, I suggest you play one of your favorite games with the sound off as an experiment. I think you'll then be convinced that sound is just as important as graphics.

Computer games use sound for three basic areas:

- Music: Much emotional content is contained in the music alone. Alfred Hitchcock knew this very well.

- Sound effects: If a car crashes or a gun fires, we expect to hear the sounds associated with these activities.

- Speech: Many games tell a story by allowing the player to listen in on conversations, or even participate. The player's communications are often typed in, but the characters in a game can speak and they expect to be heard.

I find it interesting that many programmers, even those having many years of experience with graphics and event-based programming, know very little about how to manipulate and play sounds on a computer. In many ways, sound programming is like graphics programming: object positions and rendering are used, the listener's (viewer's) position affects the result, frequencies (colors) must be handled, and a special device sits at the heart of everything (sound card/video card).

In this chapter, we'll begin our trek into the unknown world of computer audio. As with graphics, we'll need to use some math, but unlike graphics, most of the math is not necessary for simple reproduction of sound using a computer. Most games merely read sounds from files and play them at appropriate moments. Games would be very dull if graphics were used in the same way. Graphical objects need to be moved, rotated, transformed, and tested for visibility and collisions. Audio objects basically get turned on and off, become louder or softer, and perhaps move from the left to the right stereo channel. Playing sounds is actually simpler than displaying graphics.

At the beginning of this book, I explained why I selected OpenGL instead of DirectX to create our games. It would not be appropriate now to use DirectX for audio, which, by the way, does handle audio very well. Because we still want to keep a logical distance from the actual audio device, we'll need some software that can work with multiple platforms, handle the sound card, and provide us with a relatively simple interface that gives us high-level control. The OpenAL platform seems to fit the bill, and I'll present this software in detail so that it can be used in the final game we develop.

Basic Audio Concepts

Although there are similarities between how we see objects and how we hear sounds, the differences are significant. The most important concept is that objects that are seen normally reflect light from another source, rather than generating light on their own. We see by reflected light. Audio, on the other hand, is usually produced by an object that is being sensed; that is, an object that we hear is generating the sound, not reflecting it.

Of course, sound reflections are important, and contribute to the ambiance of the sounds we hear. The idea that sound sources are detected is key to audio generation. In graphics, the equivalent would be if we could only observe light sources. Things would be much simpler. Also, we don't really have an audio image—a two-dimensional pattern that can be interpreted. Instead, we have two sound receptors (ears), each of which perceives the sum of the sounds that reach them at any particular moment. This can also be thought of as another way that audio is simpler than graphics.

Sounds are essentially vibrations of the air. The intensity of the vibrations is called the *volume* or *loudness* of the sound. The duration between two consecutive peaks of the vibratory motion is called the *period*, and the number of peaks that occur in a second is called the *frequency* or *pitch* (see Figure 7.1).

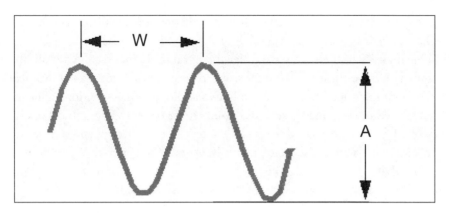

Figure 7.1
Representing a sound wave.

A sound wave is viewed as a graph of intensity vs. time. The wavelength W is the distance between two peaks; the period is the time between two peaks. The amplitudes are the distance from the peaks and troughs. The frequency is the number of peaks that pass by a stationary point in one second.

The unit of frequency is measured in Hertz (shortened as Hz), which was named after a person. This name may sound familiar to you because your computer has an execution speed that is also measured in Hertz—megaHertz (MHz equals million cycles) or gigaHertz (GHz equals billion cycles). This refers to the number of clock cycles per second.

A typical human can hear sounds that have frequencies between 40 Hz and 15000 Hz (1000 Hz equals1 kiloHertz or KHz). Some people can hear 20 KHz sounds and even higher, but as we get older, our ability to hear high-pitched sounds declines. I know this from first-hand experience! In any case, frequencies above 15 KHz are not as important as the lower frequencies in computer games because computer speakers are generally not able to reproduce these sounds. The real issue is that many people cannot hear these high-pitched sounds.

We have two ears, and normally any sound will present itself to both of them. A slight time difference will likely occur between the arrival at the left and right ears, caused by the distance you are from an object and the distance between your ears. It takes a certain amount of time for a sound to travel the short distance represented by the width of your skull. This is how you locate a sound. Most people can determine a fairly precise location for a sound even when they have their eyes closed, but only if both of their ears function properly. This fact is important in a game because an object that looks like it is at the left side of the screen should also sound like it is coming from the left.

In day-to-day life, we are surrounded by sounds, and we can actually detect many of them. What we hear is really the sum of all of the sounds that reach us at each moment in time. This makes audio rendering simpler than graphics rendering. After all, the screen requires that we compute the intensity and/or color of at least 640×480 pixels (places). For audio, we need to compute only two audio "pixels"—one for each ear. However, we need to compute these audio points more often than graphical ones. A frequency of 24 frames per second is usually enough to realistically represent moving objects on a screen. To render audio realistically, we need to generate a new intensity value at a rate that is at least twice the frequency being created, or up to 30,000 times per second! Fortunately, a sound card can do a lot of this work for us.

To store a sound on a computer, the sound must first be digitized, or *sampled*. A standard sound card can do this if you plug a microphone or other sound source into it. Sound is represented as electrical signals, which can actually look like the sound wave shown in Figure 7.1 when viewed on an oscilloscope. Sampling a signal involves making measurements at regular and frequent intervals. An electrical signal can be measured as voltages. To store a sound, we could measure the voltage being sent to the speakers every millisecond and store this measurement as a binary number. Playing the sound back requires us to convert binary numbers into voltages again, and send them to an output device.

I don't want to get into too much detail here because signal processing is a whole subject unto itself. What you actually need to know is that sampling a sound requires you to use a rate that is at least twice the highest frequency that you want to reproduce. For example, if you want to be able to hear 15KHz sounds, you have to sample the signal 30,000 times per second. If a sample is an integer (16 bits), this means that a four-minute song would require 28 Mbytes (4 * 60 * 30,000*4 bytes) to be stored. Storage space of 56 MBytes would be needed if the song is to be played in stereo. Of course, compression schemes can be used to reduce the size of sounds saved on disk. In any case, samples need to be stored as numbers, either integers or floats, and they need to be sent to a sound card.

This is where OpenAL comes in. We can create reasonable sounds for a typical game without needing to know too much about the math or physics of sound. We also won't need to know too much about the sound card we use. We do need to understand, however, the basic techniques required to use the OpenAL system.

Introducing OpenAL

Unlike OpenGL, the OpenAL library is not yet a standard that is distributed on Windows and Macintosh computers. You will probably have to download OpenAL from the Internet. The website for this book provides links to OpenAL distribution sites. The standard site belonging to Creative Labs, builders of the *Sound Blaster*, is (**http://developer.creative.com/**).

To use OpenAL, you'll need to make sure your compiler is set up so that it knows where to find the OpenAL libraries and include files. I will again provide the instructions for the Visual C++ compiler from Microsoft, but any compiler can be used. The essential operations include copying include files into the include directory, copying the .lib and .bin files into the library directory, and copying the .dll files into the system directory. To tell the compiler to load the libraries, you should follow these steps:

1. Download the OpenAL installation program. Mine was named **OpenALSDK.exe**, but this could vary.

2. Run the installation program. When complete, OpenAL software will be placed in a directory named C:\Program Files\OpenAL 1.0 Software Development Kit.

3. The include files will reside in the Include subdirectory of the directory named above. Copy these into the Visual Studio include directory *C:\Program Files\Microsoft Visual Studio\VC98\Include*.

4. The executable library files **ALut.lib** and **OpenAL32.lib** must be linked into the runtime version of your program. In Visual Studio, you do this by choosing *project->settings->link* window, and adding these libraries to the *Project Options* text box. The lib files must be copied into the compiler's lib folder, which is located at *C:\Program Files\Microsoft Visual Studio\VC98\Lib*.

5. **OpenAL32.dll** must also be made available at runtime; it must reside in the directory *C:\WINDOWS\system32*.

> **NOTE:** *These are the compiler settings needed to be able to compile programs that use OpenAl.*

OpenAL is fairly easy to understand, provided that you buy into their view of the world (the *paradigm*, we academics call it). OpenAL causes you to think in terms of three object types: sound *sources*, which make noise and have a position and velocity; the *listener*, who also has a position and velocity; and *buffers*, which are places to store the sound itself and associated parameters. OpenAL offers facilities to create these objects and to change their properties and manipulate their parameters.

The basic plan for any OpenAL program involves:

1. Performing all of the required initializations.

2. Creating sound sources and specifying their positions and velocities. This involves connecting to buffers.

3. Defining the listener, and specifying position and velocity.

4. Playing the sounds.

As a simple example, let's create a program that plays a sound that is read in from a .WAV file.

Playing a Sound File

A single sound file will have one source. Naturally, a single listener is required as well as one buffer for the single source. We'll build the smallest possible functional OpenAL program to keep things simple. The program will play a .WAV file named musique.wav each time the program is executed. Of course, you will be able to play any file you like simply by renaming the file to musique.wav or changing the name of the file in the program.

The creators of OpenAL have given us three categories of objects for implementing any audio display scheme. By object, I don't mean a C++ object, but a more generic object definition—an entity or item. The three categories are **buffers**, **sources**, and **listeners**. Each type of object has a number of attributes that can be used to characterize specific instances, such as position and orientation. Objects can be created dynamically (except for a listener object) and their attributes can be changed dynamically. In addition to these objects, OpenAL provides facilities for manipulating and displaying sampled audio.

Except for the listener, of which there is only one, all objects have a unique name that is defined when the object is created. The name is used to reference the object. These names are, in fact, unsigned integers. They are used to reference objects in all cases, and while I might have used pointers or handles, the advantage of using an integer is that the consequences of following a bad pointer are thus avoided. A bad name given to an OpenAL function simply causes an error code to be returned. Here's an example of a request to OpenAL that uses a name:

```
boolean IsBuffer ( uint buffer_name);
```

This function returns **true** if the parameter specifies a legitimate buffer name, as allocated by OpenAL. It returns **false** otherwise. Similarly, the function

```
boolean IsSource ( uint source_name );
```

returns **true** if the name passed represents a valid *source* object.

Attributes for an object can be retrieved by calling a function having the form:

```
void alGet[objecttype][parametertype] (enum Parameter, type *values);
```

These are essentially equivalent to C++ or Java accessor methods, but the syntax is a difficult syntax to explain. The *objecttype* here refers to a *buffer*, *listener*, or *source*. The *parametertype* is a letter code that refers to the type of parameter to be returned, and must agree with the **type** specified above. The *Parameter* represents a discrete enumerated type that really amounts to a list of the attributes that are possible. In other words, there are constant values supplied by the OpenAL include files for each attribute you may want to retrieve, and these are passed as the first parameter to specify what we want.

Let's look at a few examples so that this doesn't sound so abstract to you. If we need to know the current position of the listener object, here's the function call we could use:

```
alGetListenerfv (ALenum POSITION, ALfloat *position_vector);
```

In this case, the *objecttype* is a *listener*, the parameter type is a floating point vector, coded as **fv** and represented by the C type **float ***, and the *Parameter* being requested is the position in three dimensions of the listener, represented by a constant named **POSITION**. To get the **POSITION** associated with a source object, the call would be:

```
alGetSourcefv (ALuint source, ALenum POSITION, ALfloat *position_vector);
```

The first parameter in this case is the name of the *source* component that is being queried. Since there is only one *listener*, no name is needed for the listener functions. A complete description of all types and attributes can be found in the "OpenAL Programmer's Reference." Changing the value of an attribute can be accomplished using a similar collection of modifier-like functions. The naming convention is very much the same except that the modifier functions do not have "Get" as a prefix in the name. Thus, to set the position of the listener you would call:

```
alListenerfv (ALenum POSITION, ALfloat *position_vector);
```

Similarly, to set the position of a source you would call:

```
alSourcefv (ALuint source, ALenum POSITION, ALfloat *position_vector);
```

Figure 7.2 presents a visual diagram of how the OpenAL objects interact with each other. My previous discussion might seem a little confusing because of all of the details involved, so this illustration should help you follow along. Here we have a schematic representation of one possible configuration: one listener (as always), two buffers, and three sources. Each of the sources sends a sound to the listener, which represents the game player. Two of the sources use the same buffer (sources 1 and 3 use buffer 1), while buffer 2 and source 2 are connected to each other. The sources could represent any number of things that make sounds, such as musical instruments, engines, weapons, people speaking, and so on.

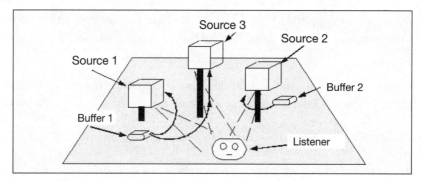

Figure 7.2
One possible arrangement of OpenAL sources, buffers, and a listener.

Now that you've been introduced to the basics, let's look at each type of OpenAL object in more detail.

The Buffer

Like buffers in other applications, an OpenAL buffer represents the space for saving data, in this case, audio data. Before a sound can be played, it must be loaded into a buffer, which is allocated using OpenAL functions. Although a buffer holds the actual sound, the sound can't be played. A buffer is not an active component in that sense, but is a structured representation for audio data that will be used by a source. As such, there are some aspects of the data in the buffer that must reside with it:

- Frequency: This is the sample rate. A typical rate would be 22050 Hz. We need to know this so that the correct number of samples can be sent to the audio device each second. If, for example, you sample sound at 8000 Hz and play it back at 16000 Hz, it will sound squeaky and high pitched, and will play twice as fast as it should.

- Number of bits: **This** is the resolution of any single sample. An 8 bit-sample allows 256 distinct values, which is relatively low resolution. A more typical resolution would be 16 bit.

- Number of **channels:** Typically, only one channel is used (what you might call monophonic, or mono). For stereo, two are needed. One channel sound allows many of the positioning features of OpenAL to be accessed. You cannot change the apparent position in 3D space of a sound that has more than one channel.

- Buffer size: This dictates the amount of physical storage (in bytes) allocated to the buffer, and also dictates how much sound will be stored in a particular buffer.

Allocation of a buffer is accomplished by calling

```
void alGenBuffers(ALsizei n,ALuint *buffers);
```

where the parameter **n** indicates the number of buffers to allocate, and the **buffers** pointer receives the address of the *names* of these buffers. This means that multiple buffers, for multiple sources, can be allocated at the same time. Note that the **buffers** parameter does not point to the buffers themselves, in accordance with the OpenAL philosophy of acting as a server for attributes and objects. A buffer is de-allocated using this function:

```
ALvoid alDeleteBuffers(ALsizei n,ALuint *buffers);
```

It should be called when you don't need the buffer anymore.

Other functions and attributes of buffer objects can be found in the programmer's guide, and in the examples that appear in this chapter. Because buffers are associated with source objects, we should look at them next.

The Source

Any OpenAL program can deal with multiple *sources*, which are analogous to objects in OpenGL. Each source has a position and velocity in 3D space, and has a sound that it is transmitting into space. I suppose it is like a speaker. The sounds from each source can be different, and are often read from .WAV files or some other type of audio file.

A source must be associated with a buffer, which is really just some space for storing the audio samples. OpenAL manages its own buffer space, although you must request it and associate specific buffers with specific sources, one buffer per source (possibly multiple sources per buffer, though). We will first create a framework for creating and manipulating sources in general.

Each source can be associated with a structure that holds the important data associated with it: the buffer code, the position and velocity of the source, and any other information that we wish. Understand that this is not OpenAL organization, but my own way of collecting OpenAL data into logical constructs:

```
/* My structures for organizing sounds */
struct SourceStruct
{
    ALuint source;
    ALuint buffer;
    ALfloat position[3];        /* Source position */
    ALfloat velocity[3];        /* Source velocity */
                . . .
};
typedef struct SourceStruct * A_SOURCE;
A_SOURCE      src;
```

The fields named **source** and **buffer** represent the specific source and the buffer assigned to it. They are in fact simply the names (integers) associated with the objects and are used to access them. We also need a function, such as a C++ constructor, that allocates and initializes a source. Since we will typically use files as the source of our audio data, I suggest that the initializer be passed the file name of the WAV file holding the sound. I will write this function in parts, and annotate each part. Here's the first part:

```
A_SOURCE new_source (char *wavFileName)
{
    A_SOURCE x;
    ALenum format;
    ALsizei size;
    ALvoid* data;
    ALsizei freq;
    ALboolean loop;
```

The types used here are essentially OpenAL standard types that can take the place of C++ types varying in size from implementation to implementation. First, we allocate a structure for the source:

```
x = (A_SOURCE)malloc (sizeof(struct SourceStruct));
```

If this succeeds, we try to create a buffer for this source:

```
if (x != NULL)
{   /* Allocate 1 buffer */
    alGenBuffers(1, &(x->buffer));
    if (alGetError() != AL_NO_ERROR)
    {
        free(x);
        return NULL;
    }
}
```

Our first special-purpose OpenAL function is **alGenBuffers()**, which allocates a buffer with a given name, in this case "1." We have saved a reference (pointer) to this buffer in our **A_SOURCE** structure named **x**.

Next, we use OpenAL to read a WAV file and extract some useful information:

```
alutLoadWAVFile (wavFileName, &data, &format, &size, &freq, &loop);
```

This function is part of the ALUT library—the audio equivalent of GLUT in OpenGL. Its job is to read and parse the header in a WAV file, among other things, and return some of the useful information. This function gives us the parameters that are needed by the buffer so that we can play the sound stored in the file. The returned parameters are:

wavFileName	The name of the sound file
format	An integer that tells us how the data is structured. The possibilities are **AL_FORMAT_MONO8**, **AL_FORMAT_MONO16**, **AL_FORMAT_STEREO8** and **AL_FORMAT_STEREO16**, with obvious meanings.
data	A pointer to an actual array of sampled audio data.
size	Number of data points in the array of data.
freq	Sample rate.
loop	Looping indicator (true/false)

The file has been read into variables and a data array. The data can now be copied into an OpenAL *buffer* so that it can be used (played):

```
al BufferData(x->buffer, format, data, size, freq);
```

Here all parameters that have the same name as the ones in the **alutLoadWAVFile()** call have the same meaning as well, and the first parameter is the name of the *buffer* to be filled.

At this point, the audio data has been read from the file, and the buffer is allocated and filled. Now we need a source object to be used to play the sound:

```
alGenSources(1, &(x->source));
```

The first parameter is the number of source objects to create, and the second is an array of names of source objects allocated. We just want one.

The way that OpenAL handles errors is to set a variable that it keeps to itself. If you want to know whether or not an error has occurred, you must ask. The function **alGetError()** will return the code for the last error that occurred, and if everything is okay, it returns **AL_NO_ERROR**. For the above *source* creation, the error checking code is:

```
if (alGetError() != AL_NO_ERROR)
{
    alDeleteBuffers(1, &(x->buffer));
    free(x);
    return AL_FALSE;
}
```

If we allocated a *buffer* for this *source*, and there was an error in allocating the *source*, the *buffer* should be freed up. This is done by the call to **alDeleteBuffers()**.If no error occurs, we can do the final step, which is to connect the newly full *buffer* to the newly allocated *source*:

```
alSourcei (x->source, AL_BUFFER, x->buffer);
{
    return x;
}
```

At this point, we have a full *buffer* and a *source* that has a position in 3D game space at which the sound will originate—a sound that was read from a file that we requested. All we need to do now is set up the position of the listener.

The Listener

A listener represents the user. Its properties describe the location and orientation in space where we are hearing the sounds produced by the sources. A listener is not created or allocated; one always exists. We simply define its characteristics. A listener structure could be:

```
struct ListenerStruct
{
   ALfloat position[3];      /* Listener position */
   ALfloat velocity[3];      /* Listener velocity */
   ALfloat orientation[6];
};
typedef struct ListenerStruct * THE_LISTENER;
```

This gives us a basic data organization for a listener. There is just one, so we can declare it as shown here:

```
THE_LISTENER me;
```

Next, we'll need an initialization function for the listener to set the position, velocity, orientation, and so on, in whatever fashion we choose: read from a file (or from the console), or just pick values we think are good:

```
THE_LISTENER new_listener ()
{
   THE_LISTENER x;

   x = (THE_LISTENER)malloc (sizeof(struct ListenerStruct));
   if (x != NULL)
   {
      alListenerfv(AL_POSITION,    ListenerPos);
      alListenerfv(AL_VELOCITY,    ListenerVel);
      alListenerfv(AL_ORIENTATION, ListenerOri);
   }
   return x;
}
```

This function returns a pointer to a new structure representing the listener, initializes the parameters, and establishes those values with the system. The OpenAL function **alListenerfv(AL_POSITION, ListenerPos)** that I described previously sets the position attribute of the listener.

We could also provide the equivalent of accessor and modifiers for the basic parameters of a *listener*. This is especially useful if the position and other parameters are to be modified frequently. An example might be if the point of view used is the driver of a moving vehicle.

Remember that our task is to read a .WAV file and play that sound on the PC. The only thing we have left to do is make the actual call to the function that plays the sound. We have encapsulated the OpenAL functions so that we can write a simple function to load the file by name and return either **true** or **false** as the file is loaded or not.

```
ALboolean LoadALData()
{
    src = new_source("musique.wav");
    if (src == NULL)
    {
        printf ("No source allocated.\n\n");
        return AL_FALSE;
    }
    return AL_TRUE;
}
```

OpenAL may have to terminate because of an error. We are asked to provide OpenAL with a function to call to do clean-up if this happens. Ours simply deletes the allocated *buffer* and *source*:

```
void KillALData()
{
    alDeleteBuffers(1, &(src->buffer));
    alDeleteSources(1, &(src->source));
    alutExit();
}
```

The main program does two things that are new. First, we must call a special initialization function before doing anything with OpenAL. This function is called **alutInit()**. It is used in an obvious way in the code presented next. The new thing is the actual call that plays the sound: alSourcePlay. This is called by passing the source of the sound to be played as a parameter. Since the *source* has been given a full buffer, it has everything it needs to play the sound:

```
int main(int argc, char *argv[])
{
    char c;

    alutInit(&argc, argv);
    alGetError();
    if (LoadALData() == AL_FALSE)  /* Load the wav data.  */
        return -1;
```

```
        me = new_listener ();
        atexit(KillALData);    /* Setup an exit procedure */

        alSourcePlay(src->source);
        scanf ("%c", &c);
        return 0;
    }
```

All that remains are the declarations for the include files and the initialized arrays with positions and orientations for the *source* and *listener*.

```
#include <stdlib.h>
#include <stdio.h>
#include <al/al.h>
#include <al/alc.h>
#include <al/alu.h>
#include <al/alut.h>
```

The project for this program resides in the **source/chapter7/openal1** directory on the website for this book.

Changing Attributes

Now that you are familiar with the basics of using OpenAL to load and play sound files, let's look at how we can do a little more by working with attributes. In particular, we write some programs to stop, pause, and play sounds continuously.

Stopping, Pausing, and Looping

The ability to stop a sound is very important, especially if the sound is a looping one, such as an engine sound. Fortunately, stopping a sound is fairly easy to do with OpenAL. Two special functions are provided—**alSourceStop()** and **alSourcePause()**. Here's the first one:

```
ALvoid alSourceStop (ALuint source);
```

This function will cause the sound being played by the given source to stop playing, and when the sound is played again (using **alSourcePlay()**) the sound will start playing from the beginning. The second function also stops a sound from playing:

```
ALvoid alSourcePause (ALuint source);
```

When the sound resumes playing, the sound will start from where it left off.

These two functions are not really needed because what they do is change the value of the **SOURCE_STATE** variable. A sound that is playing has the state **AL_PLAYING**, a sound that is stopped has the state **AL_STOPPED**, and one that is paused has the state **AL_PAUSED**. We can actually stop or pause a sound by setting the state variable associated with its source. Here's a few examples:

```
alSourcei (source, AL_SOURCE_STATE, AL_STOPPED);
alSourcei (source, AL_SOURCE_STATE, AL_PAUSED);
```

If a sound needs to be repeated, such as some music and sound textures, including engine noise, we can provide OpenAL an instruction to do this. The fact that the *loop* flag was set in the original WAV file is not necessarily transmitted automatically to the source object when it is played. We can again use **alSourcei()** to do this as follows:

```
alSourcei (source, AL_LOOPING, AL_TRUE);
```

Now the sound will be played over and over without pause. If the end of the sound is similar to the beginning of the sound, you'll get the impression that the sound is a continuous one.

The program shown next has been modified to show how a sound can be stopped, paused, and played in a continuous loop. The engine.wav sound is loaded, and then it is set to loop. Then, as it plays, you may type a number. If the number is odd, the sound will pause; if the number is even, the sound will resume. A negative number will terminate the loop, and the program will end:

```
Int main(int argc, char *argv[])
{
    int i = 0;

    alutInit(&argc, argv);
    alGetError();
    if (LoadALData() == AL_FALSE) return -1;
    me = new_listener ();
    atexit(KillALData); /* Setup exit */
    alSourcei (src->source, AL_LOOPING, AL_TRUE);
    alSourcePlay(src->source);
    i = 1;
    do
    {
        scanf ("%d", &i);
        if (i%2) alSourcePause (src->source);
        /* if (i%2)
```

```
        alSourceStop (src->source); */
        else alSourcePlay(src->source);
    } while (i > 0);
    return 0;
}
```

See the web page **chapter7/StopAndPause** for source code and workspace files.

Changing the Source Position

OpenAL allows you to specify a position and velocity for audio sources and listeners. When using audio in a game, the velocity is probably not relevant because we need to keep track of the position and velocity of all of our objects anyhow. If you have an audio system attached to your computer that can take advantage of three-dimensional audio, OpenAL's ability to specify position can lead to accurate positioning objects in the audio field. If not, at least the position data can be automatically used by OpenAL to attenuate the volume as a function of distance. This saves us from having to do this ourselves.

The attribute that we need to alter is the **AL_POSITION** attribute of the source or listener object. A position is three floating point numbers: the x, y, and z coordinates of the object. OpenAL offers us two ways to get and change these values. First, if we are saving them in an array (as in the **position** field of the **sourcestruct** structure), we can get the position vector by calling this function:

```
ALvoid alGetSourcefv(ALuint source,ALenum pname,
                ALfloat *values);
```

Here **values** is the position vector and **pname** is the constant **AL_POSITION**. If we have three variables **x, y,** and **z,** we could call this function:

```
ALvoid alGetSource3f (ALuint source,ALenum pname,
                ALfloat *x, ALfloat *y, ALfloat *z);
```

The website for this book provides sample code for this. You can download this code and experiment with changing position parameters. The program has two parts: one that allows you to specify the Y coordinate of the source as it is playing, and one that moves the source across the field from left to right.

The first part is implemented by the following code snippet in the main program:

```
SPos[0] = SPos[1] = SPos[2] = 0.0F;
alSourcefv(src->source, AL_POSITION, SPos);
do
{
```

```
        printf ("Enter Y position:(float)    ");
        scanf ("%f", &x);
        SPos[1] = x;
        alSourcefv(src->source, AL_POSITION,    SPos);
        alSourcePlay(src->source);

} while (x < 1000.0);
```

This occurs after the initializations are made to create the source and listener objects. It is interesting to type a number between -12 and 12 to see how the sound position seems to change. The sound is a car engine, by the way.

If you type a number 1000 or higher this part of the program ends and the next starts. Here, the virtual car starts at position (0, -12, 0) and drives past you to position (0, 12, 0). You can hear the sound get louder, pass you by, and disappear to the right. This is done using a cheesy timing loop, and changing the position by a small amount (0.1) every cheesy interval:

```
SPos[0] = SPos[2] = 0.0F;  SPos[1] = -12.0; x = -12.0;
alSourcefv(src->source, AL_POSITION,    SPos);
alSourcePlay(src->source);
do
{
    SPos[1] = x; x += 0.1;                  /* Change position by 0.1 */
    for (i=0; i<10000; i++)                 /* Cheesy timing loop */
    {
        z = 100.0+i;                        /* Do a bunch of */
        z1 = z*z1/(z/2.0);                  /* floating point */
        z1++;                               /* Computations. Takes time! */
    }
    alSourcefv(src->source, AL_POSITION, SPos);
    printf ("%f ...\n", x);
} while (x < 12.0);
```

The loop prints out the Y position in the console window each iteration. Keep in mind that this sample program works fine on my 2.3 Ghz PC, but may be faster or slower on your machine. There's a better way to do this using timers, as seen in the source code for *Gopher-it*.

Changing Pitch—Engine Noise

It turns out that one of the attributes of a sound being played is pitch. This happens to be useful for us, because the pitch of an engine increases as the speed (RPMs) increases. The standard sound is played with a pitch value, an attribute having the name

AL_PITCH, of 1.0. As the player goes faster (presses on the virtual gas pedal), we want the sound to rise in pitch accordingly. This turns out to be easy to do in OpenAL!

Setting the pitch value is done using this function:

```
ALvoid alSourcef(ALuint source,ALenum pname,ALfloat value);
```

An actual call to this function to produce our engine noise sound would look like:

```
alSourcef (src->source, AL_PITCH, pitch);
```

Here the floating point variable **pitch** has a value between 0 and 2. Values less than 1 pitch the sound lower. It might be possible to use a single engine sound and pitch it as a function of the estimated engine RPM, mapping idle speeds (about 500 RPM) to red line speeds (6000 RPM). It seems unlikely, though, since this range is a factor of 12 times the low value ($5 \times 12 = 60$), and not 2 times as the function allows.

We need another way to do this. One technique is to use multiple files. Let's assume that the engine2.wav file is pitched at twice that of the engine.wav file, and that source **src1** is used to play engine.wav, and a new source **src2** is used to play engine2.wav. For pitch values ranging from 1 to 2, we simply set the pitch variable on **src1** playback in the obvious way. For pitches between 2 through 4, we use **src2** in the following manner:

1. Compute **pitch2 = 2.0-(4.0-pitch)/2**. This is the pitch parameter for **src2**. It should be pitched at double the pitch of **src1**.

2. If **pitch** is between 0 and 2, adjust the pitch parameter of **src1** to **pitch**. Then, if **src1** is not playing, pause **src2** and play **src1**.

3. If **pitch** is between 2 and 4, adjust the pitch parameter in **src2** to **pitch2**. Then, if **src2** is not playing, pause **src1** and start playing **src2**.

This gives us a greater range of pitch than we had previously, and it may well be enough to stretch to the range 500 to 6000 RPM. If not, we can use three or four WAV files. In fact, the engine2.wav file was created from the engine.wav file using a computer program that changes the frequencies of sampled audio in arbitrary ways. The web page directory **chapter7/4frequencyChange** holds the Visual Studio workspace, and here's the main program, which does much of the work:

```
int main(int argc, char *argv[])
{
        int i = 0;
        float pitch = 1.0, pitch2 = 1.0;
        A_SOURCE src1, src2;
```

```
alutInit(&argc, argv);
alGetError();
if (LoadALData( "engine.wav", &src1) == AL_FALSE) return -1;
if (LoadALData("engine2.wav", &src2) == AL_FALSE) return -1;
me = new_listener ();
alSourcei (src1->source, AL_LOOPING, AL_TRUE);
alSourcePlay(src1->source);
alSourcei (src2->source, AL_LOOPING, AL_TRUE);
do
{
        i = scanf ("%f", &pitch);
        if (i < 1) break;
        if (pitch < 0) break;
        if (pitch <= 2)
        {
                alGetSourcei (src1->source,
                AL_SOURCE_STATE, &i);
                if (i == AL_PLAYING)
                        alSourcef (src1->source, AL_PITCH, pitch);
                else
                {
                        alSourcef (src1->source, AL_PITCH, pitch);
                        alSourcePause (src2->source);
                        alSourcePlay (src1->source);
                }
            } else if (pitch <= 4.0) {
                pitch2 = 2.0-(4.0-pitch)/2;
                alGetSourcei (src2->source,
                AL_SOURCE_STATE, &i);
                if (i == AL_PLAYING)
                        alSourcef (src2->source, AL_PITCH, pitch2);
                else
                {
                        alSourcef (src2->source, AL_PITCH, pitch2);
                        alSourcePause (src1->source);
                        alSourcePlay (src2->source);
                }
        }
        printf ("Pitch is now %f\n", pitch);
} while (pitch > 0.0);
return 0;
}
```

Playing Audio Data from Memory

All of the examples so far have involved playing sounds that were read in from WAV files. What if we wish to modify a sound that was read in or create a sound completely from scratch? We can certainly do the equivalent in graphics using OpenGL. Does OpenAL support the playing of synthesized audio on the fly?

Yes and no. There are no special facilities for playing raw sampled data from memory, and certainly none for assisting with audio synthesis. There is a function in ALUT called **alutLoadWAVMemory()** that will load a WAV file into a buffer from another memory location. This implies that the WAV file existed as a file in the first place and was read in previously, or that a programmer created a memory image of a WAV file containing audio data. Playing a WAV file is faster if it has been pre-loaded, and I suspect that's why this function exists. However, the function also allows you to manipulate the sound while it is saved in memory, provided you have code that knows how to decode and decompress the data stored in memory. To play synthesized audio, we would have to create a WAV formatted memory image using structures defined by the creators of the WAV format, then fill the data area with samples of the sound we wish to play.

After all of this, to quote from the OpenAL Programmer's Guide, "*This function is not guaranteed to be included with any OpenAL distribution, as it is not part of the specification of OpenAL.*" This is not a confidence builder!

So, I embarked on a small exercise to figure out how to play what I will call *dynamic audio*. What follows is material that I have not seen anywhere else. Not to say it does not exist somewhere, but I have been unsuccessful in locating something I can reference. This means that I might be violating some precept of OpenAL. It is true that I have discovered these things by experimenting with programs, but I never modified OpenGL source code.

The program we are going to write will create a sampled sine wave in memory, a digital representation of a pure tone, and play it. In fact, it will create sampled tones for frequencies from 500 Hz to 4000 Hz and play them in ascending sequence, each tone lasting about a second. Along the way, we'll discover some interesting hidden features about OpenAL. These features are useful to know for anyone who plans to use OpenAl to write a game.

Creating a Sound

First, we must know how to create a sampled sound in an array in memory. This is relatively simple, and involves no OpenAL functions at all.

A sine wave is the basic audio tone from which all others can be constructed. It has the form:

Equation 7.1 $\quad A = \sin(t)$

where A is the amplitude of the wave and t is the time at which the measurement was taken. (See Figure 7.1 again for a picture of a sine wave.) This function is periodic, which makes it good for making sounds, and it has a period of 2p. If we wish to sample at a given rate (let's say F = 11025 samples per second) and the sine wave is to have a specified frequency (let's say f=500 Hz), we could express this as:

Equation 7.2 $\quad A_i = \sin(2pfi/F)$

where A_i is the i_{th} sample. Here the code calculates this for us:

```
#define PI 3.1415926535
ucdata = (unsigned char *)malloc (size);
global_buffer = ucdata;

for (i=0; i<(int)size; i++
{
    y = (i*PI*2*frequency)/(double)freq;
    z = (sin(y)+1.0)/2.0;
    ucdata[i] = (unsigned char)(z * 255);
}
```

The array **ucdata** is an array of unsigned characters that will hold the sound we are building. The OpenAL format of this will be **AL_FORMAT_MONO8,** which is to say monophonic 8 bit, and this translates to unsigned char. The code above allocates a buffer big enough to hold about one second of data (size equals 12000) and saves it in a global buffer. I'll present more on this topic later. It then loops, filling each element in the buffer array with a sample computed according to Equation 7.2.

Now, because we use an unsigned type, there can be no negative numbers. The sine function returns numbers between -1.0 and +1.0, which is bad, so we add 1 to the sine, making the values between 0 and 2, then divide by 2 so the result is between 0 and 1. Finally, the calculated value is converted into a value between 0 and 255, which is to say 8 bits, and assigned to the element.

So much for the simple part. How do we convince OpenAL to play this? We construct a buffer using this array instead of something we read from a file. We can set all of the parameter values to reasonable settings and pass them to **alBufferData()** to create a buffer that we can connect to a source.

A rewrite of the function **new_source()** function is shown next. It creates a source that will play a sine wave of a specific frequency, which is passed as a parameter:

```
A_SOURCE new_source (int frequency)
{
    A_SOURCE x;
    ALenum format;
    ALsizei size;
    ALvoid* data;
    ALsizei freq;
    ALboolean loop;
    unsigned char *ucdata;
    int i = 0;
    double z,y;

    x = (A_SOURCE)malloc (sizeof(struct SourceStruct));
    if (x == NULL) /* ... exit */

    alGenBuffers(1, &(x->buffer));    /* Allocate a buffer */
    format = AL_FORMAT_MONO8;
    size = 12000;
    freq = 11025;
    loop = 0;
    data = (void *)ucdata;

/* Generate sound here, save in array ucdata. */
    alBufferData(x->buffer, format, data, size, freq);
    alGenSources(1, &(x->source));
    if (alGetError() != AL_NO_ERROR)  ...
    alSourcei (x->source, AL_BUFFER, x->buffer);
    return x;
}
```

The array **data** is an OpenAL construct, and must be set and passed to the functions that are called as a **void** *. Thus, it is initialized as a cast pointer to **ucdata**. At this point, if we play the source, we should hear a pure sine tone at the specified frequency. All we need to do now is write a little loop that increases the frequency and plays the new buffer each second.

This is not so easy, actually. First we need a function that changes the data in the buffer, so that we can play different frequencies by modifying the buffer we have. After some fiddling about with OpenAL, I decided that the easy way to do this was to free the source and buffer, then call the existing new_source() function passing the new frequency. The function **SetFrequencyData()** does the necessary freeing and allocating:

```
void SetFrequencyData (int frequency)
{

    alDeleteSources(1, &(src->source));
    if (alGetError() != AL_NO_ERROR) ...

    alDeleteBuffers(1, &(src->buffer));
    if (alGetError() != AL_NO_ERROR) ...

    src = new_source (frequency);
}
```

The rest is easy: the main program creates a source for 500 Hz and plays it, then loops over frequencies, changing the sine wave in the buffer and playing it repeatedly. Here's what the code would look like:

```
if (LoadALData(500) == AL_FALSE)        /* create 500 Hz. */
        return -1;
alSourcePlay(src->source);              /* Play 500 Hz */

for (i=600; i<4000; i+=100)             /* For 600..4000 Hz */
{
    SetFrequencyData(i);                /* Create the wav data. */
    alSourcePlay(src->source);
}
```

The problem is that it doesn't quite work the way we want it to. What we hear is the first 500 Hz sound being played, and that's all. You'll learn why next as we come up with a solution for this problem.

When Is a Sound Finished Playing?

The OpenAL system sends a sound to be played to the sound card. The sound is sent by passing an address of the sound data and other parameters. The sound card then takes over and does the work of sending the audio to the speakers, leaving the CPU free to do other things. Thus, when you call alSourcePlay(), OpenAL does not wait for the sound to be finished playing before returning. The function returns immediately, and you can do a lot of calculations while the sound plays. You can even create a new buffer full of sound data, for example.

My previous example tried to play a sound through an existing source while that source was busy playing another sound. The first call to alSourcePlay() was still active while all successive ones were attempted. When the sound finished playing, the entire loop had completed, and the main program was done. Thus, we heard only one tone played.

We need to know how to determine when a sound is finished playing. What we could do then is play a sound, wait for it to finish, then play the next one, and so on. It is not completely plain from the OpenAL documentation that **alSourcePlay()** operates in this way, nor is it plain how to do what we want. There is a clue, though: the manual says that when you call **alSourcePlay()**, *"The playing source will have its state changed to AL_PLAYING."* Aha! A state of a source is what I've been calling an attribute, and we can retrieve it using function the **alGetSourcei()** function. Specifically, here's the call:

```
alGetSourcei(src->source,  AL_SOURCE_STATE, &value);
```

It requests the value of the state attribute for the *source* named **src->source**. The value of this attribute will be returned as the variable **value**. If the value of this attribute is **AL_PLAYING,** the *source* will still be playing the sound; otherwise, it is finished. This is exactly what we need.

The code needed to wait for a sound to finish playing is:

```
alSourcePlay(src->source);
do
{
    alGetSourcei(src->source, AL_SOURCE_STATE, &value);
} while (value == AL_PLAYING);
```

Now we can make our program work as specified. We insert the above code after playing a sound (i.e., calling **alSourcePlay()**), knowing that when it completes, the sound will be finished playing. Here's the new version of the program:

```
int main(int argc, char *argv[])
{
    char c;
    long i=500;
    double z = 101.0;
    ALint value;
    alutInit(&argc, argv);
    alGetError();
    me = new_listener ();
    atexit(KillALData);
    if (LoadALData(i) == AL_FALSE) return -1;
    alSourcePlay(src->source);
    do
    {
```

7

```
        alGetSourcei(src->source, AL_SOURCE_STATE, &value);
} while (value == AL_PLAYING);
for (i=600; i<4000; i+=100)
{
        SetFrequencyData(i);
        alSourcePlay(src->source);
        do { alGetSourcei(src->source, AL_SOURCE_STATE, &value);
        } while (value == AL_PLAYING);
}
return 0;
}
```

It now synthesizes frequencies and plays them. The entire Visual Studio workspace is available on the website as **chapter7/5audioFromMemory**.

Cleaning Up

OpenAL allocates a bit of memory for its own purposes, and memory in a game program can be a scarce commodity. We should clean up as much as possible as soon as possible, and never allow a memory leak. Here are a few simple tips for cleaning up while using OpenAL:

1. After reading a WAV file, and after it has been copied into the source buffer for playing, we should free up the space that OpenAL used by calling the following function:

    ```
    ALvoid alutUnloadWAV(ALenum format, ALvoid *data,
                    ALsizei size, ALsizei freq);
    ```

    The actual audio data is stored in the buffer by this time.

2. When a game is finished with a *source*, the *source* should be freed using:

    ```
    ALvoid alDeleteSources(ALsizei n,ALuint *sources);
    ```

3. After the sources are deleted, delete the associated buffers (which can possess a huge amount of space) using the following function:

    ```
    ALvoid alDeleteBuffers(ALsizei n,ALuint *buffers);
    ```

4. If all sources and buffers are freed, you can close OpenAL and free all resources it has by calling:

    ```
    alutExit();
    ```

Summary

You now know enough about sound display using OpenAL to construct a complete audio system for a driving game. In fact, you also know some tricks for modifying sounds so that you can create a realistic engine sound that changes as it revs faster, and some rare methods for synthesizing sounds in memory and for special tasks. DirectX audio, which is the Microsoft implementation, is not very different from the OpenAL scheme, so you now have a solid background to pursue that if you wish.

7

Chapter 8

Using Ambient Traffic

■ Learn how to use basic stochastic navigation techniques to model ambient traffic in a game.

■ Learn how to simulate traffic so that it can drive through a basic intersection.

In Chapter 6, we discussed racing and navigation strategies, including how to control an opponent car that is racing with the player and other cars. We also learned how to control these cars so that they seem "clever." In almost all cases, the assumption was that the autonomous vehicles would operate as opponents. It's now time to explore another option for using other vehicles in games—a practice called generating— *ambient traffic*. In this case, vehicles are used as "props" in a game to make the virtual scene appear more realistic.

A great many driving games, from *Simpson's Hit and Run* to *Road Rash* to the *Burnout* franchise, incorporate ambient traffic or autonomous non-competitors. Sometimes these vehicles are merely moving obstacles, such as the ones used in *Road Rash*, but more imaginative things can also be done. For example, in *Burnout*, a major factor in the game is the slow-motion, high-speed collisions, with replay. In *Hit and Run*, the characters can actually jump on to the AI vehicles and tour the city—a passive variation of sandbox mode.

Still, an important strategy is to place traffic in a game where one would expect to see it in real life. Another important strategy is to make the traffic operate realistically, obeying the basic driving guidelines that people follow while they are on the road. Most people obey the traffic laws, more or less. Most traffic also does not all move at the same speed or in the same direction. In the real world, we have traffic lights, speed limits, left turn lanes, and four-way stop signs. We also have four-way and three-way intersections, back alleys, and parking lots. I won't cover every one of these traffic situations in this chapter, but I'll provide the basic concepts of how to simulate traffic and how to set up the logic for certain types of intersections. We'll focus on simulating more urban-like environments in this chapter but once you learn the basics, you'll be able to apply what you learn to other types of environments, such as off-road or rural situations. I'll start by introducing an important navigation modeling technique called "stochastic navigation." Then you'll learn how to model ambient traffic that can drive through intersections. Because of all of the activities taking place in an intersection, they are one of the more difficult traffic-related environments to simulate. As you'll discover in this chapter, there are many factors that must be considered.

Stochastic Navigation

The word "stochastic" means having a random component or element, and that's exactly what we want from our ambient traffic. If you look at traffic from the top of a building, each vehicle appears to operate both predictably and randomly; each vehicle predictably obeys traffic rules, but follows what looks like a random route. That's because we don't know where each car is going, since we don't control them and are watching from a distance. They all have a destination, but without knowing what the destinations are, we won't really know what any given car will do at the next intersection. And we certainly won't know what a given car will do at the intersection three blocks away. Each car might have its own plan internally, but as an observer, we wouldn't be able to decipher it. This is exactly the situation in real life. When you drive towards an intersection, you don't know what the cars ahead are going to do. To model this behavior in a game, we need the traffic to look natural, and we don't want all cars to turn left at 5th street. We certainly don't want the same cars to go around the same block for the whole game. After all, too much predictability could really ruin a game. At the same time, we need to make sure that the ambient traffic follows certain traffic laws and driving behavior so that the driving looks realistic.

Each car should have a plan for at least its next choice. If a car is going to turn left, it will need to move over into the left lane before the intersection. Each vehicle in traffic should have a short-term plan, which is updated every time it executes a planned move, such as a turn. The plan can be generated randomly, and thus random numbers can be used to control the activities of the traffic. The most likely event for traffic is to have it drive straight through an intersection, but a certain percentage of the traffic at any given intersection would make a left or right turn. To express these actions, probabilities can be used as shown here:

- Drive straight through intersection: 80% chance
- Make left turn: 9% chance
- Make right turn: 9% chance

- Make right turn at next alley: 1% chance

- Turn into next access: 1% chance

We could implement the following set of probabilities, by using this sample code:

```
if (x < 0.8) plan = GO_STRAIGHT;
else if (x<0.89) plan = TURN_LEFT;
else if (x<0.98) plan = TURN_LEFT;
else if (x < 0.99) plan = NEXT_ALLEY;
else plan = NEXT_ACCESS;
```

The code assumes that a random number, **x**, is first generated between the values 0.0 and 1.0. The first **if** statement would process most of the cars as they drive straight through the intersection.

Of course, there are other situations that we need to think about. For example, if a car enters a parking lot, it should park. Cars that turn at a corner or drive through an intersection usually disappear from view, and can be ignored from then on. A car that stays in view, such as in the parking lot situation, engages in a more complex behavior. This activity is likely initiated by a finite state machine state change.

Always keep in mind that the traffic in a driving game only needs to behave properly whenever the player is watching. After all, it takes time for the AI system to move the vehicles around sensibly. If we can avoid taking this time, we'd free up some processing time for other activities that need to be performed in the game. A few questions that come to mind include:

- Do we need to create traffic when it would likely be visible? That is, when the player's car turns a corner, do we need to invent some cars and plans for them? The option is to always keep the traffic moving, even when it can't be seen.

- How long does the traffic need to be shown after the player performs an activity such as making a turn?

- How much traffic, overall, do we need to create a realistic environment?

- How many distinct vehicles do we need, given that we're recycling them? Will the players notice the same cars are being used all of the time? Will they care?

The challenge with modeling ambient traffic is avoiding problems in cases where the player chooses to explore the environment, especially if he does so by following ambient traffic. Imagine turning a corner to find that the cars you just saw have vanished. It is better to have more of the traffic be inactive (not moving) until it is within a specific radius of the player. Naturally, if the player stays in one place too long, the traffic in his neighborhood could vanish—as it leaves the active radius it stops, and nothing can start up until the player moves closer.

When working with ambient traffic, things can get complicated very quickly. The best approach might be to give some CPU time to moving ambient traffic once in a while, each few frames. If the player is idle, ample free time will be available for this task. If traffic is within a radius of, say, five blocks of the player's car, the traffic will get a "turn" (a few cycles) each frame for movement control. Otherwise, it will get a turn based on its position in a queue and the number of free cycles. As the frame rate increases, extra time will be available to give to the traffic, unless the player engages in activity such as combat. The distant vehicles can be placed in a queue, and the front few can be given movement control each frame, and then they can be placed at the end of the queue. This will automatically give as much spare time as possible to traffic motion.

Steering Behavior

Previously, I suggested that the cars controlled by the AI code should be handled in much the same manner that players would operate their cars—using incremental left and right turns and incremental accelerations and decelerations. Players indicate their incremental movements by pressing keys, whereas the AI system simply adjusts the steering and driving parameters directly, but the effects are the same. In Chapter 6, I showed how waypoints can be used for navigation, and you learned that you need to build multiple routes through the game by hand. The AI can then steer the cars toward the driving line defined by the curves drawn between the waypoints.

There is at least one other option we can use to control ambient traffic, which is called *pursuit point tracking*[6] It involves automatically and repeatedly defining temporary waypoint-like points on the path ahead of a car. The car steers towards these points much as it would steer towards a pre-defined track. Every so often (every few frames), a new *pursuit point* is selected, which may require a modification of the steering angle. Speed is usually controlled through other means.

Pursuit points need to be determined automatically, and thus we must come up with a relatively simple way to do this. Generally, a car follows roads or lanes within a road, and this can be the major clue for the AI system for placing pursuit points. We can think of the lane as a ribbon[7] that is continuous at least between intersections, and which has branching options at those intersections. Every few frames, we can select a point at or near the center line of the lane or ribbon, and then steer towards it. This should allow the car to track a fairly straight course.

Turning a corner involves creating pursuit points more often than the ones created for a straight path. The points are created on a ribbon that bends around a corner, or by joining two perpendicular ribbons with an arc and selecting points on the arc as pursuit points. Figure 8.1 shows the options in a more graphical form. Let's take a closer look at what is going on here. In the leftmost section (a), ribbons are placed on the locations where the cars are to drive as the cars approach the intersection. For each car, we select a point on the center line of the ribbon and aim for this point. As the car comes into the intersection (b), three ribbons are used, one for each direction the car might chose to travel in—straight, turn left, or turn right. The drawing in section (c) shows an alternative approach that can be used, Here we can terminate the ribbons and connect them with short arcs. The pursuit points are ten, placed on these arcs. The drawing in section (d) shows a simple coordinate system for a ribbon where the distance is indicated along the ribbon (D), the offset is shown from the center line (O), and the height is indicated above the ribbon (L). The (D,O,L) coordinate defines a point on the ribbon unambiguously.

This method of control requires no more effort for the designer than using waypoints. In both cases, the routes must be carefully laid out, and intersections must be individually designed and set up by hand. In one case, we place waypoints. In the other case, we lay out ribbons. The effect is much the same.

8

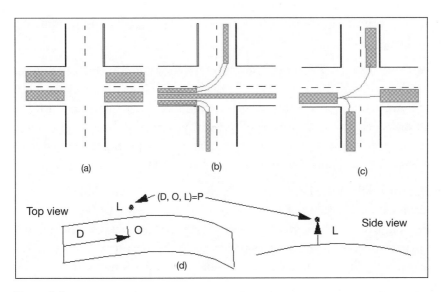

Figure 8.1
Using pursuit point tracking.

Driving through Intersections

Most activity in a traffic system occurs in an intersection. This is the place where decisions are made, turns are executed, and traffic lights and other control schemes are positioned. The AI controls, which we'll call *driving agents* from this point on, need to pay special attention to intersections. Each intersection needs to be identified by the AI system as being a special object. Traffic lights need to be switched at these locations, at least if they can be observed.

In Chapter 6, we defined a finite state machine and showed how it could be used to control a vehicle at a high level. You also learned that AI techniques can be used to control a car in the same way that the player does—by using discrete steering steps and acceleration/braking increments. Both of these techniques can be used to control ambient traffic. At the last intersection, the system will determine what each car determines it will do. If, for instance, a car wants to turn left, it will have one block in which to get into the left lane, and it will turn into the left turn lane, if there is one, when it nears the intersection. It will also plan to slow down and then stop as it approaches the intersection, although it may not need to stop, depending on the traffic controls and the state of the intersection.

Each intersection will have some sort of internal representation for the AI system. Depending on this, the cars, each having different plans, are guided through the maze of possibilities. Fortunately, there are fewer choices than it seems, and it is possible to enumerate them.

By the way, there are a few different kinds of intersections, and each has a distinct variety of choices. Figure 8.2 shows a few of the common intersection types. The one on the left shows a four-way controlled intersection that doesn't have any turn lanes. The one in the center shows a controlled four-way intersection having opposing turn lanes. The one on the right shows a T-intersection. Each type of intersection requires a certain amount of anticipation on the part of the AI system.

A few technical articles have been written on this subject of controlling intersections that we can draw on. One of the better ones is by Wang, Kearney Cremer, and Willemsen[1], and while I don't agree with everything that they suggest, the mathematical notation and some of the techniques presented in this chapter are based on their work. This work also has the added advantage of being quite recent (2004).

The authors mentioned here use a close coupling between the AI system and the environment database, which is not really unusual for a game. Normally, the AI knows about all of the objects in the game anyhow, and the database is merely an access

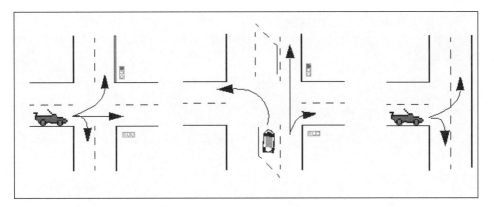

Figure 8.2
Examples of the types of intersections that can be encountered.

mechanism. However, the structure required to describe a traffic intersection might be more complex than most other objects, and there will be a large number of possible activities that can take place there. Essentially, all possible routes that can be taken through the intersection need to be either described explicitly, or at least permitted.

An intersection can be entered in multiple ways. A driving agent enters from one direction along a particular driving line or lane, and exits to another direction and lane. Lane changes, by the way, are rarely legal at intersections, so entering in one lane restricts the possible exit lanes. In our discussion of the behavior at intersections, I'll assume that you've read the material in Chapter 6 on waypoints and simple behaviors like cruising and following. In fact, I'll expand on that discussion next.

Implementing Intersection Behavior—A Walkthrough

Rather than engaging in a detailed discussion of potential implementations, let's do a more-or-less complete implementation for one of the intersection conditions shown in Figure 8.2. The other conditions would likely use a lot of the same code required to implement the first condition, although they would require some new features. The leftmost intersection shown in Figure 8.2 looks like a good example to start with. It provides all of the basic situations that can be encountered in an intersection.

The driving states that we need to support are *cruise*, *cruise_left*, and *cruise_right*. The *cruise* state involves driving into an intersection that contains traffic. *Cruise_left* is a *cruise* state where we intend to turn left at the upcoming intersection, and *cruise_right* is the state where we plan to turn right at the upcoming intersection. Each lane has waypoint control of traffic, and likely will require multiple waypoints. At least one path will be defined for normal ambient traffic, but there may be others for racing or missions if these exist.

Whenever a turn is made, the agent involved will exit from its turn state and enter a cruise state again, at least for a moment. For random cruising, a few decisions need to be made right away:

- Should the agent turn at the next intersection?

- What direction should that turn be?

We need to know some information about the next intersection in the current direction, such as what turns are possible. That information could be stored in the waypoint structure itself.

A possible waypoint organization for the intersection is shown in Figure 8.3. Here, a main waypoint named **d** is used, which represents the initial goal of an agent arriving from the left, following the arrow. If that agent plans to go straight through the intersection, as indicated by its current state (*cruise*), the waypoint after **d** will be **e**. When **e** is reached, the agent will decide what to do at the next intersection. Here's the code sample that performs this operation:

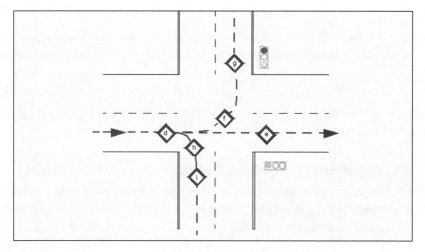

Figure 8.3
Basic controlled intersection with waypoints.

```
x = frandom ();
q = nextNode (Waypoint);
generate_turn_probabilities(PNONE, PLEFT, PRIGHT);
/* Do nothing - drive through the intersection */
if (x < PNONE) change_state (STATE_CRUISE);
```

```
else if (x < PNONE+PLEFT)
            change_state (STATE_CRUISE_LEFT);
else if (x < PNONE+PLEFT+PRIGHT)
            change_state (STATE_CRUISE_RIGHT);
else /* Error */
```

The function **generate_turn_probabilities()** looks at the turns that are possible and assigns probabilities for each one. Standard values may be 90%-10%-10% for representing the likelihood of traveling straight, left, or right. If the agent can't make a left turn, we could assign the probabilities, 85%-0%-15%. In this way, the agent never tries to make a turn that is illegal. After all, that would be embarassing.

The code I just presented merely decides what to do next, and while that is very important, the agent must also carry out the appropriate behaviors. When the agent decides what to do at the next intersection, its behavior has been decided upon, and the decisions about speed and direction can be made starting at that time. There are basically three behaviors, which are modified by traffic and the control signals at the next intersections. These are cruising through the intersection, stopping, and turning.

Basic Behavior—Cruising through the Intersection

To have an agent cruise through an intersection, we'll use a slightly embellished combination of *cruising* and *following* behaviors. That is, if a car is ahead of the agent and within a certain distance, let's say two car lengths, the agent will follow that car; otherwise, the agent will follow standard cruising behavior. We will ignore signal lights for the moment.

In cruising, two speeds need to be considered: a desired speed $\mathbf{v}_d$ and the speed that the agent is currently traveling at, $\mathbf{v}$. If the agent is moving slower than the desired speed ($v < v_d$), the agent should change its acceleration according to the following formula:

Equation 8.1 $\qquad a = \min\left(a_p, k^c p^*(v_d - v)\right)$ if $v < v_d$

This condition holds for a maximum acceleration of $\mathbf{a}_p$. If the agent is traveling faster than the desired speed ($v > v_d$), the agent will need to slow down. If the maximum negative acceleration is $\mathbf{a}_N$, the acceleration in this instance is computed as:

Equation 8.2 $\qquad a = \max\left(a_N, k^c p^*(v_d - v)\right)$ if $v > v_d$

Of course, if the agent is moving at velocity $\mathbf{v}$, there should be no acceleration at all. On the other hand, if there is a car just ahead of the agent, its speed may well determine the agent's speed. Anyone who has driven in traffic knows this, and what is needed is to control the agent's speed by having it behave as if it is *following* another vehicle. We haven't discussed this situation yet.

The basic idea is to keep the agent a specified distance behind a *leader*, which is just the car in front. The leader, or lead vehicle, is the one that is the closest to the agent. A *Proportional Derivative* controller[1,3] can be used to find the acceleration for the agent:

Equation 8.3 $a_f = max \left(a_N, \Delta s - k_f^v \times \Delta v \right)$

Here a_f represents the acceleration that we need. Δs is equal to the actual following distance minus the desired following distance (which we said was two car lengths). Δv is equal to the speed of the agent minus the speed of the leader, and $k^c p$ is a proportional constant. $k^f v$ is the derivative parameter (a good value for $k^f v$ is $2\sqrt{k_p^c}$).

In real life we usually vary the distance between our car and the next one ahead of us as a function of how fast we're moving. My mom taught me that you need six seconds of stopping time between you and the car ahead. This naturally corresponds to a different distance for every speed. If my mother is correct, it is reasonable to define the following distance as the speed of the vehicle times a constant, six, I guess:

Equation 8.4 $s_d = max \left(s_1, v*6 \right)$

Here, s_d is the desired following distance, and s_1 is the smallest allowable following distance.

I promised a practical section, so here goes. Cruising behavior can actually be thought to be simply an acceleration, and would be implemented as something like this:

```
float cruising_behavior ()
{
    float a = 0.0F;

    if (v < vd)
    {
        a = kcp *(vd - v);
        if (a>MAX_ACCELERATION) a = MAX_ACCELERATION;
        return a;
    } else
    {
        a = kcp * (vd - v);
        if (a<MIN_ACCELERATION) a = MIN_ACCELERATION;
```

```
    }
    return a;
}
```

The variables we need to know about in this code are **kcp,** which is the constant in equation 8.1 and 8.2, **vd,** the desired velocity, and the values for minimum and maximum acceleration, which can be constants.

For the "following" behavior, we need to know the speed and position of the leader as well as the values we know for cruising. Again, the behavior can be encapsulated in a single value, the acceleration, which can be computed as:

```
float following_behavior (float dist, float vl)
{
    float a = 0.0F, dv = 0.0F, ds = 0.0F;
    float kvf;

    if (dist > desired_distance)
            return cruising_behavior();
    ds = desired_distance - dist;
    kvf = 2.0F * sqrt ((double)kcp);

    dv = vl - v;
    a = ds - kvf*dv;
    if (a < an) a = an;
    return a;
}
```

We determine whether or not to perform cruising or following behavior depending on the distance between the agent and its leader. Here's the code that performs this operation:

```
p = follower (agent);
dist = distance_2pt (p.pos, agent.pos);
if (dist > 6*agent.velocity)
    a = cruising_behavior();
else
    a = following_behavior (dist, p.v);
```

You should understand that this code only implements the basic behavior. It does not take into account the traffic signals or the actions of traffic in the intersection.

Stopping the Agent at a Particular Place

How do we stop a car at the intersection? If the light is red, we certainly want it to stop. If we are turning, we'll need it too slow down or stop just before turning. Traditional physics comes to our assistance in this case. If the distance to the stopping point is **s** and the current velocity is **v**, the equation we need is:

Equation 8.5

$$a_i = \frac{v^2}{2s}$$

This acceleration is negative, meaning that the vehicle is slowing. It is also constant, and the vehicle will stop after traveling precisely distance **s**. If a_i is greater than a_N (the maximum possible negative acceleration), the car won't be able to stop in time. This can be a useful thing to know. For example, if the signal light turns amber, and the value of a_i computed at that point is less than a_N, there is no point in trying to stop. The vehicle will need to run the light. This is the point when you hope that there are no cops around to catch you!

In fact, Wang et al[1] define four conditions based on the value of a_i and another acceleration value v_d, which is the desired acceleration value for the agent. Anyone who drives probably has a preferred v_d, because accelerations greater than this could cause dismay and distress. Accelerations that are lower, on the other hand, could create impatience and discomfort. The conditions are (and I quote[1]):

- If a_i is out of the desired range in positive direction, i.e., $a_i > a_d - \Delta a$, then, we believe the desired stopping position is still far away. It is too early to respond to the traffic control signals. Otherwise,

- If a_i is out of the desired range in negative direction, i.e., $a_i < a_d - \Delta a$ and $a_i < A_N$, the vehicle is too close to the desired stopping position, so that it is impossible to stop the vehicle at the desired stopping position. Otherwise,

- If a_i is out of the desired range in negative direction, i.e., $a_i < a_d - \Delta a$, then the vehicle cannot stop soon enough at its desired deceleration rate. However, if $a_i >= A_N$, where A_N is the maximum negative acceleration, the vehicle can still be stopped at the desired stopping position. Otherwise,

- If a_i is within a small desired range around the desired negative acceleration, i.e., $a_i \in [a_d - \Delta a, a_d + \Delta a]$, the vehicle can be successfully stopped at the desired stopping position.

So, the choices are:

- Too early to begin stopping

- Too late to stop entirely

- Too late to stop for a margin of comfort (but still possible)
- Can stop within the comfort range

All of these choices will be important to determine, as you will see below.

Turning Right at the Intersection

As soon as the decision to turn right has been made, our code needs to calculate the acceleration value for the agent, a_i and decide when to start to slow down. The agent doesn't always need to come to a complete stop, so a turn velocity v_t can be used, which is often between 5 to 15 MPH. Equation 8.5 is simply modified by substituting v_t for v, and we can determine the acceleration needed to slow down by the requisite amount. The stopping behavior defined in the previous section is used to do this.

Remember, there are at least 24 frames per second, so we don't have to check more than once each 8 frames or so. Of course, we could compute a_i for 1/8 of the cars each frame, thus spreading the workload over multiple frames.

When the agent arrives at the waypoint (waypoint **d** as shown in Figure 8.2), the agent will be moving slowly. Because a decision was made to turn right, the agent switches to the path that travels though waypoints **h** and **i**, and follows the spline curve that passes through those points. At point **h**, the velocity will be increased, and the agent will accelerate to its desired new velocity according to the *cruising* or *following* state.

Most cities have traffic laws that give the right of way to cars turning right. This means that there is little need to avoid other traffic in this case, since the only competition for road space will be from facing vehicles turning left.

Turning Left at the Intersection

Left turns are essentially the same as right turns, except for the direction of the turn and the right-of-way. The agent slows, as before, to turning speed. When it reaches waypoint **d**, it switches paths to the spline path connecting **d**, **f**, and **g** (see Figure 8.2 again). Once the agent reaches waypoint **f**, it will accelerate to cruising velocity, and enter a *cruising* or *following* state.

The thorny issue of right-of-way still needs to be resolved, and will be shortly. First, we need to discuss how traffic lights are implemented.

Implementing Traffic Lights

Traffic signals are very much like a finite state machine having three states: *Green*, *Amber*, and *Red*. The transitions occur in sequence always from Green to Amber to Red, but no event is used to trigger the transition; transitions occur after timed intervals. This is why signals are not *really* FSAs; an FSA has no timer and no memory of prior states. Still, the idea is clear enough.

The way that the light is represented graphically is not important to the AI system. We just need to know that it is in a particular state. The state indicates only the illuminated color. Oh, by the way, a traffic light is not just one light, or three colors; it consists of *all* of the control signals in an intersection. If a light is green in the East-West direction, it had better be Red in the North-South direction. A controller is connected to a set of lights to keep track of this for us.

Our implementation for the game will provide multiple controllers but not all of them will be synchronized. Each controller is connected to a set of traffic signals on an intersection, or in multiple intersections. The AI system knows about all of the controllers, and updates their timers each frame. Each signal knows what control it is connected to, and therefore what color is currently active. Any number of signals can point to any controller, but for aesthetic reasons, it would be best if the signals using a single controller were far enough apart that they could not be seen at the same time.

One possible structure for a controller is:

```
#define RED_TRAFFIC_LIGHT   0
#define GREEN_TRAFFIC_LIGHT 1
#define AMBER_TRAFFIC_LIGHT 2
struct traffic_control_struct
{
/* What time will the EW light change? */
    int change_time;
/* Duration of each color */
    int ticks[3];
/* Current color for EW direction */
    int EW_color;
/* Current color for NS direction */
    int NS_color;
};
```

The traffic light associated with this controller needs to know only the color that the controller has assigned at the moment. One implementation is:

```
typedef struct traffic_control_struct * TC;
#define NORTH_SOUTH 0
#define EAST_WEST   1

struct traffic_light_struct
{
/* Controller */
    TC controller;
```

```
/* Direction the light controls */
     int direction;
/* Current color being displayed */
     int *my_color;
/* Where is this light? */
     int xpos, ypos;
/* Other stuff ...
};
typedef struct traffic_light_struct * TL;
```

Normally in an urban driving game setting, many traffic lights and many controllers would be used. Controllers can be stored in an array as shown here:

```
TC all_traffic_controls[NCONTROLS];
```

So can the lights:

```
TL all_traffic_lights[NLIGHTS];
```

All traffic controls are created at game initialization. Each should start with a random color and number of ticks remaining. The duration of the lights should be hard-coded or read from an initialization file, with the latter being preferred. The expression **all_traffic_controls[i]->ticks[RED_TRAFFIC_LIGHT]** tells us, usually in milliseconds, how long a red light would last in total. The controller controls only one direction, let's say East-West; the other direction simply follows the same time pattern with opposing colors.

The initialization of a controller to a random state, given that the durations have been read in from the parameters file, could look something like this:

```
/* Controller */
     TC controller;
/* Direction the light controls */
     int direction;
/* Current color being displayed */
     int *my_color;
/* Where is this light? */
     int xpos, ypos;
/* Other stuff ...
for (i=0; i<NCONTROLS; i++)
{
     p = all_traffic_controls[i];
/* initialize color - only red or green */
     if (frandom() < 0.0F)
     {
```

```
            p->EW_color = RED_TRAFFIC_LIGHT;
            p->NS_color = GREEN_TRAFFIC_LIGHT;
        } else
        {
            p->NS_color = RED_TRAFFIC_LIGHT;
            p->EW_color = GREEN_TRAFFIC_LIGHT;

        }
/* Set up an initial random duration */
        p->change_time =
            (int)(p->ticks[p->EW_color]*frandom());

}
```

The traffic lights themselves are graphical entities, and need to be rendered only when they are visible. The only crucial thing about a light from the point of view of the AI system is its color, and that is determined by its controller. If we want to assign random controllers to lights, the following code will suffice:

```
for (i=0; i<NLIGHTS; i++)
{
/* Choose a random controller ... */
    j = (int)(frandom()*NCONTROLS);
    q = all_traffic_lights[i];
    q->controller = all_traffic_controls[j];
    if (frandom() < 0.5)
    {
        q->direction = EAST_WEST;
        q->color= &(q->controller->EW_color);
    }
    else
    {
        q->direction = NORTH_SOUTH;
        q->color = &(->controller->NS_color);
    }
}
```

The important thing to note here is that the **color** field of the light is a pointer that points to the controller's color for the specified direction. Thus, when the controller changes the color, all of the lights that point to that color will change also. This means that the renderer does not need to know about the controller at all. It simply draws the signal light object and illuminates the correct color of light using only the traffic light reference.

Time can be expressed in frames, and each frame requires an update to the controllers to see if any lights change. I'm making the assumption here that we measure the passage of time in milliseconds using an integer value. When the **change_time** field in the controller becomes less than the current time, the E-W light should change color. The N-S light should usually be easy to determine, but amber causes a small problem. The N-S light changes amber while there is still time left on the E-W red light. Consider the code shown next for updating the controllers. Any of the controllers may need to be changed during any frame:

```
t = time_milliseconds();
for (i=0; i<NCONTROLS; i++)
{
   p = all_traffic_controls[i];
   switch (p->EW_color)
   {
     case GREEN_TRAFFIC_LIGHT:
     if (t>p->change_time)
     {
       p->EW_color = AMBER_TRAFFIC_LIGHT;
       p->change_time = t
         + p->ticks [AMBER_TRAFFIC_LIGHT]
         - (t - p->change_time);
     }
     break;
```

This means that the E-W green light changes to amber, and that this does not affect the N-S light.

```
case AMBER_TRAFFIC_LIGHT:
     if (t>p->change_time)
     {
       p->EW_color = RED_TRAFFIC_LIGHT;
       p->change_time = t
         + p->ticks [RED_TRAFFIC_LIGHT]
         - (t - p->change_time);
       p->NS_color = GREEN_TRAFFIC_LIGHT;
     }
     break;
```

The E-W change from amber to red also changes the N-S light to green:

```
case RED_TRAFFIC_LIGHT:
     if (t>p->change_time)
```

```
{
    p->EW_color = GREEN_TRAFFIC_LIGHT;
    p->change_time = t
      + p->ticks [GREEN_TRAFFIC_LIGHT]
      - (t - p->change_time);
    p->NS_color = RED_TRAFFIC_LIGHT;
}
else if (t>(p->change_time-ticks[AMBER_TRAFFIC_LIGHT))
{
    p->NS_color = RED_TRAFFIC_LIGHT;
}
break;
```

If E-W is red, two situations are possible. One is simply that red changes to green, which also changes N-S from amber to red. The other is that N-S needs to change to amber from green; this is done by seeing if the current time exceeds the change time *minus* the duration of the amber light. The E-W light does not change, so this is a special case.

Note that the situation described here is a common one but is not the only one. Intersections also have walk lights, advance turns lights, flashing lights, and many other options. The complexity of the game is, as usual, determined largely by how realistic you want it to be, and here that means how many different cases you handle.

A Complete Behavior Model

I've now presented two of the major components of the intersection driving model: the driving plan (e.g, turn right) and the traffic lights. I've also mentioned the behavior of traffic in the intersection. It's time to put these elements together to form a complete system.

The first thing that an agent must do is pay attention to the traffic lights. A response begins at some distance from the intersection; there is no point in slowing down for a red light that is a full block away. So, for distances from the intersection beyond a threshold value, the behavior is simply as described so far. It is crucial, therefore, to know that distance, which we'll call d_I. If the light turns red (well, ok, amber, then) at some point, we compute the acceleration a_i needed to stop at the intersection using Equation 8.5, where $s=d_I$. If the vehicle is too close to the intersection to stop at a comfortable acceleration, the decision is made not to stop, and $a_i = 0$.

However, sometimes the traffic signals are in the agent's favor, and it must still yield to oncoming cars, usually other agents controlled by the same processor. The AI controls must make a decision based on the current velocity and the nature of the other "traffic" that will be in the intersection. It is a simple matter to compute the time t_1 at which this agent will enter the intersection, and only slightly more complex to estimate the time t_2 when the agent will exit from the intersection. The value of t_1 is the time found by solving the elementary physics equation for t_1:

Equation 8.6
$$d_I = vt_1 + (a_i t_1^2)/2$$

Here, v is the current velocity and d_I is the distance to the intersection. Naturally, as time goes by, the values of s and v will change, and we actually get a more accurate picture of the situation. It would be simple for the AI system to save the most current value for t_1, since it is a useful thing to know for many reasons, and is strongly related to d_I.

The time of intersection exit t_2 can be estimated given the turning speed v_t and the turning radius R. A typical left or right turn is 1/4 of a circle. The distance traveled would be $\pi R/2$ and since distance is velocity multiplied by time, we see that

Equation 8.7 $$\pi R/2 = v_t t \implies t = \pi R/(2v_t)$$

and then $t_2 = t_1 + t$.

The calculation of t_1 and t_2 is performed for all cars within a specific distance of the intersection. If no other vehicle will pass through the intersection between t_1 and t_2, we are free to proceed. If there are some conflicts, we need to worry only about those that represent cars with the right-of-way over us. Those rules are usually simple:

- Going straight through is given the top priority
- Turning right is assigned the next priority
- Turning left should yield, the first car there wins, and in case of a tie, we yield to the car on the right

The basic plan is to compute $t^i 1$ and $t^i 2$ for all vehicles i. If, for some vehicle j, we have $t^j 1$ or $t^j 2$ falling between $t^i 1$ and $t^i 2$, we'll know there is a potential conflict that needs to be resolved. This means that one of cars (i or j) will need to slow down and stop when it reaches the intersection. The act of slowing one of the cars may well clear up the conflict by the time the intersection is reached, and the car may not need to stop. If there is no overlap of time intervals, the cars simply move without constraint.

8

The decisions are re-evaluated every few frames, since the situation can change quickly. It seems as if there could be loops created by this, where some vehicles alternate between choosing to move ahead and choosing to stop. Any such loops will not last long because reaching the intersection will resolve them. The right of way rules are designed to ensure that traffic flows through intersections rather than being impeded by them.

At this point, there are three distinct accelerations that may have been computed: the acceleration determined from cruising behavior, the acceleration determined from following behavior, and the acceleration due to intersection behavior. A simple rule to decide what to do with these scenarios should be fairly obvious when stated simply[3]: use the minimum value of these three accelerations as the one that will be applied to this vehicle. This is referred to as the most conservative rule, and it gives a reasonable answer in all cases, if perhaps not the *best* one.

Summary

Simulating traffic is a complex activity that can be seen in terms of a few, simpler, interrelated activities. The really time-consuming part of the process, and one that has not been very well described, would be the design of the intersections, the layout of the ribbons and waypoints, and other design activities that allow the AI system to control a large number of cars efficiently.

What is really needed to make this work well is a tool or set of tools that allow the designer to use a graphical interface to layout and connect roads and intersections using the keyboard, screen, and mouse. Tools of this sort fall into the category of *middleware*, and are generally not cheap. They are also sometimes not available, and I know of no tools for specifically creating roads and waypoints, at least not right now.

I have tried to include a fairly complete set of references to technical articles about this subject. Perhaps one of you will create the tools that we need, or perhaps someone will point out to me a program that exists that can do the job. When that happens, let me know, and I'll add the information to the website for this book.

In the meantime, you can learn a lot by downloading and reading some of the atricles in the references, and by searching for other articles that reference them. There is a website called citeseer (**http://citeseer.ist.psu.edu/**) that can look for papers that reference a particular one. In this way, you can search for articles written *after* anyone that you know is on a subject of interest, and thus find newer information.

Chapter 9

Physics for Driving and Racing Games

- Learn the basic physics involved in creating driving and racing games.

- Learn how to simulate motion for low-speed and high-speed turns.

- Apply "cheating" techniques to simplify the simulation of driving and racing activities.

The physics involved in operating objects that we use everyday, such as our cars, can get fairly complicated. Just think about how your car really works for a minute. Most automobile engines are internal combustion engines, which convert the up and down motion of the pistons into the rotational motion of a shaft. The transmission converts the basic rotary motion of the shaft into various degrees of rotational speed and power, depending on the ratio of the gears. This feeds into a differential or something equivalent that changes the speed and power again. The direction of rotation is also altered so that the wheels can be turned. The wheels have a specific size, and their size translates the rotation of the axle shaft into a linear motion where one rotation of the wheel converts into a forward motion equivalent to the circumference of the wheel. The translation of wheel motion to forward motion depends on the friction between the road and the wheel. If a vehicle is traveling on a surface that is wet ice, for example, the wheel may spin without generating any forward motion at all.

The physics involved in moving a car don't stop here. A forward force operates on a mass. A car has mass and therefore weight, and a moving car has intertia. If a car could accelerate without any opposing forces, the acceleration would lead to ever increasing velocities. There are, however, opposing frictional forces and air resistance that create a limit to how fast the car can go.

The laws of physics dictate that for a particular mass and velocity, a car that tries to turn a corner is subject to specific transverse forces that can cause it to skid if the forces exceed the friction of the tires on pavement. A car traveling fast enough can leave the ground if it reaches the crest of a hill, and may also have a rotation, if the steering wheel was turned just beforehand. A car that strikes a guard rail at a significant speed will bounce off in a particular direction, and will lose part of its speed, and therefore momentum, as a result.

Braking is yet another driving activity that involves physics. The rate of deceleration is a function of the frictional properties of the tires and the surface, and an uneven surface can cause skidding even on dry pavement. Controlled skidding into a turn can increase the speed at which the corner can be navigated—the so-called *hand brake turn* or *E-brake*.

As you can see, the physics of moving a car in the real world involve numerous factors. We'll need to explore some of these issues in this chapter so that you'll be able to create games that can be more accurate simulations. We will also discuss ways to fudge the physics so that our simulations look good enough. Many theme driving games do this, and they look good and are fun to play. Although the word "physics" might sound a little scary, the math that we'll need to use won't be too complicated. Most of the math involved you've likely seen in high school. Most people seriously underestimate the amount of math that goes into a computer game.

Basic Straight-Line Car Physics

Figure 9.1 shows the basic forces that act on a car as it moves forward in a straight line. The weight is included with this example because it affects friction. We'll be using the weight to calculate the motive force. The motive or tractive force from the engine moves the car forward. The air resistance and the rolling resistance slow the card down. The model I'm showing here is fairly simple but it does cover all of the basics.

Before we get too much further, let's review the famous physics equation that we'll be using over and over, in various forms:

Equation 9.1 $F = ma$

This tells us that force, mass, and acceleration are connected by a simple linear relationship. If the mass of the car and the net force acting on it are known, we can determine its acceleration, and hence its velocity and position as a function of time. This is essential for driving simulations, and sports games specifically.

The four forces acting on the car shown in Figure 9.1 will result in a net force that acts on the mass of the vehicle. If that net force is in the forward direction, the car will accelerate forwards; if the force is in the reverse direction, the car will slow, or accelerate backwards (decelerate). Determining the net force is achieved by using vectors. A resultant force vector is found for the major directions: front-back, left-right, and up-down. Of

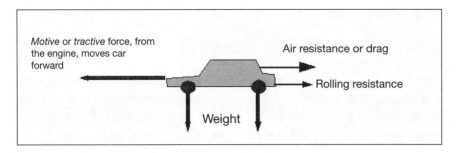

Figure 9.1
Forces that act on a car as it is moving forward.

course, we have ignored other directions here, but it is essential to consider the three directions separately in our calculations for the game for the sake of simplicity.

Finding a net force is simple for our example. We simply put a "-" sign on the magnitude of the forward forces and a "+" sign on the backward ones and then add them up. The net force is simply the difference between forward and backward forces. Later on, finding the resultant between multiple forces will be a more complex calculation, as forces interact and angles are considered in 3D.

The Nature of the Basic Forces

The forces shown in Figure 9.1 are not simple ones; they have their origins in quite complex events. The motive force, for example, is originally provided by the vehicle's engine, and is not a force in the forward direction but is in fact a *torque*—a rotational force. In a first approximation, the force in the forward direction, F_{mot}, can be thought to be proportional to the force provided by the engine, F_{eng}, which in turn is related to the throttle setting **Th**. We could say that

Equation 9.2 $$F_{mot} = k_0 F_{eng}$$

where a constant is used to relate the two forces. This only works in our one-dimensional example because force is actually a vector. To be more correct, a coordinate system needs to be defined using the car as the origin, and the X axis should be used to orient the car in the direction it is pointing. In any 3D coordinate system there are three basic coordinate vectors, each one pointing along each axis: X, Y, and Z. Each vector will be one unit in length. These vectors will be named **i**, **j**, and **k**. The unit vector along the X axis is **i** = **1,0,0**, and the force in Equation 9.2 must be aligned in this direction:

Equation 9.3 $F_{mot} = ik_0 F_{eng}$

If the only force were $\mathbf{F}_{mot}$, the car would ultimately accelerate to the speed of light. Friction or resistive forces come to the rescue here, and two are used in our current example. The first is air resistance or drag. This force is something that we tend to ignore in day-to-day life. The full expression for aerodynamic drag is[1]:

Equation 9.4 $F_{drag} = -\dfrac{1}{2} C_d \pi A v^2$

Here, r is the air density, A is the area that the vehicle presents as seen from the front (i.e., direction of motion) and v is the velocity. The air density is related to what is called *viscosity*, or thickness of a fluid. Oil is thicker than water, which is in turn thicker than alcohol, and the resistance offered by a fluid (air is a fluid for this purpose) is greater for thicker fluids. The air density will also be affected by temperature, air pressure, and so on. A simpler expression is[3]:

Equation 9.5 $F_{drag} = -\dfrac{1}{391} C_d A v^2$

Here, C_d is a constant called the *drag coefficient*. Units are represented in miles per hour (MPH) and pounds of force. This constant is measured for different shapes, for the most part, and is one reason that we have wind tunnels at race car design facilities. Figure 9.2 shows the drag coefficients for some simple shapes. A typical range of values for cars is between 0.32 to 0.38.

The two interesting things about drag are:

■ Drag is essentially a frictional force and it always opposes the direction of motion.

■ Drag is proportional to the *square* of the velocity. This means that drag is the main limit on top speed, and that it is less of a factor at low velocities.

Rolling resistance, $\mathbf{F}_{roll}$, is also a force that always opposes motion. If you do an Internet search on "rolling resistance" you'll discover that most discussions are concerned with tires on pavement, but there are internal frictions that enter into the situation. It can be

Equation 9.6 $F_{roll} = -v C_{roll}$

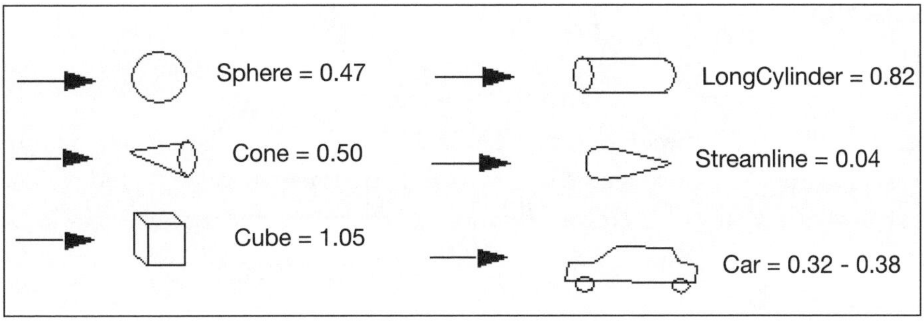

Figure 9.2
Drag coefficients of some common shapes, as measured in a wind tunnel.

very difficult to calculate the rolling resistance. Let's just say that it is a constant factor times the velocity:

In case you've forgotten, I should remind you that velocity **v** is a vector. Because the current problem considers only longitudinal forces, the Y and Z components of **v** are considered to be 0. However, velocity has components in all three directions that correspond to the speed along each of the three axes. What we usually call *speed* is simply the magnitude of the velocity vector as shown here:

Equation 9.7

$$Speed = \sqrt{v_x^2 + v_y^2 + v_z^2}$$

Now that we have examined the major forces involved in straight ahead car motion, we can add them all up and calculate the net force:

Equation 9.8

$$F_{net} = F_{mot} + F_{drag} + F_{roll}$$

Recall that F_{drag} and F_{roll} are negative. At this point, Issac Newton can help us again. We can determine the acceleration from Equation 9.1:

Equation 9.9

$$a = \frac{F_{net}}{m} = \frac{F_{mot} + F_{drag} + F_{roll}}{m}$$

The velocity is found by considering the acceleration over a time period, in our case the time between two consecutive calls to the physics program. I have been referring to this as the time between frames, and will continue to do so. The velocity at time T will be

Equation 9.10 $\quad V_T = V_{T-1} + a\,(dt)$

where **dt** is the time between frames. The final step in our simulation is to determine the car's position. We know where it is at time **T**, we know its velocity, and we know the forces that act on it. This means that we can determine the car's acceleration. Its position at **T+1** is:

Equation 9.11 $\quad P_T = P_{T-1} + V_T(dt)$

Our first level of the simulation is now complete. We can represent the position of the entire car by using its center of mass, which is a point. We position the center of mass at P_T after each frame according to Equation 9.11 and its friends, and draw the car as polygons offset from there. In our game, velocity does not matter except that it lets us compute the correct position of the car from frame-to-frame. The car's position is the aspect that matters because it tells us where to draw a car relative to the background and terrain.

We now have the ability to take a force from the engine and convert it into a position of the vehicle at any time. The simulation is vehicle-specific, as some of the constants vary by vehicle type, but we don't need to know anything else. For example, if we collect the constants in Equation 9.4 into a single constant for my 1992 Chevy Blazer[7], C_d =0.450 and A=2.213 M^2 and a standard air density of r = 1.29 kg/m^3, we can create a constant C_{blazer} = 1/2 * 0.45 * 1.29 * 2.213 = 0.642. As a first approximation, it is acceptable to set C_{roll} to about 30 times the overall drag C_{blazer}, or C_{roll} = 19.26.

Let's say (because we don't know for sure, yet) that for a Chevy Blazer F_{mot} = 3000 Newtons (a Newton is a unit of force, where 1 Newton = 1 Kg-M/sec²); this will be a maximum, of course, since it is under the control of my foot on the accelerator. Given the formulas above, it is now a simple matter to calculate the net force after each arbitrary time step, and determine position and velocity. The drag forces increase with speed, providing a negative feedback loop that automatically implies a peak velocity where the acceleration becomes zero (no net force).

Braking and Weight Transfer

My mother drives her automatic by using both of her feet but most people don't do this. When braking, you normally remove your foot from the accelerator pedal. This action removes the forward motive force. When you place your foot on the brake, this action creates a third retarding force F_{brake}. Equation 9.8 is replaced with

Equation 9.12 $F_{net} = F_{brake} + F_{drag} + F_{roll}$

in which all of the forces are in the negative direction and serve to retard motion.

I have introduced retarding forces, and I have mentioned friction several times in this chapter and have not really described friction very well as it relates to forces. The basic equation that governs frictional forces is[5]

Equation 9.13 $F = \mu N$

where N is the normal force, or the force perpendicular to the motion, and m is a constant that depends on the nature of the surfaces, called the *coefficient of friction*. The value of m varies from $m=0.05$ for ice on ice to $m=0.72$ for a car tire on asphalt pavement or $m=1.16$ for rubber on rubber[11]. The force due to braking cannot exceed the frictional force between the pavement and the wheels, so we have, approximately

Equation 9.14 $F_{brake} = -\mu\, C_{brake}$

for some constant C_{brake} that you can specify. This is an approximation, but a fair one; C_{brake} contains the normal force, which is usually constant and a function of the mass of the vehicle, and a few other potential "fudge factors."

It is important that the frictional force not be responsible for any actual motion. In real life, this cannot happen but because F_{brake} is a force; a physics engine may convert this into a velocity ($F = ma$) if the vehicle is stopped to begin with. One hazard of a simulation is that it may only account for the parts of the real world that it has been told about. Anyway, it is a strange effect of a simple bug that applying the brake to a stopped car could make the car accelerate backwards! Note that the other slowing forces are a function of velocity.

A relatively simple solution would be to make the braking force also a function of velocity, but that may be expensive. We could check to see if the only significant force is F_{brake}, and if so, set $F_{brake}=0$ and $v=0$ too. One way to do this would be to use a conditional statement such as:

9

```
if ( (Fbrake/Fnet > Fthresh) && (speed < Sthresh) )
    {
        Fbrake = 0;
        Speed = 0;
    }
```

Weight Transfer

The last time I drove home with my car (the Montana, not the Blazer) full of lumber, I had to make a quick stop to avoid hitting a deer. I was struck in the back of the head with a spruce 2×2 that appeared to be unaware that we had stopped. Why am I telling you this? Because you have probably noticed some sort of affect like this yourself. In particular, when a car accelerates from a standing start, weight is transferred from the front wheels to the rear ones (assuming a rear-wheel drive, of course). This has an interesting effect—it means that traction on the driving wheels increases, and maximum motive force is significantly greater than normal.

The reverse is the case when braking. Weight is transferred to the front. The front suspension takes more of the stress, and rear-wheel traction is decreased. Many people could not identify these issues with any accuracy, but they would know when they were not being portrayed accurately in a game. Understanding weight transfer is more important for a realistic impression that for any other reason, and for visual impression more than any other practical issue.

If a vehicle is not moving, and the center of mass of the vehicle is located at an equal distance from the front and rear axles, the weight will be distributed equally across four (usually) points of contact—the four wheels. The weight on any one wheel is

$W = mg/4$, where g is the force due to gravity and m is the car's mass. The value of g is 9.8 m/sec² in SI units or 32 ft/sec² in British/imperial measure.

If the center of mass is not at a position that is an equal distance from both axles, the front wheels have a normal force. In other words, their fraction of the car's weight is

$$w_f = d_f/(d_f+d_r) * w$$

and correspondingly, the weight on the rear wheels is

$$w_r = d_r/(d_f+d_r) * w$$

assuming that d_f is the distance from the center of mass to the front axle, and d_r is the distance to the rear axle.

This assumes that the car is stationary. It also works if the car is moving with a constant velocity, however large. On the other hand, if the car is accelerating, a virtual transfer of weight will occur to one of the other axles. Forward acceleration is a positive value, and deceleration is negative; the weight on the front axle will then be

Wf = $d_f/(d_f+d_r)$*W - $z/(d_f+d_r)$*M*a

and on the rear the weight will be

Wr = $d_r/(d_f+d_r)$*W - $z/(d_f+d_r)$*M*a

where **z** is the height (i.e., z axis value) of the car's center of mass. If you have a rear-wheel drive, it is important to have the center of mass as far to the rear of the vehicle as possible, and, of course, the opposite is true for a front-wheel drive.

A perfectly reasonable simplification we can use is to assume an equal distribution over all four wheels. Remember that we are talking about axle weights, so each wheel has half of this value in a normal situation. Later in this chapter, I'll present the rare instances when the weight transfer matters.

Transfer of Force to the Wheels: Engine and Transmission

We have used a value for motive force of 3000N for a Chevy Blazer in the example calculations we've done. This was an arbitrary value, since the manual that came with the vehicles specifies no such number. Indeed, the engine actually provides a rotational force, or torque, rather than a straight linear force. Now torque, like force, is a vector quantity but is sometimes colloquially referred to as a simple value. Think of a handle on a rotating shaft that turns a grinder or a pump. Pushing on the handle with a force of 2 Newtons yields a torque of 6 Newton-meters if the handle is 3 meters long, and has a torque of 4 Newton-meters with a 2 meter handle. In other words, the torque is the distance from the center of rotation times the force.

As a vector, torque is the cross product of the radius over which the force acts combined with the magnitude of the force. We know from collision detection that a cross product of two vectors is a vector that is perpendicular to both vectors. Figure 9.3 diagrams the idea of torque as a vector. Convention has it that if you wrap your fingers around the rotation axis so that your fingers point in the direction of rotation, your thumb will point in the direction of the torque vector.

In an internal combustion engine, the torque that the engine provides is not a constant but is a function of the speed of the engine in revolutions per minute (RPM). This function is not linear, or even necessarily predictable. It is measured on a bench at the factory, and stored in a table or drawn as a graph. Each engine type has different

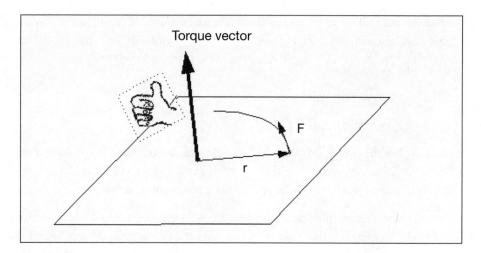

Figure 9.3
Representing torque as a vector.

properties, and each individual engine is a little different from the others. An example torque curve for my other car, a Montana with a GM 3.4 Liter V6 engine[8], is shown in Figure 9.4. The peak torque of 210 ft-lb occurs at 4000 RPM. This curve shows the maximum torque at each RPM vale, and the actual torque is a function of the throttle position, as a percentage. This graph could be stored in a table, and indexed by RPM to give torque values in a game.

Figure 9.4 is typical in that it also shows the horsepower curve. Horsepower also varies with RPM, and in fact is directly related to torque. Using English measures, the relationship is expressed as:

Equation 9.15 $$H = \frac{\tau\, RPM}{5252}$$

This means that the curves will cross over at RPM=5252. (Note: The two curves shown in Figure 9.4 have different scales.)

We're almost done with torque-talk. The torque in the curve is measured at the engine, and there are losses of between 20% to 30% that are emitted as heat. After that, the transmission and differential modify the engine torque, and then it is transmitted to the wheels.

I think we are now equipped to deal with the problem that interested us in the first place: how to find the motive force on the vehicle. According to Monster [4] we have:

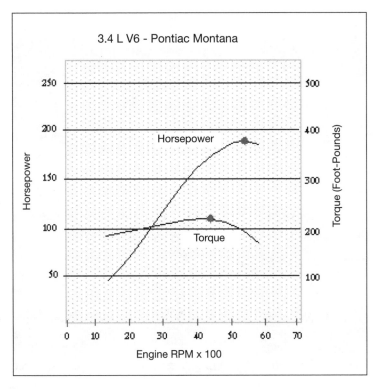

Figure 9.4
The torque curve for a Pontiac Montana which shows torque plotted against RPM.

Equation 9.16 $$F_{mot} = \frac{u\, T_{engine}\, x_g\, x_d\, n}{R_w}$$

Here, T_{engine} is the torque of the engine at the current revs, as looked up in the torque curve table; x_g is the transmission gear ratio for the current gear, x_d is the differential gear ratio, n is the efficiency of the transmission, and R_w is the wheel radius. The component u is a unit vector pointing in the direction of the car's motion. Dividing by the wheel radius R_w is the way that the torque on the rear axle is converted to force on the road surface (since distance × force = torque, then force = torque/distance).

Going back to my Montana for a numerical example, at 4000 RPM, the engine generates the peak torque of 210 ft-pounds. The gear ratios of the Montana, according to the GM website, are:

Montana Gear ratios:

1st:	2.92
2nd:	1.57
3rd:	1.00
4th:	0.71
Reverse:	2.39
Final drive:	3.29:1

In first gear, assuming a transmission efficiency of 0.7, and using a wheel radius of 13.2 inches (1.1 feet)—I just went outside and measured it—we get:

$$F_{mot} = (210 \text{ ft-lb} * 2.92 * 3.29 * 0.7) / 1.1 \text{ ft}$$

$$= 1283 \text{ lb}.$$

One pound of force is 4.448 Newtons, so this force in SI units is 5706 Newtons.

To determine overall gear ratios when multiple gearboxes are used, we multiply the values for the individual gearboxes together. That is, the transmission is connected to the differential, and if we are in second gear (1.57:1 ratio), the differential ratio 3.29 is multiplied by 1.57 to produce the final end-to-end ratio of 5.17. This means that 1 foot-pound of torque at the engine is multiplied by 5.17 by the time we get to the wheels. The sacrifice is speed, so if we have 3000 RPM at the engine we will have 3000/5.17 = 580.3 RPM at the wheels. Thus, in low gears we get low speed but high torque. The reverse of this is encountered at high gears.

How fast are we going? Each revolution of the wheel, if there is no skidding going on, takes us $2\pi r$ units in the forward direction, where units are specified by r. Also,

X RPM = X*60 revs per hour or X/60 revs per second

If we assume that the wheels are moving at 580.3 RMP, we calculate:

580.3/60 = 9.67 RPS

The wheel is 13.2 inches (33.5 Cm or 0.335 meters), and each rev will be 2.10 meters. The net result is that we are moving at 2.1*9.67 = 20.35 M/sec. Since 1 MPH = 0.447 M/Sec, the final speed amounts to 45.5 MPH.

Moving from a Standing Start

When a car is standing still and the engine is idling, a motive force will be applied according to our equations. That is, idle RPM is between 500 and 800 RPM, and will correspond to a force at the wheels. Why doesn't the car move, then? In the real-life case, we may be in park or neutral gear, the clutch may be disengaged, and/or the brake may be engaged. Most games, although not all, don't simulate those things. In a game, the car is stopped with the engine running, and when you press the accelerator the car starts to move.

Recall that the torque curve gives the maximum value of torque at a specific RPM, and that we can measure the degree to which the accelerator pedal is depressed on a scale of 0 to 1 and use this to determine the actual torque at this RPM. Given that the torque curve is stored in a table and is interpolated to retrieve a particular value, here's how we could determine the actual torque:

```
xtorque = linInterpolate (torque_curve, RPM);
xtorque = pedalPress * torque;
```

Whatever the value of **xtorque** for any positive RPM, it would result in a force on the wheels. Thus, we could try the following trick:

```
ztorque = linInterpolate (torque_curve, 500)/2.0;
```

This represents half the maximum torque at 500 RPM, and will be our minimum torque value (our zero point). I'm assuming that 500 RPM represents the idling speed of the engine, or something near to it. Any torque below this will be treated as zero:

```
if (xtorque < ztorque) xtorque = 0.0;
```

An idling vehicle will now exert zero force on the wheels, which is what we want. When the accelerator is pressed past the halfway point at idle, a force begins to be felt and the car will move. Of course, the force will immediately be 50% of that available at 500 RPM, which might be a bit of a jump. We can interpolate this to smooth the force at the start if it turns out to be a problem.

From this torque value, Equation 9.13 is used to calculate the motive force F_{mot} which can be used to compute net force, acceleration, velocity, and position from Equations 9.8 through 9.11. Some of you have been waiting to ask the inevitable question, "*Where do we get RPMs from?*" Given the current velocity, we can determine how fast the wheels are turning and back that up through the gearboxes to the engine to get the speed of the engine. This seems like a circular argument: we need RPM to get the force, which gives us the velocity; we use that velocity to compute the RPM value. How can this be?

This is an example of a differential equation. Here we have equations for two unknown values and we need to solve both of them at the same time. I'm trying to give you the idea without doing all of the math, but what we're doing here is a step-wise solution to differential equations that describe the situation. We take a force, figure the next position and velocity, and then compute the next RPM from that velocity. The next step starts with the newly computed RPM and uses this value to compute a new force, and so on. This process can be unstable at times and all of the game programmers I spoke with tell me that it needs a little tweaking to make it work, depending on the situation.

The equation for finding RPM is:

$$RPM = RPM_{wheel} * x_g * x_d * 60 / 2\pi$$

Now RPM is a function of the wheel rotation, which is in turn a function of car velocity. As a starting point, the simple way to get moving is to assume that the car is moving. This works okay at the outset, and then after a few iterations of the simulation things work out correctly. So, if we assume that the car is moving at 5MPH, which is 17.6 inches per second, this would mean that a 15 inch wheel (47.1 inch circumference) would turn once every 2.7 seconds, or 160 times per minute. We now feed this back through the gear train to get engine torque, then we apply that to get a force.

Motion in Two Dimensions

The first thing to mention here is that motion in two and three dimensions is actually the same as in one dimension. We already have Equation 9.1, which governs everything. For practical reasons, it is very important to consider each dimension independently, and the vector nature of forces certainly allows this. The good news is that everything we have learned so far about forces and accelerations along the vehicle axis remains the same, without need of modification.

Motion in two dimensions concerns two basic aspects of driving. First, and most common, is the idea of turning, which means having a race track or driving area that is other than a straight line. This includes everything except drag racing, I think. The second aspect is that of collisions. Hitting a guard rail while crossing a bridge will impart a slowing force in the longitudinal direction. This action will also provide a *transverse* force that has actually two different aspects: one that will cause the car to bounce away from the rail, and one that may impart a rotation to the car, a torque, if you will. Both are important to a realistic simulation, even in a basic game.

All of these aspects of transverse force evaluation and non-linear motion will be discussed, but this is not to say that all of these aspects have to be implemented in any particular game. As the designer, and sometimes as an implementor, you get to decide where the simulation ends and where the pretending begins.

Low Speed Turns

Let's assume we'll be working with a rear-wheel drive car where only the front wheels turn. At low speeds, the wheels will roll without significant slippage in the direction that they are pointed. For example, consider a right turn; the right front wheel is at an angle of q degrees to the long axis of the car and the left front will be at a slightly smaller angle. If left alone, a moving vehicle in this mode will turn in a complete circle. The radius of the circle traveled by the outer (in this case, left) wheel is slightly larger than the radius traveled by the inner (right) wheel, and so the wheels point in the direction tangent to the circle. The outer wheel is at a shallower angle. It is doubtful that this needs to be simulated explicitly.

The input to the steering portion of the game is most often in the form of key presses. The control is discrete, where each key press changes the direction by a fixed amount in the selected direction, left or right, specified by an angle. A normal person can only press a key a few times each second, so there is little chance of exceeding the maximum steering angle very quickly. *Not* pressing a key causes the steering angle to revert to a previous state, ultimately zero degrees. The amount of each increment is a matter of experimentation, and it is important to ensure that key presses are not allowed too often. That is, a fast machine can allow a significant degree of oversteer.

The minimum turning radius is a function of the maximum angle of the wheels and the wheelbase. For the 2004 Montana with a wheelbase of 120 inches (10 feet), and assuming a 45 degree max wheel angle, we'll get the situation shown in Figure 9.5. This figure indicates that the turning radius **R** is 14.14 feet. In fact, according to the car specs, the steering diameter is 39.7 feet, radius = 19.85 feet. We can then compute the wheel angle as **arccos (L/R)** = arccos (10/19.85) = 59.7 degrees.

The maximum angle that a wheel can be turned is equal to about 60 degrees. At 24 frames per second, a little on the slow side, it would be possible to press a key once every three or four frames, and one second is probably how long it would take to turn the entire 60 degrees. This means that six key presses over a second would put us in the minimum turning radius configuration. Each press adds about 10 degrees to the turn, and if we go more than 4 frames without a press, the radius decreases by 10 degrees (at least). Or we could decrease by 10/4 (2.5) degrees per frame until the turning angle becomes 0, and add 10 degrees for each key press, resulting in a greater variety of turning angles that could actually occur.

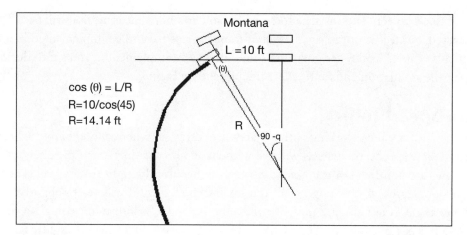

Figure 9.5
Using the wheelbase and turning radius to compute the maximum wheel angle or vice versa.

This is leading up to the ability to determine the car's position from frame-to-frame while turning. We can do this in a first approximation by simply assuming that the car travels in a straight line between frames, but in a direction determined by the steering angle. This means that the car will be moving at a tangent to the turning circle between frames, and we can compute position essentially as we did before but with a discrete change of direction.

The other way to compute position is to assume a curved trajectory, compute an angular velocity, and determine the position along the curve. This is actually an approximation too, since the turning angle is really changing between frames and the trajectory is really not a circular one at all. In this case, the angular velocity is used to change the car's orientation only, while the speed remains constant or under control of a separate key.

Driving on the tangent lines, it is clear that we need to be able to change the direction of the car quickly and easily using the velocity vector or a direction vector and scalar speed. A velocity vector is a vector in which each component is the velocity along one of the coordinate axes. Let's just look at the basic idea of direction vectors and changing the direction by an angle. We only need 2D for this. The vector V_0 in Figure 9.6 represents a velocity in the +X direction that is tangent to the curve S shown.

Let V_0 = (2.0, 0.0), and note that we need to rotate V_0 by 45 degrees clockwise. One possible way to do this would be to use a 2D rotation matrix, as we learned in Chapter 3. Doing this looks like:

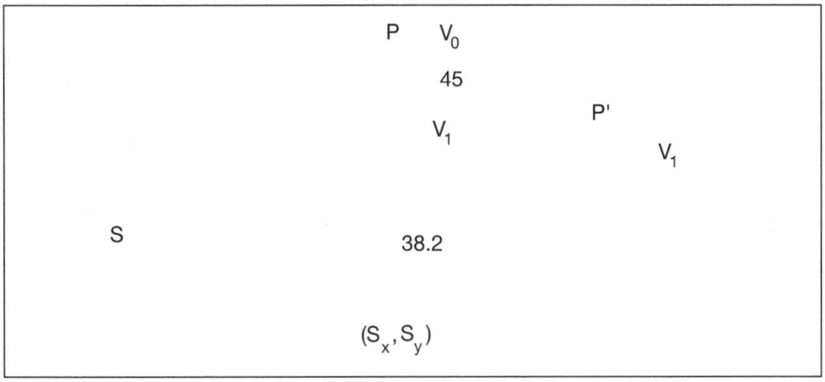

Figure 9.6
Geometry of a low-speed turn.

Equation 9.17
$$\begin{bmatrix} x \\ y \end{bmatrix} = \begin{bmatrix} cos45 & sin45 \\ -sin35 & cos45 \end{bmatrix} \begin{bmatrix} V_{0x} \\ V_{0y} \end{bmatrix} = \begin{bmatrix} 0.707 & 0.707 \\ -0.707 & 0.707 \end{bmatrix} \begin{bmatrix} 2 \\ 0 \end{bmatrix} = \begin{bmatrix} 1.414 \\ -1.414 \end{bmatrix}$$

That looks pretty close, actually. Computing the norm of the vector V_1 gives us the speed, 2.0! Perfect. We can compute the next velocity vector by pre-multiplying the previous one by the rotation matrix. If the car is located at the origin of V_0, point P (0,0), after one unit of time the car will move to (1.414, -1.414) by this estimation.

Now let the radius of the circle **R** equal 3, and assume that the time interval between start and end was one second, which means that the vehicle travels two units. The circumference of the circle is 18.84 units, and two units of travel should be 2/18.84 * 360 = 38.2 degrees around the circle. Again, assuming that the point **P** is (0,0), a rotation of 38.2 degrees clockwise puts the car at point **P'** on the circle. This is expressed as:

Equation 9.18
$$cos(90 - 38.2) = \frac{x}{3} \longrightarrow x = 1.855$$

$$cos(90 - 38.2) = \frac{y + 3}{3} \longrightarrow y = -0.642$$

This value of (x,y) is the position determined from following the curve of the circle, and is significantly different from the one we got by using the tangent. One reason for this is that the assumption was that the turning angle was 45 degrees at the beginning of the turn, and that the turn was made instantaneously. If we divide the angle in half (from 0 degrees to 45 degrees in one second averages to 22.5 over that second), we get a final position of (1.84, 1.04) using Equation 9.17. This is much closer to what I assume is the right answer of (1.855, -0.642). If we break up the one second interval into more reasonable, smaller, pieces, the answer will hopefully converge to a fairly accurate one.

The thing is that we rarely drive in circles, and if we do the tangent method will get us back to the starting point anyway, just with some inaccurate spots. It is an approximation that works well enough at low speeds.

The trigonometric calculation shown in Equation 9.18 is correct for what it's worth, but is not in a general form, and may lead to problems when computed in some cases. Since we know where the center of the circle is (S_x, S_y), what the radius is (**R**), and that the car is moving at speed **V**, we can calculate the angular velocity, a measure or rotational speed, as:

Equation 9.19
$$\omega = \frac{V}{2\pi R}\ 360$$

Here the units are specified in degrees per time unit. We compute the angular motion as a fraction of that in one time unit and rotate the position of the car by that angle around the center. That is, if the time interval between two frames is **δ** seconds, the car will be rotated an angle of **δ*ω** degrees about the center. We then rotate the car about the center by this angle. To do this, we translate the car by $(-S_x, -S_y)$, rotate by and then translate back by (S_x, S_y). Now the car is where it should be after the move.

High Speed Turns

At some high enough velocity, the tires can start to slide as well as roll. The orientation of the wheels and the car can be in different directions, as in a skid. If you have ever done this, or seen high-speed skids in movies, you may have noticed smoke. This is a side effect of a large amount of frictional force being converted into heat in the rubber tire. In other words, trying to make a tire slide involves a lot of friction, and that implies a large force opposing the motion. It would be good to calculate this force and include it in the overall melange of forces acting on the car.

Naturally, wheels prefer to roll (i.e., they have a low resistance to rolling) rather than slide, and the sliding happens when the brakes are applied or when the turning radius is too small for the speed. In this latter case, the wheels will be turned so that, for a short time, there is a difference between the direction that the tire is pointed and the direction of travel or velocity vector. This difference is called the *slip* angle, and is referred to as **a** in the literature and in the equations coming up next (yes, we have more).

In fact, there is a small slip angle for a brief time whenever the steering wheel is turned. The force of friction on the tires in this case is what causes the car to turn. The force depends on the slip angle and the weight on the particular tire, since normal forces contribute to frictional force. For relatively small angles, this force is related to α by:

Equation 9.20 $F_{corner} = C_a * \alpha$

The term C_a is a value called the *cornering stiffness*.

Figure 9.7 shows the definition of the angle α. It is clear that a wheel can only roll along its circumference, which in a linear direction would be perpendicular to its narrow axis (width) in the plane of the four wheels. A basic concept of physics is that forces, and therefore accelerations, can be broken up into orthogonal vector components. Thus, for a car that is turning, there are components in the forward (longitudinal) direction and the side-to-side (lateral) direction. The lateral force is represented by F_{corner} and it is related to **a** due to the math involved; for small angles, it is approximately true that $\sin(\alpha) = \alpha$.

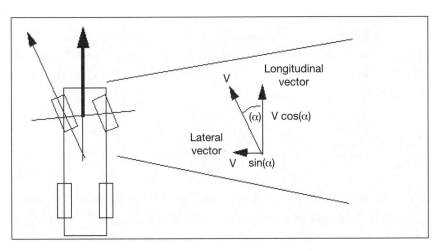

Figure 9.7
Forces that act on a car as it is turning.

So, who really cares? The fact that F_{corner} exists allows a car to turn at all. General knowledge, I guess. However, something that is rather important is determining when a car begins to *drift*, or slide into a corner. Some people call this a skid, but there are other definitions of skid, like slamming on the brakes or accelerating harder than the tires can permit. Anyway, at some speed and turning configuration, the tires begin to slide in addition to turning, and control of the car becomes difficult. Because it is usually the case that the front tires are turned more in the direction that the car is traveling, it is the rear ones that begin to slide. This means that the car starts to rotate about its center of mass, apparently in an effort to get the front wheels lined up with the rear ones.

The car starts to drift when the centripetal force pushing the car outwards from the center of the circle or the turn exceeds the frictional force of the tires. At that point, the tires start to slide with the rear ones sliding first. The centripetal force is computed as

Equation 9.21 $$F_c = \frac{mv^2}{r}$$

where r is the radius of the circle, m is the vehicle's mass, and v is the velocity. The frictional force that prevents the wheels from sliding is, like all frictional forces, a function of the normal force and the coefficient of friction of the surfaces as in equation 10.13: $F = \mu N$

The normal force N is the weight of the car in Earth's gravity, and typical values of 'm for rubber on pavement are between 0.5 and 0.8. Recall that in Figure 9.5, $\cos(\theta) = L/R$ where θ is the steering angle and L is the wheelbase. Thus, $R = L/\cos(\theta)$ and when the drift begins we have:

Equation 9.22 $$\frac{m \cos \theta \, v^2}{L} = \mu N$$

As the velocity increases or the angle θ increases, the drift gets worse. The force causing the drift is the excess of centripetal over frictional force, or $F_e = m \cos \theta \, v^2/L - uN$. The acceleration that this force causes on the car of mass m is $a = F_e/m$.

The fact that this causes the rear wheels to drift more than the front is quite difficult to calculate, but we could assume that there is a ratio that we can use to assign the sliding force between the front and rear wheels. We could arbitrarily assign a ratio of 30/70 front/back assignment of force. We could use the steering angle as a percentage of maximum: a zero angle would give a 50-50 assignment of force, whereas 100% would assign all of the excess to the rear wheels. We could also use the slip angle, where greater slip angles assign more excess force to the rear wheels.

In any case, it is clear that higher speeds will cause drifting, as will increased turning angle (decreased turn radius).

Cheating—How to Fake Physics

Games cheat about details a lot. The goal, after all, it to make the player feel happy about the game, its realism, its goals, and that it is fair. A driving simulation has to be realistic about all of the details, largely because the players will know if it is not and be unhappy as a result. I do not wish to offend anyone, but truthfully, a perfect simulation would not be the most interesting game for most players. I could also write a very large book just about how to conduct the simulation; the physics would be quite complex. I propose a compromise along the usual game design lines—let's cheat.

Perhaps it would be more aesthetic to call our cheating *approximation* or *simplification* instead of cheating. The idea it to make it look like you are doing it right without going through all of the actual detailed calculations. After all, the calculations take time, and you have to get a lot of details right. As long as the action in the game *looks* right, what does it matter? This is one of the distinctions between a driving simulation and a theme driver; the simulations actually gets the details right, the theme driver may or may not, but the correctness is not the issue. Playability is the issue. Simulation games are fun partly because they are accurate, and the players expect the accuracy and *make* it part of the enjoyment. This chapter has been about how to get the physics right, but it should be clear that I could go on for the rest of the book on the same subject. There are a lot of details, and a lot more we could talk about.

On the other hand, games like *Mario Kart* that don't have accurate physics are a lot of fun to play for many people. Why do these games work so well? They provide a combination of real physics calculations with a set of simplifications that permit game play to seem real. The simplifications are a set of rules that are applied in specific circumstances. The rules can get specialized depending on the type of game you are developing, but I can cover some of the basic ones in the remainder of this chapter to help you get started.

Controlling Speed

The typical user-speed control is a key. A player makes a car go faster by pressing the key and releases the key to make the car go slower. The scheme we described for speed control earlier in this chapter used a relatively complex feedback scheme between the engine RPM, the gearboxes, and the wheels. What I suggest here as a cheat is a simple linear speed control or table look-up.

Using Linear Control

In this scheme, each time the forward key is pressed, we add a simple increment to the current speed. Of course, if we are going as fast as possible—a normal situation—we don't increase the speed. When the forward key is not being pressed, the vehicle slows down by a fixed amount each second. If the forward increment is 0.2 meters/second, for example, and the player can hit the forward key five times per second, the player's car can go 1 meter per second faster each second. Deceleration should probably be at the same rate. For example, if the forward key is not pressed, we decrease speed by 1 m/s each second in the above case.

In general, we adjust the velocity each frame. If the speed increment is ΔS per press, if **k** presses are allowed every second, and if the current frame rate is **F** frames per second, the deceleration will be $(k\,\Delta S)/F$ in the current frame. The minimum speed is 0, of course. Because speed should not change instantly, this change in velocity will be spread over a few frames.

Using Table Look-Up

The idea here is to implement a more complex function than a linear one while not requiring significantly more processing time. It would be possible to build a simple array that would be indexed by speed and that would return an acceleration that would be used when traveling at that speed. The same table could be used for acceleration and deceleration, or we could have different tables. Using different tables would not matter from a performance perspective.

On the other hand, the table could contain multipliers for the simple linear values we computed previously. For example, the new way to compute the deceleration for a particular speed S might be **accTable[S]*(k ΔS)/F**. The numbers in **actable[]** will be between 0.0 and 1.0 and will reflect any non-linearities in the acceleration curve.

It is not unusual for the starting acceleration to be slower than those seen for higher speeds. This is a direct result of the torque curve giving higher torques at RPMs between 3000 and 4000. The values in **actable[]** will be smaller than 1 for the low speeds, and should peak at or near 1.0 at speeds corresponding to the places where the car is most responsive.

Controlling Direction

Each time a left or right turn key is pressed, the vehicle should change direction. When the turn key is released, the vehicle will stop changing direction and straighten out, continuing in the new current direction. Straightening the vehicle should occur over a few frames, just as deceleration does.

For each key press, the *turn angle*—the desired angle of the wheels—should be equal to the desired change in the vehicle direction. It should change by a specified amount. Negative angles, for instance, could be for left turns and positive angles could be for right turns. A maximum turning angle must be enforced. Then, in each frame, we compute how much the car changes its direction according to the specified turn angle, given that any vehicle can only change direction just so fast. Here is a relatively simple and obvious way to implement this:

```
if (left_key_pressed)
{
   if (turn_angle > MIN_TURN_ANGLE)
   {
      turn_angle -= turn_increment;
      if (turn_angle < MIN_TURN_ANGLE)
         turn_angle = MIN_TURN_ANGLE;
   }
} else if (right_key_pressed)
   if (turn_angle < MAX_TURN_ANGLE)
   {
      turn_angle += turn_increment;
      if (turn_angle > MAX_TURN_ANGLE)
         turn_angle = MAX_TURN_ANGLE;
   }
} else if (abs(turn_angle) > 0.1)
{
   if (turn_angle < 0)
   {
      turn_angle += straighten_increment;
      if (turn_angle > 0) turn_angle = 0;
   } else
   {
      turn_angle -= straighten_increment;
      if (turn_angle < 0) turn_angle = 0;
   }
}
change_car_direction (turn_angle*frame_factor);
```

The last line results in the actual change in the direction of the car in the specified way. The setting **frame_factor** represents the amount of change that can occur within the time duration of one frame. Note, for example, that if **turn_angle** is zero, the change will be zero. The car straightens out to a zero change according to the parameter **straighten_increment**, and the user-specified changes in angle are spread over a few frames.

Skidding

Faking a skid is a matter of knowing a few simple parameters: how sticky the driving surface is, how fast the car is moving, and how much the car is turning.

The surface is specified by the location on the terrain model, and is a design feature of the game. Some games take place entirely on dry pavement; others have ice, rain, snow, gravel, grass, and a host of other surfaces. We need a simple way to parameterize the surface. One such way is to use a small scale of *stickiness*: 0 is very sticky, 1 is very slippery, and all surfaces have a value between 0 and 1. Of course, stickiness is really about friction, and the vehicle contributes to this. (Some cars have really good tires but others don't.) Thus, each car modulates this stickiness by a factor that reflects the car's parameters. This can be done by giving a car a number between 0 and 2 that will be multiplied by the surface stickiness to get the total stickiness. The result of the multiplication is cropped to be between 0 and 1. The higher the stickiness value, the more likely a skid will occur.

The speed at which a car is moving can, again, be converted to a number between 0 and 1 by dividing the current speed by the maximum speed. This number represents the percentage of maximum speed that the car is moving, and provides, in some sense, a way to compare vehicles to each other. The faster a car is moving, the more likely it is to skid.

In a similar fashion, the measure of how much a car is turning can be expressed as the current turning angle divided by the maximum (or minimum). Here we take the absolute value of the maximum of **turning_angle/MAX_TURNING_ANGLE** and **turning_angle/MIN_TURNING_ANGLE**. This will be a number between 0 and 1, and again, the larger the value, the more likely a skid will occur.

Now we have three numbers, each between 0 and 1. We can combine these in many ways: we can add them, average them, multiply them, and so on. Just to give a practical example, let's average them, which results in a value S_{val} between 0 and 1. What we do with this number is also up to us, and I think some experimenting with it is very likely to be needed. Still, here's an idea: if $S_{val} < 0.7$, no skid will take place. If $S_{val} > 0.7$, a skid will take place with a probability related to the size of S_{val}. We could code this as:

```
if (Sval < random()) do_skid (Sval);
```

The size of the skid is related to **1.0-S**$_{val}$, and will determine the amount by which the direction of the car changes. An easy way to change the car's direction is to instantly add a value to the **turn_angle** variable in case of a right turn skid, and subtract it in case of a left skid. The effect of this will be that to specify a turn in the opposite direction will actually correct the skid quickly, but will also permit an over-correction, resulting in a skid in the opposite direction. Skidding is an exception to the turn angle limits, by the way; a skid can result in the **turn_angle** becoming greater than the maximum allowed. This is because the turn is not a function of the physical limits of the vehicle, but instead is an exceptional case resulting from exceeding the speed at which the car can stay safely stuck to the pavement.

Collisions

As we have seen, resolving the effects of a collision can be a complicated process. All of the forces acting on a car are resolved every time unit, and the net forces are used to determine accelerations, and hence motions.

We are essentially cheating by using table look-up values instead of having to calculate net forces. In particular, forward motion and steering are essentially done by table look-up. The only forces that are used are now those caused by collision. We just have to make the result of a collision look good, not actually reflect the real physics of the situation. There are really three aspects of a collision from this perspective that we need to consider: the effect of the collision on speed, direction, and orientation.

The effect on speed is a function of the current speeds and directions of travel of the objects involved in the collision. We can think of the resultant speed as a vector sum of the velocities of the two objects if they are both moving; we have seen a vector sum before. If one object is a building or other fixed object, the moving object bounces off of it so that it reflects like a light beam for shallow angles, and stops completely for angles over about 45 degrees.

The effect on direction has partly been described, but there are other cases. If a vehicle is hit perpendicular to the direction of motion (*T-boned*), it will be forced to slide at an angle not possible otherwise. We therefore need to treat collisions as a special case, permitting forces and accelerations in special ways for a few frames. We could, for instance, have a special acceleration vector and velocity vector that are usually all 0, but if a collision happens, the values in the vector will be filled in according to the collision; the velocity vector is the velocity imparted by the collision, and the acceleration is that which will slow the vehicle from that velocity. Since these are both zero in most cases, they will not affect the vehicle unless a collision occurs. The velocity vector will move the vehicle in a direction opposite to the impact, and the acceleration vector will restore the vehicle to normal motion, and restore the velocity vector to all zeros.

In a very similar way, we can control the vehicle's orientation. If our car is hit near the rear wheels on the driver's side, the impact will impart a rotation to our car that will change its orientation as a function of time, and will do so almost independently of our steering control. This can be implemented as a *moment vector* that is again usually zero. When a car is struck, a force at a point along the car is converted into a moment arm, stored in the vector as a rotational velocity. When this vector is non-zero, we use it to compute the orientation of the car as a function of time; that is, all of a sudden, the direction that the car is pointing will change every frame by an amount specified in the moment vector.

The values in this vector decrease by a fixed amount each frame so that the car stops spinning after a time, and the magnitude of the rotation is a function of the intensity of the collision and is independent of the other aspects, like the change in velocity and direction of motion. All three effects occur at the same time.

Becoming Airborne

There's no way to determine whether a car has all four wheels on the ground or not without real physics to tell us. When a moving vehicle crests the top of a hill, it may go airborne for a second or so. How can we arrange this? We can make a special case for this as before.

The crest of a hill is marked by the game designers, and this makes it easy to tell when the car reaches it. At that point, the car enters the airborne state, and a path through the air is computed. Basically, what we need to know is where the car will land and how long that will take. At the moment the car goes airborne a vector is computed that gives a vertical velocity to the car that is proportional to the car's speed up the hill. The effect is that the car continues to move up even though the ground falls away. This vector is recomputed each frame, decreasing the upward velocity and causing the car to fall. While in the airborne state, the steering and acceleration controls do not work, but the engine sound should continue to reflect the engine speed.

The direction of motion and speed of the car will change quickly when it hits the ground; the transition from airborne to normal occurs when the car hits the ground (i.e., any terrain polygon) and the car's speed will, at that time, be the horizontal speed while airborne, and its direction will be its direction of motion at that moment. The engine speed now takes over, and must quickly become compatible with the car's speed. If the car's engine is moving very quickly and the car is moving slowly, the car speeds up and the engine slows down according to a schedule that needs to be computed at that time. The car will be moving in a direction that may be in opposition to the steering control, so the same process takes hold for steering: the car's direction of motion changes from the direction it was moving while in the air to the direction indicated by the wheels. If the two directions are vastly different, we may decide to roll the car over, or at least to make a squealing noise and display some smoke around the wheels.

Summary

This chapter has given you enough information to build a relatively detailed simulation of a car. You've also learned how to approximate those aspects that are not really important to simulate, but which should still look right. A complete simulation is not given as code, but the website for this book provides links to car simulations at various levels of detail that you can play with. Some of these resources are also listed in the references section at the end of this book. Many of these come with source code.

The implementation of these features can be done in many ways, and doing all of them is impossible. The *Manic Mars Racer* game that we'll be developing later in this book will show you one way to build physics into a real system.

I'll end this chapter by providing you with some resources that can help you implement physics in your own games. Table 9.1 provides units and conversions to help you work with the physics equations. Table 9.2 provides gear ration data for actual transmissions.

9

Table 9.1   Units and Conversions

	Metric	Imperial
Distance	Kilometer (Km)	Mile (Mi) = 1.6093 km
	Meter (M)	Foot (Ft) = 0.3048 m
	Centimeter (Cm)	Inch (In) = 2.54 cm
Speed	Meters/second (M/s)	Feet/sec (ft/s)
	Kilometers/hour (kph)	Miles per hour (MPH) = 1.609 km/h0.2778 m/s = .447 m/s
Mass	Kilogram (Kg)	Pound* (lb) = 0.4536 Kg)
Force	Newton (N = Kg*M/s²)	Pound = 4.45N
Power	Watt (W = N*M/s)	Foot-pounds/second = 1.356 W
		Horsepower = 745.7 W
Torque	Newton-meter (N*m)	Foot-Pounds (ft-lb) = 1.356 N.m
Force of Gravity		9.8 m/s² = 32.1 lb/s

Table 9.2   Gear ration data for actual transmissions. (Data provided for 2004 vehicles.)

Car	Auto/ Std	1st	2nd	3rd	4th	5th	rev	Diff.
Sunfire	Std	3.58	2.02	1.35	0.98	0.69	3.31	3.94:1
	auto	2.96	1.62	1.00	0.68		2.14	3.63:1
Grand Prix	auto	2.92	1.57	1.00	0.71		2.39	3.05
Mustang GT	Manual	3.37	1.99	1.33	1.00	0.67	3.22	3.27:1
Explorer	Auto	3.22	2.32	1.55	1.00	0.71	3.07	3.55:1
Focus	Auto	2.82	1.50	1.00	0.95			3.73
	Manual	3.15	1.93	1.28	0.95	0.756		3.61
Taurus	Auto	2.77	1.54	1.00	0.69			3.96
Honda Element	Std	3.533	2.042	1.355	1.028	0.825	3.583	4.765
	Auto	2.864	1.535	1.081	0.738		2.00	4.438
Mazda Miata	Manual	3.14	1.89	1.33	1.00	0.81		4.30
	Auto	2.45	1.45	1.00	0.73			4.10
Totota Rav4	Manual	3.833	1.904	1.333	1.038	0.820	3.583	4.235
	Auto	3.943	2.197	1.413	1.030		3.145	3.120

Chapter 10

Simulating Continuous Time

- Learn how to simulate continuous time in a game using a basic game loop.

- Learn how to write programs for the Win 32 API using device contexts and Windows.

- Learn about double buffering and other means to eliminate flickering.

The simple games we developed in Chapters 2 and 3 used a basic stepwise time increment feature. This is the type of time control used in some of the old arcade games like *Frogger*. You've probably figured out that this approach won't work very well for driving and racing games that have any degree of sophistication at all.

Time on a computer is not continuous. A computer has a clock that sends timing signals to the CPU, and the unit of time is therefore an instruction execution. All of that aside, we just have to make it *look* like time is continuous, and that means we need to generate graphical frames and play them at a high enough rate. Television plays pictures at 30 images per second, and motion pictures are displayed at 24 images per second. This range is acceptable for games, although many modern games running on fast machines can achieve a frame rate of 60 frames per second or higher.

I have taught classes on computer game development for many years, and I find that my students encounter a few major conceptual difficulties when it comes to a subject such as simulating continuous time. It takes real effort to be able to make it appear as though time is passing smoothly in a game at a similar rate to the real world. The physics simulations we discussed in Chapter 9 depend on equations involving time, and their success at predicting positions and velocities depends on game time having similar properties to time in the world.

We'll begin our exploration of continuous time using the GLUT interface. Ultimately, however, we'll want to take advantage of the native Windows interface. This will help us gain efficiency improvements, use the Windows timer functions, and get control of the main loop. As you should recall, GLUT has a loop that controls time and the game functions, and most programmers resent giving up this control.

As we explore both simulated time and real time, I'll introduce the minimal native Windows code needed to open a window, create timers, and manipulate the operating system. We will also see how to connect this small amount of native code to OpenGL so that we can continue to use the graphics scheme that we are used to.

To help you learn how to simulate continuous time, we'll walk through a set of five demo programs in this chapter. We'll start with Demo 1, which creates a simple 3D environment with a vehicle (a prism) that you can move around using the numeric keypad. Then, we'll continue to modify this program and develop other versions to allow the program to run under Windows without GLUT. I'll also show you how to use double-buffering techniques to eliminate flicker.

The Game Loop and Time

As you learned in Chapter 2, a game loop can be organized in a few distinct ways. One important goal is to have the game run at the same speed on all computers. It is very irritating to have a perfectly good game run at three times its normal speed on a new computer. In fact, the *turbo* button on older computers was intended to be used to account for this problem. The *Gopher-it* game has a timer that allows it to use one-second steps on any normal computer. We want the same for continuous time on a PC.

> *Interesting side note:* Have you ever played *Space Invaders*? It is a very old arcade game, designed by Toshihiro Nishikado in Japan in 1978. If you played this game, you will recall that as you destroyed the alien space ships, the game would play faster and faster. Near the end it moves very quickly indeed. This may seem like a design feature, but actually it is caused by the fact that fewer objects can be processed more quickly, and by blowing up the alien ships, you permit the CPU to move the fewer remaining objects more frequently. What seemed like a cool design feature of the game was actually a timing issue.

Within the game loop we render a new frame, determine collisions and compute responses. We also determine the activity of AI-controlled objects. These activities are expected to take a significant amount of time. We could set up our code so that each time the game loop executes one iteration, the elapsed time gets computed and is used as a delta. This effectively means that a variable amount of time will elapse between any two arbitrary frames. Ideally, this amount of time will be less than 1/24 of a second, and the variations will not be visible to the player.

Before I show you how to construct the main loop in this manner, I should tell you about an alternate scheme. It is also possible to force the loop to have a frame rate no greater than a certain value. That is, if we wish to set 30 frames per second as the game's nominal speed, we could set a timer to execute a callback every 1/30 of a second. If a frame takes a lot of calculation, it may take longer than this, but the frame rate will never be greater than the one specified. Implementing this scheme is easier if we use GLUT, so let's start with our GLUT version first.

A basic implementation of a main loop in C includes calls to the base routine in all of the important subsystems of the game. Note that in the code shown next I have excised collision detection from the AI system. This is because it potentially takes a great deal of time (and time is the subject at hand). It could possibly take as much time as the rest of the AI system needs. In the code shown next, each line in the loop could easily take the same amount of time:

```
while (true)
{
    detectCollisions();
    AIandMovement();
    render();
    sound();
    t = deltaTime();
    gameTime += t;
}
```

If nothing is really happening in the game, this loop could run very fast. Rates of well over 60 frames per second could be achieved. This should not cause any problems because the motion of objects will depend on the global value **gameTime**, which represents the time setting for our game. Thus, the objects will move with appropriate speeds on any processor, fast or slow.

A fixed frame rate can be achieved by causing the loop just shown to go idle if it executes its code in less than the specified time. A global variable named **delay** is used that holds the correct elapsed time for each iteration. If the loop finishes early, it idles (waits, delays) until the specified time has passed:

```
float dt;
dt = deltaTime(); gameTime = 0.0;
while (true)
{
    detectCollisions();
    AIandMovement();
```

```
        render();
        sound();
        dt = deltaTime();
        sleep(max (0, delay - dt);
        gameTime += dt;
}
```

If the **delay** variable is set to 1/30, we will get at most, 30 frames per second. The **deltaTime()** function returns the real time duration since the last this function was called. You might now be wondering, how do we tell what time it is on a PC so we can implement the **deltaTime()** function? Let's look at a few ways for doing this and select the best one.

The **DWORD timeGetTime(void)** function returns the system time, which is the elapsed time since Windows was started. The units returned are represented in milliseconds, which is good, but the resolution can be as large as 5 milliseconds, which is bad.

The **DWORD GetTickCount(void)** function does effectively the same thing as **timeGetTime()**, but it has some drawbacks, especially with respect to performance. My advice is to not use this function.

The system functions **QueryPerformanceCounter()** and **QueryPerformanceFrequency()** could also be used; **QueryPerformanceCounter()** has a higher time resolution, sometimes under a microsecond, but takes longer to call, and the time value must be normalized before using. This is not really a place for such detailed comparisons. Look these up, if you like, but let's use a pretty good scheme based on **timeGetTime()**.

Our main loop will want to use as much of the CPU as the game needs at all times. The amount of calculation will vary from frame-to-frame, though, and we need to know how much actual time has elapsed between calls to the physics routines and the renderer. For example, we need to know how far things have moved so they can be drawn in a new position, and this means knowing their velocities and how much real time has elapsed. A function that returns a delta time, the time since the last time it was called, is a very useful thing to have:

```
/* needs winmm.lib and mmsystem.h */
float deltaTime ()
{
        static float prevTime = 0.0f;
        float current, delta;

        current = timeGetTime() * 0.001f;
        delta = current - prevTime;
```

```
        prevTime = current;
        return delta;
}
```

The **deltaTime()** function returns a real number that represents the number of seconds between calls to the function. We can use this to sequence events and determine game time. The speed of a game is often measured in frames per second—the number of times the screen is redrawn each second. The frame rate can be calculated using the following function:

```
int frameRate ()
{
    static int frames = 0;
    static float lastStart = 0.0F;
    static int tmp = 0;

    lastStart += deltaTime();
    frames++;
    if (lastStart > 1.0F)
    {
        tmp = frames;
        frames = 0;
        lastStart = 0.0F;
    }
    return tmp;
}
```

Continuous Time in *Gopher-it*—Using GLUT

As an illustration of how to use "continuous" time in a simple game, let's modify the *Gopher-it* game we developed earlier in the book by eliminating the discrete time step. In fact, I propose we eliminate most of the game and simply create a demo, but it will at least be one that you can understand quickly. First, we'll remove all of the maze walls, fuel-ups, and gophers, along with their textures. We don't need them and they take a lot of time to render. The program we'll create is called **Demo1**.

To implement continuous time, I'll use GLUT in a straightforward way. In the version that we wrote for Chapter 4, timers were set to enable one second steps, and callbacks were used to move the player and the police each time increment, which was about one second. Instead of this, I now create a callback (tick) every 1/30 second to get the video frame rates. Every tick, the callback executes an iteration of a simple game loop and performs the AI, graphics, and sound. The original timer code has been modified.

Instead of three timers, one for each vehicle, we now have just one. Here's the old code to give you a frame of reference:

```
void start_ai_timers ()
{
    glutTimerFunc (COP1_INTERVAL, moveCop1, POLICE1);
    glutTimerFunc (COP2_INTERVAL, moveCop2, POLICE2);
    glutTimerFunc (PLAYER_INTERVAL, timedAILoop, 0);
}

void moveCop1 (int a)
{
    ...
    glutTimerFunc (COP1_INTERVAL, moveCop1, POLICE1);
    ...
}

void moveCop2 (int a)
{
    ...
    glutTimerFunc (COP2_INTERVAL, moveCop1, POLICE1);
    ...
}

void timedAILoop (int a)
{
    ...
    glutTimerFunc (PLAYER_INTERVAL, timedAILoop, 0);
    ...
}
```

Each function in this original code shown here controls the motion of one of the moving objects. The time values, such as **PLAYER_INTERVAL**, are significant fractions of one second, usually 0.9 or so, although they are a little different from each other to make the behavior appear random.

The new code looks like this:

```
void timedAILoop (int a)
{
    float dt;                       // Time since last frame.

    if (ENDOFGAME) return;
```

```
    glutTimerFunc (PLAYER_INTERVAL,timedAILoop, 0);
    // How long since the last frame was drawn?
    dt = deltaTime();
    movePlayer (dt)
    display ();
}
```

Here, **PLAYER_INTERVAL** is set to 33 milliseconds (1/30 second). This is the new "main loop" where the moving objects are alternately moved and displayed. Actually, there is no loop because the code schedules the GLUT timer to call itself. In this function, the single **timedAILoop()** function moves all of the moving objects, rather than having three timers, one for each. Each player possess their own velocity, so the objects can move at different speeds and directions without changing the timer.

Continuous Motion

A significant change has taken place in the structure that represents objects. To implement continuous time we must be able to support arbitrary motions. For example, in 33 milliseconds, a car could travel 30 feet (assuming it is traveling at 60 miles per hour), 10 feet (if it is traveling at 20 miles per hour), or an arbitrary distance in an arbitrary direction. The previous version of *Gopher-it* did not permit this, and moved a car one step per time. This is one of the reasons the game was dull.

The new object structure we'll need to support arbitrary motions is shown here:

```
struct objectStruct
{
    float posx, posy, posz;      // Position on the board
    float vx, vy, vz;
                                 // Velocity
    float dx, dy, dz;
                                 // Orientation: Wher
                                 // are we pointed?
    float steer, accel;
                                 // Keyboard instructions
    float speed, bearing;
    unsigned char exists;
                                 // Still there?
    unsigned char *icon;
};
typedef struct objectStruct OBJ;
```

The idea is to update object position, velocity, and orientation each frame based on the previous values and the user input. I am going to keep things very simple for the first demo program that we create so that I can emphasize only the new aspects. In particular, the new demo provides only a player-controlled car.

The player begins with the car at location (300,300) on a grid of 700×700 locations. Initialization is performed in the function **initializeAI()**. In this code, **player** is an **objectStruct** structure:

```
player.exists = 1;
player.dx = 1.0f; player.dy = 0.0f; player.dz = 0.0f;
player.vx = 0.0f; player.vy = 0.0f; player.vz = 0.0f;
player.posx = 300; player.posy = 300;
player.posz = 0.0f;
player.speed = 0.0f; player.bearing = 0.0f;
```

The keyboard callback is changed so that it calls an AI function that sets counters. Each time the forward key is pressed, an AI function named **enterUserMotion()** is called:

```
enterUserMotion(0.0F, 0.1F);
```

The first parameter indicates an increment to the steering (left is negative and right is positive). The second parameter indicates an increment in motion (forward is positive and braking is negative). In the case just shown, the **player.accel** value is incremented by 0.1; the maximum value is 1.0, or 100%. The maximum **player.steer** value is 1.0 for full right turn, and -1.0 for full left turn, with 0.0 being the norm. Between two frames, it is possible that multiple key presses can occur, although in 1/30 of a second such a thing is not likely.

The function named **timedAILoop()** has a call to the function that moves the player's vehicle, **movePlayer()**. As you should recall, this function call should be made every 33 milliseconds or so, but the actual value is passed to the function. The **movePlayer()** function does more than just determine the next position of the player. It also applies restoring values to the steering and acceleration inputs so that, for example, the car does not move forever if the forward key is typed once. Finally, **movePlayer()** computes new values for the velocity and orientation vector given the current ones and the steering and acceleration values. The function as seen in the demo is:

```
void movePlayer(float dt)
{
    OBJ *ptr;
    float x, y, speed=0, angle=0;
```

```
if (ENDOFGAME) return;
if (player.exists)
{
   ptr = &player;  // this object

   // Compute next position based on velocity
   x = ptr->posx + ptr->vx*dt*90;
   y = ptr->posy + ptr->vy*dt*90;
   ptr->posx = x;
   ptr->posy = y;
   speed = ptr->speed;
```

This determines the position of the player using velocity and time. The numerical
constant is set to 90 in the code above, and those in the code below are determined by
experimentation, rather than by computing a correct physical simulation. Next, we
restore the steering and acceleration to zero gradually, if no key is pressed. For example,
steering is restored by 1/30 of a unit per frame, meaning the wheels straighten in a
second. Each press of a turn key (4 or 6) results in a steering value being increased or
decreased by 0.1:

```
// Apply restoring values to velocities and steering
if (ptr->steer < 0)
   ptr->steer += 1.0F/30.0F;
else if (ptr->steer > 0)
   ptr->steer -= 1.0F/30.0F;
if (fabs((double)ptr->steer) <= 1.0F/30.0F)
   ptr->steer = 0.0F;

if (ptr->accel < 0)
   ptr->accel = 0.0f;
else if (ptr->accel > 0)
   ptr->accel -= 1.0F/60.0F;
if (fabs((double)ptr->accel) <= 1.0F/60.0F)
   ptr->accel = 0.0F;
speed = ptr->accel;
ptr->speed = speed;
```

Finally, the bearing (direction the car is moving), orientation, and speed are determined
for use during the next frame:

```
// Update velocity based on steering and acceleration
    angle = ptr->steer * MAX_STEER_ANGLE;
    ptr->bearing += angle;
    ptr->dx = cos((double)(ptr->bearing*TO_RADIANS));
```

10

```
    ptr->dy = -sin((double)(ptr->bearing*TO_RADIANS));
    ptr->vx = ptr->dx * speed;

    ptr->vy = ptr->dy * speed;
  }
}
```

The final item of interest (in my opinion, at least) is the function that draws the player's vehicle. In the original game, I simply gave quad coordinates to the OpenGL function, **glVertex3f()**. This time I've created arrays to hold the coordinates of the quads, as would be the case if they were to be read from a file. They are drawn using this simple loop:

```
glColor3f (r, g, b);
cosa = (float)cos((double)(angle*TO_RADIANS));
sina = (float)sin((double)(angle*TO_RADIANS));
for (i=0; i<24; i++)
{
    xx =  cosa*X[i] + sina*Y[i] + x;
    yy = -sina*X[i] + cosa*Y[i] + y;
    glVertex3f (xx, yy, Z[i]);
}
```

The angle specified in this code represents the orientation of the vehicle, in this case, a simple prism. The prism is rotated to align with the specified orientation so that the car stays aligned with its bearing vector.

The source code for this demo, along with a Visual Studio workspace, can be found in the Chapter 10 section of the website for this book, and is named **Demo1**. The large prism in the center of the plane is there to make it easier for you to orient yourself when running the demo. The cube "car," as shown in Figure 10.1, has a blue vector attached to it that points in the direction of orientation; this is also the direction of motion. The keyboard controls motion: 4 and 6 are left and right turns, 8 accelerates the car forward, and 2 is the brake. I have drawn a grid on the driving surface so that you can get some feeling of motion.

Note that this is essentially the same visual space that was used for *Gopher-it*. The drops are the same, the basic code is the same, and we still are using GLUT. On my computer, there is a somewhat irritating flickering horizontal bar that moves up the screen sometimes, like a TV with bad vertical hold. Perhaps there's a way to get rid of this.

Figure 10.1
Screen shot from the first continuous time demo.

Using the Win32 Native API

The OpenGL *GLUT* system allows us to create windows and manipulate them and their contents irrespective of the host system, more or less. This means that our game should run properly on PCs, MACs, Linux, and Unix—any system that supports OpenGL. Unfortunately, this portability has a downside—the code doesn't run as quickly as we want it to. The flexibility of GLUT comes at the price of some compromises in the performance area, and this may well cause some difficulties. In addition, if we want to use some of the interesting features of the Microsoft DirectX system, we'll need to know at least a little about how to setup and use a Window on a PC running a Microsoft operating system.

Many books have been written on this subject. Many of these books weigh over ten pounds and contain a thousand pages or more. What I am prepared to do here is merely get you started so that you can experiment with this on your own. Material will be added to my website on a regular basis that will support you in your studies, and of course the Web already contains a vast amount of material on this subject[1,2,3].

10

Recall that *GLUT* allows us to define and draw a window on the screen. This window will hold the graphics for a game, and will be the host for the interaction with the player. We want to know how to do these things on a Windows PC without using *GLUT*. In Chapter 3, we learned how to use GLUT, and so I suggest that we use the same basic set of steps to learn how to use the Windows API. It seems to me that there are really four parts to creating a window: initialization, creation, the event loop, and callbacks.

Initialization

In Chapter 3 you learned that the initialization stage of a GLUT program involves two calls: **glutInit()** and **glutInitDisplayMode()**. The important task that these functions perform is that they send critical setup information to the operating system. The operating system must know the details of all resources. A window, with its connected memory, display space, and other facilities, is a resource.

In the Windows API, the initialization step amounts to telling the system about a window by filling in the members of a structure. Multiple window types are available, which Windows confusingly calls *classes*. Each class has a structure that contains vital information. The common element that connects windows of the same class is that they share the same windows procedure (see **WndProc()** below).

The structure that holds the vital information is named **WNDCLASSEX** (it used to be called **WNDCLASS**) and it holds the following data fields:

UINT size;	Size of this structure, in bytes. Set this to **sizeof(WNDCLASSEX)**.
UINT style;	Predefined window styles are provided, each represented by a predefined constant and a set of parameters. We don't need to know much about this field; simply specify a **0** here.
WNDPROC lpfnWndProc;	A pointer to the window procedure that will handle relevant events. This field is usually set to a function named something like **WndProc**.
int cbClsExtra;	This is the number of extra bytes to allocate following this window-class structure. You might use these for task-specific variables. This field should almost always be set to **0**.
int cbWndExtra;	The number of extra bytes to allocate following the window instance. The system initializes the bytes to zero. This field should be set to **0**.
HINSTANCE hInstance;	This is a handle (pointer to a structure) to the *application instance*. The system will give this to us. It should be set to **hInstance**, the first parameter to **WinMain**.

HICON hIcon;	A handle (pointer) to an icon. It serves as a small graphical symbol for this class. If this is **NULL,** the system will provide the handle. It should be set to **NULL,** or to **LoadIcon(NULL, IDI_APPLICATION).**
HCURSOR hCursor;	Yet another handle that describes the cursor that will be used in this window. It should be set to **LoadCursor(NULL, IDC_ARROW).**
HBRUSH hbrBackground;	A background color or texture to be used to draw the window. You can use a standard-named color (like **COLOR_GRAYTEXT** or **COLOR_HIGHLIGHT**) or you can use **(HBRUSH)(COLOR_WINDOW+1)** for a change.
LPCTSTR lpszMenuName;	Set to **NULL** to have no default menu.
LPCTSTR lpszClassName;	A string name by which this window class shall be known. You can use a constant such as **"SimpleWindowClass"**
HICON hIconSm;	A handle for a small icon to be used in the upper-left corner of the window. You can use **NULL** or **LoadIcon(NULL, IDI_APPLICATION).**

By now you might be wondering: what's with all of the weird variable names? They come from a standard called *Hungarian notation*. The basic idea is that there is a set of prefix letters that identify the variable type followed by a variable name. For example, in the variable **lpfnWndProc** the prefix is **lpfn**, meaning that it is a (long) pointer to a function, and the name is **WndProc**. Some developers claim that this scheme reduces programming errors, and others deny it. I don't really care; I just think it's ugly. Still, you must use the existing names that are defined by Windows. Other than that, call variables what you like.

It is necessary to first create an instance of the above specified structure **WNDCLASSEX**. You can then initialize the fields as I have suggested. The next step is to call a function to "register" the class with the system. This would be done in the standard Windows main program named **WinMain**. The code for this is:

10

```
WNDCLASSEX windclassex_instance;
    ...
    /* Initialize fields, such as: */
windclassex_instance.style = 0;
    ...
k = RegisterClassEx (&windclassex_instance);
if(k == 0)
{
      /* Registration failed */
    ...
}
```

To use the **WNDCLASSEX** structure, you must include the basic Windows include file Windows.h. The above code is more or less equivalent to the following **GLUT** code:

```
glutInit (argc, argv);
glutInitDisplayMode (GLUT_RGB);
```

Window Creation

The next step is to create the window. The Windows API provides a function named **CreateWindowEx()** to do that. A call we could use for our purposes is:

```
windowHandle= CreateWindowEx( 0,      /* Style of window */
   "SimpleWindowClass",                /* Window class */
   "The title of my window",           /* Title for upper bar */
   WS_OVERLAPPEDWINDOW,                 /* A window style param */
   CW_USEDEFAULT,                       /* Coordinates for the */
   CW_USEDEFAULT,                       /* Upper left corner */
   300,                                 /* Window width */
   500,                                 /* Window height */
   NULL,                                /* Parent handle */
   NULL,                                /* Menu handle */
   hInstance,                           /* First Parameter to WinMain */
   NULL);                               /* Additional data */
```

If the **CreateWindowEx()** function returns **NULL** (that is, **windowHandle** above is 0), we'll know that the call failed. This means that a window was not created and an error message should be displayed.

Finally, to actually draw the window on the screen, you must add the following boilerplate code:

```
ShowWindow(windowHandle, SW_SHOWNORMAL);
UpdateWindow(hwnd);
```

The GLUT calls to do the equivalent things are as follows. (I presented them in Chapter 3 but included them here for convenience):

```
glutInitWindowPosition(x, y);
glutInitWindowSize(300, 500);
glutCreateWindow("The title of my window");
```

The Event Loop

By now you should know what the event loop is. Recall that it's a loop that continuously deals with computer events like key presses and mouse moves. Microsoft calls this a *message loop*, and the basic one is so trivial that it is a wonder that you need to provide it at all. It looks like this:

```
while(GetMessage(&message, NULL, 0, 0) > 0)
{
    TranslateMessage(&Msg);
    DispatchMessage(&Msg);
}
return message.wParam;
```

GetMessage() returns the next message (event), such as a key press or mouse motion. If there are none, **GetMessage()** goes to sleep (blocked) until there *is* one, then returns it. **TranslateMessage()** does some extra work with keyboard events that is not relevant to us, and **DispatchMessage()** sends the fixed-up message to the destination window. A great many programs can use the code above exactly as-is. This loop is a part of the **WinMain** procedure, the main program.

The equivalent GLUT code is

```
glutMainLoop();
```

Callbacks

GLUT has a collection of functions that are called to process key presses and mouse events. You get to code the specifics and decide what to do in each case. In the Windows API, the window procedure does all of this, or at least coordinates things and provides the operations that deal with user inputs. As I mentioned in the previous section, the function that handles this work is named **WndProc()**. Here's a simple example:

```
LRESULT CALLBACK WndProc(HWND windowHandle,
    UINT message, WPARAM wparam, LPARAM lparam)
{
    switch(message)
    {
      case WM_CREATE:              // Open window
        break;
      case WM_CLOSE:               // close window
            DestroyWindow(windowHandle);
```

```
        break;
    case WM_PAINT:                          // Draw in window
        break;
    case WM_DESTROY:                        // destroy window
        PostQuitMessage(0);
        break;
    case WM_SIZE:                           // resize the window
        break;
    default:
        return DefWindowProc(windowHandle,
            message, wparam, lparam);
    }

    return 0;
}
```

This code would need to be completed for a specific application, but I'm showing the essential stuff here. Note that the event (message) is specified as an integer, and that there are pre-defined constants in an include file (such as **WM_CLOSE** and **WM_DESTROY**) that represent specific events. The **WM_CLOSE** event, in particular, indicates that the close box was clicked by the user. To process this event you would want to clean up any open files and allocated storage. Calling the **DestroyWindow()** function destroys the window and its children, and causes a **WM_DESTROY** message, which is handled by the code shown here also. **PostQuitMessage()** causes the program to end.

Remember that all windows having the same class use the same windows function, but the value of the **windowHandle** will be different for each window in the class.

Using GLUT, recall that we had functions such as **keyPress()** and **mouseClick()** that are registered with OpenGL using the **glutKeyboardFunc()** and **glutMouseFunc()** functions.

You've now seen how to setup and draw a window using the native API, and not using OpenGL. Naturally, we still want to use OpenGL to draw within the window. Let's see how to do that next.

A Hook to OpenGL

We have seen that GLUT provides a connection between OpenGL and the part of the operating system that manages the window system. This is true on Linux and Unix as well as Microsoft systems, by the way. If we want to use the native system to deal with the display, how does OpenGL talk to the system? We need a connection in software between the graphics operations of OpenGL and the window in which the picture is to be displayed, a window that was created outside of OpenGL and without knowing specifically what was going to be done with it.

Device Contexts

We need to know a little more about how the operating system uses a window. In particular, we need to know something about a *device context*, the *wgl* routines, and the *rendering context*. Let's start with a Microsoft definition:

> *A device context is a Windows data structure containing information about the drawing attributes of a device such as a display or a printer. All drawing calls are made through a device-context object, which encapsulates the Windows APIs for drawing lines, shapes, and text. Device contexts allow device-independent drawing in Windows. Device contexts can be used to draw to the screen, to the printer, or to a metafile.*
>
> —Microsoft Developer's Network[5]

Referred to as a *DC*, the device context is a clear indication of what Microsoft is capable of in terms of design. Windows keeps track of the graphics and display hardware you have connected to your computer and it knows where the drivers are. To draw things, we simply need to get a device context for the device we want to use. In our game program, the DC is a handle used to get at the window, which is being drawn on the screen device using a graphics card. Now, I am old enough to have written code using DOS, and doing this required specialized knowledge about the graphics system, the card being used, and how to write to specific registers on the card using their addresses. Believe me when I say, "Ugh."

Another advantage of the Windows approach is that when a new high-powered graphics card gets installed, a program that uses the DC still works, and can actually take advantage of any new features on the new device.

To get a device context from Windows, we use one of their special calls:

```
hDC = GetDC(hWnd);
```

This is a little cryptic for those not familiar with the Microsoft incantation syntax. Here's a clearer example:

```
deviceContextHandle = GetDC (windowHandle);
```

10

This does the same thing, of course. The **windowHandle** was given when a window was created, and the device context handle is used to draw into that window. This is all we need to do. If we were using DirectX, and many programmers do, then the device context would be passed to the DirectX graphics calls when drawing to the window. However, when using OpenGL, we need to complete one more step to connect the two systems.

Rendering Contexts

A rendering context is an OpenGL construct that completes the connection to the system. On Microsoft systems, a rendering context specifies a device context that will be the target of the drawing operations, and it acts as a portal for graphics commands. It knows about Windows, and it knows about OpenGL, and so it acts as a kind of translator. A program wishing to use OpenGL must create a rendering context. There can be many rendering contexts that exist at any one time, but only one of them is marked by the system as *current*, and that's the one that will be used whenever something is drawn onto the screen.

In a practical sense, we can think of the connection as looking like the ones shown in Figure 10.2.

The rendering context is, in any case, very much an OpenGL thing, although we access it using a handle just as we do with device contexts. There are a few basic functions for manipulating rendering contexts that we need to know about. These functions are the so-called *wiggle* routines, named for the **WGL** (Windows Graphics Library) prefix on the function names. The most important WGL routines are:

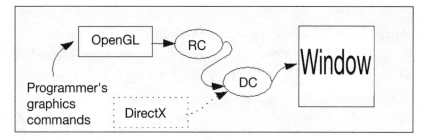

Figure 10.2
The conceptual view of using a rendering context.

HGLRC wglCreateContext (HDC hdc);
Creates a new rendering context that uses the given (passed) device context. Note: The pixel format of the DC must be compatible with that of the rendering context (RC). See below.

BOOL wglDeleteContext (HGLRC hglrc);
Deletes an open rendering context **hglrc**.

BOOL wglMakeCurrent(HDC hdc, HGLRC hglrc);
Makes a rendering context named **hglrc** the current one, associated with the device context **hdc**. If **hglrc** is NULL, this means that there should no longer be a current rendering context.

BOOL wglDeleteContext (HGLRC hglrc);
Deletes an open rendering context **hglrc**.

HGLRC wglGetCurrentContext(VOID);
Returns a handle to the current rendering context. Only one current handle can be used.

There are a total of 16 wgl functions, but the ones just shown should be the only ones that we need.

A *pixel format* is a specification of what the pixel values mean. For example, we could use 24 bits to store a pixel, packed into a 32-bit word in RGB order with a transparency value tacked on. There is an integer code on Windows that means exactly this, and there are many other possible pixel formats. The device context must use the same kind of pixels as does OpenGL, and so the pixel format of the DC must be set before we create a rendering context from it. This is done using the function shown here:

```
BOOL SetPixelFormat(
    HDC   hdc,
    int   iPixelFormat,
    CONST PIXELFORMATDESCRIPTOR *  ppfd);
```

You may look this up on MSDN, of course. What we need to know is that Microsoft suggests the format descriptor (a structure) be set up as follows: (copied directly from MSDN):

```
PIXELFORMATDESCRIPTOR pfd = {
    sizeof(PIXELFORMATDESCRIPTOR),        // size of pfd
    1,                                    // version number
    PFD_DRAW_TO_WINDOW |                  // support window
    PFD_SUPPORT_OPENGL |                  // support OpenGL
    PFD_DOUBLEBUFFER,                     // double buffered
    PFD_TYPE_RGBA,                        // RGBA type
    24,                                   // 24-bit color depth
    0, 0, 0, 0, 0, 0,                     // color bits ignored
    0,                                    // no alpha buffer
    0,                                    // shift bit ignored
    0,                                    // no accumulation buffer
    0, 0, 0, 0,                           // accum bits ignored
    32,                                   // 32-bit z-buffer
    0,                                    // no stencil buffer
    0,                                    // no auxiliary buffer
    PFD_MAIN_PLANE,                       // main layer
    0,                                    // reserved
    0, 0, 0                               // layer masks ignored
};
HDC  hdc;
int  iPixelFormat;
```

We now need to find a match between existing pixel format codes and the structure we have just defined:

```
iPixelFormat = ChoosePixelFormat(hdc, &pfd);
```

Finally, we make this the pixel format for the device context:

```
SetPixelFormat(hdc, iPixelFormat, &pfd);
```

You must set a device context's pixel format before creating a rendering context.

Organizing the Code

We've now discussed everything needed to get an OpenGL program to execute properly on a Windows system without using GLUT. Of course, it is especially important in Windows code to put things in the right place, and to do things in the right order. Here's a summary:

WinMain:

- Create the window and save the handle to it for further use (**CreateWindow**).

- Make the window visible (**ShowWindow**).

■ Use a Windows message loop to translate and dispatch the messages that come in.

WndProc:

■ Setup the necessary event processing: creation, painting, resizing.

■ Process mouse and keyboard actions.

Most of the activity related to OpenGL will take place within **WndProc**. Games are mostly driven by events, so it is natural that the event handler will get some exercise.

In particular, here is the activity associated with specific events:

WM_CREATE:
When a window is created, all of the OpenGL facilities must be initialized. This may require a rendering context, so one is created. It is best if this rendering context is kept around, so it should be static or global. I have created a modular game interface between windows and OpenGL; the function to be called here is named **myInitOpengl(h)**, and it is passed the windows handle.

WM_DESTROY:
When the window is destroyed, we finalize OpenGL, close any open files, release storage, and so on. Do not forget to delete the rendering context.

WM_PAINT:
This is the hard one, but most of the work can be done in a function that would have to exist whether we used GLUT or WGL. This event means that the window is to be re-drawn. We need to set up a rendering context and make it current, call all of the drawing functions, and then release the rendering context.

WM_LBUTTONDOWN, WM_RBUTTONDOWN, WM_LBUTTONUP, WM_RBUTTONUP,
These are the mouse controls. In the GLUT version of the demo, this simply results in the game ending. In other cases, it can result in increased motion, change or direction, object selection and manipulation, and so on.

WM_CHAR:
This tells us that a character was typed on the keyboard. This is how we control speed and direction in the demo, and so we must pass the value of the character that was typed to the speed/direction control function. The character that was typed is stored in the **wParam** parameter to the **WinProc()** function. For example, '8' means accelerate, '4' means turn left, and so on according to the numeric keypad.

10

Demo2: Drawing Using OpenGL and WGL

My goal in this chapter is to permit a game to interact with the player in real time while using the basic Windows toolset and interface. The good news is that we are almost there. In this section, we'll put together a complete program that displays game-like images without calling GLUT routines. In the next section, we'll incorporate real-time motion.

Actually, all of the stuff we need has been discussed. It's now time to simply put everything together. We can use the previous demo that implemented a prism-shaped vehicle on a planar grid. In fact, I started this project by copying the exact source files from the demo1 directory into **Demo2**. All references to GLUT were then deleted, and a windows project (not a console project) was created to house the modified code. The required **WinMain** and **WndProc** routines were then added to the project.

I will state at the outset that I am going to make some people upset. The code shown in this section does not use the normal notation found in Windows C programs. There is one main reason for this. As a teacher, I find that students sometimes recall patterns more easily than concepts. The standard pattern for the Windows main program includes the Hungarian notation for variables, and this code is easily recognizable by programmers who have written a few such programs. By changing the appearance, I hope to knock some of you out of old habits and force you to look at the code again. I also want to eliminate some of the confusion that I find trips up programmers who are not experienced Windows programmers. It should not matter at all that my variable names or indentation differs from that seen in Windows programming books and on most websites.

As **WinMain** really just creates a window for us (at least for now that's all it does!), the actual code we'll be interested in is in **WndProc**. If you look at the code for the previous demo, there are just a few key things to note. A basic initialization routine is used that calls the AI and graphics initializations: this function was called **initializeAll()**, and the same function still exists in the new demo. There is a function that draws the current version of the screen, which is called **display()**. The version now used is almost unchanged from the version used in the first demo program. Additionally, I've included a function to deal with mouse clicks and one to deal with keyboard data entry.

GLUT used to do a couple of things we must do using windows calls. Creating the window is one; the main event loop was another; and finally, it handled mouse and keyboard events. We do that ourselves now in the following very obvious way:

```
LRESULT CALLBACK WndProc(HWND windowsHandle,
    UINT message, WPARAM wParam, LPARAM lParam )
{
```

```
HDC deviceContextHandle;
static HGLRC renderingContextHandle;
PAINTSTRUCT ps;

switch(message)
{
case WM_CREATE:
  renderingContextHandle =
  OpenGLinit(windowsHandle);      // MY CODE
  return 0;
```

On creation of the window, the function **OpenGLinit()** is called. This will be shown later, and serves to create the correct pixel format so that OpenGL can run correctly on Windows:

```
case WM_PAINT:
  deviceContextHandle = BeginPaint(windowsHandle,&ps);
  wglMakeCurrent( deviceContextHandle, renderingContextHandle );
  OpenGLdisplay();
       // MY CODE
  wglMakeCurrent( NULL, NULL );
  EndPaint( windowsHandle, &ps );
  return 0;
```

Whenever the window is to be painted (drawn), we get a rendering context and make it current. Then, **OpenGLdisplay()** is called, which I wrote to display the current situation in the demo. Here it will be a static image drawn from the component parts, just as in the real moving version. It also calls the initialization routines if needed (when the demo starts):

```
case WM_CHAR:
     keyPress ((unsigned char)wParam); // MY CODE
     return 0;
```

Whenever a key is pressed, this code sends the value of that key to the same function we used last time to control motion and direction. The only change is that we don't need the position parameters (x, y) anymore so I removed them:

```
case WM_LBUTTONUP:
case WM_RBUTTONDOWN:
         mouseClick ();                  // MY CODE
```

10

When a mouse click happens, we call the same basic function as we did before. A mouse click simply ends the program, so I let it fall through to the next part of the **case** statement:

```
case WM_DESTROY:
    wglDeleteContext( renderingContextHandle );
    terminateAll ();            // MY CODE
    PostQuitMessage( 0 );
    return 0;
  }
  return DefWindowProc (windowsHandle,
      message, wParam, lParam );
}
```

Finally, when the window is closed or destroyed, we call the standard Windows clean-up code, and also call our own **terminateAll()** function to clean up after ourselves.

The lines of code shown here with a comment that says **MY CODE** are the lines that reference functions specific to this demo. The **OpenGLinit()** function does only initializations that we have discussed, but I've included it here to make it as complete as possible:

```
HGLRC OpenGLinit( HWND windowsHandle )
{
   static PIXELFORMATDESCRIPTOR pfd =
   {
     sizeof (PIXELFORMATDESCRIPTOR), 1,
     PFD_DRAW_TO_WINDOW | PFD_SUPPORT_OPENGL,
     PFD_TYPE_RGBA, 24, 0, 0, 0,  0, 0, 0, 0, 0,
     0, 0, 0, 0, 0, 32, 0, 0, PFD_MAIN_PLANE, 0,
     0, 0, 0
   };

   int pixelFormat;
   HDC deviceContextHandle;
   HGLRC renderingContextHandle;

   deviceContextHandle = GetDC( windowsHandle );
   pixelFormat =
      ChoosePixelFormat( deviceContextHandle, &pfd );
   if (pixelFormat == 0) exit(0);
   SetPixelFormat(deviceContextHandle, pixelFormat, &pfd);
```

```
renderingContextHandle =
    wglCreateContext( deviceContextHandle );
ReleaseDC( windowsHandle, deviceContextHandle );
return renderingContextHandle;
}
```

The **OpenGLdisplay()** function calls the old display function we used in **Demo1**, but also checks a flag and initializes everything if needed:

```
void OpenGLdisplay( )
{
    static int init = 1;

    if (init)
    {
        init = 0;
        initializeAll ();
    }

    display ();
}
```

And that's it, really. When this demo is executed, it displays the screen shown in Figure 10.3. As I mentioned, the car, the grid, and all of the other items are drawn just as they were in the more interactive demo 1; we are just not letting them move yet.

Continuous Time in Win32

The time has come to put everything together. We'll modify demo 2 to permit the cube car to be moved in real-time by the player. What are we missing? We need to incorporate the scheme for controlling the passage of time.

To get continuous time to work with Win32, we need one more piece of information—one that is not obvious from the available documentation. We could use the timer code we wrote before, but a problem resides (for those of you uninitiated in Windows) in the message loop. Here it is again:

```
while (GetMessage(&message, NULL, 0, 0))
    {
        TranslateMessage( &message );
        DispatchMessage( &message );
    }
    return( message.wParam );
}
```

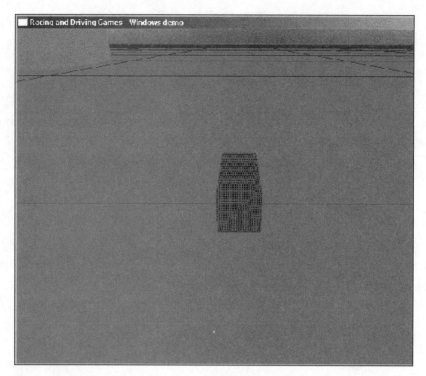

Figure 10.3
Demo 2 screen shot.

The function **GetMessage()** retrieves a message and returns 0 if it encounters a **WM_QUIT** message (end the program); this will, obviously, cause an exit from the loop. The **TranslateMessage()** and **DispatchMessage()** functions make certain that keyboard messages are dealt with correctly and that the messages are sent to the correct handler or child window.

The problem, from a timer's point of view, is with **GetMessage()**. This function actually *waits* for a message to be sent. There is no other way to wake it up and continue the main loop other than to send a message. Thus, we really have only a few choices if we want to simulate continuous time: we can have a timer function send a message in order to wake up the main loop, or prevent the main loop from locking up while it is waiting for a message.

The logic of using a timer to send a message is clear, and it would be my personal choice if it were not for the fact that timer messages are associated with a low priority. A timer message may be postponed for too long, resulting in missed collisions or irregular or incorrect frames.

It is very common to change the main loop so that it does not use **GetMessage()** at all. The alternative is **PeekMessage()**, which looks for a message without pausing. If a message is available, the return value is nonzero; otherwise it is zero. If a message was seen, **PeekMessage()** returns basically the same information as does **GetMessage()**. The basic distinction, in addition to the no-waiting thing, is that **PeekMessage()** has a fifth parameter that specifies what is to be done with the message; it can either be removed from the message queue or it can be left in the queue.

Here is what we'll do: we'll call **PeekMessage()** instead of **GetMessage()**, and we'll exit from the loop if we see the **WM_QUIT** message. If there isn't a message, we'll execute the game code for another frame; otherwise, we'll execute the translate-dispatch code as before.

Our "new" message loop becomes:

```
while(1) // While true do (usual simulation loop!)
{
    if (PeekMessage(&message,NULL,0,0, PM_REMOVE))
    {
        if(message.message == WM_QUIT) break;
        TranslateMessage(&message);
        DispatchMessage(&message);
    }
    else // No message
    {
        timedAILoop(); // Draw game frame
    }
}
return(message.wParam);
```

Note that we must specifically check for the **WM_QUIT** message in the loop because **PeekMessage()** does not do that. This loop will not be delayed by a specific amount of time, like we did when we used GLUT. The main loop shown here will call our demo code whenever it is not doing anything else. We can't wait with our code either, because it would be possible to miss a message! Hence, the function we call in the main loop to link to our demo is:

```
void timedAILoop ( )
{
    float dt;          // Time since last frame.

    if (ENDOFGAME) return;
    dt = deltaTime();  // How long/last frame
```

```
        movePlayer (dt);
        movePolice (dt);
        display ();
}
```

This is almost identical to the function we used previously, with cosmetic differences only. If we wish to maintain a specific frame rate, we only do any real work if we're close to the next frame time. In that case, we would do as follows:

```
void timedAILoop ( )
{
    float dt;                       // Time since last frame.
    static accumtime = 0.0f;

    if (ENDOFGAME) return;
    dt = deltaTime();               // How long/last frame
    accumtime += dt;
    if (dt >= FRAMETIME)
    {
        movePlayer (dt);
        movePolice (dt);
        display ();
        accumtime -= FRAMETIME;
    }
}
```

The program that uses this code has only been changed slightly from the **Demo2** version, but is vastly different in function. The car cube now moves under user control, with mouse and keyboard events enabled. This program can be found on the website for this book in the **chapter10/demo3** directory. It now has the functionality of the GLUT version without the overhead and restriction of having GLUT do the main loop. On the other hand, **Demo3** only runs under Microsoft Windows systems.

I do not own a Mac, but I'll maintain the website so that readers can submit code and improve what I have. An obvious improvement would be to write this demo so that it runs on Xwindows, and again for the Mac. Any takers?

Handling Flicker

Both the GLUT OpenGL continuous time demo and the Windows demo display a noticeable flicker while they are being executed. This is caused by the visual effect of clearing and redrawing the screen many times per second. Small changes in illumination or even interference between colors or intensities, if they happen at rates similar to those on TV and movie frame display, will be seen by our visual system as motion. In a game, this is very irritating.

The standard mechanism for preventing flicker is something that we computer science types call *double buffering*. The idea is to draw the next frame into a structure in computer memory (a *buffer*) instead of onto the screen directly. Only when the image is complete in every respect do we then tell the system to display this new frame. What is happening is that there are two frames in memory and a pointer to each one, let's say **P1** and **P2**. The physical display can be told to show the image found at **P1**, and this can be done very quickly. We then draw into **P2** and tell the system to display **P2**. Then, we draw **P1** and then draw **P2**, and so on, forever. The time needed to draw on the screen and the fact that we can see a visual artifact of that drawing causes the flicker, so this buffering scheme removes the flicker completely in most cases.

It turns out that both GLUT and Windows do most of the work for us; we just have to tell the system to do it.

Double Buffers Using GLUT

Double buffering using GLUT requires two simple steps. First, when the display mode is set (**glutDisplayMode**) the **GLUT_DOUBLE** bit must be set, as follows:

```
void initializeGraphics( void )
{
/* First, we initialize & set the display mode */
   glutInitDisplayMode (GLUT_DOUBLE | GLUT_RGB);
        . . .
```

This tells GLUT not to display directly to the screen, but to one of two internal buffers. GLUT always draws to one buffer while displaying the other. Then, when the screen is to be updated, we must tell GLUT when to display the buffer we just drew. In our display function, this occurs after the call to **glFlush()**:

```
void display(void)
{
   ...
   glFlush();
   glutSwapBuffers ();
}
```

The **glutSwapBuffers()** function merely changes pointers from the internal buffer to the screen buffer.

10

This completes our demo program. The Demo 4 directory holds working code that will illustrate the GLUT no-flicker program.

Double Buffers Using Win32

As usual, using Windows directly is more complex. We must set up the pixel format so that the "**double buffer**" property is set. This is a flag that tells Windows device contexts to do double buffering, very much as GLUT does. We do this using this code:

```
HGLRC  OpenGLinit( HWND windowsHandle )
{
    static PIXELFORMATDESCRIPTOR pfd =
        {
                sizeof (PIXELFORMATDESCRIPTOR), 1,
                PFD_DRAW_TO_WINDOW | PFD_SUPPORT_OPENGL |
                PFD_DOUBLEBUFFER,
                PFD_TYPE_RGBA, 24, 0, 0, 0,  0, 0, 0, 0, 0,
                0, 0, 0, 0, 0, 32, 0, 0, PFD_MAIN_PLANE, 0,
                0, 0, 0
            };
    . . .
    pixelFormat =
        ChoosePixelFormat (deviceContextHandle, &pfd );
    . . .
```

Now, as when using GLUT, the drawing will be done to a buffer instead of to the screen. To display the buffer, we call the **SwapBuffers()** function, and this is done in our case in the message loop, as follows:

// The Windows message loop.

```
while(TRUE) // Do our infinate loop
{
// Check if there was a message
    if (PeekMessage(&message,NULL,0,0,PM_REMOVE))
    {
        if(message.message == WM_QUIT) break;
// If the message wasnt to quit
        TranslateMessage(&message);
        DispatchMessage(&message);
    } else // if there wasn't a message
    {
        timedAILoop ();
// Double buffer
```

```
        SwapBuffers (deviceContextHandle);
    }
}
```

Because the buffer is not displayed until the **SwapBuffers()** call is made, we must do the swapping whenever the window is painted too, especially the *first* time. This happens in the **WndProc()** function where the **WM_PAINT** message is handled:

```
case WM_PAINT:
    OpenGLdisplay();
    SwapBuffers (deviceContextHandle);
    . . .
```

The code for a complete program can be found in the Chapter 10 Time/Demo 5 directory.

Summary

In this chapter, I have shown you how to conduct a simulation in real time. In a driving game, this means that you now know how to display the vehicles in their correct screen positions quickly enough so that it appears as if they are moving. Combined with the ability to control the vehicle's speed and direction, this is really the heart of any driving game.

This is also the end of Part II of this book in which we discussed advanced techniques for AI, audio, and graphics for game creation. In the next part of the book we'll focus on some advanced techniques including the development of the *Manic Mars Racer* game.

10

Chapter 11

Cinematography for Driving and Racing Games

- Learn how a camera can be controlled by a game to give an exciting representation of the action.

- Use a third-person camera view to capture standard driving game play action.

- Use other camera views, including first-person ground level view and a ceiling view, to capture other action.

The good news is that we've almost arrived at the point where we can roll up our sleeves and start building the fun project for this book—the *Manic Mars Racer* game. The bad news (actually this really isn't bad news) is that we still need to cover a few topics—cinematography and terrain mapping—before we'll be ready to build our game.

The Mars racer game that we'll be developing in this book is a real 3D interactive driving game. This game will allow you to drive, collect objects, and race a Martian on a model of the Martian surface. Before we start building the game, we'll need to look at cinematography in this chapter and then terrain mapping in Chapter 12.

Anyone who has been to a movie has some first-hand experience with cinematography. This popular art form incorporates the art and science of lighting, framing, and photographing. Good cinematography can vastly improve an otherwise mediocre film, and bad cinematography can destroy an otherwise very good one. *Casablanca* and *Lawrence of Arabia* are films touted as having some of the best cinematography of all time. Compare these films, for example, to the *Blair Witch Project*, and you'll likely agree that there is no comparison.

So how does cinematography apply to a game? Games don't have real cameras or lights, but they do have virtual ones. Where the camera is placed and how it views and follows the action can be very important for game play. After all, if you can't see the cars in front of you, you will very likely hit them. What we will be discussing in this chapter might well be called *interactive* cinematography because the camera and lighting placement may well change as a function of what the player does.

It is also true that people don't seem to like the same things. Some people like to drive from the perspective of a real driver, inside of the car behind the steering wheel. Some, like me, prefer a vantage point higher and behind the car, such as is the one used in *Mario Kart*. Still others want to be at bumper level on the car or to the side, as if watching from the audience. A good game will allow players to make many choices like this to optimize their enjoyment.

Determining the shot angles and camera placement in a game may seem very simple but it isn't in the general case. It is true that the camera position and direction are simply specified parameters to OpenGL or DirectX. Determining values for those parameters is not so easy, and is really not even a graphics issue. Cinematography is not a part of the renderer; it is a part of the AI system. You'll learn why in this chapter.

My strategy in this chapter is to show how different types of cameras can be used in a game to improve game play. I'll introduce the different techniques and we'll create a set of six demo programs so that you can see how the different techniques are coded. As you work through the chapter, take a little time to play with the different demos so that you can better understand the results produced by the different camera views.

Using Third-Person Cameras

The standard camera position for a driving game is behind and above a car, looking forward, to the front of the car. This is the view shown in Figure 11.1. I think you can see why this view is popular. Notice how the front section of the car is shown to help position the viewpoint. The region in front of the car is also clearly visible, allowing the player to see the targets and the obstacles. The extra height shows that the field of view is wide, allowing the player to see further than if the point of view were in the cockpit. In addition, the player can see over small obstacles such as other cars.

This camera view resembles the one used in the well-known game *Tomb Raider*. The controls also operate like the controls used in the *Tomb Raider* game. If the right turn control is pressed, the car will turn right, and the camera will look right also because it follows the car. The point of view always moves with the vehicle, which is very important. The car should be in view at all times, and the controls should produce an obvious and immediate effect on the car and the camera.

Figure 11.1
The traditional camera position used in the *MiniMayhem* driving game.

Implementing the Simple Third-Person Camera

In this section, I'll explain the techniques needed to implement a third-person camera. A little bit of math will be required. Then, I'll present some code examples and we'll create a sample program named 'Demo 1 that you can experiment with. Later in the chapter, we'll create additional demo programs to try out other camera views.

To implement a third-person camera, we need to know where the player's car is. We can specify this location as a 3D vector: $P = (P_x, P_y, P_z)$. This is normally the position of the center of mass. We can also represent the velocity as $V = (V_x, V_y, V_z)$ and the orientation as $A = (A_x, A_y, A_z)$. The vector A points in the direction of the long axis of the car from the center of mass to the front grill. As shown in Figure 11.2, the vector $-A$ points towards the rear of the car, and $-2A + P$ is a point behind the car. Finally, if the Y-axis represents the vertical orientation, the Y coordinate of the camera should be raised above the car by a known amount. A height of three or four times the car's height would likely be okay.

11

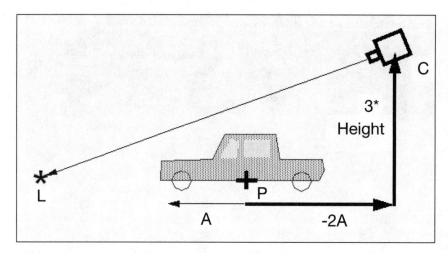

Figure 11.2
Computing the first-person camera position.

Our simple camera could be placed at the following location:

Equation 11.1

$$C_x = P_x - 2A_x$$

$$C_y = P_y + 3*\text{Height}$$

$$C_z = P_z - 2A_z$$

You may recall from Chapter 3 that we need two things to determine the camera location—the camera position as computed above, and a way to determine the direction in which the camera is pointed. OpenGL refers to this as the *look at* or *focal point*; we'll call it L=(L_x, L_y, L_z).

One possibility is to set the focal point to a fixed distance in front of the car. Given the orientation vector **A**, we could do the following calculation:

Equation 11.2

$$L_x = P_x + 2A_x$$

$$L_y = P_y$$

$$L_z = P_z + 2A_z$$

In this case, whenever the car turns, the focal point changes in a very mechanical way. In fact, this yields a somewhat unrealistic, although quite familiar, appearance in which the car looks stationary at the same place in the field of view.

Let's look at a practical example. In Chapter 10, we wrote some demonstration programs to show continuous motion in a simple driving environment. In those demos, there had to be a camera positioned to view the actions of the game in progress, or else nothing could have been seen. Here is the code that positions the camera in those demos, exactly as it appeared:

```
getPlayerPosition (&x, &y);
getPlayerOrientation (&dx, &dy);
gluLookAt( x-5*dx, y-5*dy, 4,
           5*dx+x, 5*dy+y, 0.0,
           0.0, 0.0, 1.0 );
```

From Equation 11.1 and Figure 11.2, and using the code above, we can see the correspondence easily enough. The first three parameters to **gluLookAt()** represent the C_x, C_y, and C_z values (the camera position); we see that $P_x = x$, $P_y = y$, $A_x = d_x$, $A_y = d_y$ and 3*Height is 4. The second set of parameters to **gluLookAt()** represents the point in space that the camera is looking at, which were named L_x, L_y, and L_z in Equation 11.2. Again, we see that the parameter names translate as before. The multiplier to A_x and A_y is now 5 instead of 2.

The complete program that implements the third-person camera (Demo 1) can be found on the website in the subdirectory **Chapter 11**. The example provided is the same as the **Demo 4** program presented in Chapter 10. Why? Because the camera model presented there is a basic one—the simplest possible. We will develop the material in this chapter from that point, so before you read on, I suggest that you play with the demo to get a sense of how the camera works.

We're now ready to make a change to the first demo program by using the velocity vector instead of the orientation. We'll create a new program named **Demo 2** that can be found on the website for this book (see the **Chapter 11** subdirectory). How does velocity enter into the camera control scheme? We can select a time **t** in the future, and have the focal point be the location of the car's relative position at that time. Of course, the focal point will be found assuming that the velocity does not change—an unlikely event but a simple assumption. Thus, the focus moves about relative to the car giving the view a more realistic appearance. For instance, if the car slows down, the focus will be too far in front, as if the camera is reacting with a slight delay—a very human thing.

11

For a few reasons, including simplicity, I will use speed instead of velocity, and use the orientation as direction. Later we'll use velocity directly. Determining the camera position will be done in the same way as before. The look-at location, as indicated by L_x and L_y in the equations above, is computed in the display function as

```
lx = x + speed*dx*90*0.033;
ly = y + speed*dy*90*0.033;
lz = 0.0;
```

where **speed** was retrieved from the AI system, 90 is the factor by which speed in screen units relates to the physics equation (determined by a little experimentation), and 0.033 is the expected duration of a frame. Do not use the actual frame interval because small variations in time are magnified on the screen and the image will become very jerky and bouncy.

If you look at the code in

Demo 2 you will see some curious material that is commented out. For example, the function **getPlayerVelocity()** in the AI system looks like this:

```
void getPlayerVelocity (float *x, float *y)
{
//*x = *y = player.speed;
//*x = sumSpeed/NSPEEDS;
/ *y = sumSpeed/NSPEEDS;
}
```

The commented code is a part of an extension of this scheme. This extension uses a *moving average* instead of a single speed sample. The player's speed will naturally change. At 30 frames per second, it will change every 0.033 seconds. This allows quite a lot of variation. The *moving average* is the average speed over that past **NSPEEDS** frames, and will not vary as rapidly as the current speed.

The way to calculate the moving average of the speed is very simple in principle: keep the last **NSPEEDS** speed values in an array, and then whenever the speed is requested, sum the values in the array and divide the sum by **NSPEEDS**. We can use a faster way to keep the current sum and get it updated each time. Here is the **setPlayerVelocity()** function that can be used to do this:

```
void setPlayerVelocity ()
{
    sumSpeed -= speedData[speedIndex];
    sumSpeed += player.speed;
```

```
        speedData[speedIndex] = player.speed;
        speedIndex = (speedIndex + 1) % NSPEEDS;
}
```

The global variable **sumSpeed** holds the current sum of the past **NSPEEDS** speed samples, which have all been stored in the array **speedData[]**. Each time a new sample is made, **setPlayerVelocity()** is called; the speed sample saved at the longest time past is subtracted from the sum, and the current speed is added to it. This is needed to maintain the correct sum of the past speeds. The current speed is then saved in the array. The array **speedData[]** is maintained as a circular list. There are **NSPEEDS** elements, and the one to be removed is always at the same location as the one to be added. The index variable **speedIndex** wraps around the end. For example, let's say that **NSPEEDS** is 10 and **speedIndex** is 9 at the moment, which is at the end of the array. We update element 9 of the array and increment **speedIndex** modulo **NSPEEDS**; **speedIndex** becomes:

```
(9+1) mod 10 = 10 mod 10 = 0
```

The overall effect is to smooth the speed values so that there is less variation from sample to sample. This function could be extended so that it computes the moving average of the X and Y component of the velocities just as easily. This smoothing is commented out in the **Demo 2** program, but is easy to restore, and I encourage you to experiment with it and use various values for **NSPEEDS**.

The down side to this speed-based camera system relates to a focus problem that can occur. If the car goes backwards, the focus could be behind the car. This is unfortunate, since the camera is behind the car too; the car itself can't be seen in this case. A possible solution is to move the camera to the front of the car if the velocity is negative. Another simpler and more obvious solution would be to force the focus to stay in the front by giving it a base position at zero velocity.

A Practical Third-Person Camera

We've now created two demo programs to use a third-person camera. Along the way, I identified quite a few problems with our initial camera design. The examples were designed to get us started, but to eliminate the problems, we'll need a more complete implementation that supports various properties and situations. This time, let's define the camera properties very carefully and then try to determine how to accomplish what we need. The description can be vague initially, as long as all of the gaps are filled before code is written.

Here's my list of properties:

1. The camera will normally follow behind and above the player's vehicle, and will normally be pointed so that the car, or at least the front of the car, can be seen along with the road and future path of the vehicle. Obstacles should be visible while the driver still has a chance to do something to avoid them.

2. When the car speeds up, the camera should move upwards and focus further ahead because we'll need to see more at higher speeds.

3. Similarly, when the car slows down, the camera should move lower.

4. When the car turns, the camera should allow the car to move in the field of view slightly in a direction opposing the turn. This improves the illusion of motion by providing a short lag.

5. When the car accelerates, the car should for a brief time move away from the camera; when the car slows, it should get closer to the camera for a second or two.

6. If the car should spin, the camera should not follow it around. Instead, the car should stay in the field of view, and the player should be able to watch the spin take place. When the car stops or proceeds in a linear fashion again, the camera should take up its traditional position above and behind the car.

The first five items are quite a bit simpler to implement than the final one. We've actually taken care of the first property already, so we can start with the second property. We'll implement the properties by creating a set of demo programs, which you can find in the Chapter11 subdirectory on the website for this book.

Raising and Lowering the Camera

Figure 11.2 shows what is minimally needed for a velocity dependent camera—the second property from my list of the six properties. Once the basic height and focus of attention are defined, we can determine the basic geometry of the situation. When the car speeds up, the camera should rise. Instead of a constant of 3*height being used as the height of the camera, we compute 3*height*F(v), where F(v) is some function of the vehicle's velocity. The precise function to be used depends on the field of view, the maximum velocity, and the general scale of objects in the scene. A table look-up could be used that would eliminate the complex function calculation. For velocities between 0 and approximately 1/3 maximum, we could simply use F(v) = 1. For velocities from 1/3 to maximum, we could ramp the height to twice normal.

This means if we use speeds in miles per hour or kilometers per hour, we will need relatively few table entries. For a top speed of 200 MPH, we need at most about 140 entries—one for each MPH over 70. In fact, we can "bin" the values and use less space. *Binning* is the operation of taking a number and finding a bin in which to place it; a bin has a range of values that belong in it. For example, a set of bins may be used that have a size of 5 MPH, and speeds in each value in the same 5 MPH range will be placed in the same bin. We need about 28 entries in the table (140/5). The bin 0 represents the first step above 1/3 max speed, and the first increase in camera height; the last bin, 27, represents a height multiplier of 2. Each bin is 1/14 bigger than the one before, with bin 0 being 1-1/14. This can be generalized in the obvious way.

The table is indexed by (speed-70)/5. As the speed decreases, the height of the camera will also decrease. The calculation in **C** is:

```
ind = (int)(speed - 70)/5;
if (ind < 0) factor = 1.0;
 else factor = F[ind];
Cx = Px - 2*Ax;
Cy = Py + 3*Height*F[ind];
Cz = Pz - 2*Az;
```

Since we already have the table **F** all built, we can also adjust the focal point to be more distant if moving fast and nearer when moving slowly:

```
Lx = Px + 2*Ax*F[ind];
Ly = Py;
Lz = Pz + 2*Az*F[ind];
```

The Demo3 program found in the Chapter 11 subdirectory implements these techniques. However, there are a few differences that need to be discussed. First, instead of using a table for F, I used a function (I just multiply by 4), because it is easier and we don't need the extra efficiency bought by using the table. Secondly, I have moved all of the code for determining the camera position and focal point into the AI system; we now call a single function to determine these things each time a frame is computed. That function is called cameraParameters(), and the version written to implement the current demo is:

```
void cameraParameters(float *cx, float *cy, float *cz,
    float *lx, float *ly, float *lz)
{
void cameraParameters(float *cx, float *cy, float *cz,
    float *lx, float *ly, float *lz)
{
    float x, y, dx, dy, vx, vy;
```

```
getPlayerPosition (&x, &y);
getPlayerOrientation (&dx, &dy);

*cx = x - 5*dx;
*cy = y - 5*dy;
getPlayerVelocity (&vx, &vy);
*cz = 4.0f+((vx+vy)/2)*4;  // Height varies as speed

*lx = x + 2*dx*4;
*ly = y + 2*dy*4;
*lz = 0.0f;
}
```

Using this function will make it much easier to isolate the code responsible for camera control. As the camera system becomes more complex, this isolation becomes more important from a software engineering perspective.

Camera Turn Lag

We can implement lag using a number of different approaches. Lag could sometimes be thought of as *momentum* or *inertia*. A simple idea here is to factor in the previous camera focal point, as if the camera is keen to keep looking where it is. Let's say that the previous focal point is $L' = (L'_x, L'_y, L'_z)$. We'll also let a variable α have a value between 0 and 1. A compromise position between the new focal points as computed by Equation 12.2 and the previous position L' would be:

Equation 11.3 $M = aL + (1-a)L'$

If $\alpha=1$, the previous point has no effect on the new one and, oddly, if $\alpha=0$, the new calculation has no bearing on the new focal point. A good value for α is the fraction of the maximum possible turning angle that is being used at the moment. Thus, if the wheel is 50% left then $\alpha=0.5$. The code for the update of the focal point is now

```
Lx = a*(Px + 2*Ax*F[ind]) + (1-a)*lpx;
Ly = a*Py + (1-a)*lpy;
Lz = a*(Pz + 2*Az*F[ind]) +(1-a)*lpz;
```

where the previous focal point is **(lpx, lpy, lpz)**.

There are other possible solutions. We could compute the yaw angle (i.e., left-right) of the camera as a function of α; that is, we decrease that angle in proportion to the current steering angle. I propose to let you experiment with ways to implement many of the camera motions described here.

In the code shown in the **Demo5** program for this chapter, you'll find see the following function:

```
void cameraParameters(float *cx, float *cy,
        float *cz,float *lx, float *ly, float *lz)
{
        float x, y, dx, dy, vx, vy;
        static float lastx, lasty, lastz, alpha=0.1f;

        getPlayerPosition (&x, &y);
        getPlayerOrientation (&dx, &dy);
        *cx = (x - 5*dx);
        *cy = (y - 5*dy);
        *cz = 4.0f;
        getPlayerVelocity (&vx, &vy);

        *lx =  alpha*(x + 2*dx*4) + (1-alpha)*lastx;
        lastx =  x + 2*dx*4;
        *ly =  alpha*(y + 2*dy*4) + (1-alpha)*lasty;
        lasty =  y + 2*dy*4;
        *lz = 0.0f;

        *cz = 4.0f + ((vx+vy)/2)*4;
}
```

The **Demo5** program can be found in the Chapter 11 directory on the website. It essentially introduces the time lag into the camera pointing logic that we have been working with in the pervious demo programs.

The effect is most obvious when the vehicle is changing its orientation but not moving forward. As you execute the demo, note that the camera focal point lags behind the vehicle a little, giving the illusion of a human operator. The height adjustment with speed is also in effect. As the value of the variable **alpha** changes to become closer to 1.0, the lagging effect vanishes.

11

Spin

I coded the six demo programs presented in this chapter so that the vehicles can't spin. I can, however, give you a quick plan for how to implement this feature.

The physics part of the AI system will know what the angular velocity (or momentum) of the vehicle is. The camera system has a threshold value T_ω that it applies; if the angular momentum ω is less than T_ω, we follow the standard mechanism for camera control. If the $\omega > T_\omega$, the system enters *spin mode* where the camera should position itself relative to the center or mass of the vehicle, which is not spinning, in the direction of the net linear velocity. The camera will not stay behind the car, but will continue to look ahead of it. The current orientation of the car is not relevant to the camera position when the vehicle is in spin mode.

Using a First-Person Ground Level Camera

Many game designers realize that players like to have the ability to change the camera position. For driving games, one of the popular positions that players like to switch to is the one where the camera is near the ground level looking forward. I call this a *bumper camera* (see Figure 11.3). This camera placement gives the effect of speed and turning motion much more than we get with the other camera positions. Fortunately, this feature is very easy to implement as well. On the down side, we'll now have more than one camera mode, and so we have to implement a control mechanism and a simple state machine for the camera. Adding this code isn't difficult, but it does require a little more work.

The top part of Figure 11.3 shows the camera view that will be added to our Demo4 program. The bottom part of Figure 11.3 shows the bumper camera view that is used in the game *MiniMayhem*. Before you read how the camera is implemented, I suggest you compare these views to the ones shown in Figure 11.1.

Figure 11.3
Incorporating ground-level camera views.

First, let's discuss what we need to do to implement the state machine. We'll need to define two states: one for the normal camera mode (**CAMERA_STANDARD**) and one for ground level mode (**CAMERA_BUMPER**). The user can select ground level mode by typing 'v' on the keyboard, and change back to standard mode by typing 'b' the 'v' was chosen to mean "view" and 'b' was chosen because it is physically next to 'v' on the keyboard. The keyboard handler **keyPress()** needs to be modified to accept the 'v' and 'b' character inputs. This function now calls a new function named **setCameraState()** when these characters are seen. Let's construct another demo (**Demo4**) to illustrate some of the newer ideas, like the bumper cam.

The bumper camera implementation itself is simple: we place the camera at the front of the car at a low height, say 0.5 units, looking forward to the same point as before except it will also be set at a height of 0.5. The view is therefore parallel to the driving surface. All of the new code is shown here:

```
#define CAMERA_STANDARD 300
#define CAMERA_BUMPER   301
int camera_state = CAMERA_STANDARD;
   . . .
void keyPress (unsigned char key, int x, int y)
{
   if (key == '6')
      enterUserMotion (0.1F, 0.0F);
   else if (key == '4')
      enterUserMotion (-0.1F, 0.0F);
   else if (key == '8')
      enterUserMotion (0.0F, 0.1F);
   else if (key == '2')
      enterUserMotion (0.0F, -0.1F);

   else if (key=='v') setCameraState(CAMERA_BUMPER);
   else if (key=='b') setCameraState (CAMERA_STANDARD);

   else if ((key=='q') || (key=='Q'))
      game_over ();
}

void setCameraState (int state)
{
   camera_state = state;
}

void cameraParameters(float *cx, float *cy, float *cz,
```

11

```
      float *lx, float *ly, float *lz)
{
  float x, y, dx, dy, vx, vy;

  getPlayerPosition (&x, &y);
  getPlayerOrientation (&dx, &dy);

  if (camera_state == CAMERA_STANDARD)
  {
    *cx = x - 5*dx;
    *cy = y - 5*dy;
    *cz = 4.0f;
    *lx = x + 2*dx*4;
    *ly = y + 2*dy*4;
    *lz = 0.0f;
    *cz = 4.0f + ((vx+vy)/2)*4;
  } else if (camera_state == CAMERA_BUMPER)
  {
    *cx = x + dx;
    *cy = y + dy;
    *cz = 0.5f;
    *lx = x + 2*dx*4;
    *ly = y + 2*dy*4;
    *lz = 0.5f;
  }
}
```

Of course, now that we have two camera states, we will be implementing more of them, and adding them to our final demo program, **Demo6**.

Fixed Cameras and Camera Placement

We'll finish up this chapter by creating a program that incorporates multiple cameras—multiple auto-switching cams, bumper cam, and ceiling game. As you play with the demo, you'll be able to switch between the different cameras by pressing the 'v' key.

Motion pictures use many kinds of camera placements, and many of them use fixed cameras rather than moving ones. Sure, a driving game involves motion, but there are many places where a fixed camera can be used to an advantage. If nothing else, they're relatively easy to implement and give the player some extra choice. Players like choices.

Fixed and other sorts of cinematic cameras are sometimes, perhaps even most frequently, used for replays. In some games this is a special selling feature; the game *Burnout* and its successors have sophisticated replay for showing the (inevitable) collisions that take place between the player and ambient traffic. These collisions are very well done using a very clever physics system, and are played back in slow motion after they take place from various perspectives.

Ceiling Camera

This is a top-view camera that shows a significant portion of the field of play from a great height (see Figure 11.4). Sometimes ceiling cameras are fixed, and sometimes they follow the vehicle. Either type is easy to implement. For example, here's the code needed to add a ceiling camera to our **Demo5** program. Inside of the `cameraParameters()` `function` we add:

```
case CAMERA_CEILING:
        *cx = 300.0; *cy = 300.0;
        *cz = 150.0;

        *lx = x;
        *ly = y;
        *lz = 0.0f;
        break;
```

This setting follows the players's car using a camera at a height of 150 units. Figure 11.4 shows how this view appears in the demo program (right side) and in the *MiniMayhem* game (left side). In both examples, I have circled the car so that you can see where it is located.

Multiple Fixed Cameras

Using multiple fixed cameras can be an interesting setup, but it is hard to control a vehicle using them. Imagine that four cameras have been set up at widely separated points on our driving plane. Each one has a significant height, say twice the height of a standard follow camera, and each one follows the vehicle by using a lead point as a focus. It is possible for the player to shift from one camera to another using the keyboard, but it is also possible to automatically shift from one camera to another by always using the one nearest to the car.

We now officially have too many camera modes for keyboard commands, so we'll now modify the interface so that typing the same key ('v') will toggle between modes. First, the **setCameraState()** function is modified so that it increments a global static camera state variable:

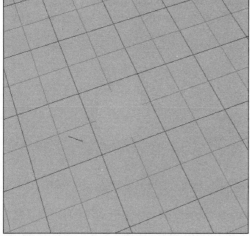

Figure 11.4
Using a ceiling camera to create a top view.

```
void setCameraState ( )
{
    camera_state = camera_state+1;
}
```

The **keyPress()** handler function simply calls this function whenever a 'v' character is typed. The function **cameraParameters()** has been modified to use a **switch** statement instead of a chain of **if** statements:

```
void cameraParameters(float *cx, float *cy, float *cz, float *lx, float *ly,
        float *lz)
{
        . . .
```

```
          switch (camera_state)
          {

default:
case CAMERA_STANDARD:
          . . .
case CAMERA_BUMPER:
          . . .
case CAMERA_CEILING:
          . . .
          }
}
```

To add a new camera mode, we only need to add another constant name with a consecutive numerical value, and add a new case to the statement.

In particular, we want to now add four cameras that behave as I just described, where the nearest camera is used to observe the player's vehicle. This case is as follows:

```
case CAMERA_FIXED_AUTO:
     d1 = abs(x-camx[1]) + abs(y-camy[1]);
     cam = 1;
     d2 = abs(x-camx[2]) + abs(y-camy[2]);
     if (d2 < d1)
     {
        cam = 2; d1 = d2;
     }
     d3 = abs(x-camx[3]) + abs(y-camy[3]);
     if (d3 < d1)
     {
        cam = 3; d1 = d3;
     }
     d4 = abs(x-camx[4]) + abs(y-camy[4]);
     if (d4 < d1) cam = 4;

     *cx = camx[cam]; *cy = camy[cam]; *cz = 20.0;
     *lx = x; *ly = y; *lz = 0.0;
     break;
```

These modifications can be seen in detail in the final **Demo6** program. As always, feel free to play with and modify this code to see what you can make it do. In particular, you could change the magnification on the perspective transform to show the car larger in the field, and you could see if a Euclidean distance as opposed to a 4-unit distance would make any difference.

Many of these camera techniques will be used in the *Manic Mars Racer* program that will be described in Chapters 13 and 14. You should look for these techniques in the games that you play, because many of them will certainly be there.

Summary

You have learned how a camera can be controlled by a game to give an exciting representation of the action. There are many specific methods of controlling a camera that have been discussed, although most will not appear in every game. At this point, you should appreciate that the camera control system presents the entire game to the player through the graphics system; the view that the player sees is completely seen through the game camera.

The cinematographic methods presented in this chapter are only the basics. Any particular game can expand on these methods, just as a particularly artistic motion picture can advance the state of the art in movies. I expect advances yearly as the skills of game developers advance.

Chapter 12

Creating Terrains

- Learn how to design and implement a realistic terrain for a driving game.
- Learn how to render objects including the Mars rover that we'll use for the Mars racing game.
- Use elements such as quad trees and ROAM to improve texture mapping.

A driving game that involves racing across a perfectly flat plane with no trees, buildings, or scenery of any kind would become boring sooner or later. The scenery gives the game ambiance and a sense of place. Racing through the streets of Paris is something I never really wanted to do in real life, but this fantasy may be interesting to some. A more important function of the scenery, to be practical, is to provide a feeling of motion. It's no fun to drive at 200 miles an hour if there is no sense of speed, no way to tell that you are moving. There's nothing like a tree flashing past your window to give you a healthy sense of velocity.

That being the case, it's time to learn how to add some ambiance to our games. We'll learn how to design our landscapes to contain graphical elements that we can render easily (because I'm lazy) and that can be replaced with more complex, interesting scenes later (because you may not be lazy). I'll also describe the topography of our track; normal race tracks are pretty flat, but Grand Prix tracks are planed around European city streets. This will also be our plan.

In the first part of this chapter, I'll focus on the basic techniques of creating terrains. In the second part of the chapter, I'll present the sets and props that we'll be using in the *Manic Mars Racer* game that we'll develop in Chapters 13 and 14.

Representing Terrains

Cars have always been designed to run over flat, smooth surfaces such as paved roads and salt flats. When designing and implementing a racing game, it is likely that the race will be run over pavement, maybe even on a race track. Race tracks tend to possess no significant changes in elevation at all.

And that is the crux of terrain modeling and representation: the ability to deal with changes in elevation realistically. A perfectly flat plane is easy to represent but is a very unrealistic environment because very few real places are perfectly flat. Here's what we'll need to do:

1. Design a terrain on which to play our game.

2. Build a model of our terrain for use in the virtual game environment.

3. Find textures that can be used to give the terrain a realistic appearance.

4. Determine how to render the terrain model and textures quickly enough so that the environment can be displayed in real time.

We'll do each phase completely but not exhaustively, and then look at the details that may improve things in the general sense.

Designing a Terrain

What does it mean to design a terrain? It actually involves describing and creating a surface in three dimensions on which a game will be played. There are basically three ways we can do this:

- Use real terrain, measured and mapped and converted into computer data.

- Build a surface using an interactive program such as Maya, 3D Studio Max, or more specifically, Terragen.

- Build a pseudo-random mathematical surface by summing "bumpy" functions such as sine, cosine, and Gaussian functions.

There are relatively few ways to represent a terrain surface. The most common is to create a grid of height values, which is what game folks call a *height map* or *height grid*. Robotic vision people use something related called a *depth map*, which is a 2D grid of distances from the camera or viewpoint; this can be converted into a height map very simply. The computer representation of a height map is a two dimensional array of height values. Generally, the XZ plane is considered horizontal, with Y values representing heights.

Figure 12.1 shows what a simple height map represents and how it is stored. On the left side, the checkerboard grid represents the spacing on the X-Y axis, and the black bars show the height at each grid point. Heights are stored as integers in a 2D array.

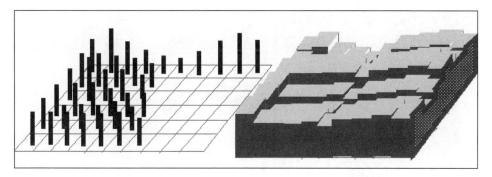

Figure 12.1
Using a height map to create a terrain.

On the right side, the same map is drawn as adjacent prisms. The top surface of each prism is the specified height above X-Y.

Each element of a two dimensional array holds a number that represents a height. Heights for locations that lie between array cells are computed by using an approximation, interpolating between nearby values. Bilinear or cubic interpolation are the two schemes generally implemented. However, it is quite common to polygonalize the height map before using it. With this approach, the terrain is actually set up as a set of triangles or quads like any other object in the game.

Creating "Random" Terrain

You might think that the simplistic way to create a terrain map would be to generate random level values and store them in an image. This is the first thing that occurs to many people when they are asked for a method for creating random terrains. This fails because a terrain rarely changes height quickly, whereas random numbers vary across the possible range without regard for neighboring values.

It would be possible to create a smoother terrain by using neighboring values as a mean and selecting a small standard deviation. The result would be a fairly smooth terrain, probably too smooth for someone not born in Kansas. Still, it would work for some situations. Figure 12.2 shows a random and locally random terrain created using these two methods.

Figure 12.2a shows a completely random set of height values between 0 and 255, whereas Figure 12.2b shows the same image after ten passes of averaging the local 3×3 regions. It is fairly obvious that Figure 12.2b is a much more likely representation of a real terrain field.

The code that creates the smoothed random field is shown here:

12

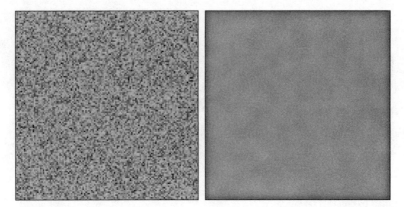

Figure 12.2
Comparing a random terrain with a locally random terrain.

```
for (i=0; i<ROWS; i++)
    for (j=0; j<COLS; j++)
        terrain[i][j] = (float)(rand()%256);

for (k=0; k<10; k++)
  for (i=0; i<ROWS; i++)
  {
        for (j=0; j<COLS; j++)
        {
                x = terrain[i][j];
                if (i-1 >= 0) x += terrain[i-1][j];
                if (i-1 >= 0 && j-1 >= 0)
                        x += terrain[i-1][j-1];
                if (i-1 >= 0 && j+1 < COLS)
                        x += terrain[i-1][j+1];
                if (i+1 < ROWS && j-1 >= 0)
                        x += terrain[i+1][j-1];
                if (i+1 < ROWS)
                        x += terrain[i+1][j];
                if (i+1 < ROWS && j+1 < COLS)
                        x += terrain[i+1][j+1];
                if (j+1 < COLS) x += terrain[i][j+1];
                if (j-1 >= 0) x += terrain[i][j-1];
                terrain[i][j] = x / 9.0f;

        }

    }
```

It's better to use random parameters to smooth functions to create synthetic terrain (see Figure 12.3). For example, we could sum up a few sine and cosine functions of various frequencies to create a smooth varying surface. We could let the landscape be represented as a height grid, a matrix of grey level (integer) values representing the height of the surface at fixed intervals in the X and Y directions. We could then write this grid to a file in an image format, in this case PGM.

Here's the code that performs this work:

Figure 12.3
Using a synthetic terrain.

```
float terrain[ROWS][COLS];

void generateHeights( void )
{
    double height;
    int i,j;

    for(i=0; i<ROWS; i++)
    {
        for(j=0; j<COLS; j++)
        {
            height =  4.0 * sin(i/8.0 + j/12.0) +
                      6.0 * sin((i+7)/31.0 ) +
                      7.0 * cos((j-50.0)/18.0);
```

12

```
                terrain[i][j] = (float)(height+17);
         }
     }
}
```

The *Demo 1* directory in the *Chapter 12* subdirectory on the website for this book contains a program that creates synthetic terrain files using the methods I just presented. The files created consist of 128 rows of 128 elements, each element uses a height value expressed as an integer. You may, of course, alter the parameters of the software to create new and larger terrain samples.

Rendering the Height Grid

Since the terrain values are expressed on a regular grid, a simple way to draw the surface is to think of groups of four samples as rectangles and to draw them in OpenGL as QUADS. A function to do this is shown here:

```
void drawTerrain ( )
{
    int x,y,z;
      static int LOADED = 0;
      FILE *f;

      if (!LOADED) // Load the terrain file if necessary
      {
            f = fopen ("terrain.txt", "r");
            for(x=0; x<ROWS; x++)
                    for(y=0; y<COLS; y++)
                    {
                            fscanf (f, "%d", &z);
                            terrain[x][y] = (float)z/8.0f;
                    }
            fclose (f);
            LOADED = 1;
      }


      glColor3f(0, 0.5, 0.1);
      glBegin(GL_QUADS);
      for(x=0; x<ROWS; x++)
      {
            for(y=0; y<COLS; y++)
            {
```

```
                glVertex3f(SCALE*(x+1), SCALE*y,
                    terrain[x+1][y]);
                glVertex3f(SCALE*x, SCALE*y, terrain[x][y] );
                glVertex3f(SCALE*x, SCALE*(y+1),
                    terrain[x][y+1] );
                glVertex3f(SCALE*(x+1), SCALE*(y+1),
                    terrain[x+1][y+1] );
            }
        }
        glEnd();
}
```

There are a few key issues about this code that I need to point out. First, the terrain file is read in the first time this function is called; this could also be done during an initialization stage, but I wanted to modify as little code as possible from the equivalent Chapter 11 demo.

The next point is the scaling that I do, both in the plane and the heights. When the surface was created, the values ranged from 0 to 128 or so; this is too large a range for the scene because the building is 40 units tall. Thus, the height values are decreased by a factor of eight as they are read in. The playing surface as originally defined was 700×700 units, while the terrain model is 128×128 units. This implies a scale factor of 700/128= 5.46875, which happens to be the value of the constant **SCALE** in the code just presented. This scaling means that the terrain covers the playing surface as precisely as is possible.

If the scaling function is called from the **display()** function, some unintended consequences occur. The surface will be drawn but the car, camera, and the grid lines will still be defined to be at z=0. This means that the car and our point of view will be *beneath* the surface rather than on top of it. We need to ensure that everything we want to place in the game's virtual world will sit on top of the terrain surface. This can be done in many ways, but a simple one (I like using a simple approach as long as it is fast enough) is to first write a function that tells us what the height of the surface is at any point (x,y):

```
float getz (float x, float y)
{
    float z;

    if ( (x/SCALE < ROWS) && (y/SCALE<COLS) )
      z = terrain[(int)(x/SCALE)][(int)(y/SCALE)];
    else z = 0.0f;
    return z;
}
```

Now whenever we draw the player, we need to make certain that the vehicle is drawn at a height of **getz(x,y)** where the vehicle position is **(x,y)**. Inside of the **drawPlayer()** function we put the code:

```
z = getz (x, y);
glBegin (GL_QUADS);
prisma (theta, 2.0, 1.0, 1.0,
x,  y,  z,  .9, .9, .9);
glEnd();
```

This will ensure the car is in the right place, but the camera won't be; we'll be looking up at the car moving overhead. This positioning is found in the display function and needs to be fixed. We can do this by simply getting the height at the camera position and add this height to the computed camera height above terrain level:

```
cameraParameters(&cx, &cy, &cz,&lx, &ly, &lz);
lz = lz + getz (cx, cy);
cz = cz + getz(cx, cy);
gluLookAt (cx, cy, cz,
          lx, ly, lz, 0.0, 0.0, 1.0);
```

Finally, we want to draw the grid on the surface of the terrain so that we can see motion and contour. This means modifying the **drawGrid()** function so that it draws individual line segments (rather than the entire 700-long grid lines) so that the line endpoints are at the correct height:

```
void drawGrid()
{
     float i, j, z;

   // Turn the lines GREEN
   glColor3ub(0, 255, 0);

   for(i = 0; i <= 700; i += 50)
   {
     glBegin(GL_LINES);
       for (j=0; j<700; j+=50)
       {
             z = getz (j, i);
             glVertex3f (j, i, z);
             z = getz ((j+50.0), i);
             glVertex3f(j+50.0, i, z);
```

```
            z = getz (i, j);
            glVertex3f(i, j, z);
            z = getz (i, j+50.0);
            glVertex3f(i, j+50.0, z);
        }
      glEnd();
   }

   glColor3ub(255, 0, 0);
   for(i = 25; i < 700; i += 50)
   {
       glBegin(GL_LINES);
       glVertex3f (0, i, 0);
       glVertex3f(700, i, 0);
       glVertex3f(i, 0, 0);
       glVertex3f(i, 700, 0);
       glEnd();
   }
}
```

Now we can compile and play the demo again. Note that the green grid lines are now on the terrain surface, whereas the red ones are on still on the z=0 plane.

Figure 12.4 shows the **Demo 2** game that we have been building in this section. You'll find the game in the Chapter 12 subdirectory on the website for this book. As you play the demo, try to drive off of the terrain edge for a bit and then turn around. You will

Figure 12.4
A scene in Demo 2 where the player drives on the surface of a terrain model.

see the terrain surface floating above the x-y plane, and cutting the building (the grey prism) part of the way up from its base. When you drive back into the playing surface your car will automatically move up to the level of the terrain. Figure 12.5 shows what the surface looks like from a distance. Notice that the building is cut off by the surface and that there is a grid on the ground as well as on the surface.

Figure 12.5
The rendered terrain model seen from a distance and below.

Speeding Up Terrain Rendering

The implementation used in the demo seems fast enough but there is really not that much going on. If we needed to render a lot of objects and we used more complex AI techniques, such as a couple of autonomous vehicles, the game would slow down quite significantly, and we would need some acceleration of the terrain display. How can the display be speeded up? Two specific OpenGL possibilities are immediately available to us.

The first speedup option involves using a quad strip instead of individual quads. Using this technique, the terrain is built on top of a regular grid or mesh, and in OpenGL this begs to be drawn as quad strips or even triangle strips. This would imply sending only half of the vertices down the OpenGL pipeline. Let's assume that we want to send the quads from left-most to right-most; the use of a quad strip implies sending the left edge, then the right edge. The quad is implied from this by connecting the top and bottom vertices to each other, respectively, creating a quad. The next quad needs only to specify the next two vertices (the ones on the right of the quad), and so on across the entire row of quads. Then we send another row, and so on. Only half of the usual number of vertices needs to be sent to the graphics card.

When rendering a grid using quad strips, the OpenGL programming guide (Page 37) states: "(specifying quad strips) *draws a series of quadrilaterals (four sided polygons) using vertices v_0, v_1, v_3, v_2, then v_2, v_3, then v_4, v_5, v_7, v_6, and so on. N must be at least four before anything is drawn, and if n is odd then the final vertex is ignored.*"

Given this, the **drawTerrain()** function should be re-written as:

```
for(x=0; x<ROWS; x++)
   {
   glBegin(GL_QUAD_STRIP);

   for(y=0; y<COLS; y++)
   {
     glVertex3f(SCALE*x, SCALE*y, terrain[x][y]);
     glVertex3f(SCALE*x, SCALE*(y+1),
         terrain[x][y+1]);
     glVertex3f(SCALE*(x+1), SCALE*y,
         terrain[x+1][y]);
     glVertex3f(SCALE*(x+1), SCALE*(y+1),
         terrain[x+1][y+1]);
   }
   glEnd();
   }
```

This code and the code used for normal quads is in the **Chapter 12/Demo 2** directory; you can comment out the part that you don't want. However, you should try them both out to experience first-hand that the quad strip version is faster.

The second speedup option is to use a *call list*. The idea here is to compile (collect and pre-process) the terrain quads in advance, and to make a procedure call. This can only be done if the quads are unchanging, and that is certainly the case with terrain. Using this method, the terrain quads or quad strips are processed in a similar way as before, but only once and then they are saved internally. Finally, a simple call is made to display the saved quads. Here's the code:

```
static int COMPILED = 0;
static GLuint  quadStripList;
. . .

if (!COMPILED)
{
```

12

```
quadStripList = glGenLists(1);
glNewList(quadStripList,GL_COMPILE);
glColor3f(0, 0.5, 0.1);
for(x=0; x<ROWS; x++)
{
    glBegin(GL_QUAD_STRIP);
    for(y=1; y<COLS; y++)
    {
        glVertex3f(SCALE*x, SCALE*y,
            terrain[x][y]);
        glVertex3f(SCALE*x, SCALE*(y+1),
            terrain[x][y+1]);
        glVertex3f(SCALE*(x+1), SCALE*y,
            terrain[x+1][y]   );
        glVertex3f(SCALE*(x+1),
            SCALE*(y+1),
            terrain[x+1][y+1]);
    }
    glEnd();
}
glEndList();
COMPILED = 1;
}
glCallList (quadStripList);
```

The **COMPILED** flag indicates that the terrain model has been "drawn" into a memory array. It is initially false (0). This means that the code that draws the quads into an OpenGL *list* will be executed. This code simply allocates an integer identifier and the needed underlying data via a call to **glGenLists()**. Then, the **glNewList()** function is called, effectively opening the list for writing. From that point, every quad drawn (by calling **glVertex3()**) is written to memory. A call to **glEndList()** (following the call to **glEnd()**) finalizes the list. Now a call to **glCallList()** is made, which passes the index of that list. This results in the terrain being drawn. The complete task is really very convenient (and fast). The code for this is also found in the **drawTerrain()** function in **Demo 2**.

Mapping Texture onto the Terrain

Now that you know how to draw a basic terrain, we're ready to learn how to create the terrain that we'll be using for the *Manic Mars Racer* game that is represented in the next two chapters. The **Demo 2** program we've been building has a green color painted onto the quads, representing the terrain. This does not look at all like grass, especially because a set of grid lines are drawn over it. What we need for a proper driving game is a surface that looks like a driving surface: a road, ice, or dirt. Simple color won't accomplish this; we need texture. The terrain that we'll be creating for the Mars racer game will use a sandy-reddish texture on the terrain so as to approximate the rusty world portrayed in the images sent to Earth from the Mars rovers such as Pathfinder and the others.

The **Demo 3** directory contains a Visual C++ project that renders a texture to the terrain model (see Figure 12.6). This represents our attempt to model the Mars desert. How do we map this texture on the terrain quads? We'll use the same technique that we used in Chapter 4.

The same method can be used to draw grass or pavement or any other texture onto a terrain.

Figure 12.6
The Mars surface texture image.

```
void drawTerrain ( )
{
    . . .

/*  Basic quad terrain */
    glColor3f(1., 1., 1.);
```

```
glBindTexture (GL_TEXTURE_2D, dirtTex);
glBegin(GL_QUADS);
for(x=0; x<ROWS; x++)
{
    for(y=0; y<COLS; y++)
    {
        glTexCoord2f (1.0, 0.0);
        glVertex3f(SCALE*(x+1), SCALE*y, terrain[x+1][y]);
        glTexCoord2f (0.0, 0.0);
        glVertex3f(SCALE*x, SCALE*y, terrain[x][y]    );
        glTexCoord2f (0.0, 1.0);
        glVertex3f(SCALE*x, SCALE*(y+1), terrain[x][y+1] );
        glTexCoord2f (1.0, 1.0);
        glVertex3f(SCALE*(x+1), SCALE*(y+1),
        terrain[x+1][y+1]);
    }
}
glEnd();
}
```

Of course, the texture image has to be read in and the usual setup has to be performed, as before. The Mars ground texture has been supplemented by a red sky and I removed the grid lines, resulting in the demo in the *textured terrain* directory.

Creating Objects

The only objects used in the demos presented so far is the building (which does not present an obstacle to the player), and the player's vehicle, which is a simple prism. Prisms are easy to draw, and because the building is also drawn as a prism, no complex objects have been used yet (unless you count the terrain). If the player's vehicle were, say, a Corvette or a pickup truck, we would need a way to represent it as an object in the game, and to read it in if it were complex enough to require more than a few polygons.

Most objects are stored as files in a 3D polygon format of some kind. There are many such formats, the most common being *.3ds* and *.obj* formats. Files of these types are created by programs that are used to generate 3D models—programs such as Maya and 3D Studio Max, which are both commonly used by game developers to create objects for games. I have chosen the *obj* format to describe here, but others are available on the Internet and you should become familiar with the source code for all of the important systems.

The Alias Wavefront OBJ Format

This format represents text-based files that support both polygonal and free-form geometry. The Java 3D system allows use of the .obj file format also, and this means you can create virtual reality environments using Java. The Sun Java3D documentation contains a useful set of documentation on this format. The file must be able to specify the polygons that comprise any object that may be needed within any game, and it must also be able to allow the specification of color and texture. The file, therefore, contains vertices, and collections of vertices that make up the polygons.

The file, however, consists of text rather than binary information. This is useful to us, as it means that we can create *.obj* files by using a text editor, and that is a serious advantage when testing the programs that read these files. One of the things that can occur in a *.obj* file is a comment—a text description of what is going on. This is exactly the same as a comment in C or C++ code.

Basic OBJ File Elements

Any line in an *obj* file that begins with a '#' character is a comment, right to the end of the line. Here's an example:

```
# This is a vertex
```

In a *.obj* file, this line would be completely ignored by a reader program.

A vertex is represented as a line in the file beginning with the 'v' character, followed by the three coordinates of a point in 3D space, represented as real numbers:

```
v float float float
```

These vertices can be thought of as providing the x, y, z coordinates. In addition, the vertices are given numbers starting at the first vertex specified in the file, which would be numbered 1, in ascending order as they appear. This format allows us to reference these vertices later, when collecting them into polygons, for instance.

A line that begins with the characters 'vn' represents a normal vector, again in 3D space:

```
vn float float float
```

Also as before, the first normal vector in the file is numbered as 1, the next one is 2, and so on. This is a texture coordinate, again numbered from 1 in ascending order.

12

```
vt float float
```

Lines beginning with 'f' define *faces* of polygonal objects, or simply polygons as we have called them:

```
f int int int ...
f int/int int/int int/int . . .
f int/int/int int/int/int int/int/int ...
```

The integers are numbers of vertices, texture coordinates, or normals. For example, the line

```
f 1 2 3
```

means that we are defining a three vertex polygon (triangle) from vertices 1, 2, and 3. The second integer would be a texture coordinate, if there was one, and the third would be a normal. So the line

```
f 1/1 2/5 3/8
```

defines a triangle using vertices 1, 2, 3 that correspond to texture coordinates 1, 5, and 8, respectively. Some texture and smoothing methods require that normals be specified. By the way, polygons have to be convex; this means that a line drawn between any two points on the perimeter of the polygon may lie completely inside of the polygon. Simple polygons such as squares, triangles, and so on are convex. The points that define the vertices of the polygon must be in a plane, too; this means that the polygon is *flat*.

Let's Build a Pyramid

Let's create a simple model and then display it as a way to become familiar with the obj format. A pyramid is a very simple 3D shape that would be an excellent choice. If we build it using a cube as a kind of scaffold, the coordinates will be easier to determine.

Figure 12.7 shows a unit cube at the origin of the (X,Y,Z) axes and shows a pyramid, although not a regular one, that can be drawn inside of it.

There are four vertices and four faces. The vertices can be listed in any order, but are numbered from 1 in ascending order. Here is a suggestion:

```
v 0 0 0
v 1 0 0
v 0 1 0
v 0 0 1
```

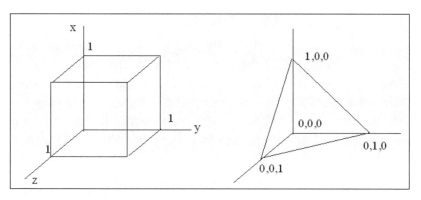

Figure 12.7
Creating a simple pyramid in OBJ format.

The faces are obvious enough. For example, one is (0,0,0) to (0,0,1) to (1,0,0); as vertex numbers, this is from 1 to 4 to 2, and in the file it is written as:

```
# vertices
(0,0,0) to (0,0,1) to (1,0,0)
f 1 4 2
```

The others are:

```
# vertices (0,0,0) to (0,1,0) to (1,0,0)
f 1 3 2
#vertices (0,0,0) to (0,1,0) to (1,0,0)
f 1 3 4
# Final face, vertices (1,0,0) to (10,1,0) to (0,0,1)
f 2 3 4
```

We'll create a file named **pyramid.obj** that contains these lines. Display this and see what you have! To do this, you'll need a display utility that understands **OBJ** files. There are many, but not all are free. We could, of course, write one. Or we could download one or two of them from the Internet. Here are a few to consider:

- Quick3D Viewer **www.quick3d.com**.

If you pay Quick3d for this program, you'll see fewer windows and have fewer buttons to click when invoking it. Two other viewers that I have downloaded and used are:

- browz 3d **http://users.skynet.be/bk232951/appbrowz3d.html**

- 3d photo browser light **www.mootools.com/plugins/us/3dbrowserlight/index.htm**

12

A Complex Object—A Mars Rover

The Mars racer game that we'll be creating will need to use rovers as vehicles. We'll want to have a vehicle in OBJ format that can be drawn into the game. My brother is a bit of a modeling genius, and created the rover model shown in Figure 12.8 in a surprisingly brief amount of time. This will be a part of the game, and you can use it—it is available on the website for this book. The image shown on the left in Figure 12.8 is the actual image that we'll be using in the game. The image shown on the right is the actual rover that was sent to Mars.

Figure 12.8
Creating the Mars rover from the game by using the actual rover as a starting point.

The details will be available in the source code for the book, and will be described in the next two chapters. However, the basic idea is quite simple: the objects used in the game, including the rover, are read in as OBJ files in the format explained previously. Then, the objects are drawn in the place of the rectangular prism that I have used in the demos. Since the rovers are simply collections of triangles, the differences between the old and the new program are minor; we simply draw all of the triangles in a collection (an array, for example) instead of drawing the quads that comprise the prism.

The demo is starting to look like a game, now.

Using Level of Detail (LOD)

The demos that I have provided on the Internet all use a terrain grid that is merely 128 by 128 points; this requires approximately 16384 points or 8192 triangles. As the terrain area gets larger, the number of triangles grows as the square of the number of vertices in a size of the terrain rectangle. If we let the model grow to 1024×1024, we would need to render half a million polygons each frame, 24 frames per second. This would require six million polygons per second.

At some point, for some number of terrain polygons, our hardware will not be able to keep up, and the frame rate will drop. We must do something to avoid this. It's really the same basic game problem over and over—things are fast enough until a certain degree of complexity is reached, and then we have to do something clever so that the computer has the time to do the needed calculations. The something clever we're going to do this time relates to creating different *levels of detail* or *LOD*.

The idea is quite simple in concept but can be tricky to implement correctly. At large distances and in relatively smooth regions where the terrain does not change much visibly and changes are coarse, we use large-ish polygons and low resolution textures. As we get closer to a particular terrain feature, more details become visible and we must use smaller polygons to represent the surface. This is simple to implement in some cases because we can take a large right triangle and make it into two smaller ones, and four still smaller ones, very efficiently.

Because this is really a book about *driving* games and LOD is not an essential topic in that context, I won't go into significant detail here. I will give you a few leads about where to find more about the basic methods, and you can do the rest.

Basic LOD—Multiple Models

First, let's look at the simplest way to implement LOD. Consider the situation of a simple object, such as a car. This object can consist of thousands of polygons, which can take significant time to draw. If the car is far from the camera, most of the polygons can't be seen anyway, and the time used to draw them is wasted. The simple solution is to use a distance threshold, not unlike that used to determine whether an object can be seen at all.

The object having the high polygon count is drawn when the object is near enough to the camera so that the polygons can actually be seen. Simply put, if the distance between the center of the object and the viewpoint is less than D_t, we draw the large model; otherwise, we use a model of the object that has many fewer polygons. Naturally, this means creating multiple 3D models of each object, reading them into memory, and calling them up when needed. This is normally faster in a real-time sense than using the same model all of the time.

We can use more than two models and more than two thresholds; it all depends on how complex the objects are and what quality of rendering is needed. This method can be applied to terrain in a simple way: distant terrain is displayed as a merger of adjacent polygons, and nearer terrain is displayed at full resolution. There are problems at the interfaces where different levels of detail meet, and a smoothing must take place. This simple method is the first logical step to understand the processes involved in determining the level of detail needed. This method is often referred to as *discrete level of detail*.

12

Quad Trees

A *binary tree* is, as you probably know, a data structure where each element in the structure has pointers to two other nodes, called *children*. This branching repeats as often as needed. Binary trees are good for simple numeric data including alphabetic information such as names, and many other applications in Computer Science. A *quad tree*, on the other hand, is like a binary tree but each node has four children and the tree is designed to store 2D information, such as that associated with images and terrain. Figure 12.9 shows a simple illustration of a binary tree, and a quad tree. A quad tree recursively tessellates the terrain model, creating a multiple resolution approximation of the underlying height field. The binary tree is shown on the left in Figure 12.9. Each box in the figure is a node that holds data. Visiting the nodes in a particular order retrieves the data in alphabetical order (as an example). The quad tree is shown on the right. Here each node represents four other nodes at a lower level. A quad tree is used for spatial data.

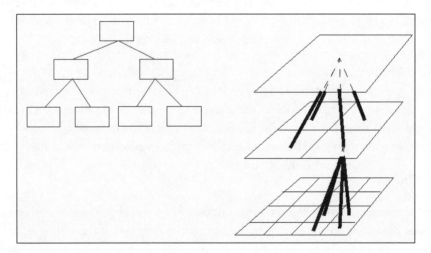

Figure 12.9
An example of a binary tree and a quad tree.

A data structure that could be used to implement a quad tree is:

```
struct QTstruct
{
    struct QTstruct *upper_left, *upper_right;
    struct QTstruct *lower_left, *lower_right;
    float value1, value2, value3, value4;
}
```

The data values in the quad tree node can be used to store composites of values seen at the lower level. The lowest level consists of individual pixels, for example. We could let **value1** be the pixel intensity value in that case. The next level up has four pixels below, and so we could have **value1** be the average of the pixel values of those four pixels. Carrying this on up the tree, the top level has a value that represents the average intensity of the whole image.

As a multiple resolution terrain model, the quad tree is a natural implementation. At any level other than the lowest, we can use the upper-left coordinate of the upper-left part of the quad, the lower-left coordinate of the lower-left quad, and so on to give a polygon (quadrilateral) that can be used to replace the four smaller ones at the lower level. This can be done at any level in the quad tree, so we could have as many different levels of detail as we like.

This is but one way to reduce the number of vertices or to *simplify* the mesh. If we look at any particular quad in the terrain mesh, it can be thought of as having up to eight triangles, as shown in Figure 12.10, or as few as two. On the left, you can see that the nine vertices or eight triangles belong to any quad tree terrain block. On the right, the figure shows the possible configurations of blocks resulting from deleting various vertices.

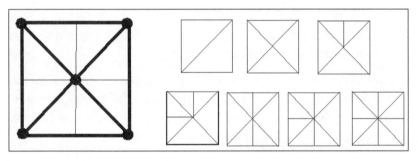

Figure 12.10
Arranging a quad into as few as two triangles or as many as eight.

12

We can simplify the arrangement of the quad tree by removing vertices that represent a height difference that can't be seen from the camera point. There are nine vertices that could belong to any given quad and removing them one at a time yields one of the configurations on the right of the figure, modulo a rotation. Algorithms for LOD are often simply ways to determine which of the vertices are to be kept and which are to be removed, and most of these algorithms are based on quad trees.

An LOD Algorithm—ROAM

There are a half-dozen algorithms for implementing LOD on terrain that we could discuss, and in fact, one whole book has been written on the subject (See [11]) as well as numerous technical articles (E.G. [1,5,8]). We don't have the time or space to cover everything, so let's pick one to look at here—*Real Time Optimally Adaptive Meshes* or **ROAM**.

All LOD algorithms need to have some elements in common. These elements include:

- A method to merge vertices and edges in the initial, low-level height map into a lower resolution version. Looking at this top-down will show you how to easily split a high-level low-resolution polygon into a greater number of higher resolution ones.

- An efficient way to represent all levels of detail (resolutions) in a data structure, and effective ways to manipulate (traverse) that data structure.

- A fast way of determining at which points in the mesh we need to use a different level of detail. These are often based on the distance from the view point to the polygon, either directly or indirectly. Indirect measures can be such things as deviation or variance—a measure of how much the vertex or edge varies from the raw mesh or the next detail level up or down.

The ROAM algorithm can be characterized by the methods that are used to solve the three problems I just stated. Let's take a closer look.

1. **How to split polygons.** A polygon in ROAM is always a triangle, a right triangle, in fact. Given that, splitting it in half is a simple matter of creating a new vertex at the center of the hypotenuse and creating a new edge from the new vertex to the opposite vertex, something like the one shown in Figure 12.11.

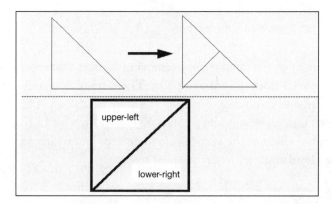

Figure 12.11
Splitting a right triangle in half and using two high-level triangles to store an entire mesh.

This action naturally creates two new right triangles, which in turn can be split again in precisely the same manner—recursively, one might say. The top of the *binary triangle tree* that we can create in this fashion is a high-level low-resolution triangle that contains half of the polygons in the terrain mesh, assuming the entire mesh is square. We need two such high-level triangles to store the entire mesh as shown in the bottom portion of Figure 12.11.

The lowest level of the tree has the most detail, and is in fact the original height map. I think (hope) that the idea is clear enough: we have a number of levels in the triangle tree, each representing a level of detail. The terrain can be drawn at any of those levels, or in combinations of levels such that the level of adjacent triangles differs by at most one (1). See [12] for details on the triangle tree.

2. **Representing levels of detail.** I've already talked about how to represent different levels of detail in a quad tree. ROAM uses a binary triangle tree. For our purposes, we'll need a little more detail. We'll use a binary tree that can hold pointers to the two sub-triangles at any but the lowest level. Traditionally, binary triangle trees are drawn with the main hypotenuse at the bottom, as shown in Figure 12.12.

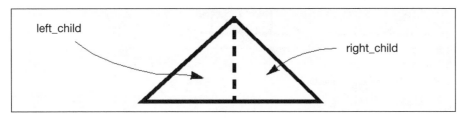

Figure 12.12
Creating a binary triangle tree with right triangles.

We still need more information to be efficient. Sometimes levels will be mixed; that's okay, because when using triangles we know that we won't have gaps along the edges as long as the difference in levels is one or less. Still, we may need more information than just the children, as shown in Figure 12.13.

A tree node structure consists of at least five pointers, one for each of the labeled triangles as shown in Figure 12.13. You could add more data to this structure, but keep in mind that there may be many thousands of them existing at any one time. Indeed, a static allocation structure should be considered, or at least a reclamation scheme that lets the program re-use freed nodes quickly. This structure yields the hierarchical representation[6] shown in Figure 12.14.

12

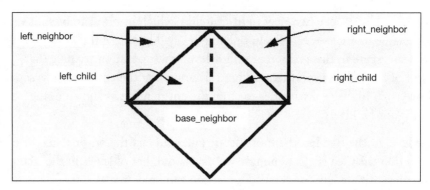

Figure 12.13
Using more information than just the children.

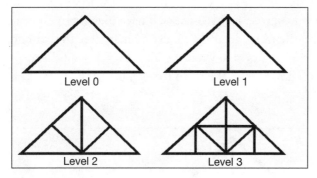

Figure 12.14
Using a hierarchical representation.

3. **Determining error/deviation/variance.** We now must have a measure for visible error in a mesh approximation. The original paper that described ROAM [2] used a measure that turned out to be relatively slow. ROAM does not actually demand that a particular measure be used, and it appears that one called *variance* has been used successfully; a good example is found in [10]. Variance is the distance between the interpolated height value at the midpoint of the hypotenuse of a given triangle and the actual height values as obtained from the actual height map at that point. I think that this is a pretty intuitive measure of variation and requires very little overhead. The calculation is:

$$v = \left| actualHeight - \frac{(lowerLeftHeight + lowerRightHeight)}{2} \right|$$

Here, **lowerLeftHeight** and **lowerRightHeight** are available from the triangle tree. The **actualHeight** value is determined by a looking it up in the actual height map.

It would be cool if we could use this calculation directly, but recall that the values of **lowerLeftHeight** and **lowerRightHeight** are themselves most often interpolations (unless you're at the lowest level of the tree). This creates an error that is too great (try it and see!), so we have to keep the values from lower levels of the tree. In fact, the best way to do this is to have a distinct *variance tree* that stores only the **v** (variance as computed above) value for each triangle at each level of the triangle trees.

Finishing Up ROAM

The ROAM algorithm can now be described simply, in terms of the previous bits and pieces:

1. We create a variance tree for each of the two level 0 triangles forming the rectangular region of terrain to be rendered, recursively down to the lowest level. This will not change unless the height map changes, so it can actually be done ahead of time and saved as a file (unless it's too big, of course).

2. Create a tessellation of the height map and save as a triangle tree. Using the variance tree, split a triangle if the variance at the top level is greater than a predetermined threshold. This threshold can be a function of distance to the region, if you like. This is done recursively, applying the threshold and splitting to the children down to the lowest level.

I have not provided code for this, as there are plenty of samples in the references (especially [6] and [10]).

Geomorphing

In some implementations of LOD, the terrain looks fine when stable but has a problem when you start to move. As the polygons are modified to reflect new distances and camera positions, especially when the camera is attached to a vehicle, we have the problem that new vertices will be added to the terrain grid, and these will seem to "pop" into existence. As higher levels of detail are needed, multiple vertices can simply come into existence—a disturbing thing when you are trying to drive and shoot at the same time.

This effect is called popping for obvious reasons, and can be observed in many driving games, especially older ones that involve off-road driving. It can be reduced by using higher polygon counts, but this defeats the purpose.

12

Geomorphing aims to reduce popping by not allowing rapid changes to the polygon geometry. It does this by modifying a quad gradually rather than all at once when a threshold is passed.

How can we change the grid gradually? Take a look at Figure 12.15. The left portion of the figure shows a terrain patch at a distance of 110 units from the camera, where the threshold for a switch in resolution is T=100. On the right, we have the same patch at a distance of 90 units. In the center is the patch at a distance of 100 units, or halfway between the left and right patches. The new subdivided vertices are half way between the values of the images on the left and on the right, and there is a continual interpolation of the left to right height values of the new nodes as the distance changes. We get to decide at what distance the *morphing* begins and at what distance it ends; distances of 90 and 110 for this are as good as any for this example.

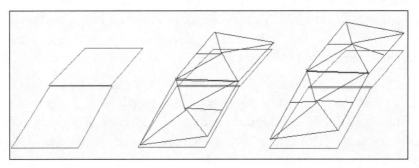

Figure 12.15
Using simple geomorphing.

The actual interpolation is done using a number I refer to as **alpha**, but other writers call it a *blend factor* or *merge ratio*. An **alpha** value of 1 means that no interpolation is to be done because the vertex is at its actual height according to the distant polygon map. An **alpha** value of 0 means that we use the near polygon map. Any value in-between means that an interpolation is used. The formula for the interpolation is to compute the vertex height as:

Equation 12.1 $z = (alpha * distantZ) + (1-alpha)*nearZ$

In the method here, **alpha** varies as distance **d** from the polygon vertex. If **d>=110** (in this example 110 is the far threshold distance), **alpha = 1**. If **d<=90, alpha = 0**. Otherwise, **alpha = (d-90)/(110-90) = (d-90)/20**.

The threshold distances for this process are a matter for determination in a particular scene. It is very much a matter of relative scale and how fast objects can move. In the above example, if the distance between 90 and 110 can be traveled in one or two frames, the distance would be too small, and perhaps a distance of 80 to 140 would be a better range. I should point out that this is a simple way to do geomorphing, and that there are other published implementations that involve storing **alpha** in the quad tree with the vertices. (See refs. 6, 9, 13).

A Hint for Creating Buildings, Trees, and Other Objects

There are basically two ways to build a structure in a computer game. One is to build it from polygons, just as the Mars rover was built. Programs like Maya and 3D Studio Max are commonly used to create new 3D graphical objects. The second way is to build a simple cube or prism and texture map a building image onto its sides. This is hardly worth mentioning, much less covering in a whole section of a chapter. There is, however, a third, less well-known technique to display stationary objects in a game: *billboards*.

A billboard is a two-dimensional surface that has an image mapped onto it. We actually discussed something like this in Chapter 2. However, a simple image drawn on a simple rectangle is sort of cheesy, especially if you can drive past it and see that its perspective changes incorrectly and that it is in fact of zero thickness. The clever thing to do is to place two of these at right angles to each other, like the ones shown in Figure 12.16.

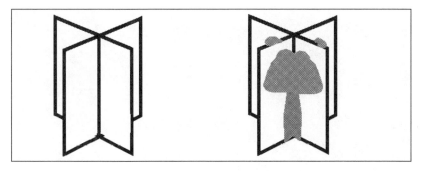

Figure 12.16
Using billboards placed at right angles.

12

Now we map an image onto each rectangle. As an example, a tree, shrub, or if we're especially clever, a burning torch or campfire could be used. When we move around the object, we see it from slightly varying perspectives and it appears more realistic. By the way, this trick works best if the background color of the images mapped to the billboards is transparent!

Another way to do something very much like this is to either rotate the billboard so that it always faces the camera, or to paint textures on spherical or cylindrical billboards [14].

Summary

In this chapter we have looked at the terrain surface on which driving games take place, and how to render and texture the terrain in real time, as a vehicle moves over it. We've also examined the construction and display of game objects such as cars, trees, and buildings, and how to read them from files. We even learned a few tricks about how to use levels of details to save some rendering time.

I think that the time has come to use everything we have learned about driving games and actually design and build one. That's what we'll do in the next two chapters.

Chapter 13

Designing the *Manic Mars Racer* Game

- Create the High-Concept Design document and the Technical Design document for the *Manic Mars Racer* (*MMR*) game.

- Learn what features will be provided in the *MMR* game.

- Learn how the basic features will be implemented.

We're now ready to apply the techniques that we've been discussing—3D graphics, collision detection, AI, audio, physics, and time simulation—and develop our Mars racing game. We have, of course, written a simple game already in the first part of this book, but that game differed in a great many ways from a real driving game, especially because it used a step every second instead of a continuous flow of frames. In this chapter, we'll design a driving game that we'll implement in Chapter 14. Actually, many of the implementation techniques, such as game physics, AI control, cinematography, terrain mapping, and so on, have already been covered in the book, so our work of putting the game together will progress quickly. The Mars racer game will not, of course, be of the same quality as a game such as *Mario Kart* or *Crazy Taxi*, but it will have the same basic components implemented in the same basic way.

Because of the recent interest in the planet Mars, created partly by the different probes and robot vehicles sent there, I thought it would be fun to write a game that takes place on Mars. After all, we have effectively sent three vehicles there—enough for a race. Also, because some of the probes that we have sent to Mars have been creating fairly good maps of Mars' surface, I thought that we could use actual data of the Martian terrain as the playing surface for our game. We can even obtain 3D models of the Mars Landers and use them as the vehicles to be raced in our game. My thinking is that a racing game that takes place on an unusual surface like Mars would add a new dimension to a racing game.

The basic *idea* behind the game is to have a race between strange vehicles on the surface of Mars. Of course, there is always a big difference between an idea and a design, as you will soon see. A design contains a complete description of all the game situations and their resolutions, a list of all assets, and a complete plan for all activities. In Part I of this book, I showed you that there are two basic documents used to design a game—the High-Concept Design document and the Technical Design document—so let's now create these documents.

Manic Mars Racer—The High-Concept Design Document

This section provides the complete High-Concept Design document for *Manic Mars Racer*. Make sure you look these design guidelines over closely before you get wrapped up in the implementation details. You can use the approach that I take here to design one of your own games.

1. Game Analysis—*Manic Mars Racer* (*MMR*) is a 3D racing/driving game that takes place on Mars. Two vehicles will be used in the game—the player's vehicle and an opponent vehicle. The drawings for both of these vehicles are shown in Figure 13.1.

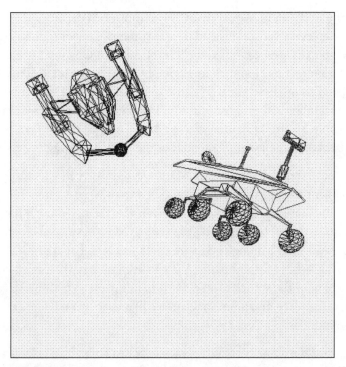

Figure 13.1
Graphical models of the Martian vehicle (left) and the player's Rover (right).

1.1 Basic Game Concept

MMR is a single-player game in which the player drives a mobile Mars probe. The game doesn't actually have a road or track for the player to follow, but there are rules and goals that the player needs to consider. First of all, the player needs to gather rock samples and other objects. As the player gathers these objects, he or she will accumulate points. The player's goal is to collect as many points as possible.

An opponent (a Martian) will be collecting things also, and if the opponent collects an object the player loses out on it, as well as the points that are associated with the object. At some point, the game becomes a race against the Martian as the player tries to get back to the starting point.

1.2 Game Characteristics

The game is based on a set of basic ideas as follows:

- **Simple competitive mission that involves collecting objects**

- **Basic off-road race in low gravity**

- **Use of actual Mars data in the game—a nice environmental message**

- **Uses the element of speed to encourage the player to race around to gather points**

1.3 Game Information

Manic Mars Racer is a 3D theme-racing game for the PC platform. It takes place off-road on a Martian landscape. The competition in the game is based on both speed and strategy.

1.4 Brand Analysis

MMR is not a licensed game, but players will recognize the landscape. One design consideration is that many people expect Mars to look like a huge beach (no water, of course). We'll take advantage of this. Also, the search for life on another planet often starts on Mars. Finally, the names and shapes of the Mars Landers are well known and recognizable.

1.5 Competitor's Analysis

I know of no other racing game that takes place on Mars. *MMR* has aspects of off-road racers, and also provides mission-like tasks. Other games that compete in this genre might be:

- *SODA Off-Road Racing*: Although this game provides off-road racing features, it simply takes place at traditional locations and landscapes.

13

- *FUEL*: A game created by friends at Firetoad Software that includes driving, boating, and many off-road racing features. This game has more features than *MMR* but it doesn't take place on another planet.

- *Wild, Wild Racing*: A game developed by Rage Studio in 2000 that uses dune buggies.

1.6 Story Concept

Humans have been sending junk to Mars for the past 30 years or so. The residents of Mars are really getting annoyed about this. Quite frankly, they've had enough. Some well-organized and enterprising Martians have managed to repair and energize an old Mars rover left by the humans called *Pathfinder*. The Martians are very creative and handy, so they've added controls to allow them to drive their new possession. They drive around the surface of Mars and try to collect the junk that the humans have left behind. Why? Because the Martians lack many essential materials needed to construct complex electronic and mechanical equipment, even though many Martians are quite clever. They plan to build a shield out of the material they collect to prevent humans from dropping any more trash on their planet.

Unfortunately, this shield would keep humans from being able to land on Mars in the future. The shield would also keep humans from being able to communicate with the Martians. (By now you should realize that all of the junk left behind has really put the Martians in a bad mood.) We don't want to be locked out of Mars. Our strategy is to send someone there (the player) to gather the junk we've left behind and remove it before the Martians can gather it themselves and build their shield. Of course, while we are there, we'll also want to pick up some valuable Mars rocks for our collection back home. (Just imagine how valuable those Mars rocks would be if you could bring them home and sell them on eBay!)

1.6.2 Game Play

The game begins as the player has their vehicle at the Mars base. The player is assigned the task of picking up a certain number of debris (objects) and a certain number of rock samples. The player receives points for picking up these various objects. The player leaves the base and starts towards the Martian debris collection area (home site). This area is home to the largest debris pile on the planet. The player uses a small map showing the location of desired rocks and debris relative to the player's current position. Desirable collectables are placed on a route that leads to the Martian home site.

The more debris the player collects, the more the Martians will take notice and will want to steal what the player is collecting. If the Martians spot the player, they may chase the player or not, depending on how much the player has collected at the time.

The player may return to the base and drop off collectables, but that takes time and fuel. If the Martians chase the player, a race ensues where the Martians will try to get to the player's base first and block the entry to the repository so that the player can't save their points. If the player gets to the Martian home site, there will certainly be a race back as the Martians chase the player away.

The Martians are also collecting debris, but not rocks. The longer the game lasts, the less debris remains to be collected.

2 Game Design

2.1 Game Structure
The player is always in the driver's seat of a Mars rover, and drives over the tops of objects to collect them. The terrain looks like a desert or a beach with red sand, rocks, and sky. Dust blows by from time-to-time. For entertainment value, the odd beach ball, umbrella, and so on, are provided.

The screen that the player will see shows the view from above and behind the player's vehicle (a Mars rover), or from a vantage point high in the sky looking down. On the upper-right of the screen is a small symbolic map showing the location of the rocks and debris to be collected, the player's current position and home base, and the position of the Martian (sometimes) and the Martian home base.

The screen also shows the vehicle's current speed, points collected, and time elapsed.

2.2 Detailed Game Play
The player controls a small vehicle using the arrow keys. The vehicle is initially located at the human base on Mars. The viewpoint can be moved from the cockpit to behind the vehicle.

2.3.1 Mission Mode
In mission mode, the player can attempt to collect parts and materials on the Martian surface, as indicated by the map in the upper-right area of the screen. Each object collected is worth points. When a certain number of points have been acquired, the player can return to the base. Also, the player's car might become attractive to the Martians at some point, who will try to steal it from the player.

2.3.2 Race Mode
When the player reaches the cache of parts collected by the Martians, the Martians will chase the player back to his base. The Martians will attempt to steal their stuff back and will take everything the player has collected if the Martians can force the player to stop.

13

2.5 Core Controls
The controls supported are simple mouse and keyboard actions:

8 or (Arrow UP)	Accelerate the player's car forward
4 or (Arrow LEFT)	Move the player's car to the left
2 or (Arrow DOWN)	Accelerate the player's car backward
6 or (Arrow RIGHT)	Move the player's car to the right

A mouse click on the END icon will terminate the game.

3 Characters and AI
The only character in the game will be the Martian, and he will remain in his vehicle at all times.

4 Sound
The sound for this game will be relatively simple. A low-level background sound of wind blowing will be used to give an impression of distance and isolation. The engine sound will also be more or less constantly playing, but will vary according to the speed and gear of the vehicle. Some other required sounds are:

- Voice message from mission control. These must be obeyed or points will be lost.

- A sound to indicate an object has been collected

- The sound, in 3D, of the Martian rover

- Music, as selected by the player

- Collision sounds as needed if the player collides with rocks, buildings, or Martians

- Sounds indicating that the Martian is stealing objects

Sound will be low resolution, and some sounds, like the sound of the Martian vehicle, will be positional.

5 Key Feature Summary
Here's a summary of the key highlights of the game:

- *MMR* provides an exotic location (Mars)—one that's recently been in the news and is known to most players

- Features simple play that is suitable and entertaining for smaller children and older ones

- Supports two modes: mission and race
- Provides an easy interface that uses standard controls

A Casual Description of the Game

Our *MMR* game has two modes: search and race. The game begins with the player driving a vehicle of some kind, perhaps a dune buggy, out of a garage located at a human base on Mars. A small display is provided in one corner of the screen that shows a small region of the surface where the player's vehicle is located. The display also provides the player with a graphical location for finding objects to be retrieved and it also shows where the Martian vehicle is located, if it can be seen.

The player's job is to collect junk metal from the surface of Mars. This debris is from the many probes that humans have sent to Mars over the years. The player must bring the junk back to the base so that it can be taken away; otherwise, the Martians will get it. The Martians wish to use the junk to build some device of unknown, but nefarious, purpose. The player drives from point-to-point on the surface, collecting the bits and pieces of Earth hardware to be found.

The Martian will mostly ignore the player, but the more material the player has in his car, the more interesting the player will become to the Martian. The player won't know how much stuff they can collect before the Martian tries to come after it, and the player won't have enough time to return to the base with everything they find. At some point in the game, the Martian will see the player and give chase, at which point the game becomes a race. The player must get back to the base before the Martian can steal the player's objects.

Objects are worth different points depending on their composition and size. As the player, your score is a function of time and how many points worth of junk you collect.

The Terrain

I have chosen an actual location on Mars where this drama will take place: the *Valles Marineris*. The Mars Orbiter Laser Altimeter (MOLA) collected the data, which was processed into an image by the MOLA team at Goddard Space Flight Center, and it is located between 30 and 80 degrees West longitude and centered at the equator. This is a very low resolution image, but at least it's real. We'll need to get creative and play with this image a little so that it works for our game. The mapping of this actual location is shown in Figure 13.2.

13

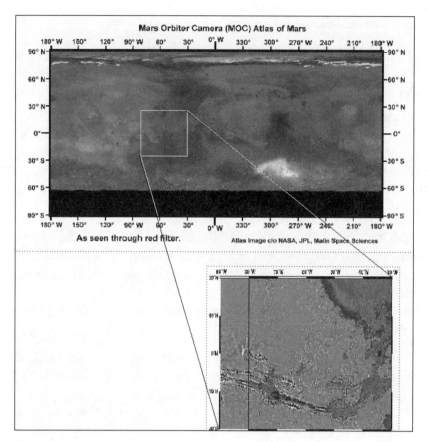

Figure 13.2
A map of the Martian surface showing the global location of the site of the game.

Of course, the image itself can't really be used as a terrain model. What we need is an image that shows heights. Unfortunately, we only have an image that shows light reflections from the surface. There is a relationship but not a simple one. We'll use height measurements, even though the probe that makes them operates at a low resolution. Each height measurement represents hundreds of meters. Who would know, though? We are only creating a game, after all.

The grey image shown in Figure 13.2 can't be used directly for the reason that the illumination creates shadows that would be mistaken for low areas. A mountain would be bright on one side and dark on the other, and this does not represent the actual heights present. What we'll do is create a height map of actual Martian height measurements taken with the MOLA instrument. I don't have the raw data, so I downloaded an image of the height map from the Internet. (The image is shown in the lower-right part of Figure 13.2.) This is a little perverse because we're going to convert from raw data (heights) to an image (found on the Web) to heights (a height map file) and then to an image again (shown on the screen when the game is playing). Playing with data in this fashion is very common when building games.

You could modify the data files so that the game would use any particular portion of the Martian surface. Just download the data file that you want to use, convert it into a terrain file, and save it using the appropriate name.

The Human Base

We will need a few simple models for our game, including:

- A "garage" for the dune buggy

- A space craft so we can get home

- A shelter I chose a quanset, which is a half-cylinder structure of the sort that they use in Antarctica.

We could also use a fence and some lights. Our game doesn't involve fighting, so we won't need any weapons.

The Martian Base

My idea is to design the Martian base so that it looks like a post apocalyptic, rag-tag collection of stuff, sort of *Waterworld*- like. The Martians are building a shield so there should be smoke and fire and the sound of metal being beaten and shaped. The game won't require any character animation. Recall that character animation is difficult to do well. It is certainly too difficult for a first or second project for one or two people. This means we won't have aliens walking about or building things. We won't even need to show aliens driving the car.

Artifacts and Props

The barren surface of Mars has a few interesting things that we want the player to experience, including the two bases. We also need to show the debris items that are being collected. These are pieces of space craft, and thus should be painted metallic with insignias on them. They must be small enough to carry in a dune buggy.

The portions of the terrain that count as artifacts—boulders and smaller rocks as we have seen from the Mars Lander images—are scattered all over the surface of Mars. They could interfere with our driving if they are large enough.

13

Collisions

The vehicles could collide with only a few objects:

- Colliding with a debris item is how the object is collected. Such a collision won't impede the player's progress, but after the player collides with an object, the object needs to be displayed in the player's car.

- Colliding with a rock or boulder causes damage, and changes the player's course.

- Buildings at the bases are typical obstacles, and force the player to drive around them.

- Cliffs act like boulders and buildings.

- The only moving object in the game other then the player's car is the Martian vehicle. This makes the collision detection fairly simple. When the Martian collides with the player's car, some of the player's collected items are transferred to the Martian's car. The precise number of points transferred is random. The result is that the Martian gets more stuff, and the player becomes a less appealing target.

Manic Mars Racer—Technical Design Document

Now that we've finished the High-Concept Design document, it's time to put together the Technical Design Document. This document will help us flesh out the details of how we implement the key features of our design.

1 Introduction

This document describes in detail the technical design of the PC version of the *Manic Mars Racer* game.

1.1 Objectives

The purpose of this document is to provide a plan for the implementation details and to clarify and specify all of the design decisions that have been made. This document will aid in the development of each individual component as well as the integration of the components.

1.2 Intended Audience

This document is produced primarily for the developers of the game *Manic Mars Racer*. *(A lie—it is really designed so that you can see how the design proceeds and how the document is structured!)*

The managers of the development company and the producers will also use the document to assess the state of the *Manic Mars Racer* project.

2 Game Architecture

This section briefly describes the overall structure of *MMR*. The various components of the system communicate through a broadcast/listening style message system—one that is not actually parallel, but that sends simple messages through basic function calls. Thus, no part of the system has direct access to variables or functions of any other.

The format of a message is:

```
<header>
   Type
   Size (bytes) of body
<body>
   Data
<trailer>
   Characters "abcd"
```

This form of communication limits the interaction between the components, and encourages independence and data privacy.

The game is written in C and uses OpenGL for graphics and OpenAL for audio. All three of these tools are cross-system portable, and will allow the game to be ported to run on Linux, Macintosh, or Unix platforms with minor work.

Game AI

The AI used keeps track of objects, allows time to advance smoothly, and generally controls all aspects of the game. It uses both the physics engine and the game timer and communicates with other modules as needed. This module *is actually* the game, and uses the other modules to display the game objects and to receive information from the player. The game AI receives events from the event listener generated by the other sections and sends messages to give instructions to the other sections.

Sound

The sound engine plays the music and sounds for the game. It only receives messages from the event listener. It does generate some sounds on demand, such as engine noise as a function of RPM, but mostly it plays sound objects that have been read in as .WAV files.

13

Input

User input is generally in the form of keyboard input, and this is given directly by the system to the input module. Mouse clicks are also sent in to the input module. This module receives no messages, only input data from the user which it sends directly to the event listener to inform the AI module of what has been requested. This will affect the next game state.

Main Game Loop

The structure of the main game loop looks as follows:

```
while(TRUE)
{
Event_Purge();
    GameAI_Run();
    Graphics_Run();
    Sound_Run();
    Input_Run();
}
```

The **Event_Purge()** function cleans up the used messages, following when each module's **run()** function is executed. Inside of each function, the first action involves checking to see if there are any messages that the component cares about. The component then acts on those messages and updates the states accordingly.

3 Event Manager

3.1 Overview

The event manager component consists of two modules: the **EventManager**, which is really just a queue, and the data module, **Event()**. **EventManager()** is the module through which all the other components communicate. It has two basic functions: **add()**, which allows a new message to be posted, and **front()**, which allows the messages to be viewed from the beginning of the queue. The messages are maintained in a circular, linked list of **Event** structures.

3.2 Module Definition

Module EventManager() Description

eventManagerInit()	Constructor to set up initial empty event list.
add()	Adds a new **Event** to the queue.
front()	Returns the **Event** to the front of list.
Empty()	Returns **true**, when done going through list.
Clear()	Deletes used messages.

Module Event( ) Description

An event is a structure as follows:

```
struct EventStruct {
   UINT Type  /* This is the type of message that it contains */
   UINT Size  /* Size of the data block, in bytes */
   Void* Data /* This is the data of the message cast to a void pointer */
};
typedef struct EventStruct * EVENT;
```

It includes creation and destruction functions:

Allocate an event structure.

```
EVENT newEvent (UINT type, UINT size)
```

Free an event structure.

```
void freeEvent ();
```

4 Input Manager

4.1 Overview
This module is responsible for setting up the keyboard and mouse input devices and for obtaining data from the keyboard. The input manager sends the data to the event manager for use inside the game. The input manager uses GLUT to access the keyboard.

4.2 Module Definition

Module InputManager( )

inputInit()	Initializes the system, creates buffers, and sets up GLUT interfaces.
setEL()	Sets up access to the event manager.
acquire()	Acquires keyboard (called, for example, if the device is lost).
run()	Polls devices for buffered data and sends data to the event manager.
cleanup()	Releases buffers, devices, and interfaces.

13

4.3 Events
The events that are created by this module are:

KB_INPUT	Key that was pressed by the user.
	Keeps track of the up or down state of the key.

MOUSE_PRESS	Mouse button that was pressed.
	Up or down
	X location
	Y location

5 Front-End

5.1 Overview

The front-end module creates and displays screens and menus and deals with the input and state changes when the game is in the beginning, pause, and post game states. It sends events to the graphics module to display the appropriate screens. Information collected in the front-end screens about user choices and setup tasks are stored in the game state and the input event mapper.

The front-end manager is composed of sequences of screens, which are image representations of menus. Each screen allows the user to specify certain parameters that will control the way the game is run (e.g., sound off) or parameters that control the way the game is played by the user (e.g., vehicle selection). The module **frontEndManager()**deals with input events from the event manager and handles screen flows.

5.2 Module Definition

Module FrontEndManager( )

Init	Sets up access to event manager, game state, and input event mapper.
Run	Takes all input events currently in the event manager and forwards them to the current screen.
OnMainMenuScreenExit (menu item)	Sets a new current screen or new game state depending on what menu item on the main menu screen triggered the exit.
OnNewGameScreenExit (menu item)	Sets a new current screen or new game state, depending on what menu item on the new game screen triggered the exit.
OnConfigScreenExit (menu item)	Sets a new current screen or new game state, depending on what menu item on the configuration screen triggered the exit.
OnHighScoresScreenExit (menu item)	Sets a new current screen or new game state, depending on what menu item on the high-score screen triggered the exit.
OnCreditsScreenExit (menu item)	Sets a new current screen or new game state, depending on what menu item on the credits screen triggered the exit.

OnPauseScreenExit (menu item)	Sets a new current screen or new game state, depending on what menu item on the pause screen triggered the exit.
OnEndGameScreenExit (menu item)	Sets a new current screen or new game state, depending on what menu item on the end screen triggered the exit.

Module Screen

Init()	Sets up access to game state and the input event mapper.
ResetFocus()	Sets the menu items to the default focus.
ProcessInput ()	Processes key presses depending on the current menu item.
	This includes setting the focus on the correct menu item, changing the value of text fields or scroll bars, updating stored information, and exiting the screen.
SetExitCallback()	Sets a pointer to the function to invoke when this screen exits.
Display()	Sends display event containing information about this screen.

5.3 Events

The events that are created will include (there may be others as needed):

Event Name	Data
DISPLAY_SCREEN	Identifier of screen to display.
	Focus state for all widgets on the screen
	Value for widgets

6 Game AI Module

6.1 Overview

The AI section of the game does most of the basic bookkeeping associated with the game play—state management, determining what is drawn, determining where objects are drawn, providing alien car control, supporting object motion, controlling the timing, and managing static objects and consumable resources. It works closely with a large set of other modules that will be described shortly.

The main part of this module is actually the main program for the game. It includes all the data structures and initializations, and it knows what all of the resources are and where they are. It also initializes all of the other modules. It then steps through the

13

pre-game, game play, and post game sections as indicated by the user through the interface. It checks for relevant events and updates internal flags and states appropriately. Then it invokes the correct function sequences to accomplish the tasks of the current portion of the game. This description may seem vague, but this module starts out at the highest levels of the game and works its way down to the lowest levels.

Function	Description
InitAll()	Start all the other units.
InitializeEvents()	Sets up access to the event manager.
Run()	Depending on the current game state, performs the appropriate action.
CollisionCheck()	Performs collision detection.
GameoverCheck()	Checks for a game termination state and determines who wins.
CollisionResolution()	Processes a collision that has occurred by determining what happened.
RunFrontEnd()	Runs the front-end.
RunPreGame()	Performs the game startup actions.
PlayGame ()	Plays the game.
GameOver()	Displays the termination menus, performs the cleanup operations, and displays the high score.

6.2 Initial State

6.2.1 Summary

This is a storage unit for high level information, such as:

- Current high-level state

- Player's name

- Player's vehicle

- Sound on/off and volume

Seven high-level game states are supported: **Initialize, Begin, Pre, Post, Playing, Pause,** and **Clean.**

Initialize: Data files are loaded and the variables and data of the game are set up. When finished, this state will change to **Begin.**

Begin: The splash screen is displayed, and the menu scheme allows the user to select parameters and then start the game. When the user chooses to start a game, the state is switched to **Pre.**

Pre: The renderer is told about all the objects. The world is loaded and the game is set up to be played. When this is done, the game state becomes **Playing**. There is no input to be acted on in the **Pre** state.

Playing: The game is actually being played and the user is interacting with the system. The user can **Pause** and enter the **Post** state automatically when someone wins.

During the **Playing** state, the game will perform the following actions:

1. Update the internal state using an FSA based on the messages received.

2. Calculate where the AI controlled objects, mainly the alien, will move to.

3. Perform collision detection on the alien and the player—the only moving objects.

4. Resolve any collisions based on the current level of physics used by the system.

5. Inform the sound system of any sounds to be played or synthesized.

6. Provide the graphics system engine with the new positions of the objects, orientations, and camera positions.

Post: Display statistics to the player, indicate the score and who won, clean up storage and files, and update the high score.

Pause: The player selects a pause state, and must now be given the choice to continue or exit to the main menu. No time passes for the player or the AI, so game activity effectively ceases. Thus, the game can be sent to either the **playing** or the **Begin** states.

Clean: When the game is over, the memory is cleaned up and the game exits gracefully.

6.2.2 Class Description

Class: CGameState

Function	Description
GetState()/SetState()	Retrieves or stores the game state.
GetPlayerName()/SetPlayerName()	Retrieves or stores the player's name.
GetVehicle()/SetVehicle()	Retrieves or stores a selected vehicle.
GetTimeLimit()/SetTimeLimit()	Retrieves or stores the time limit.
GetVolume()/SetVolume()	Retrieves or stores sound volume.

13

6.3 Terrain/World Representation

6.3.1 Overview
Three data files represent the layout of the game and its props. These files are:

- Terrain file

- AI layout file

- Objects file

The player sees a rendering of scenery and objects that represent the surface of Mars, the vehicles, and the target objects. Each of the these files holds a different aspect of the world. The AI sees the game as a set of fixed objects, moving objects, and cells for collision testing and waypoints. These normally can't be seen, but there should be a way to render them if you want to.

6.4 Sound Assets
We require .WAV files for the following events and sound textures:

- Collision between player and alien car

- Collision between player and rock

- When the player's car falls off cliff/rock

- Player's engine

- Alien engine

- Screech—corner on hard surface (3-4 choices)

- Player picks up an object (multiple choices)

- Rattling noise such as objects bouncing around in the vehicle

- Spinning tires in the sand

- Construction noises at the alien base (hammer, anvil, welding, grinding)

- Alien base—loudspeaker announcements

- Alien base—flames

- Player base—humming.

- When alien steals stuff from player

- When objects fall off of vehicle

Summary

I have provided you with templates for the two main design documents used in game development. I also provided you with a concrete example of the content of these documents for a game that we're actually going to build. It's important to have a clear idea of what you are proposing to build before you get started. This is like a house plan or the blueprint for a machine; you can change it later, but you need a picture of the proposed result. This is true if you want to succeed, whether the game is a professional one or just a game for your enjoyment only.

13

Chapter 14

Coding the *Manic Mars Racer* Game

- Implement the messaging system for the Mars racer game.
- Create the graphics and state machine for the game.
- Create the terrain and implement the game AI.

Sadly, we're almost done.

You have learned how to draw pictures with OpenGL and to play sounds using the OpenAL system. You also know how to move graphical objects around the screen under the control of key presses. You know how to simulate a car, how to control vehicles so that they appear to be driven, and how to race. Finally, you've learned how to control a camera and how to build a terrain that the car can drive on top of. We have even built some very practical demos to experiment with implementing these features. The time has come to put everything together and build our masterpiece.

The Mars racer game has been designed in some detail, as you've seen in Chapter 13. You should now have some idea of how to make this game work. As with the sample games and demos that have been introduced in this book, the source code for *MMR* is available on the website for this book. You'll find everything you need in the *Chapter 14* directory. Without being too self-serving, I think that this game, although it has some flaws and provides only limited game play, is one of the coolest games published in a book. I designed it for this book and it was implemented by Deifante Walters and Eric Yeung—two students in my *Video Game Programming* class (Computer Science 585) at the University of Calgary; they were assisted by Mike Slywka, who worked mainly on the terrain model. The idea was to show all of the basic elements of a real driving game; many books just put together game components into a basic playable mess (or BPM), as I call it.

Our task now is to look at the essential and interesting parts of the Mars game so that you have a roadmap to help you navigate the code. Before we do this, you should download and play the game for about fifteen minutes to make sure that you have a good idea about the gameplay, graphics, narrative, and AI. Try to crash the vehicle (there's no prize). You can use the website to tell me about bugs. Perhaps you will even suggest a fix if you find a bug. Once you play the game, the material presented in this chapter will make more sense.

Oh, and do have some mercy on us. We attempted to create a fairly complex game project without any budget and very limited time. There *will* be bugs, and the game is incomplete. I'm hoping that many readers will download the source and modify it to add features and improve the game. Think of this as the final class project. If you do have feedback, let me know and I will upload the best of the mods I receive to the website for this book

Implementing the Messaging System

Let's first look at how the messaging system is implemented for the game, because the messaging system serves as the heart of the game. The design presented in Chapter 13 states that messages will be passed from module to module in the game to permit the distinct components in the game to communicate with each other. *MMR* uses a variation of the scheme presented in the book, *AI Programming Gems*. A message is just a simple block of data; you can think of it as a string or a C structure. When a game object wants to send a message, it uses the following function:

```
void aiSendMessage(enum MessageName mnName,
    unsigned int uiSender, unsigned int uiReciever,
    void* pvData, int iNumBytesData)
```

This function can be found in the source file AI.c. The message name is a selection from a list of predefined message names, and represents the type of the message being sent. Each game object receives a unique ID, which is used by the messaging system to find out which game object should receive the message. Because the number of game objects for *MMR* is not large, the system builds a message list and searches it using a simple linear search.

At the other end, the receiving game object creates an **OnMsg(<messageName>)** block. This block can occur inside a specific state block or in the global scope of the state machine. This block is used to provide a specific action when the game object is in a certain state, but will have a default action at other times.

The receiving object will know what game object sent the message because of the ID of the message. The last two arguments in the **aiSendMessage()** function are for optional data. The key press messages make use of this data to specify what key was pressed, for example. When sending a message like this, the calling function is responsible for cleaning up the memory. In the key press example, the calling function uses a regular variable that is cleaned automatically. This also brings out an important design choice of the messaging system: when using **aiSendMessage()**, the call is synchronous. If the user presses a key that makes the player move, the updating code in the player will be run before the **keyDown()** function exits.

When a message is sent with **aiSendMessage()**, it is routed to the proper game object with this function that is found in AI.c:

```
void aiRouteMessage(MessageObject* moMessage)
```

This function does a few things. Its first task is to check to make sure that the object to receive the message is still around:

```
pgo = aiGetGameObjectFromID(&g_singleAI, moMessage->uiRecieverID);
if(!pgo)return;
```

The next thing that happens in an immediate message is that the message is delivered to the proper game object using the following function:

```
int aiRouteMessageHelper( GameObject* pgo,
    enum GameObjectState currentState ,
    MessageObject* pmoMessage)
```

This function just calls the proper state machine function based on the game object:

```
if( aiRouteMessageHelper( pgo, pgo->currentState, moMessage) == 0)
{
//Current state didn't handle message, try global state
   aiRouteMessageHelper(pgo, gosGlobal, moMessage);
}
```

Here you can see how the global state works. If a message is sent and the return value is 0, we'll know that the current state didn't handle the message. We can try with the global state and the current state doesn't have to change. The next block allows the state machine to decide upon a specific state:

14

```
//check for a state change
   while(pgo->iForceStateChange)
   {
      memcpy(&moTempMessage, moMessage,
                 sizeof(MessageObject));
//Create a general message for iniatlize and cleaning up the state change
      moTempMessage.uiRecieverID= pgo->uiObjectID;
      moTempMessage.uiSenderID = pgo->uiObjectID;

      pgo->iForceStateChange = 0;

//Let the last state clean up
      moTempMessage.mnName = ExitMessage;
      aiRouteMessageHelper(pgo, pgo->currentState,
                 &moTempMessage);

//set the new state
      pgo->currentState = pgo->nextState;

      //Let the new state initalize
      moTempMessage.mnName = EnterMessage;
      aiRouteMessageHelper(pgo, pgo->currentState,
                 &moTempMessage);
   }
```

The code checks to see if the game object and the state machine want to make a state change. If so, the current state is cleaned up by telling it to run its own **OnExit** block. This happens in the first call to **aiRouteMesageHelper()**. The second call runs the **OnEnter** block of the next state. The current implementation can get caught in an infinite loop this way, but the current game doesn't have any state changes in **OnEnter** blocks; so this doesn't happen.

The system also provides support for delayed messages. These are stored and sent to game objects on the first update loop after the delay time has expired. One use for this would be the expiration of a power up. You can see how this code works by looking at the source for the function **aiProcessSpeedUpStateMachine()**.

At each AI update, the system checks for messages that have expired and sends them to their respective game objects. They are then removed from the linked list. The callee game object is not responsible for cleaning up the pointer here either, as the system will clean the memory after the call is made using this function:

```
void aiRemoveDelayedMessage(DelayedMessageNode* pdmnRemove)
```

At the end of the game, all pending delayed messages are cleaned up with the following function:

```
void aiRemoveAllDelayedMessages()
```

Using a Nifty Finite State Machine Scheme

The implementation of our state machine also makes use of an idea presented by Steve Rabin in the original *Game Programming Gems* book[1]. As you saw in the previous chapters on AI, FSAs are very useful for many of the game tasks that make the game appear clever. You should recall that a finite state machine has both a small number of states that it can be in and a set of transitions between those states. Actions of an AI object depend on the state that it is currently in. A state machine implementation requires the ability to define the current state, to define transitions between states, and the ability to execute specific code depending on the current state.

Rabn's scheme uses C preprocessor directives. First, a FSA is enclosed within a **BeginStateMachine** and an **EndStateMachine** directive. A particular state is defined using a **State(name)** directive and the machine enters a new state by invoking the **SetState(name)** directive. Within a state definition, there is an **OnEnter** directive to perform initialization and an **OnExit** directive to clean up after execution. We can also respond to messages (**OnMsg(messagename)**) and send messages (**SendMsg()**).

As one simple example, here's how the FSA can be coded for traffic lights (see Chapter 8 for more information):

```
t = time_milliseconds();
BeginStateMachine
OnEnter
{
   SetState (randomTrafficLight();          // Red,green,amber at random
}
State(GREEN_TRAFFIC_LIGHT)
{
1f (t>p->change_time)                       // Green to Amber change
{
     p->EW_color = AMBER_TRAFFIC_LIGHT;
     p->change_time = t + p->ticks [AMBER_TRAFFIC_LIGHT]
             - (t - p->change_time);
     SetState (AMBER_TRAFFIC_LIGHT);
}
```

14

```
    }
State (AMBER_TRAFFIC_LIGHT)
{
    if (t>p->change_time)
    {
      p->EW_color = RED_TRAFFIC_LIGHT;
      p->change_time = t + p->ticks [RED_TRAFFIC_LIGHT]
          - (t - p->change_time);
      p->NS_color = GREEN_TRAFFIC_LIGHT;
      SetState (RED_TRAFFIC_LIGHT);
    }
}
State (RED_TRAFFIC_LIGHT)
{
    if (t>p->change_time)
    {
      p->EW_color = GREEN_TRAFFIC_LIGHT;
      p->change_time = t + p->ticks [GREEN_TRAFFIC_LIGHT]
          - (t - p->change_time);
      p->NS_color = RED_TRAFFIC_LIGHT;
      SetState (GREEN_TRAFFIC_LIGHT);
    }
    else if (t>(p->change_time-ticks[AMBER_TRAFFIC_LIGHT))
    {
        p->NS_color = RED_TRAFFIC_LIGHT;
    }
}
EndStateMachine
```

There are many **#define** directives that are used in this code for implementing the FSA. They can be found in the file AI.c. These directives make the state machines very easy to write because they provide a clean definition of every state they define. Using this approach also gives us an optional block of code that will be executed once upon entry to the state and one for exiting as well. When the state machine receives a *message*, it can be caught in the current state or in a global state. These few ideas, along with a message passing system, run the entire AI for *MMR*. Almost every thing that can be thought of as an object in the game has one of these state machines embedded within it.

Implementing the Graphics

Naturally, we used OpenGL for all of the display elements of the game. The visible playing area is a Martian scene, and has a predominantly red tint. A sky box is used that is textured with clouds and mountains. This was created by taking a typical Earth scene and building a sky box in a normal way. The texture images were then edited, and the tint was altered in favor of red. Almost any image manipulation tool will allow this, including *the Giml* and *PhotoShop*.

Most of the graphics in the Mars racer game are standard techniques, as you learned in Chapters 3 and 4. There are just a few exceptions, however, which I'll present next— the particle graphics dust effects and the heads up display.

Dust Devils and Smoke

In the game, I use something new that I call the "dust devil" effect. Sounds cool, right? This effect creates the small dusty balls that seem to blow around the Martian surface while the game is playing. We implemented it using an OpenGL extension called **GL_ARB_point_sprite** that allows the user to supply a 3-D coordinate, and OpenGL will apply a screen-aligned texture at that position. The dust devils are actually small graphical textures created using an image editing program, and they are saved as a PNG image file. The textures are loaded using this function:

```
int initRenderingContext()
```

The function is included in the source file, Rendering.c. The actual function that loads the dust textures is

```
int GenerateOpenGLImage(Image *image, const char * szTextureName)
```

which is found in Images.c. To keep things as simple as possible, the dust devils use the same code infrastructure as all other game objects (the other option would be to manage them separately). The other two textures used in this way are the exhaust from the vehicles and the dust raised by the wheels. The texture images are shown in Figure 14.1. The image on the left is the dust devil. The image in the center shows the impact of dust that has been raised by a spinning tire and the image on the right represents the exhaust smoke that is emitted. The code for creating these particular particles is found in the file AI.c:

```
OnMsg(InitMessage)
{
    aiSendDelayedMessage (TimerMessage,
      ((SmokeParticleInfo*)pgo->pvExtra)->lTota LifeSpan, pgo->uiObjectID,
        pgo->uiObjectID, 0, 0);
    aiPlantGameObject(pgo);
```

14

```
    ((SmokeParticleInfo*)pgo->pvExtra)- >v3dInitalPositon.fY =
      pgo->v3dPosition.fY;
    SetState(gosIdle);
}
```

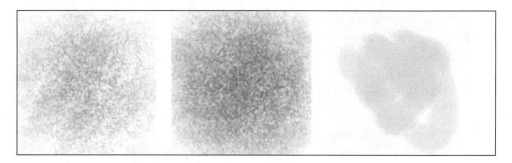

Figure 14.1
Texture images used in the game.

When these particles are created, they send a message to themselves to tell them to die. They also plant themselves firmly on the ground.

Each particle has a limited life span and we find out how much time is left by subtracting the time that has passed since the last update from its entire life span. The x and z components of a particle's position are updated based on the amount of time that has passed. Each particle has a set direction that it goes in the x-z plane. The object is then planted on the ground and moved up by one unit. We do this so that they remain visible. It has the bad side-effect of making them follow the terrain very closely, but we decided to do this to keep things as simple as possible. The code that does this is:

```
State(gosIdle)
   OnMsg(UpdateMessage)
   {
      float fDeltaT = 0;

      ((SmokeParticleInfo*)pgo->pvExtra)->lRemainingLifeSpan -=
        aiGetFrameTimeDelta(&g_singleAI);
      fDeltaT = (((SmokeParticleInfo*)pgo->pvExtra)->lTotalLifeSpan -
((SmokeParticleInfo*)pgo->pvExtra)->lRemainingLifeSpan)/1000.0f;

      pgo->v3dPosition.fX = ((SmokeParticleInfo*)pgo->pvExtra)-
>v3dInitalPositon.fX + pgo->v3dDirection.fX*pgo->fSpeed*fDeltaT;
      pgo->v3dPosition.fZ = ((SmokeParticleInfo*)pgo->pvExtra)-
>v3dInitalPositon.fZ + pgo->v3dDirection.fZ*pgo->fSpeed*fDeltaT;
```

```
        pgo->v3dPosition.fY = 999;
        aiPlantGameObject(pgo);
        pgo->v3dPosition.fY += 1;
    }
```

When the particle receives its own message, it kills itself. Each particle is created instantly, but is faded in and out during its lifetime so that the effect remains visually appealing:

```
fHalfTotal = (float)((SmokeParticleInfo*)g_singleAI.pVisibleObjects[i]->pvExtra)
    ->lTotalLifeSpan/2.0f;
        fParticleAlpha = 1.0f -
        (fabs((float)((SmokeParticleInfo*)g_singleAI.pVisibleObjects[i]->pvExtra)-
>lRemainingLifeSpan - fHalfTotal)/fHalfTotal);
```

Other particles in the system start at full intensity and then fade out, but because dust devils wouldn't look right popping up, they are faded in and out through their lifespan.

Quaternions

The word *quaternion* seems designed to strike fear into the hearts of all who avoided freshman mathematics. (Another such word is *tensor*, which we don't need here but which is related to the quaternion.) Quaternions are used in *MMR*, and so I need to at least describe them very briefly here. If you wish to pursue the subject, see the references for this chapter.

What you need to know is that quaternions are a mathematical formulation that permits us to perform certain graphics calculations very efficiently. In particular, we'll use them for rotations. A quaternion is a set of four numbers: (x, y, z, w). The numbers x, y, and z are actually complex numbers, but for our purposes, we just don't care. We can think of the (x, y, z) part as defining an axis of rotation, and the w part is the amount of rotation. There are other interpretations that could be used. In any case, here is a quaternion:

Equation 14.1 $Q = xi + yj + zk + w$

This quaternion is also sometimes written as the real part **w** and a vector **v** consisting of (x, y, z):

Equation 14.2 $q = (w, v)$

14

The key thing about quaternions is that they can be used to represent rotations. A rotation matrix has nine elements, whereas a quaternion has only four, so we already get a savings in space. A quaternion (x, y, z, w) represents the rotation matrix as shown here:

Equation 14.3

$$\begin{matrix} w2 + x2 - y2 - z2 & 2xy - 2wz & 2xz + 2wy \\ 2xy + 2wz & w2 - x2 + y2 - z2 & 2yz - 2wx \\ 2xz - 2wy & 2yz + 2wx & w2 - x2 - y2 + z2 \end{matrix}$$

Another interesting thing is that we can compose two rotations (first rotation A then B) by multiplying their quaternions. This is also more efficient than multiplying the rotation matrices. Quaternion multiplication is defined as Equation 14.4:

Equation 14.4 $Q = xi + yj + zk + w$

where the vector v is as defined in Equation 14.2 . Note: $q_1{}^*q_2$ is not equal to $q_2{}^*q_1$, as they would be with matrix multiplications.

An interesting and useful fact is that quaternions are understood by OpenGL, and we can specify rotations and orientations to OpenGL in the form of quaternions. Thus, a simple four-component quaternion can represent orientations and rotations. In particular, they can be used for camera models and for rotating graphical elements on the screen (as shown in the following section). DirectX knows about them, too. We're going to use them to create the radar screen in the "heads up" display next.

The Heads-Up Display (HUD)

The HUD is fairly simple. The text and radar are loaded and displayed in similar fashion; the only difference is the logic applied when displaying them. Both are initialized in Rendering.c as shown here:

```
int initRenderingContext()
```

This function call, found in Images.c, loads a PNG format image file with the name specified and puts it in the **image** structure:

```
int GenerateOpenGLImage (Image *image,
        const char * szTextureName)
```

Each time the screen is refreshed, the HUD must be updated. The text part is simple: we know the x and y screen position of the text, and we just write the text there. The radar is a little more complicated. The function to draw the radar is found in Rendering.c and is called:

```
void drawRadar();
```

There are a few ways that the radar screen could be constructed. The first technique would be to take all the objects in their global position, then scale and draw them. The result would be like a map of the area where only the player and alien would move on the radar. A little more complicated technique would be to make the player the center of things. This would require that the positions of objects would have to be relative to the player. The player would need to be at coordinates (0, 0, 0)—the center of the radar—and all other objects would be transformed into "radar coordinates" using a simple translation and scaling operation, as I explained in Chapter 3. With this implementation, the player would be stationary on the radar and everything else would move. The "up" direction on the radar/map would always correspond to North on the map or a similar direction, depending on which direction is up (North) in the implementation.

I wanted a radar that would turn with the player, so that the forward direction of motion of the player's vehicle would always be "up" on the radar. To accomplish this, we do things the same way as before, but we add the orientation of the player into the mix as well. The angle between the player and the objects is computed and is used to display the object representations in the radar display. This takes more computation but gives a display that is more like what we see in other games, and so is in some sense traditional.

This function first uses the player's orientation to find a "global" orientation. This orientation will make sure that the radar displayed on the screen is always facing the same way. That is, the blips on the radar will rotate when the player turns (note the use of quaternions):

```
pv3dFacing = malloc(sizeof(Vector3D));
memcpy(pv3dFacing ,
    &g_singleAI.pgoPlayer->v3dDirection,
    sizeof(Vector3D));
quatRotateVectorMod
    (&g_singleAI.pgoPlayer->quatOrientation,
     pv3dFacing);
pv3dFacing->fY = 0;
```

14

```
v3dSetMod(&v3dNorth, 0, 0, 1);
v3dNormalizeMod(pv3dFacing);
pquatRadarRotation = vectorsToQuaternion(pv3dFacing, &v3dNorth);
quatConcatMod (pquatRadarRotation,
    &g_singleAI.pgoPlayer->quatOrientation,
    pquatRadarRotation);
```

This code assumes North is the same as the positive z direction. We find a rotation from the player's orientation to this North with the **vectorsToQuaternion()** function call. We then make a new rotation from the concatenation of this quaternion and the player's rotation quaternion.

The next process is to get a scaling from the global coordinates to radar coordinates. The beginning of the function starts this process with:

```
int iMaxX = g_singleRenderingState.pTerrain->fXSize;
int iMaxZ = g_singleRenderingState.pTerrain->fYSize;
```

These two lines of code find the size of the map in global coordinates:

```
iMiddleX = g_singleRenderingState.imgRadarBackground.uiWidth/2;
iMiddleY = g_singleRenderingState.imgRadarBackground.uiHeight/2;
iScaleX =  iMaxX/g_singleRenderingState.imgRadarBackground.uiWidth;
iScaleY =  iMaxZ/g_singleRenderingState.imgRadarBackground.uiHeight;
iMaxX/=2;
iMaxZ/=2;
```

This block sets the variable that will be used to take a position in world coordinates and put them in radar coordinates.

Now we draw the static radar background as shown here:

```
glWindowPos2i(
 (glutGameModeGet(GLUT_GAME_MODE_WIDTH)-
   g_singleRenderingState.imgRadarBackground.uiWidth),
  (glutGameModeGet(GLUT_GAME_MODE_HEIGHT) -
   g_singleRenderingState.imgRadarBackground.uiHeight));
glDrawPixels(
   g_singleRenderingState.imgRadarBackground.uiWidth,
   g_singleRenderingState.imgRadarBackground.uiHeight,
```

```
      g_singleRenderingState.imgRadarBackground.uiGLFormat,
      GL_UNSIGNED_BYTE,
      g_singleRenderingState.imgRadarBackground.uiImageData);
```

It is not positioned particularly nicely, just crammed as far to the upper-right as possible.

Using this global orientation and applying some scaling, we can now draw our objects. For each one that will be drawn, we must determine where to draw it. In this radar, everything is relative to the player. That is, the player is at the center of the radar at all times. We must find the object's position relative to the player's position. This is done in the following code block:

```
pv3dToObject = v3dSubtract(
   &g_singleAI.pRadarGameObjects[i]->v3dPosition,
   &g_singleAI.pgoPlayer->v3dPosition);

quatRotateVectorMod(pquatRadarRotation, pv3dToObject);
iPaintX = (-(int)pv3dToObject->fX + iMaxX)/iScaleX;

iPaintY = ((int)pv3dToObject->fZ + iMaxX)/iScaleY;
```

We get the position of the other game object relative to the player using the subtraction. We then rotate this vector using the quaternion we created before, and finally, we find out where the object should be painted using the scaling integers created previously. Finally, it is a simple matter of determining what type of object it is, then drawing the associated blip on the radar.

The final process is to draw each of the object types on the radar. There are a few stipulations before we can draw them. The most simple is a distance check as shown here:

```
if(v3dLengthSquared(pv3dToobject) > 90000)
{
   free(pv3dToObject);
   pv3dToObject = 0;
   continue;
}
```

If the object is too far away, then we don't draw it on the radar.

14

Creating The Terrain

Creating the terrain turned out to be more of a challenge than I had thought it would be. It was not difficult to create the triangulated height map, but it was very difficult to create a height map that represented actual Martian terrain. There is a small amount of altimeter data that has been collected from an instrument in orbit around Mars, the *Mars Orbiter Laser Altimeter* that was mentioned in Chapter 13. Some of this information has been collected into height map images[3]. The images were presented on the Web in color, with certain colors representing high places and different colors representing low ones (see Figure 14.2). I edited the image, converting the colors into grey levels, and smoothed out the irregularities (Look on the website for color versions of all of the figures in this book, especially this one). The result is the image shown in the right side of Figure 14.2.

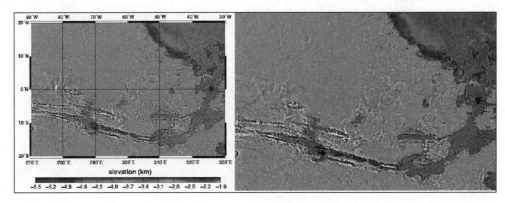

Figure 14.2
Topography of Valles Marineris (Mars Orbiter Laser Altimiter) and the edited image using a height map.

The game reads in the height map as a PNG image and triangulates it, creating the basic terrain that is seen when you play. The terrain is covered in a texture called *Perlin noise* to give it a rough appearance, and then the objects are place onto the surface (see Figure 14.3).

If you wish to replace the terrain used by the game, all you need to do is create or download a PNG file with the desired height map in it. The image should be grey level only, and white colors will act as high points and dark ones will act as low points. Just for fun, you can use pretty much any lunar image photographed at local noon. I have provided a tool that converts PNG images into height maps that *MMR* can use. This tool is a program called PNG2Hmap. An example of its use is PNG2Hmap mars, where **mars.png** is in the current directory; the output will be a file called **mars.hmap**.

Figure 14.3
The Martian terrain where the actual height data and Perlin noise texture is rendered in real time.

PNG2Hmap takes a PNG and converts it to a height map. The PNG image supplied must have only a gray scale channel. RGB elements or transparency will cause the image to be rejected. PNG2Hmap takes one command-line argument. This is the name of the PNG to be converted without extension. The output files will be one Logfile.txt and a height map. The name of the height map will be the same as the PNG., but with the 'hmap' suffix.

PNG2Hmap can be downloaded from the **Chapter 14** directory, where the game binaries and sources also live.

Perlin Noise

Natural textures tend to consist of a mixture of large and small variations in combination. For example, look at some mountains, or leaves and branches in a tree, and you will see large scale and small scale variations that combine to give the natural appearance. The Perlin noise function represents an effort to simulate natural textures, and it does so by adding up a set of random noise functions having different scales.

14

A noise function is usually just a random number generator designed to return numbers from a particular statistical distribution. The random number generator that is used by C, for instance, generates a floating point number between 0.0 and 1.0, with any particular value having the same chance of being generated. This is called a *uniform* distribution.

By the term *scale*, I mean how far apart the numbers will be placed on a spatial grid. A *large scale* (or low resolution) feature is one that has a large distance between samples, and conversely a *small scale* (high resolution) feature has the generated points near each other. A Perlin noise generator consist of multiple noise generators that each create points at different scales, which are then smoothed into curves and added together. Take a look at Figure 14.4.

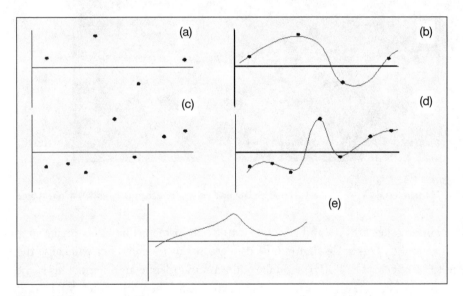

Figure 14.4
Perlin noise in one dimension.

In this figure, you can see the noise generated and placed at points one unit apart (Figure 14.4.a) and at a half unit apart (Figure 14.4.c). A smooth curve is drawn through each set of points using an interpolation method (see Appendix B). The purpose of this is to estimate the value of the noise function between the actual samples. Then all of the curves are added together at each point. In Figure 14.4, this means summing the values of the interpolated curves at every point on the resulting curve (Figure 14.4.e). The result has features at high and low resolutions. Naturally, a proper job of creating Perlin noise would require that more than two noise functions be used. Typically, we need between six and twenty functions to do a good job[4].

Ray Casting

How do we make certain that the cars will always sit on the ground? The way most often used is called *ray casting*, where a line is drawn from the vehicle to the terrain surface. The collision of this ray and the terrain is where the car will sit. There is a little y added to the final result so the car will sit on the terrain instead of in it. In the actual code, we use the following function that is found in AI.c:

```
void aiPlantGameObject(GameObject* pgo)
```

This function puts every thing on the ground. There are quite a few cheats along the way, though. To make sure that the ray origin is not under the terrain, the y value of its origin is set to a high number. Otherwise, there will be no ray-terrain collision, and that is not a good thing. The actual position of the collision point is found in Terrain.c:

```
Vector3D* getCollisionPoint(Terrain* pTerrain, Ray3D* pRay3D)
```

Because of the design philosophy of the game and the fact that ray-terrain collisions were not needed for any thing else in the game, this function assumes that the ray **pRay3D** will always be facing down. This fact is used to cull the number of polygons that the ray collision will be tested against. We do the culling by finding the few polygons around the ray origin if its y component were 0. This can only be done if the ray is facing pretty much straight down, because the ray origin and collision point in this case will not differ by a large amount in the x and z components. We then cycle through the subset of triangles and collide the ray against each. The first triangle that hits is used for the collision point and the point of collision is returned.

The ray-triangle test is found in **Vector4D.c**:

```
Vector3D* v4dRayTriangleCollision(const Ray3D* pRay,
    const Triangle* pTriangle)
```

The basic idea is that first there is a test against the plane that the polygon is in, then we test to see if this collision point is in the triangle. This algorithm is explained in Chapter 5.

Implementing the Game AI: The Martian

14

Like all game objects, the Martian AI is based on a state machine. Each state either involves a decision or performs a task. For the decision-making states, the AI assesses the environment and attempts to make a decision based on the information that it is given. For this game, the AI is simple and performs three basic functions: collecting metal objects, chasing the player, and returning to the base. The goal of the game is to ultimately collect as many metal objects as possible. The first priority of the AI is to collect metal objects. However, once the player has collected a certain amount of items, the alien will begin to chase the player until the player finds the player base to drop off its items. If the player has not collected enough items to warrant the alien's attention, the alien will concentrate on collecting metal objects and dropping them off at the alien base. Here is the code that performs these tasks:

```
State(gosLook)
    OnMsg(UpdateMessage)
{
    AlienInfo * pAlienInfo = pgo->pvExtra;
    PlayerInfo * pPlayerInfo =
       g_singleAI.pgoPlayer->pvExtra;
    switch(pAlienInfo->iAIPriority)
    {
    case aipCollectMetalObjects:

      pAlienInfo->pgoClosestMetalObject =
       aiGetClosestMetalObject(pgo, g_ppGameObjects,
              g_iNumOfMetalObjects);

      if(pAlienInfo->pgoClosestMetalObject &&
         pAlienInfo->pgoClosestMetalObject->iActive
         && pAlienInfo->pgoClosestMetalObject->iAlive
         && pAlienInfo->pgoClosestMetalObject->objectType
            == gotMetalObject)
      {
        SetState(gosCollectMetalObjects);

        if(pPlayerInfo->iItemsOnBoard >= 5)
        {
          AL_UpdateGO(g_singleAI.pgoPlayer,
              &g_pSoundSources[alChase]);
          AL_PlaySoundEffect(alChase);
          pAlienInfo->iAIPriority = aipChasePlayer;
          SetState(gosChasePlayer);
        }
      }
      else
      {
```

```
          if(!pAlienInfo->pgoAlienBase)
            pAlienInfo->pgoAlienBase =
                  getAlienBase(&g_singleAI);
          SetState(gosReturnToBase);
        }
        break;
    case aipChasePlayer:
        if(pPlayerInfo->iItemsOnBoard >= 5)
        {
          AL_UpdateGO(g_singleAI.pgoPlayer,
                    &g_pSoundSources[alChase]);
          AL_PlaySoundEffect(alChase);
          pAlienInfo->iTimesToCollideWithPlayer =
            rand()%5;
          SetState(gosChasePlayer);
        }
        else
        {
          pAlienInfo->iAIPriority =
            aipCollectMetalObjects;
          SetState(gosLook);
        }
        break;
    case aipReturnToBase:
        if(!pAlienInfo->pgoAlienBase)
        {
          pAlienInfo->pgoAlienBase =
            getAlienBase(&g_singleAI);
        }
        SetState(gosReturnToBase);
        break;
    default:
        break;
    }
}
```

During the player chase, the alien will attempt to track down the player. If the alien collides with the player, the alien will bump the player and steal some of the player's cargo and have some of their points deducted. The player must avoid the alien and find the base to drop off their cargo as quickly as possible:

```
State(gosChasePlayer)
    OnMsg(UpdateMessage)
    {
```

14

```
      PlayerInfo * pPlayerInfo = g_singleAI.pgoPlayer->pvExtra;
      if(g_singleAI.pgoPlayer && pPlayerInfo->iItemsOnBoard>=5)
        doChase(pgo, g_singleAI.pgoPlayer);
      else
        SetState(gosLook);


      aiPlantGameObject(pgo);
    }
    OnMsg(CollideMessage)
    {
      . . .
        // dislodge the player when collided
        aiRotateGameObject(pgoOtherObject, (float)floor(radians2degrees(fAngle)));
        aiMoveGameObject(pgoOtherObject, (pgoOtherObject->fSpeed*aiGet
          FrameTimeDelta(&g_singleAI)/1000.0f)*2.5f);

        // steal items
        if((pAlienInfo->iItemsOnBoard + iNumObjectsToSteal) < pAlienInfo-
          >iItemsCapacity)
        {
          RockInfo * pRockInfo = pgoOtherObject->pvExtra;
          pAlienInfo->iItemsOnBoard += iNumObjectsToSteal;
          pPlayerInfo->iItemsOnBoard -= iNumObjectsToSteal;
          pAlienInfo->fItemsWeight += pRockInfo->fWeight;
          SetState(gosLook);
        }
        else
        {
          pAlienInfo->iItemsOnBoard = pAlienInfo->iItemsCapacity;
          pPlayerInfo->iItemsOnBoard -= iNumObjectsToSteal;
          SetState(gosReturnToBase);

        }
        // deduct points
        if((pPlayerInfo->iPoints - iPointsDeducted) > 0)
        {
          pPlayerInfo->iPoints -= iPointsDeducted;
        } else
          pPlayerInfo->iPoints = 0;


        . . .

        SetState(gosLook);
      }


    }
```

Extended (EAX) Audio

The EAX(tm) API adds reverberation capabilities with occlusion and obstruction effects to the DirectSound(tm) component of DirectX and OpenAL. Although DirectX and OpenAL provide a number of useful audio effects such as Doppler effect, roll-off and direction, EAX provides important environmental effects such as reverberation, reflections, and sound occlusion or obstruction by intersecting objects. The user can still hear the sounds but has no idea of the environment where the sounds are located without these effects.

EAX is an added API extension to OpenAL. The 3D audio world is setup through OpenAL. EAX properties are attached to sound sources to provide reverberation, occlusion, and obstruction effects. These effects add together to give the user a sense of audio realism. They provide depth to simulate a believable audio world.

We use EAX because it offers environmental effects. EAX properties are attached to the sound sources globally. However, since our terrain is very wide open and there are not very many audio interactions, our usage of EAX is very simple. As shown in the code next, the EAX environment setup is relatively easy:

```
// determine EAX support level
if (alIsExtensionPresent((ALubyte *)"EAX2.0") == AL_TRUE)
{
   g_iEAXLevel = 2;
} else
{
   if (alIsExtensionPresent((ALubyte *)"EAX") == AL_TRUE)
   {
      g_iEAXLevel = 1;
   }
}

if (g_iEAXLevel != 0)
{
   g_pfPropSet =
     (EAXSet) alGetProcAddress((ALubyte *)"EAXSet");
   if (g_pfPropSet != NULL)
   {
      g_lGlobalReverd = -1000;
      g_pfPropSet(&DSPROPSETID_EAX_ListenerProperties,
                 DSPROPERTY_EAXLISTENER_ROOM, 0,
                 &g_lGlobalReverd, sizeof(unsigned long));
      g_ulEAXVal = EAX_ENVIRONMENT_AUDITORIUM;
      g_pfPropSet(&DSPROPSETID_EAX_ListenerProperties,
```

14

```
                    DSPROPERTY_EAXLISTENER_ENVIRONMENT, 0,
                    &g_ulEAXVal, sizeof(unsigned long));
        }
    }
```

Extending MMR

The Mars racer game presented in this chapter is completely playable. It also contains all of the assets and code you'll need, and you should be able to compile it using multiple compilers on different systems. However, the game is designed to be a starting point and there are definitely features that you could improve upon and add. You can very easily extend the game by downloading the source code from the website and either build a Visual Studio 6 project or use the existing .Net project that I provide. You can edit the code to implement features of your choice.

Let me give you some suggestions. I'm not especially happy with the *game over* conditions. I am not at all certain how many points worth of junk the player should have to collect, and I think that the objects that are far away from the base should be worth more points than those closer to the base. This aspect of the game needs some experimental work, I think. I had intended that the player would have to return to the base for fuel once in a while, and you could build that feature in also.

Adding some missiles could be a cool feature. You could create multiple Martians and allow the player to shoot at them. I didn't build weapons into the game because I didn't want to add a complete chapter on weapons for space reasons. If you incorporate weapons you should allow the Martians to shoot back. Perhaps you might want to add a shield to protect the player from the missiles. You could also take away points when damage or fuel leaks occur.

I mentioned that you could convert any image into a height map and use it in the game. For example, you could use terrain from the Moon, Venus, The Sahara Desert, or Butte Montana.

The Martian AI is still a bit primitive right now. Whether or not you choose to arm him, you could add more of the behaviors that we discussed: chase, hide, follow, avoid, and so on. I wanted the Martian base to be more intricate, perhaps with a smelter, flames and smoke, noise and activity. A little animation can go a long way. Someone else suggested that the Martian should be heard to mutter to himself as he drove past, collecting junk: "Darned humans, always littering …." You could even have him say "ouch" when he picked up something big or sharp.

Even a well developed game will have some elements that you think are missing or lame. This is your chance to see what you can do to customize a real PC game. You can even put your name, or your child's name, or even an image of your house, into the game itself. I have been developing the concept of a "me-game" that allows a lot of this sort of customization using your own text and images to make everything look familiar. Kids really seem to enjoy seeing themselves and their friends in a real game.

Summary

I have provided you with a complete racing game for which the source code is available on the website. Read though it, and study it! Above all, modify it. That's the best way to learn how it's done.

And above all, have fun.

14

Chapter 15

The Bonus Game—*Charged!*

- Learn how to use the techniques presented in this book to create a "miniature" RC-style racing game.
- Learn how the *Charged!* game is designed and what key features are provided.

To end this book, I wanted to present a driving game that was developed by some of my students. The game is called *Charged!* It provides an excellent example of what can be developed in a short amount of time with limited resources (five people working on it for 13 weeks). The design and development team consisting of Chris Clark, Ricky Pusch, Beatrice Kwok, Mike King, and Chad Birch chose to use DirectX rather than OpenGL to build their game. This was another reason I wanted to include the game in this book. You'll now be able to experiment with two different games implemented using two different graphics systems—OpenGL and DirectX. *Charged!* also uses a third-party physics engine called ODE (Open Dynamics Engine)[1], which I'll introduce in this chapter.

I'll quickly introduce you to the game in the first part of the chapter and then we'll explore it in more detail. We'll look at the goals for the game and then we'll discuss all of the components of the game's design—controls, cinematography, environment interaction, race mechanics, AI, and so on. You'll find that many of the game's features are designed around using concepts presented in this book. Playing this game and examining the code for the game will give you additional insight for how you can go about creating your own driving and racing games. The code and other resources for this game can be found on the website in the directory named **Chapter 15 Charged!**

Introducing *Charged!*

Charged! is a racing game that pits a single human-controlled car against the game's AI player. Each car will be a miniature one, akin to a remote-controlled (RC) car. The first car to navigate the obstacles of the game's world and complete the required number of laps wins!

Game Concept

Charged! is a single-player racing game that places the human-controlled vehicle against AI-controlled vehicles of predetermined intelligence. Each car resembles an RC car in terms of sound, appearance, size, and feel (see Figure 15.1). Cars race around an environment similar to those of real RC cars—a house. The player must avoid obstacles, look for shortcuts, perform jumps, and out-drive the AI cars to succeed in the game. This game runs on a PC. Because it is difficult to have two players on a PC at one time, the game won't provide an option to play against another human player. The development time to incorporate such a feature would have exceeded the thirteen week period that we had to develop the game.

Figure 15.1
A typical screen from the game *Charged!*

In addition to simple racing mechanics, batteries are placed on the track in convenient places. A car can drive over a battery to increase its power level. This allows the player to gain speed bursts in order to push past competition or fly down a straightaway. In some cases, boosts will be required to perform certain beneficial tactics, such as shortcuts.

Game Goals

The goals for *Charged!* that the design team set out to achieve include:

- Provide a quick, quirky racing engine that (more or less) accurately depicts the physics and feel of an RC car.

- Use a level design that makes the player truly feel they are playing in a miniature environment.

- Develop the game using easy-to-pick-up but hard-to-master gameplay mechanics for controlling the power meter.

- Provide some form of interactivity with the levels, including knocking over a few select household items upon collision.

- Include level shortcuts which reward the player for smart use of the power meter.

- Implement AI techniques that don't feel unfair, but provide a suitable and tunable racing challenge.

- Provide a reward for winning races, perhaps including new colors of cars or different AI settings.

Game Design

The game only has one mode which allows the player to race against an AI opponent. The player is placed at the starting line and given a three-second countdown, at which point the race begins. The race is fairly standard in that completion of a predetermined (tunable) number of laps will win the race. There is one level/course available for racing.

Driving Engine

The game emulates the RC nature of the cars, but allows for some over-the- top performance to keep the atmosphere of the game light. All cars, whether human or AI-controlled, follow the same rules of the game engine based on certain parameters (such as top speed, acceleration, traction, and so on) of the car being driven. The game provides jumps for the player to perform, and the game emulates the appropriate physics.

Traction can be accidentally or intentionally lost in order to slide. This can be useful for keeping speed high around corners, but may cause the player to lose control of their car on straightaways.

Controls

The controls are configurable in the game settings. The default settings for the controls are as follows:

15

- Up arrow: Accelerate

- Down arrow: Brake/reverse

- Left arrow: Steer left

- Right arrow: Steer right

- Space bar: Emergency brake

- Alt key: Boost

- Ctrl key: Honk the horn

Using the e-brake will cause a car to slow down, but it also will immediately make a car go into a sliding state. This can be used to deftly maneuver around corners while maintaining high speeds.

Charge Bar/Battery Meter

The big feature of *Charged!* is the Charge Bar—a battery meter that affects how the player's vehicle operates (see Figure 15.2). It indicates how much charge the battery contains, and is equivalent to a fuel gauge. At the beginning of the race, the player has a full Charge Bar (i.e., full fuel tank). At all times when driving normally, the Charge

Figure 15.2
The Charge Bar (the red rectangle at the top of the screen) is displayed as half charged.

Bar will slowly drain. When boosting, the Charge Bar will rapidly deplete. This excess energy drain is required to gain speed so rapidly. The player will be warned once the Charge Bar reaches a very low level. If the Charge Bar fully depletes, the player will no longer be able to boost and the top speed of the vehicle will be drastically reduced.

To keep the car powered and to continue to allow the player to boost, the player must drive through power-up batteries placed along the track. Different styles of batteries will refill the Charge Bar with different amounts of charge. If the Charge Bar is full, the player can still pick up batteries but won't gain any additional charge. Players can use this strategy to minimize the number of batteries that trailing opponents can collect. To keep the racing fair, however, the batteries will be scattered in such a way that the leading player cannot simply collect all the batteries, which would force the Charge Bar of trailing opponents to run out with no method of recovery.

Cinematography

The controls are not camera relative; camera motion will emphasize the dynamic nature of the vehicle. The field of view varies with the speed of the vehicle; the faster the player drives, the farther back the camera will be. This technique was essentially described in Chapter 11. In the event of the e-brake being applied or the player spinning out, the camera will slowly rotate around to the back of the car. This gives the player ample time to correct their movement without dealing with a jerky camera. The camera favors keeping the view towards the forward race track.

Vehicle-Environment Interaction

The interaction between the vehicles and the environment is important to create both an enjoyable and believable game. The majority of the race track is made of static objects that will not themselves respond to contact. However, the vehicles, as well as a few small objects on the track, are moveable objects. The player's vehicle can bump into opponents or into walls with a minimal interaction of just being pushed away. If the player hits an opponent or part of the race track at a large enough relative speed or angle, the player's car will cause a crash. In this case, the cars will tumble for a short time before returning to a stable state. Vehicles will always quickly return to an upright orientation so that they can continue the race.

Parts of the track will allow vehicles to jump off the track. The vehicles will fly through the air but will retain the majority of their orientation so that they can have a good landing. A car will not be able to crash on the landing of a jump due to momentum tilting their car too much or not enough. When a vehicle makes a sliding turn that is both too fast and too sharp, or perhaps bumped by an opponent, the vehicle may go into a short roll. By bumping other vehicles, it may be possible to push them into a bad path where they miss a power-up or crash into an obstacle.

15

Race Mechanics

The beginning of each race starts with the player and opponents at the starting line. A three-second countdown to the start is displayed and then the racers take off. If the player presses their acceleration at just the right time during the countdown, they will receive an extra boost of acceleration just off the starting line. This resembles many other games, such as *Mario Kart*. As with all races, each participant has a rank. To win a single race, the player needs to pass the finish line first after completing the required number of laps. As the player races, their current time is displayed on the screen (see the *Layout and Feel* section for more information).

Artificial Intelligence

Opponent vehicles operate under the same physics as the player's vehicle. An AI-controlled car may attempt to retrieve batteries to keep them from the opponents. Depending on the difficulty of the AI, an AI-controlled car may decide to use jumps and other shortcuts to get ahead. An AI-controlled car may decide to go out of its way to pick up a power-up if its Charge Bar is running low. With multiple AI-controlled opponents, each adversary will be somewhat hostile to each other, but mostly they will be focused on the player's vehicle.

Reward

The game offers rewards for finishing the race under some set times. The player can unlock new colors for their car and possibly new models of car with improved speed and control ratings. If the player properly executes a shortcut, they can skip portions of the level and increase their lead on their competitors. They also get the exhilaration of going airborne and shooting off of a jump.

Layout and Feel

I've already mentioned that *Charged!* is based on a theme involving toy cars. The graphical style of the game is designed to reflect a miniature environment. The game's design emphasizes more of a colorful and entertaining look and feel rather than presenting a realistic environment. The cars themselves are portrayed as toys, like real remote control cars. Different styles are included for the user to choose from, but all of the styles are based on remote control cars. The game level is situated inside a house, and the cars all travel throughout the house through three different environments. These environments are given in the form of three different rooms in the house: kitchen, television room, and a child's toy room.

Rooms

Figure 15.3 shows some of the different rooms used in the game. The kitchen room is bright in appearance, and feels more open and spacious as compared to the two other rooms. It has a smooth floor so that the boost feature can easily be used while still allowing some hazards to be incorporated, such as a fallen chair or a wet floor.

Figure 15.3
Some rooms in which the game is played—(top) kitchen; (bottom) dining room.

15

The television room is situated on a carpeted floor and provides more obstacles. This room is slightly darker than the other two rooms and has a certain ambience to it since the television is turned on, giving the impression that a television is being watched in low light. The possibilities in this room are plenty, such as magazines strewn around for jumping off of, coffee table legs to steer around, and various other obstacles.

The child's toy room is the most difficult to race in because of all of the obstacles it contains. This room has a lowered section, giving some variety to the racing, as the cars will need to go down some stairs and up a ramp. This room is the most colorful and contains many obstacles made out of children's toys such as wooden blocks, dolls, and so on. This room can be expanded to include more elaborate obstacles, such as jumps and shortcuts, because they could be created out of the available toys in the room.

Heads-Up Display (HUD)

As in many racing games, *Charged!* displays statistical information such as speed, position, and timings using a heads-up display. The HUD also contains the Charge Bar, which is shaped like a battery. When using the boost feature, an indicator will appear on the screen to emphasize the larger drain on the battery. When the battery is running low, a warning will also show. A small overhead map is also provided so that the player can assess their position (see Figure 15.4). The cars will be shown on this map as small colored points.

Front End

The menu system is simple and easy to use. It allows the user to either start the game, change some options, or exit. The options menu includes a volume control, a difficulty level setting, a battery life setting, and a method for changing the number of laps in a race. Through the battery life and difficulty, the user can change the overall difficulty of the game to what they prefer. The user will also be able to choose the look of the car they want to drive, choosing between different colors and models. Figure 15.5 shows the initial splash screen for the game.

Sound Effects

Sound effects provide effective cues for knowing when a car is accelerating, being damaged, or approached by another car. Crashing, skidding, and squeaking sounds confirm how the automobile is interacting with the environment. An engine hum is played throughout the game, giving some ambience that the car is running. It is kept low in volume and frequency to create appropriate balance. Also, for a fully dynamic system, the presentation of each sound can change according to the state of the environment. For instance, two collisions may sound differently due to differing velocities during impact.

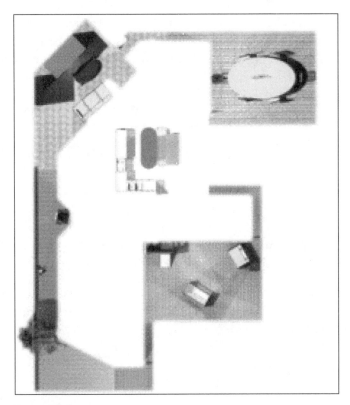

Figure 15.4
The map of the game universe on the head's-up display.

Figure 15.5
The initial splash screen for *Charged*!

15

Volume gives speed and distance cues. When a car is far away, its engine sounds soft and faint, but the closer it comes, the louder it will become. Also, during acceleration, another sound clip will be added to generate the sound effect of the engine gradually increasing in frequency.

The sound clip will be lengthened or shortened depending on how long the player presses the accelerate button. Eventually, the sound will even out as top speed is reached. When the acceleration button is released, a clip of reducing the frequency will be played. Acceleration in the reverse gear produces a different sound.

When two objects collide, the momentum during impact will determine which sound to play. If two cars were moving slowly before collision, low-frequency bumping sounds will be played. If they were moving quickly in a head-on collision, on the other hand, a crashing sound will arise. Similarly, when landing from a jump, a crashing sound will accompany the moment of impact. Skidding will occur during sudden stops.

Many other effects will be included to appropriately simulate the feel of a racing game, such as sounds for passing the finish line, sounds for counting down at the beginning of a race, and sounds for giving a car a boost.

Implementation of Key Features

Charged! was implemented using DirectX and other tools that have not been previously discussed. Rather than go into detail on those subjects, I propose to describe a few key aspects of this game and how they were done.

Physics Using ODE

The physics simulation in the game was conducted using a free engine called the *Open Dynamics Engine*, or ODE. This engine consists of a large collection of C/C++ code modules that implement the math associated with rigid body dynamics, which is all about determining forces on and motion of objects that do not significantly bend or compress. This would normally include more of the objects in a driving game.

The letters "ODE" also stand for many other things, like "ordinary differential equation," so a Web search may produce too many incorrect hits if you are looking for more information on this topic. Check out the official ODE web site at **http://ode.org/**, and download the system for free. It would not be appropriate to go through the details of ODE here, but you should examine the source code for *Charged!* to see a major example of how the engine is used in a practical application. The basic idea is quite simple, though. Here's a bit of code that handles the force of gravity acting on a simple object:

```
#include <ode.h>
int main()
{
 // the container for all the stuff that will interact in this world
  dWorldID dwid;

  double dGravityY = -9.81; // in m/s/s
  double dXPos=0, dYPos=3, dZPos=0;

  dBodyID dbidBox; //necessary for every object
  dMass dmBox; //the mass properites of the box
  double dXLength=1, dYLength=1, dZLength=1;
  double dBoxWeight=3;

//init - create the 'world', set the gravitational force. Create
//an object and give it a position.
  dwid = dWorldCreate();// create the world
  dWorldSetGravity(dwid, 0.0, dGravityY, 0.0);


  dBodyID = dBodyCreate(dwid);
  dBodySetPosition(dbidBox, dXPos, dYPos, dXPos);
  dBodySetLinearVel(dbidBox, 0, 0, 0);
  dBodysetAngularVel(dbidBox, 0, 0, 0);

  //choose one of the following 2
  dBodySetRotation(dbidBox, identityMatrix4x3);
  dBodySetQuaternion(dbidBox, identityQuaternion);

  dMassSetBoxTotal(&dmBox,dBoxWeight, dXLength, dYLength, dZLength);
  dBodySetMass(dbidBox, &dmBox);

  while(bGameNotDone)
    {
      drawWorld();
      // choose one of the following 2 for updating objects
      dWorldStep(dwid, dTimeDelta); // slow but more accurate
      //dWorldQuickStep(dwid, dTimeDelta);// faster but less accurate
    }

  //clean up
  dBodyDestroy(dbidBox);
  dWorldDestroy(dwid);
  dCloseODE();
  return 0;
}
```

15

Going Airborne

Being airborne isn't any different than driving along the ground. The physics simulation is allowed to handle the car flying through the air. The force of gravity always acts on the car (we must apply suspension forces to counter these, and keep the car's wheels on the ground realistically), so being in the air isn't really a special case.

When airborne, the wheels will attempt to touch the ground, and they will not be able to find ground within their allowed range of movement. They will move out as far as possible along the suspension axis and not apply any counter forces. Therefore, the car will not be able to counter the gravitational force, and will fall.

Collision Detection

The collision detection facility of the ODE package is used to actually generate the collisions for our objects. We have a variety of objects that have internal designation as *LevelObject*. These objects represent walls, floors, tables, and so on. We also have code objects that represent things like the batteries and cars. Each object gets assigned a unique collision ID by ODE's system, and we just save that variable in the C++ class for that object. We also store a pointer back to our *LevelObject* or *Battery* or *Car* in ODE's system, using a void pointer they provide. When we generate collisions, ODE provides the collision IDs of the two colliding objects, and we can use a combination of the void pointer and the assignment of the collision ID to our objects to determine which object collided with which, and what "type" they are.

In addition, each object class has a data structure that indicates which sounds should be playing on various types of collisions. Playing the sounds for collisions is easy once the data structure is in place, and the system is set up to be as flexible as we need it to be.

The Hardest Part of the Implementation

The most difficult aspect of the game's implementation to get right (according to the students who developed it) was the steering and friction model. The challenges that come with trying to get a car to skid, steer, and slide in a realistic manner are huge. In fact, the steering model never achieved the final form that was desired. When you play the game you'll notice some abnormal behavior at times.

Summary

This chapter presented a complete game in C++ that used DirectX. The game shows what can be developed in 13 weeks by a small group of dedicated programmers using the techniques presented in this book. It uses a shareware physics engine called ODE to provide a clever simulation of a small radio-controlled toy car. I strongly suggest that you look over the source code and compare it with the code for the Mars racer game to see the differences between using OpenGL and DirectX.

References and Resources

References

Chapter 1

1. Mark J. P. Wolf and Bernard Perron (Eds.), *The Video Game Theory Reader*, Routledge, New York, 2003.

2. Mark J.P. Wolf (Ed), *The Medium of the Video Game*, University of Texas Press, Austin, TX, 2001.

3. Donald A. Norman, *The Invisible Computer*, The MIT Press, Cambridge, MA, 1998.

4. Donald A. Norman, *Things That Make Us Smart: Defending Human Attributes in the Age of the Machine*, Perseus Books, Cambridge, MA, 1993.

5. Jakob Nielsen, *Usability Engineering*, Academic Press, San Diego, CA, 1993.

6. Coffee break arcade. Internet Flash, Java, and Shockwave Driving games: **http://www.coffeebreakarcade.com/racing.htm**

7. Download racing games for the PC from TerraGame: **http://www.terragame.com/racing/index_1_sort2.html**

Chapter 2

1. *Funk & Wagnalls Standard College Dictionary* (Canadian Edition), Fitzhenry & Whiteside Ltd., 1978.

2. Mike McShaffry, *Game Coding Complete*, 2nd Edtion, Paraglyph Press, Scottsdale, AZ, 2005.

3. Daniel Sanchez-Crespo Dalmau, *Core Techniques and Algorithms in Game Programming*, New Riders Publishing, Indianapolis, IN, 2004.

4. Andrew Rollings and Dave Morris, *Game Architecture and Design*, New Riders Publishing, Indianapolis, IN, 2003: **http://www.theswapmeet.com/articles/morris.html**

5. K. Salen and E. Zimmerman, *Rules of Play—Game Design Fundamentals*, The MIT Press, Cambridge, MA, 2004.

6. Rudy Rucker, *Software Engineering and Computer Games*, Addison-Wesley, Reading, MA, 2003.

7. Brian Yap, *Analytical Perspectives in Game Design: Architecture*, 1999: **http://numbat.sourceforge.net/numbbatV2/architecture.html**

Chapter 3

1. D. Dalmau, *Core Techniques and Algorithms in Game Programming*, New Riders Publishing, Indianapolis, IN, 2004.

2. D. Eberly, *3D Game Engine Design*, Morgan Kaufmann, 2001.

3. J. Foley, A van Dam, S. Feiner, and J. Hughes, *Computer Graphics* (2nd Ed.), Addison-Wesley, Reading, MA, 1990.

4. T. Moler and E. Haines, *Real-Time Rendering*, A. K. Peters Publishing, 1999.

5. J. Neider, T. Davis, and M. Woo, *OpenGL Programming Guide*, Addison-Wesley, Reading, MA, 1993.

6. OpenGL Architecture Review Board, *OpenGL Reference Manual*, Addison-Wesley, Reading, MA, 1992.

7. A. Watt and Fabio Policarpo, *3D Games—Real Time Rendering and Software Technology*, Addison-Wesley, Reading, MA, 2001.

8. Damiano Vitulli, Space Simulator on-line (texture mapping) tutorials: **http://www.spacesimulator.net/tut3_texturemapping.html**, 2003.

9. OpenGL Resources, Purdue University: **http://www.cs.purdue.edu/homes/sun/Teach/535/usefulInfo.html**

10. Official OpenGL resource page, Silicon Graphics: **http://www.opengl.org/documentation/spec.html**

11. OpenGL Home Page, SGI: **http://www.opengl.org/**

12. Windows.programming intro for PC: **http://www.flipcode.com/tutorials/tut_windows01.shtml**

13. OpenGL Guide (graphics3d): **http://www.flipcode.com/tutorials/tut_windows01.shtml**

14. GLUT Tutorial: **http://www.lighthouse3d.com/opengl/glut**

Chapter 4

1. J.R. Parker, *Algorithms for Image Processing and Computer Vision* (CD included), John Wiley & Sons, New York, NY, 1998.

2. J. R. Parker, *Practical Computer Vision Using C*, John Wiley & Sons Ltd., New York, NY, 476 pages (diskette included), 1994.

3. D. Eberly, *3D Game Engine Design*, Morgan Kaufmann, 2001.

4. J. Foley, A van Dam, S. Feiner, and J. Hughes, *Computer Graphics* (2nd Ed.), Addison-Wesley, Reading, MA, 1990.

5. OpenGL Architecture Review Board, *OpenGL Reference Manual*, Addison-Wesley, Reading, MA, 1992.

6. J. Neider, T. Davis, M. Woo, *OpenGL Programming Guide*, Release 1, Addison-Wesley, Reading, MA, 1993.

Chapter 5

1. E.G. Gilbert, D.W. Johnson and S.S. Keerthi, "A Fast Procedure for Computing the Distance between Complex Objects in Three Dimensional Space," *IEEE Journal of Robotics and Automation*, Vol.4, 1988, Pages 193-203.

2. A. Gregory, M. Lin, S. Gottschalk and R. Taylor, *H-Collide: A Framework for Fast and Accurate Collision Detection for Haptic Interaction*, Proceedings of IEEE Virtual Reality Conference, 1999.

3. Gino van den Bergen, *GJK-engine*, 1999: **http://www.win.tue.nl/~gino/solid/**

4. A. Watt and F. Policarpo, *3D Games: Real-Time Rendering and Software Technology*, Addison-Wesley, Reading, MA, 2001.

5. Gino van den Bergen, *Collision Detection in Interactive 3D Environments*, Morgan-Kaufman/Elsevier, 2004.

6. M. Lin and J. Canny, *Efficient Collision Detection for Animation*, Third Eurographics Workshop, 1992.

7. Brian Mirtich, *V-Clip: Fast and Robust Polyhedral Collision Detection*, ACM Trans. Graph. 17, 3 (Jul. 1998), Pages 177-208.

8. J. D. Cohen, M. C. Lin, D. Manocha, and M. K. Ponamgi, *I-COLLIDE: An Interactive and Exact Collision Detection System for Large-Scale Environments*, Proc. ACM Interactive 3D Graphics Conf., Pages 189-196, 1995.

9. T. Hudson, M. Lin, J. Cohen, S. Gottschalk and D. Manocha, *V-COLLIDE: Accelerated Collision Detection for VRML*, Proceedings of VRML 97.

10. S. Gottschalk, M. Lin and D. Manocha, *OBB-Tree: A Hierarchical Structure for Rapid Interference Detection*, Proceedings of ACM Siggraph 96.

11. Jeff Erickson, Leonidas J. Guibas, Jorge Stolfi and Li Zhang, *Separation-Sensitive Collision Detection for Convex Objects*, proceedings of the tenth annual ACM- SIAM Symposium on Discrete Algorithms, Pages 327–336, 1999.

12. Julien Basch, Jeff Erickson, Leonidas J. Guibas, John Hershberger and Li Zhang, *Kinetic collision detection between two simple polygons*, proceedings of the tenth annual ACM-SIAM Symposium on Discrete Algorithms, Pages 102 –111, 1999.

13. Joe van den Heuvel and Miles Jackson, *Pool Hall Lessons: Fast, Accurate Collisions Between Circles or Spheres*, Gamasutra, January 18, 2002.

14. Wolfram Research, *Point-Line distance, 3-dimensional*: **http://mathworld.wolfram.com/Point-LineDistance3-Dimensional.html**

15. **http://www.ams.sunysb.edu/~jklosow/quickcd/QuickCD.html**

16. Subodh Kumar, Dinesh Manocha, Bill Garrett, Ming Lin, *Hierarchical Back-Face Culling*, 7th Eurographics Workshop on Rendering, Pages 231-240, 1996.

17. Foley, van Dam, Feiner, and Hughes, *Computer Graphics*, Addison-Wesley, Reading, MA, 1990.

Chapter 6

1. Joe Adzima, *AI Madness: Using AI to Bring Open-City Racing to Life*, Gamasutra, January 24, 2001: **http://www.gamasutra.com/features/20010124/adzima_01.htm**

2. HonglingWang, Joseph K. Kearney, James Cremer, Peter Willemsen, *Steering Autonomous Driving Agents Through Intersections in Virtual Urban Environments*, International Conference on Modeling, Simulation and Visualization Methods, Las Vegas, Nevada, June 2004: **http://www.cs.uiowa.edu/ %7Ehowang/pubs/steeringOnIntersection.pdf**

3. Craig Reynolds, *Steering Behaviors for Autonomous Characters*, Game Developers Conference, San Jose, CA. 1999: **http://www.red3d.com/cwr/steer/**

4. Larry D. Pyeatt, Adele E. Howe, *Learning to Race: Experiments with a Simulated Race Car*, Eleventh International Florida Artificial Intelligence Research Symposium, 1998.

5. Robert Dunlop, *Introduction to Catmull-Rom Splines*: **http://www.mvps.org/directx/articles/catmull/**

6. Yue Wang, Dinggang Shen and Eam Khwang Teoh, *Lane Detection Using Catmull-Rom Splines*, IEEE International Conference on Intelligent Vehicles, 1998.

7. Ranck, Steven, "Computing the Distance into a Vector," *Game Programming Gems*, Charles River Media, 2000.

8. Robot Auto Racing Simulator web site: RARS: **http://rars.sourceforge.net/**

9. Brian Stout, *The Basics of A* for Path Planning*, *Game Programming Gems*, Charles River Media, 2000.

Chapter 7

1. Nigel Chapman and Jenny Chapman, *Digital Multimedia*, John Wiley & Sons Ltd, 2000.

2. Ben Gold and Nelson Morgan, *Speech and Audio Signal Processing*, John Wiley & Sons Ltd, 2000.

3. Loki Software, *OpenAL Specification and Reference,* Version 1.0 Draft Edition, June 2000: **www.openal.org/openal_webstf/specs/oalspecs-specs.pdf**

4. Creative Technology Limited, *Creative OpenAL Programmer's Reference*, Version 1.0, 2001.

5. OpenAL home page: **http://www.openal.org/**

6. Chad Armstrong, *OpenAL Tutorial,* Sept. 2002: **http://www.edenwaith.com/ products/ pige/tutorials/openal.php**

7. Mason McCuskey, *Beginning Game Audio Programming*, Premier Press, April 2003.

8. Steven W. Smith, *The Scientist and Engineer's Guide to Digital Signal Processing*, California Technical Publishing, 1997: **http://www.dspguide.com/**

9. Mark Kyrnin, *Understanding Computer Audio, Part II: Surround Sound,* 2004*:* **http://compreviews.about.com/cs/soundcards/a/ CompAudioPt2.htm**

Chapter 8

1. Hongling Wang, Joseph K. Kearney, James Cremer, Peter Willemsen, *Steering Autonomous Driving Agents Through Intersections in Virtual Urban Environments*, 2004 International Conference on Modeling, Simulation, and Visualization Methods (MSV 04), CSREA Press.

2. Xiaopeng Fang, Hung A. Pham and Minoru Kobayashi, *PD Controller for Car-Following Models Based on Real Data,* First Human-Centered Transportation Simulation Conference, 2001: **www.vrac.iastate.edu/~fang414/ Publications/ PD_controller.doc**

3. J. J. Craig, *Introduction to Robotics: Mechanics and Control*, Addison-Wesley, Reading, MA, 1989.

4. J. Cremer, J. Kearney, and Y. Papelis, *Hcsm: A Framework for Behavior and Scenario Control in Virtual Environments*, ACM Transactions on Modeling and Computer Animation, Vol. 3, Number 7 1995.

5. J. Cremer, J. Kearney, and P. Willemsen, *Directable Behavior Models for Virtual Driving Scenarios*, Transactions of the society for computer simulation international, Vol. 2 number 6 1997.

6. J. Wit, C. Crane, D. Armstrong, and J. Duffy, *Autonomous Ground Vehicle Path Tracking, Proceedings* of the 32nd Southeastern Symposium on System Theory, March 2000.

7. P. Willemsen, J. Kearney, and H. Wang, *Ribbon Networks for Modeling Navigable Paths of Autonomous Agents in Virtual Urban Environments*, Proceedings of IEEE Virtual Reality Conference, Pages 79–86, March 2003.

8. P. J. Willemsen, "Behavior and Scenario Modeling for Real-Time Virtual Environment," Ph.D. thesis, The University of Iowa, 2000.

9. R. Sukthankar, "Situation Awareness for Tactical Driving," Ph.D. thesis, Robotics Institute, Carnegie Mellon University, 1997.

10. Stephane Donikian, *How to Introduce Life in Virtual Environments: An Urban Environment Modeling System for Driving Simulation*, 1996: **citeseer.ist.psu.edu/donikian96how.html**

11. N. Farenc, S. Raupp Musse, E. Schweiss, M. Kallmann, O. Aune, R. Boulic, D. Thalmann, *One Step towards Virtual Human Management for Urban Environment Simulation*, ECAI 98 Workshop of Intelligent Virtual Environments, 1998: **http://citeseer.ist.psu.edu/farenc98one.html**

12. Bruno Arnaldi, Remi Cozot, and Sephane Donikian, *Simulating Automated Cars in a Virtual Urban Environment*, Eurographics workshops on Virtual environments 95, Barcelona, Spain, Pages 171-184, 1995.

13. Yiorgos Chrysanthou and Mel Slater, *Incremental Updates to Scenes Illuminated by Area Light Sources*, Rendering Techniques 97 (Proceedings of the Eighth Eurographics Workshop on Rendering), Julie Dorsey and Phillipp Slusallek editors, Springer Wien, New York, Pages 103-114, 1997.

14. B. Artz, *An Analytical Road Segment Terrain Database for Driving Simulation*, Driving Simulation Conference, Sophia Antipolis, France, Pages 274-284, Sept. 1995.

15. S. Bayarri, M. Fernandez, and M. Perez, *Virtual Reality for Driving Simulation*, Communications of the ACM, Pages 72-76, May, 1996.

16. M. Tambe, W. Johnson, R. Jones, F. Koss, J. Laird, P. Rosenbloom, and K. Schwamb, *Intelligent Agents for Interactive Simulation Environments*, AI Magazine, Pages 15-39, Vol. 15, No. 1, 1995.

Chapter 9

1. D. M. Bourg, *Physics for Game Developers*, O'Reilly & Associates, Sebastopol, CA, 2002.

2. http://vettenet.org/torquehp.html

3. Paul Haney (Pub.), *Inside Racing Technology, 2000*: http://www.insideracingtechnology.com/index.html

4. Marco Monster, *Car Physics for Games*, Nov. 2003: http://home.planet.nl/~monstrous/tutcar.html

5. R. Feynman, R. Leighton, M. Sands, *The Feynman Lectures on Physics*, Addison-Wesley, Reading, MA, 1963.

6. R. Weidner and R. Sells, *Elementary Classical Physics* (2nd. edition), Allyn and Bacon, Inc, Boston, 1973.

7. Mayfield Motorsports, Index to Coefficient of Drag for Many Vehicles Plus Index to Horsepower vs. Speed Curves, 2001: http://www.teknett.com/pwp/drmayf/ tbls.htm

8. http://www.gm.com/automotive/gmpowertrain/engines/gmpow/la1_truck.htm

9. Chris Hecker, *Rigid Body Dynamics*, series on Physics in *Game Development Magazine*, 1998: http://www.d6.com/users/checker/dynamics.htm

10. Brian Beckham, *Physics of Racing Series:* http://phors.locost7.info

11. Glenn Elert, *The Physics Hypertextbook™*, © 1998-2004: http://hypertextbook.com/physics/mechanics/friction/

12. GT3 Shrine—*How To Drift RWD Cars*: http://pergatory.net/gt3/howtorwd.html

13. Ted Zuvich, *Vehicle Dynamics for Racing Games*, Game Developers Conference, March 22-26, 2000.

Chapter 10

1. Brook Miles, *The Forger's Win32 API Tutorial* vers. 2.0, 1998: http://www.winprog.org/tutorial/

2. Michael Root and James Boer, *DirectX Complete*, McGraw-Hill, 1999.

3. Herbert Schildt, *Windows 98 Programming From the Ground Up*, Osbourne McGraw-Hill, 1998.

4. Amol Kakhandki, Getting Started With OpenGL, 2002: http://www.codeproject.com/opengl/opengltry.asp

5. Microsoft Developer's Network, *Device Contexts*: **http://msdn.microsoft.com/ library/default.asp?url=/library/en-us/vccore/html/_core_device_contexts.asp**

6. Microsoft Developer's Network, *Rendering Contexts*: **http:// msdn.microsoft.com/library/default.asp?url=/library/en-us/opengl/ ntopnglo_4kfn.asp**

7. Robert Dunlop, *Writing the Game Loop*: **http://www.mvps.org/directx/articles/ writing_the_game_loop.htm**

8. Dave Astle and Kevin Hawkins, *Beginning OpenGL Game Programming*, Thomson, Boston, MA, 2004.

Chapter 11

1. Ting-Chieh Lin, Zen-Chung Shih, and Yu-Ting Tsai, *Cinematic Camera Control in 3D Computer Games*, WSCG 2004, February 2-6, 2004, Plzen, Czech Republic.

2. Nicolas Halper, Ralf Helbing, Thomas Strothotte, *A Camera Engine for Computer Games: Managing the Trade-Off Between Constraint Satisfaction and Frame Coherence*, Computer Graphics Forum Volume 20, Issue 3 (2001).

3. Daniel Sanchez-Crespo Dalmau, *Core Techniques and Algorithms in Game Programming*, New Riders, Boston, MA, 2004.

4. John Funge, *AI for Games and Animation: A Cognitive Modeling Approach*, A.K.Peters, Natick, MA, 1999.

Chapter 12

1. P. Lindstrom and V. Pascucci, *Visualization of Large Terrains Made Easy*, Proceedings of *Visualization*, Pages 363-370, 2001.

2. Mark Duchaineau, Murray Wolinsky, David E. Sigeti, Mark C. Miller, Charles Aldrich, Mark B. Mineev-Weinstein, *ROAMing Terrain: Real-time Optimally Adapting Meshes*, Proceedings of IEEE Visualization, Pages 81-88, October 1997: **http://www.llnl.gov/graphics/ROAM/roam.pdf**

3. Willem H. de Boer, *Fast Terrain Rendering Using Geometrical MipMapping*, 2000: flipCode article at **http://www.flipcode.com/ tutorials/geomipmaps.pdf**

4. R. A. Apu and M. L. Gavrilova, *Adaptive Mesh Generation for Real-Time Terrain Modeling*, Proceedings of the twentieth annual symposium on Computational geometry, Brooklyn, New York, Pages 447-448, 2004.

5. Peter Lindstrom, David Koller, William Ribarsky, Larry F. Hodges, Nick Faust and Gregory A. Turner, *Real-Time, Continuous Level of Detail Rendering of Height Fields*, *SIGGRAPH 96*, Pages 109-118, August, 1996.

6. Brian Turner, *Real-Time Dynamic Level of Detail Terrain Rendering with ROAM*, April, 2000: Gamasutra at **http://www.gamasutra.com/features/20000403/ turner_01.htm**

7. Ben Discoe, *The Virtual Terrain Project:* **http://www.vterrain.org**

8. S. Rottger, W. Heidrich, P. Slusallek, and H. Seidel, *Real-Time Generation of Continuous Levels of Detail for Height Fields*, *WSCG'98*, Pages 315-322, 1998.

9. Marco Monster, *Terrain Rendering for OpenGL Games*, August 2001: **http://home.planet.nl/~monstrous/terrain.html**

10. Seamus McNalley, *Treadmarks* (battle tank combat and racing game): **http://www.treadmarks.com**

11. D. Luebke, M. Reddy, J. Cohen, A. Varshney, B. Watson, and R. Huebner, *Level of Detail for 3D Graphics*, Morgan Kaufmann series in *Computer Graphics and Geometric Modeling*, 2004.

12. Seamus McNally, *Binary Triangle Trees and Terrain Tessellation*, Longbow Digital Arts, 1999.

13. Daniel Wagner, *Terrain Geomorphing in the Vertex Shader* (excerpt from *ShaderX2—Shader Programming Tips and Tricks)* Wordware, April 2003: **http://www.gamedev.net/reference/articles/article1936.asp**

14. António Ramires Fernandes, Billboarding Tutorial, LightHouse 3D: **http://www.lighthouse3d.com/opengl/billboarding/**

Chapter 13

1. Bourg, D., *Physics for Game Developers*, O'Reilly, Sebastopol, CA, 2002.

2. Elert, G., *Acceleration Due to Gravity on Mars*, Retrieved Feb. 11, 2005 from The Physics Factbook Web site: **http://hypertextbook.com/facts/2004/JahshirahRossi.shtml**

3. Fernandes, A. R. (n.d.). *Glut Tutorial*. Retrieved Feb. 07, 2005 from OpenGL at Lighthouse 3D—GLUT Tutorial website: **http://www.lighthouse3d.com/opengl/ glut/**

4. Rabin, S., *Designing a General Robust AI Engine*. In M. DeLoura(Eds.), *Game Programming Gems*, Pages 221-236, Charles River Media, Rockland, MA, 2000.

5. Rabin, S., *Recursive Dimensional Clustering: A Fast Algorithm for Collision Detection*. In S. Rabin(Eds), *Game Programming Gems 2*, Pages 228-238, Charles River Media, Hingam, MA, 2001.

6. Rabin, S. (2002). *Implementing a State Machine Language*. In S. Rabin(Eds.), *AI Game Programming Gems*, Pages 314-320, Charles River Media, Hingam, MA, 2002.

7. Rabin, S., *Enhancing a State Machine Language through Messaging*. In S. Rabin(Eds.), *AI Game Programming Gems*, Pages 321-329, Hingam, MA, Charles River Media, 2002.

8. Shreiner, D., Woo, M., Neider, J., & Davis, T., *OpenGL Programming Guide* (4th Ed.), Addison-Wesley, New York, 2003.

9. Snook, G., *Real-Time 3D Terrain Engines Using C++ and DirectX 9* (1st Ed.), Charles River Media, Hingam, MA, 2003.

10. Van Verth, J., & Bishop, L., *Essential Mathematics for Games & Interactive Applications: a Programmers Guide*, Morgan Kaufmann, San Francisco, CA, 2004.

Chapter 14

1. J. Shankel, J., *Rendering Distant Scenery with Skyboxes*, In *Game Programming Gems 2*, Pages 416-420, M. DeLoura (Ed), Charles River Media, Hingam, MA, 2001.

2. Eric Lengyel, *Intersection of a Ray and a Triangle* in *Mathematics for 3D Game Programming & Computer Graphics*, Pages 116-118, Charles River Media, Hingham, MA, 2002.

3. Center for Mars Exploration, *Maps, Panoramas, and Globes*: **http://cmex-www.arc.nasa.gov/CMEX/data/images/Maps.html**

4. David S. Ebert, F. Kenton Musgrave, Darwyn Peachey, Ken Perlin, and Steven Worley, *Texturing And Modeling: A Procedural Approach*, 2nd Ed., AP Professional, July 1998.

5. Steve Rabin, *Designing a General Robust AI Engine* in *Game Programming Gems*, Mark DeLouria (ed), Charles River Media, 2000.

6. Russel Smith, Open Dynamics engine: **http://ode.org/**

Resources

Chapter 1

The following list of downloadable driving games and demos are resources for Chapter 1.

The top 10 list of games:

1. *Crazy Taxi*—**http://www.pcgameworld.com/download.php/id/3153/folder/demos/filename/ctdemo.zip**

2. *Colin McRae Rally*—http://downloads.gamezone.com/demos/d1582.htm

3. *Simpson's Hit & Run*—http://www.gamershell.com download_3196.shtml?
   q=hit++run

4. *Mario Kart*—http://www.gamershell.com/download_4135.shtml

5. *Road Rash*—http://www.topdownloads.net/themes/view.php?id=2617

6. *Driver*—http://www.game-revolution.com/download/pc/racing/driver.htm

7. *Gran Turismo IV*—http://www.ugo.com/channels/games/trailer/
   player.asp?articleID=10691

8. *Need for Speed*—http://www.pcgameworld.com/download.php/id/4670/folder/
   demos/filename/nfsu_demo_eagames_australia.exe

9. *Project Gotham Racing*—http://xboxmovies.teamxbox.com/xbox/415/PGR2-
   Xbox-Live-Trailer

10. *Burnout*—http://eu.playstation.com/iw_images//assets/video/burnout2/
    burnout2_02.mov

Twenty Five Other Games You Can Download:

1. *Hotrod Championship Drag Racing*
   Date: 03-1998
   http://www.programfiles.com/Default.asp?LinkId=14587

2. *Burnout: Championship Drag Racing*
   Date: 03-1998
   http://www.downseek.com/download/9460.asp

3. *Andretti Racing*
   Date: 03-2001
   http://downloads.gamezone.com/demos/d2071.htm

4. *Open Kart*
   Date: 05-2001
   http://www.cgonline.com/downloads/openkart-01-d1.html

5. *Hot Wheels Mechanix*
   Date: 09-2001
   http://www.demo-files.com/view.php3?929

6. *Off-Road Redneck Racing*
   Date: 06-2001
   http://www.avault.com/pcrl/demo_temp.asp?game=redneckracing

7. *Leadfoot*
   Date: 06-2001
   http://www.cgonline.com/downloads/leadfoot-01-d1.html

8. *Ski-Doo X-Team Racing*
   Date: 08-2001
   http://www.game-revolution.com/download/pc/racing/ski_doo.htm

9. *Super 1 Karting*
   Date: 01-2002
   http://www.pcworld.com/downloads/collection/0,collid,824,pg,1,00.asp

10. *Space Haste*
    Date: 01-2002
    http://www.pcworld.com/downloads/collection/0,collid,824,pg,1,00.asp

11. *Wacky Wheels*
    Date: 01-2002
    http://www.pcworld.com/downloads/collection/0,collid,824,pg,1,00.asp

12. *Dirt Bike 3D v1.5*
    Date: 02-002
    http://www.pcworld.com/downloads/collection/0,collid,824,pg,1,00.asp

13. *Bikez II v1.21*
    Date: 02-002
    http://www.pcworld.com/downloads/collection/0,collid,824,pg,1,00.asp

14. *Star Wars Episode I: Racer*
    Date: 02-2002
    http://www.pcworld.com/downloads/collection/0,collid,824,pg,1,00.asp

15. *Carmageddon 2*
    Date: 06-2002
    http://www.pcworld.com/downloads/collection/0,collid,824,pg,1,00.asp

16. *Need for Speed Hot Pursuit*
    Date: 08-2002
    http://www.3dgamers.com/news/more/1034617318/

17. *4x4 EVO lution*
    Date: 10-2002
    http://downloads.gamezone.com/demos/d8345.htm

18. *Midtown Madness*
    Date: 10-2002
    http://www.pcworld.com/downloads/collection/0,collid,824,pg,1,00.asp

19. *Castrol Honda Superbike 2000*
    Date: 08-2002
    http://downloads.gamezone.com/demos/d1587.htm

20. *Need for Speed: High Stake*
    Date: 12-2002
    http://www.topdownloads.net/games/view.php?id=196

21. *Extreme Burnout*
    Date: 01-2003
    http://games.tucows.tierra.net/preview/296523.html

22. *Midnight Club II*
    Date: 09-2003
    http://www.3dgamers.com/dl/games/midnightclub2/
    midnight_club2_demo_install.exe.html

23. *Tough Trucks*
    Date: 09-2003
    http://www.pcgameworld.com/download.php/id/5200/folder/demos/
    filename/toughtrucks_setup.exe

24. *Driv3r*
    Date: 06-2004
    http://www.pcworld.com/downloads/collection/0,collid,824,pg,1,00.asp

25. *Juiced*
    Date: 08-2004
    http://www.pcgameworld.com/download.php/id/5384/folder/demos/
    filename/juiced_demo_final.zip

Chapter 9

Here are some driving simulations that you can obtain from the Internet:

Racer is a free cross-platform car simulation project (for non-commercial use). It uses professional car physics papers to achieve a realistic feeling. Cars, tracks, and such can be created relatively easy (compared to other, more closed, driving simulations). The 3D and other file formats are, or should be, documented. Editors and support programs are also available to get a very customizable and expandable simulator. OpenGL is used for rendering. Visit **http://www.racer.nl/** for more information.

The *Rigid Body Dynamics* site was created by Chris Hecker. He wrote four articles about rigid body dynamics for *Game Developer Magazine* and he posts them on this site as PDF files. You'll also find downloadable programs to illustrate the physics concepts discussed. Visit **http://www.d6.com/users/checker/ dynamics.htm**.

Car Physics Demo v. 0.8—Marco Monster provides a cool demo of car physics, and downloadable examples. There is also a downloadable game called *Downtown Drivin'* and a host of other interesting items. Visit **htttp://home.planet.nl/ ~monstrous/download.html#cardem08**.

Appendix A

High-Concept Design Document for *Gopher-it*

This appendix presents the high-concept design document for the *Gopher-it* game presented in Chapter 2. You can use this design document as a template to work out the designs for your own games.

1 Game Analysis

Gopher-it is a 2D maze-based interactive puzzle game that focuses on race and avoidance. It is not an especially unique game, but it requires no licenses.

1.1 Game Concept

Goal: Introduce the basic game play and essential characters.

Gopher-it is a single player game in which the player drives a small car embedded within a maze. The goal is to collect as many points as possible, which is achieved by visiting all sites in the maze as quickly as possible. The other vehicles present in the maze are police cars that will seek out the player. The player will lose if he or she is caught by one of the police cars.

1.2 Game Goals

Goal: Outline what the game is designed to do.

- Provide a simple strategy for the gameplay
- Illustrate simple game implementation concepts
- Use a clear architecture
- Use aspect of speed to gain points

1.3 Game Information

Goal: Provide a short summary of the game genre/hardware.

Gopher-it is a simple 2D puzzle game with sound for the PC platform. It uses OpenGL so that it can be easily ported to other platforms.

1.4 Brand Analysis

Goal: Explain how the game is branded; what do players know and expect in advance?

Gopher-it is an arcade style game that is similar to *Frogger* in basic play and graphical presentation. Players should have seen these sorts of games before, so the action and interface should be familiar. (Actually, *Gopher-it* is introduced for teaching purposes, as a simple 2D example of a time stepped driving game.)

1.5 Competitor's Analysis

Goal: What are the similar and competing games?

This game is actually designed to be an eduactional tool to explain some of the basic concepts presented in this book. It therefore doesn't have any real competition but it has some game play features that are found in other popular games as listed here:

Tetris: *Tetris* is is more abstract than *Gopher-it*. Both games, however, use similar motion controls and they both have similiarities in how the speed of play is implemented.

Slither: Both games use similar speed and interactive controls. Both games also require that the player think ahead a few moves to be successful.

Pac-Man: Both games have step-wise motion and maze action.

Frogger: Both games contain the strategy of avoiding cars and, of course, running down small animals.

1.6 Story Concept

Goal: Provide a description of the narrative. Our game has none.

The narrative is simple. You, as the player, must run down small mammals on the road. The police have been called to track you down and stop you. This part of the document should describe the story behind the game.

1.6.1 The Setup

Goal: Present the previous actions to the story of the game.

This part of the document should describe any actions that have taken place prior to the player beginning the game. For instance, why do you want to drive over gophers? Why do the police chase you? Why is your car in the position that it is?

1.6.2 Story Overview

Goal: Present narrative for the game situation, player relationships, attitudes, and so on.

In more complex stories, this section is used to describe the details of relationships between players and player types, weapons and systems, and complex activities and the reason for them. Again, in this simple game, we have none.

2 Game Design

2.1 Game Structure

Goal: Describe how the game is organized from the player's perspective.

There are two modes of play. The first is avoidance mode, in which the player attempts to collect points while eluding the police cars, which are actively chasing him. The second is chase mode, in which the player attempts to catch and capture a police car. The player has some choice in selecting the mode, but not total control; the mode is a side effect of position and history.

The overall objective of the player is to collect points. One point is collected for each gopher captured, and ten points are collected for each police car.

2.2 Gameplay

Goal: Describe how the game is played.

The game is played on a small grid, 18x16 cells in size. The player controls a small red car, initially located at the 7,1 position in the grid, using the numeric keypad. One step in any of the four neighboring directions can be made each turn, which initially takes one second.

Black portions of the grid are walls, and cars cannot pass through them. If the car enters a square having a gopher on it, the gopher is collected and a point is awarded.

The player cannot move at will. Every second or so, the last move indicated by the player will be conveyed to the game, and so the gameplay has a clock-like feel.

2.2.1 Avoidance Mode

There are two police cars on the grid, initially in the area of 7,15. They will move towards the player's car and attempt to capture it. If one succeeds, the game is over. The police cars move a little faster than the player's car.

2.2.2 Chase Mode

If the player reaches a square occupied by a gas station, the station vanishes and the player becomes indestructible for 15 turns. This is indicated by a musical theme. The player can now seek out the police cars and capture them for a 10-point bonus. The police cars will not avoid the player, but move a little slower. When the musical theme stops, the player becomes vulnerable to capture again, and the police cars resume their chase.

2.7 Core Controls

Goal: Describe the user interface.

The controls used in the game are simple mouse and keyboard actions:

8: (Numeric keypad UP)	Move the player's car up
4: (Numeric keypad LEFT)	Move the player's car left
2: (Numeric keypad DOWN)	Move the player's car down
6: (Numeric keypad RIGHT)	Move the player's car right
Mouse click	End the game.

3 Characters and AI

This game has no actual characters. There are gophers that are simply present to provide a means to score points. When the player's car runs over a gopher (i.e., occupies the same square as does the gopher), the gopher icon vanishes from that square and a point is given to the player.

The police are simple automatons that always drive towards the player's vehicle. If they collide with the player, the game is over and the player loses. If the player collects a power-up (by driving over a gas pump icon), the play police begin to avoid the player, and if a player-police collision occurs, the police car disappears.

4 Sound

The sound for *Gopher-it* must be simple and yet descriptive. There are six basic sounds required:

- A beep each time the player moves, or can move (clock tick).

- A clunking sound to indicate that the player has collected a gopher.

- A siren to indicate that the player has collected a police car.

- A musical theme to indicate that the player's car is invulnerable.

- Applause to indicate that the player has won the game.

- Laughter to indicate that the player has lost the game.

Sound will be low resolution, non-positional.

5 Expanded Gameplay

We may describe levels here, and plot extensions for each level. This game has only one level. A second level might have a different arrangement of roads and a different goal. Such features would appear in this section.

6 Key Feature Summary

- Speed and puzzle solving

- Simple play, suitable and entertaining for smaller children

- Two modes of play, indicated by audio

- Easy interface, clock-like action

Appendix B

Math Tutorial for Developing Driving and Racing Games

Mathematics is a necessary prerequisite to building a computer game because computers are basically calculating devices, and games are essentially simulations of real world activities whose mathematical properties we understand. I confess that this insight comes from Albert Einstein, who said, "Physics is mathematical not because we know so much about the physical world, but because we know so little: it is only its mathematical properties that we can discover." The sad truth about games is that we can only easily manipulate their mathematical properties at this stage.

I am not a math teacher (I *do* have a math degree, if that means anything) but I am a teacher, and I think I can winnow the required material that you need to know to work with the game code presented in this book down to a bare minimum of math. It's not that I don't like math. I actually do like math but I also realize that math is not everyone's "cup of tea." This appendix presents the minimum amount of math that I think you'll need to understand to work through the code and examples presented in this book. Some of the math is actually physics, but the physics is expressed as equations, so I think I'm safe putting it in this appendix. Also, my degree is in *applied* mathematics, so I feel that I'm qualified to explain at least low-level physics math (although it has been a long time since I got my degree!).

Elementary Trigonometry

Trigonometry is all about triangles. After all, the "tri" in trigonometry means triangle. Trig defines the relationships between angles and the lengths of sides of triangles. I will show you just enough trig to be dangerous, and then leave the details of "why" (always a philosophical question) for your own study.

You can think of an angle as a difference in direction, such as on a compass. This angle can be measured between any two lines that intersect, and there are two main measures of angle magnitude: *degrees* and *radians*. Let's consider a clock. A horizontal line can be drawn from the clock center to the number 3. We'll consider this line to be our baseline—the hour hand of the clock. We'll call the angle created by this line zero, either zero degrees or zero radians. As I think you can visualize, the angle between this horizontal line and a moving minute hand will increase as the minute hand advances until it moves all the way around the clock face and meets the 3 o'clock line again. It then becomes zero once more. The total number of degrees in a complete rotation around the circle is 360 degrees (because of an old Babylonian number system); the number of radians in the same circle is 2π.

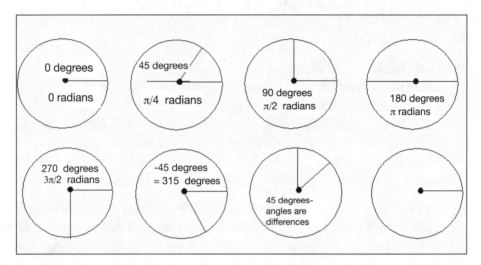

Figure B.1
Using degrees to measure angles.

Let's use degrees as a measure of angles from now on (see Figure B.1). Note that negative angles are used: -45 degrees is +315 degrees (because 360 - 45 = 315). Also note that angles represent differences between two directions, although sometimes a standard reference is made to a zero angle. That's a lot of words for a simple idea. I have noted that a lot of people think that trig is hard, and I wish to leave you with a working collection of operations, so please bear with me. Someone somewhere is likely having trouble with this.

The sum of the angles inside of any triangle is a constant 180 degrees as shown in Figure B.2.

If we know any two angles, we can compute the third angle. On the other hand, the lengths of the sides of a triangle do not have any similar property: an equilateral triangle can be one inch or one mile on each side; the angles will all still be 60 degrees.

Trig allows us to compute the lengths of sides of a triangle given some of the other sides and angles. To do this, we need to know the values of some simple functions,

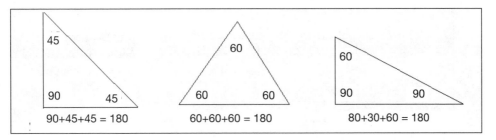

B

Figure B.2
The sum of angles in a triangle is always 180 degrees.

called *trigonometric* functions. The ones named *sine*, *cosine*, and *tangent* are the most important. To determine the value of these functions we can look them up in a book or, better yet, use a scientific calculator or computer.

Here are some very simple but very important rules to know when using these functions. These rules all apply to any *right* triangle (a triangle with a 90 degree angle in it). The *hypotenuse* is the side opposite to the right angle:

- The sine of any angle in a right triangle equals the length of the side opposite to the angle divided by the length of the hypotenuse.

- The cosine of any angle in a right triangle equals the length of the side adjacent to the angle (not the hypotenuse) divided by the length of the hypotenuse.

- The tangent of any angle in a right triangle equals the length of the side opposite to the angle divided by the length of the side adjacent to the angle.

Let's look at some examples. Our first example is shown in Figure B.3. Here we have a triangle that has the three angles: 90, 60, and 30. The basic trigonometric relationships that are created are shown in Figure B.3.

We already know the values of sine, cosine, and tangent (or *sin*, *cos*, *tan*, as they are abbreviated) for any angle. We can use one of the equations and solve for what we don't know. In other words, if we have one length, we can find the other lengths.

Let's apply what we now know about trigonometric relationships and solve a simple problem. Assume that the sun is 25 degrees above the horizon at the moment. How long will the shadow be that is thrown by a 100 foot tall building?

As usual, the solution to the problem can best be found by creating a good drawing of the problem. (In computer science, you should always assemble a very clear statement of the problem to be solved. This usually leads you right to the solution!) Our current problem can be represented as shown in Figure B.4.

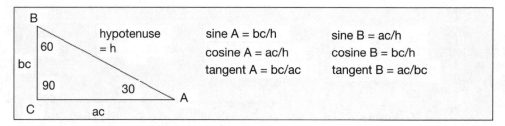

Figure B.3
Basic trigonometric relationships.

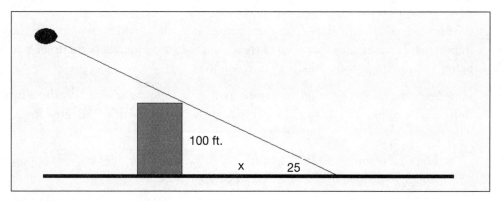

Figure B.4
Determining the length of a shadow using trig.

Here we know what the angle and the side opposite the angle is, and we wish to determine the side adjacent to the angle. The trigonometric function that uses the adjacent and opposite sides is the tangent. The equation here for calculating what we need is:

Equation B. 1 $\tan 25 = 100/x$

Next, we solve for x as shown here:

Equation B. 2 $x = 100/\tan 25$

My calculator says that tan 25 is approximately 0.47. We can thus conclude that the shadow length (x = 100/0.47) is 212 feet. Does this seem correct? Well, if the sun were higher, the shadow would be shorter. So, if the sun were at 45 degrees, we'd have x =100/tan 45 = 100/1.0 = 100 feet. What this says is that if we almost double the angle of the sun, the shadow will be much shorter (less than half the length of the shadow when the sun was sitting at 25 degrees). Well, this seems consistent. This problem is quite typical of the sort of problem that we'll encounter in a game. We'll know an angle and the length of a side, and we'll need to compute the length of another side. Depending on which side we wish to compute, we'll use a sin, cos, or tan function.

Now that you know how basic trig properties of angles are used to solve problems, let's move on to straight lines.

Straight Lines

Most of you will be familiar with the Cartesian coordinate system used to represent a plane. Most of you can also see the logical extensions into three and more dimensions. Each point, line, triangle, and object in a game is specified in terms of coordinates in a system of this type. A point is expressed as three numbers (x, y, z); a line segment is expressed using two points, a triangle is expressed using three points/three segments, and so on.

A common equation for a straight line is the slope-intercept form as shown here:

Equation B. 3 $y = mx + b$

In this case, m is the line's *slope* $(\Delta y/\Delta x)$ and b is the *intercept*, or the y coordinate of the point where the line crosses the y-axis. Any values of x and y that satisfy this equation lie on the line. The main problem with this form of the line equation is that it does not work for vertical lines for which the slope would be infinite. We need to either treat the vertical as a special case, or adopt a different line equation. The general form of the line is

Equation B. 4 $Ax + By + C = 0$

where at least one of A or B components must be non-zero. Now, there is a single line that can be drawn through any given two points; in other words, two points are needed to define a line. It is a common process to determine the equation of the line that passes through two points (x_1, y_1) and (x_2, y_2). Here's how it works:

1. If x_1 and x_2 are different, the slope $m = (\Delta y/\Delta x) = (y_2 - y_1) / (x_2 - x_1)$.

   The two-point form of the line equation is:

Equation B. 5 $y = y1 + [(y2 - y1) / (x2 - x1)] \cdot (x - x1)$

2. If x_1 and x_2 are the same, the line equation will be $x = x_1$.

Which Side of a Line Is a Point on?

Given the equation of a line, any point is either on the line itself or on the line's left or its right. Let's assume that the choice of left and right are arbitrary because we mostly care about determining whether two points are on the same side of a line. It turns out that if we substitute the coordinates of a point (r, s) into the equation, the result will be 0 (on the line), negative (to the right) or positive (to the left). If two points result in the same numerical sign when plugged into the line equation, we'll know that they are on the same side.

Distance

The distance between a point **P** and a line **L** is easy to determine. First, we choose the shortest distance, and that means that the line from point **P** to the line **L** makes a right angle (90 degrees). If **P**=(r, s) and **L** is the line in Equation 11.2, the distance between **L** and **P** will be:

Equation B.6
$$d = \frac{|Ar + Bs + C|}{\sqrt{A^2 + B^2}}$$

Where Do Two Lines Intersect?

Since we have two lines, we'll have two equations, each like the one shown in Equation B.4. If the lines aren't parallel, they will intersect at the point (x,y), which gives us a solution to both equations. Thus, to find this point, we solve the pair of equations simultaneously.

Two lines are parallel if they have no intersection, and so the system of equations has no real solution in that instance.

What Line Passes between Two Points?

It seems clear that a unique line passes between any two points that you may select. Given points $P_0 = (x_0, y_0)$ and $P_1 = (x_1, y_1)$, what's the equation of the line through P_0 and P_1? A good way to determine this requires that we first notice that Equation B.4 can be rewritten as:

Equation B. 7   y = -(A/B)x-C/B

When we rename -(A/B) as **m** and -C/B as **b** we get the slope-intercept form of the line of Equation B.3:

y = mx + b.

The variable **m** represents the slope of the line, or the angle it makes with the x-axis. The **b** variable is the point on the y-axis where it intersects the line. In any case, we now have two constants (and two points) in the equation. This means the equation can now be solved. That is, we can solve the following pair of equations for **m** and **b**:

Equation B. 8 $y_0 = m^*x_0 + b$
$y_1 = m^*x_1 + b$

Let's apply what we know to a sample problem: what line passes through the points (1, 1) and (5, 5)?

The equations are: $1 = m^*(1) + b$ and $5 = m^*5 + b$. Substituting for **b**, we get: $b = 1-m = 5-5m$. Solving for **m** gives $m = 5-5m-1$; $4m = 4$, or $m=1$.

Now, take a point on the line (5,5) and the newly discovered value for **m** and solve for **b**:
$5 = m^*5 +b \rightarrow 5 = 1^*5 +b \rightarrow 5-5 = b$, or $b=0$

The equation of the line through (1,1) and (5,5) is therefore: $y = 1x+0$ or just $y = x$

Here's an important fact worth mentioning: The slope **m** is really the change in **y** divided by the change in **x** as we sample any two points on the line. Recalling our trig and looking at the Figure B.5, we can see a useful relationship emerging.

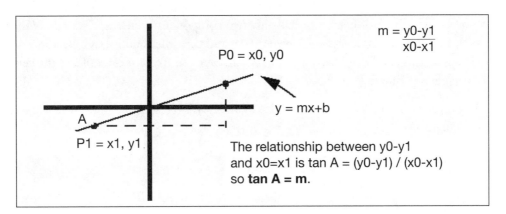

Figure B.5
An example of how two points determine a line.

The fact that **tan A = m** means that the angle **A** can be found in the tangent tables or it can be calculated as the *inverse tangent (arctangent)* of **m**. This is denoted as **atan(m)**.

What Is the Angle between Two Lines?
Lines form angles with each axis, and with each other. It is sometimes important to determine what the angles are, so we can apply a trigonometric equation or a vector transformation. Let the two lines be $y = m_1x+b_1$ and $y = m_2x+b_2$. Assign the labels **1** and **2** so that $m_2 > m_1$. It can be shown that the angle **Z** between the two lines is given by:

Equation B. 9

$$\tan Z = \frac{m_2 - m_1}{1 + m_1 m_2}$$

What Is the Equation of a Line Perpendicular to Another?

The trig fact we just discussed makes it easy to find the equation of a line perpendicular to some other line. The equation of our line is **y=mx+b**, and **tan A = m**. The line perpendicular to this has an inverse slope: that is, its slope will be **1/m**. All we need to do is find **b**, and to do that we simply select any point on the original line (x',y') and use slope **1/m**. We then solve for the new **b' = y' − x'/m**.

Vectors

A vector is a set of values or coordinates that are specified in a given order. The number of values is called the *dimension* of the vector. A point in 2D Cartesian space is a two-dimensional vector, and a point in 3D space is a three-dimensional vector. Vectors are usually drawn as little arrows with a length and direction, as shown back in Figure B.1. Since a two-dimensional vector has only two component values (x, y), we draw them such that the start of a vector is always (0,0) and the other end is (x,y). Vectors are always relative, and can have an origin where ever you like; for example, at the center of a vehicle or animated object.

The length (also called the magnitude) of a vector **P=(x, y)** is denoted by $\|P\|$ and is computed as:

Equation B. 10

$$\|P\| = \sqrt{x^2 + y^2}$$

The reason for this is easily seen by looking at Figure B.6. The **x** and **y** values are really two sides of a right triangle, and the length is the hypoteneuse. Simple trig will show us that the angle **θ** of the vector relative to the x-axis would be found as:

Equation B. 11

$$\theta = \text{atan}\left(\frac{y}{x}\right)$$

We can make a vector have a length of 1 without changing its direction; this is called *normalizing the vector*. Having a unit vector pointing, say, in the orientation direction of a car happens to be very useful, and we can make it any length we like by multiplying it by a new length. Anyway, normalizing is shown here:

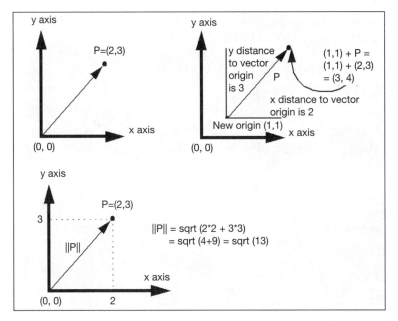

Figure B.6
A vector drawn at the origin (upper left). Placing the start of the vector at another point (1,1) means adding the point to the vector (upper right). The length of a vector is the hypotenuse of a right triangle (bottom).

Equation B. 12

$$x' = \frac{x}{\|P\|}$$

$$y' = \frac{y}{\|P\|}$$

Multiplying a vector by a number means multiplying all components of the vector by that number. What does this do to the length? Let's see. If we have a unit vector pointing along the x-axis, its coordinates will be (1, 0) and its length will obviously be 1. If we multiple this vector by 2, giving us (2, 0), the length will become:

$$L = (2{*}2 + 0{*}0)^{1/2} = 4^{1/2} = 2$$

It seems that multiplying a vector by a constant increases the length of the result by that constant factor. As I said earlier, we can give a unit vector any desired length.

We add two vectors by summing the coordinates in each corresponding dimension. For example, the sum of (1,0) and (0,1) is (1+0,0+1) = (1,1).

A line through a point **(a, b)** parallel to vector **(u, v)** is given by

Equation B. 13 $(x, y) = (a, b) + t \cdot (u, v)$

where **t** is any real number. We can think of the phrase "parallel to" as meaning the same thing as "in the direction of," and so it makes sense that any point that is is some multiple of **(u,v)** offset from **(a,b)** will be on the line.

Dot Product

The dot product between two vectors is a scalar number. It is computed in a couple of possible ways:

Equation B. 14 $A \cdot B = \|A\| \|B\| \cos \theta$

$$A \cdot B = \sum_{i=1}^{n} A_i B_i$$

Why is this useful? Well, first we can quickly calculate the angle between two vectors by computing the inverse cosine of the dot product divided by the products of the norms. More importantly in the game domain, it is used in *back face culling*. The dot product of the normal of a polygon, even a triangle, with the vector from the camera to one of the polygon's vertices is greater than zero if the polygon is facing away from the camera. Polygons that face away from the camera cannot be seen, so this calculation is a simple visibility algorithm.

Amazingly, the dot product is invariant under rotation. Two vectors of fixed length with a specified angle between them have the same dot product as do any other two vectors having the same length and the same angle between them no matter what absolute angle either of them has.

Cross Product

A cross product, or *vector product*, between two vectors **A** and **B** results in a vector that is perpendicular to both **A** and **B**. If we know all of the components of **A** and **B**, the cross product **C = A x B** is computed as shown here:

Equation B. 15

$$C_x = A_y B_z - A_z B_y$$

$$C_y = A_z B_x - A_x B_z$$

$$C_z = A_x B_y - A_y B_z$$

Why is this useful? Well, for one thing, we can find a normal vector to a polygon (a triangle in particular) by finding the cross product between two adjacent edges. This is, in turn, used in illumination algorithms and shading. Another use for a cross product is for the computation of torque.

The Plane

A plane is a line that has another dimension, giving it area. This is opposed to a 3D line, which is a line *within* another dimension. I'll present this in more detail later.

An equation that defines a general plane is:

Equation B. 16 $Ax + By + Cz + D = 0$

Notice that this is the equation of a line, but with an extra variable **z**. In fact, most of the properties of a line are also properties of a plane: they have slopes (with respect to an axis), they can meet at an angle, and so on. A plane divides space into two parts, as a line divides a plane. We can determine which side of a plane a point is on by substituting the point's coordinates into the equation of the plane, as we did with the line, and look at the sign of the result. There are, however, a couple of interesting new things.

Keep in mind that planes are essential to games because a polygon (quad or triangle) is a plane in 3D space, or at least a part of a plane. Everything that we draw is a plane, and properties of planes are used to render our images.

Normal to a Plane

A normal to a plane is a line or vector that is perpendicular to the plane in all orientations. The vector (A,B,C) is a normal to the plane Ax+By+Cz+D=0; at least it points in the direction of the normal, which is the important part. As we saw in the earlier section on cross products, we can compute the cross product of any two adjacent edges of any polygon that lies in the plane, and this product will be a normal to the plane too.

Back-Face and Culling

Just as a point (x, y) was on one side or the other of a line depending on the sign of the result of a substitution of (x, y) into the line equation, a point (x,y,z) can be located on one side or the other of a plane surface according to the sign of the plane equation. If Ax + By + Cz + D < 0, I say the point (x, y, z) is North of the plane surface; if Ax + By + Cz + D > 0, the point (x, y, z) is South of the plane.

I briefly mentioned back-face culling when I discussed the dot product. In general, half of all polygons in a scene will not be visible by the camera. Eliminating these will obviously improve the performance of the scene renderer.

What I said before was that the dot product of the normal of a triangle with the vector from the camera to one of the polygon's vertices is greater than zero if the polygon is facing away from the camera. We get the plane's normal using the cross product, and computing the dot product to a vector from the camera's position to a point on the plane. If the angle is between 90 and 270 degrees, the polygon is facing the camera—the dot product will be negative. Otherwise, the triangle is not facing the camera, and can be ignored.

Transformations

The transformations I am about to discuss in this section are essentially geometric. We'll look at reflection, scaling, and translation transformations.

Reflection

Given the functional equation y = f(x), it is possible to reflect the function about the y-axis by changing the sign on the x variable, as this equation shows:

Equation B. 17 $y_{reflected} = f(-x)$

Consider the equation of a line as in Equation B.4: **Ax * By * C = 0**. This can be converted into the form **y = f(x)**. Using some simple algebra, we get:

Equation B. 18 $y = f(x) = -(Ax+C)/B$

The reflection of this line about the y-axis is **f(-x)**, which is to say:

Equation B. 19 $y = f(-x) = (Ax-C)/B$

Reflection about the x-axis involves changing the sign on the **y** variable, such as:

Equation B. 20 $y = -f(x)$

Scaling

A change in size or scale is done by multiplying the scaled coordinates by a scale factor—a real number specifying the magnitude of the change. In addition, the scale factor can be different for each coordinate, meaning that scaling, like reflection, is actually dependent on the axis.

Scaling parallel to the x-axis is accomplished by multiplying the **x** variable by the scale factor:

Equation B. 21 $y = f(\text{factor} * x)$

It is possible to scale in each axis by a different amount, but it is not often useful to do so.

Translation

Translation involves changing the positional coordinates or variables. For a shape, this means that the object seems to change position. Each axis has a different translation, and the translation itself is accomplished by adding a distance to the variable. Moving a function or object along the x-axis by **a** units is done with this equation:

Equation B. 22 $y = f(x + a)$

This can be undone by adding **-a** to all **x** values. To perform a translation along the y-axis, we add the translation to **y** as shown here:

Equation B. 23 $y = f(x) + a$

Basic Matrix Operations

A matrix is a two-dimensional array of numbers that usually represents a set of linear equations. There is a specific way of manipulating matrices that is not always intuitive for a beginner. This is a problem in game development because there are many useful algorithms that use matrices: rotation of graphical objects, shortest path through a graph, and most splines. In fact, when you think about it, an image is just a huge matrix of pixel values.

A matrix has a certain number of rows and columns, and is defined by those values: a rotation can be accomplished using a *3x3* matrix, for instance, specifying 3 rows and 3 columns. Here how it looks:

Equation B. 24

$$M = \begin{bmatrix} 1 & 2 & 0 \\ 3 & 1 & 0 \\ 0 & 0 & 1 \end{bmatrix}$$

Elements in a matrix are indexed by using two integers: the row then the column. Thus, in the matrix M above, the value of the element at (1,2) is 2, and the value at (2, 1) is 3.

Adding matrices together can only be done only if the two matrices have the same number of rows and columns. Then, the sum is simply the sum of the corresponding elements:

Equation B. 25

$$\begin{bmatrix} 2 & 1 \\ 4 & 0 \\ 3 & 1 \end{bmatrix} + \begin{bmatrix} 3 & 2 \\ 1 & 6 \\ 2 & 3 \end{bmatrix} = \begin{bmatrix} 5 & 3 \\ 5 & 6 \\ 5 & 4 \end{bmatrix}$$

Multiplying matrices is much more difficult than adding them, and much less intuitive. Basically, an element in the product is the sum of the products of elements in a row of one matrix and a column of the other. The simplest case is a 1 row matrix multiplied by a 1 column matrix. The result is a 1x1 matrix, and the calculation is:

Equation B. 26

$$\begin{bmatrix} 1 & 2 & 3 \end{bmatrix} \begin{bmatrix} 1 \\ 2 \\ 3 \end{bmatrix} = \begin{bmatrix} 1 \times 1 + 2 \times 2 + 3 \times 3 \end{bmatrix} = \begin{bmatrix} 14 \end{bmatrix}$$

This same pattern is repeated in a general NxM matrix multiply for each element in the product. That is, if we multiply matrices A and B giving C ($C = A*B$) then:

Equation B. 27

$$C_{i,j} = \sum_{k=1}^{N} A_{i,k} B_{k,j}$$

The number of columns of A and the number of rows of B must be equal for the multiply to be possible. Note that this is a vector dot product of a row or A with a column of B. The pattern of the row X column is illustrated in Figure B.7. Here, the shaded row and column on the left side of the '=' multiply together element by element and then are added together to yield the shaded cell on the right of the '=' sign.

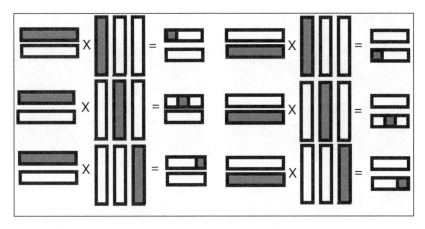

Figure B.7
Rows and columns that are multiplied to create elements in a matrix product.

It is also important to note that AxB is not the same as BxA when A and B are matrices. In other words, the order of how matrices are multiplied matters. In particular, since matrices can be used to represent scaling, translating, and rotating an object, you must remember to pay attention to the order. The expression RxTxSxA, where A is an object, R is a rotation matrix, T is a translation matrix, and S is a scale matrix, performs the scale first, then translates, then rotates. This is quite a different thing from SxTxRxA.

Matrices are often represented as two-dimensional arrays in programming languages. A typical example would be:

```
float rotationMatrix[4][4];
```

If the array bounds are not known at compile time, we must allocate the storage and create a 2D structure. In C this is simple:

```
// Allocate and return a 2D matrix with specified bound
float ** allocateMatrix (int N, int M)
{
    float **spine;
    float *vec;
    int i,j;

// The 'spine' is a 1D array containing pointers to each row.
    spine = (float **)malloc (N*sizeof(float *));
    if (spine == NULL) return NULL;
```

```
// Now allocate the rows and assign the pointer to
// row i to spine[i]
   for (i=0; i<N; i++)
   {
      vec = (float *)malloc (M*sizeof(float));
      if (vec == NULL) return NULL;
      spine[i] = vec;
   }
   return spine;
}
```

Interpolation

Interpolation is the act of determining what numerical values belongs at a particular point between some known values, assuming that there is a known behavior of the surface involved. For example, if at time T=0 we measure a voltage of 2.0 volts, and at time 1.0 we measure 3.4 volts, what was the voltage at time T=0.5? Well, we don't actually know, but if we assume that the voltages follow a linear function (a line) then a good guess would be 2.6 volts. If you see that right away, you probably already have an insight into interpolation. If you do not, read on.

Figure B.8 shows the interpolation example that we just discussed. There are two measurements that we know of, and we connect them with a straight line segment. To determine the voltage at T=0.5, we move along the line on the horizontal (T) axis to T=0.5 and read off the height of the line at that point. In fact, we can read off the value at any time between 0 and 2 under the assumption that the line is an accurate represen-tation of the real situation.

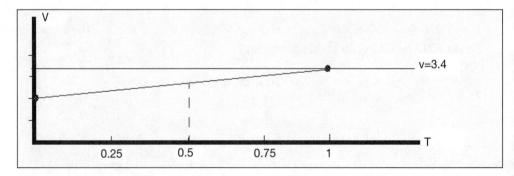

Figure B.8
Using linear interpolation.

The mathematical statement of this is: given two data points y_0 and y_1 that correspond to x values x_0 and x_1, assume that $x_1 - x_0 = 1$ (if it isn't, it is always possible to multiply by a scale factor F so that it is). Now any point between x_0 and x_1 can be expressed as a value $0 <= a <= 1$. For any such a, the function value y_a at that point is given by:

Equation B. 28 $$y_\alpha = (1 - \alpha)y_0 + \alpha y_1$$

If a line is not correct, we can use any other function we choose as an *interpolation function*. Linear interpolation is usually a fair first approximation, but it is quite jagged when there are many lines connecting multiple points (*piecewise linear* they call it). Using a polynomial can result in smoother curves, though.

There are many other interpolation functions you could choose, so there is no way I could show you all of them. In my opinion, the most useful, other than the linear one, uses a cubic polynomial to approximate the data. A big advantage with cubic interpolation is that there is a high degree of continuity possible between adjoining segments. However, to get this benefit we need more data points with which to build the interpolation: four points, in fact. We never use cubic interpolation if we have only a very few data points.

What are the four points? Well, assume that y_0 and y_1 are as before, and we scale the distance between them again to be 1.0, so a is as before too. Now also take the point that follows y_1 and call it y_2; also use the point before y_0, and call it y_{-1}. The interpolation between y_0 and y_1 is computed as follows:

Equation B. 29
$$\beta = \alpha^2$$

$$a_0 = y_2 - y_1 - y_{-1} + y_0$$

$$a_1 = y_{-1} - y_0 - a_0$$

$$a_2 = y_1 - y_{-1}$$

$$a_3 = y_0$$

$$y_\alpha = \alpha\beta a_0 + \beta a_1 + \alpha a_2 + a3$$

How do we get the first and last segments interpolated? Standard practice is to guess! Add an extra point before the first one so that the slope agrees with that of the first segment, and do the same at the end. Either that or use a linear interpolation at the beginning and end.

Basic Physics

Some would define physics as the science that describes how the universe operates. From the smallest objects (perhaps quarks) to the largest (galaxies), physics can be used to describe how objects interact, how things move, and how the universe changes as a function of time. However, it is important to remember that physics is based on observation. There is no way to derive the laws of physics from first principles; we must watch, describe, and verify or falsify everything we see. I say this to underscore the difference between mathematics and physics. Einstein once said that "As far as the laws of mathematics refer to reality, they are not certain; and as far as they are certain, they do not refer to reality." We will look at some basic phsyics that we can use in a driving game, and try not to look too far past to the (really interesting) details underneath.

For a computer game, especially a driving game, the key equation in physics is:

Equation B. 29 $F = ma$

Force equals mass multiplied by acceleration. This might seem like a simplification but it describes almost everything we want to simulate in this book.

There is, naturally, more to it. What we need to do is to find an equation that defines the magnitude and direction of every force that acts on an object, in our case usually a vehicle. We then resolve the forces, treating them as vectors, so that we have one force remaining. This force acts on the vehicle, and since the vehicle has a mass it will accelerate according to Equation B.29. This is a simplification but it will do for our discussion here.

Consider a car that is accelerating forward because its engine is moving it. A set of forces will act on it to slow it down: friction with the road, wind resistance, and engine friction. One force will push it forward. These forces are in simple opposition, making it simple to resolve them: subtract the frictional forces from the motive ones and compute a resultant. This is the remaining force, and will serve to accelerate the car forward.

Forces and accelerations are actually vectors. A force acts in a specific direction, and this would be indicated by a vector of three components, each representing a force in the three cardinal directions x, y, and z. Resolving the forces is simply a matter of adding the vectors, and the sum is the resultant net force as shown in Figure B.9.

Most forces, the simple ones at least, can be treated as if they act on the center of mass of the vehicle. This gives us a common point to act as the origin of the force vectors. On the other hand, some forces do not behave like this. If a car is struck by another car, the forces do not share the same origin. If my minivan is hit on the passenger front

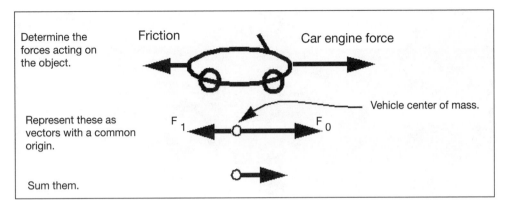

Figure B.9
Forces acting on a car, drawn as vectors.

fender by a Fiat at 90 degrees to my direction of motion, for example, the force applied to the front of my car causes it to rotate (see Figure B.10).

This is another way to apply a force that causes a different response. The force is applied at an offset to the center of mass. The result is rather like a lever or a crank, where a small force is amplified by the distance from the fulcrum or shaft, which here is the center of mass. This kind of force is called a *moment*, and it results in a new kind of force label (*torque*) and a rotational motion rather than a linear force.

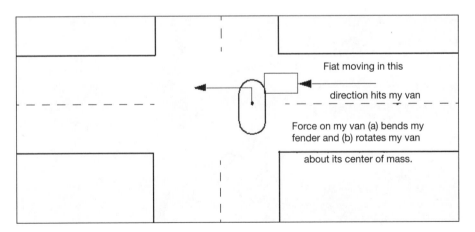

Figure B.10
How torque can be used to describe a vehicle collision involving linear motion.

Index